The Mayan in the Mall

THE MAYAN IN THE MALL

Globalization, Development, and the Making of Modern Guatemala

J. T. WAY

Duke University Press Durham & London 2012

© 2012 Duke University Press
All rights reserved
Printed in the United States of America on acid-free paper ∞
Designed by Jennifer Hill
Typeset in Arno Pro by Keystone Typesetting, Inc.

Library of Congress Cataloging-in-Publication Data
appear on the last printed page of this book.

For my mother

CONTENTS

ACKNOWLEDGMENTS

As this book was in copy editing, my mother, Nancy Way, passed away. I dedicate it to her with love and gratitude. A brilliant, talented person and dear friend, my mother taught me to write, and worked tirelessly on helping me to edit the introduction to this work. I remember the day she gave me my first typewriter, an old black Royal, when I was seven, and remember the many manuscripts she pored over with me since. It was one lasting gift in a lifetime of gifts. Thank you, Mom.

Present throughout the production of this project has been Gil Joseph. Mentor, advisor, and friend, Gil has been an integral part of this project and of my life. Too, Ralph Lee Woodward Jr., deserves more thanks than I can give, as does Laura Briggs. Michael Denning, Stuart Schwartz, James Boyden, James Scott, Pamela Voekel, Colin MacLachlan, Kevin Repp, Roseanne Adderley, Gertrude Yeager, and Nancy Yanoshak have all helped me enormously, as did Florence Thomas of the Department of History at Yale University.

Behind every book is a support team, and this one is no exception. Thanks and *abrazos* to Shannan Clark, Alison Bruey, Bethany Moreton, Michael Jo, Guillaume Aubert, Masha Salazkina, Emma Wasserman, Kate Holland, Carol Craycraft, James and Ralph Laws, Lewis Pittman, Carlos Villacrés, Alejandro Conde Roche, Charley Mack, Susan Nanes, Michael Polushin, Shedrick Cade, George Trumbull, Gladys McCormick, Martin Nesvig, and Jordana Dym. Kathleen Mallanda, my fellow traveler, merits a shout-out (and monument) all her own. I am also indebted to Jill Calderón, Rigoberto Ajcalón Choy, Liz and Rubén González, Henry Pamal García, Enrique "Kike" Aguilar, the Fogarty family, Bill Forward, Helen

Vickers, Pascale Daime, Ana Cayax, and the community at the Atitlán
Multicultural Academy. The entire Way family has my gratitude, too.

Guillermo Nañez Falcón, Carla Ericastilla, Ricardo Stein, Tani Adams,
Lucrecia "Lucky" Paniagua, Thelma Porres, Anabella Acevedo, Lucía Pellecer, Anaís García, Claudia Alonzo, Barbara Kohnen, and the staff at CIRMA,
the Archivo General de Centroamérica, and Duke University Press helped
enormously. I also thank Arturo Taracena Arriola, Víctor Hugo Acuña, Liz
Oglesby, and Paula Worby for aid, advice, and support. Special acknowl-
edgement is due to Carlos Melgar Zamboni, who shared his extensive
private collection of documents from three vendors' associations with me.
These historical treasures as well as the many hours don Carlos spent with
me have added a grass-roots dimension to this book that otherwise would
have remained largely veiled.

I also thank my union, GESO. I cannot possibly name everyone, but
Dave Sanders tops the list. Thanks, too, to Wendy Walsh, Lis Pimentel,
Anita Seth, Stephen Vella, Carlos Aramayo, Brendan Walsh, Rachel Sulkes,
Kristie Starr, Scott Saul, Shafali Lal, Louise Walker, Robert Perkinson,
Kieko Matteson, Jeffrey Boyd, and the whole family: you know who you
are. For grants, thanks to the Mellon Foundation, the Yale Center for
International and Area Studies, and the Fulbright-Hays program. Finally,
the Tepoztlán Institute for the Transnational History of the Americas has
kept me inspired and always reminds me of the kind of academy in which
I'd like to work.

Departments of Guatemala. Not to scale.

Highways of Guatemala. Only major routes are indicated. The P.A.H. is the Pan-American Highway, commonly called the Inter-American Highway in Mexico and Central America. Not to scale.

Municipalities of the Department of Guatemala. These municipalities make up the Guatemalan metropolitan area. All show some degree of urbanization. Neighboring departments are indicated in bold, uppercase lettering. On the right-hand side of the municipality of Amatitlán is Lake Amatitlán. Not to scale.

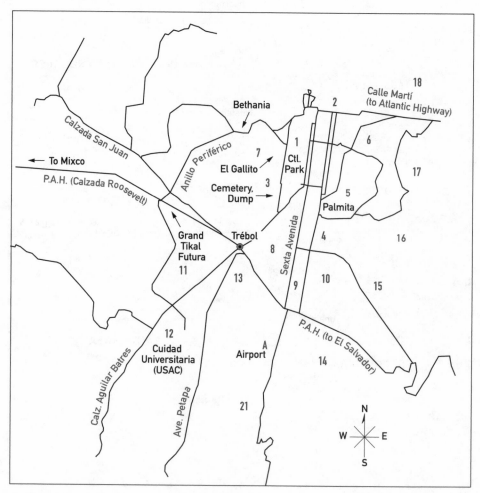

Overview of Guatemala City. Only major streets and highways are shown. Large numbers indicate city zones. Not to scale.

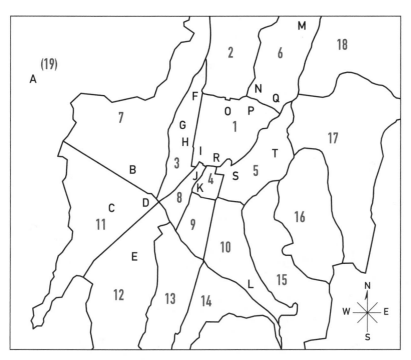

Municipal Markets of Guatemala City, 1972. Large numbers indicate city zones.
Source: *Esquema director de ordenamiento metropolitano* (EDOM) *1972–2000: Plan de desarrollo metropolitano* (Guatemala: Municipalidad de Guatemala, 1972). Note that many zones lacked markets. Not to scale. *Legend:* A: Florida. B: Mercantil. C: Roosevelt. D: Guarda Viejo. E: Reformita. F: Sauce. G: Gallito. H: Cervantes. I: Presidenta. J: Granero. K: Terminal. L: Villa de Guadalupe. M: Candelaria. N: Parroquia. O: Central. P: Colón. Q: San Martín de Porres. R: Sur 2. S: Palmita. T: Asunción

Welcome to Guatemala, center of the *mundo Maya*. A country above all else indigenous, the nation relies on tourism, and the Maya are its top attraction. Making up about half the population, they speak twenty-two languages, with names like K'iche', Kaqchikel, and Mam. They dazzle the foreign eye with woven *traje* outfits and handmade wares. Their very bodies bespeak a pre-Columbian past, a past of pyramids, of priests and sacrificial stones. Tourists move among the Maya in the volcanic highlands and experience a Shangri-La where it seems that time has stood forever still. "My God," a visitor from the United States recently commented to me. "We could be in Tibet."

Welcome to another Guatemala, one in which a mammoth shopping mall and hotel complex, Grand Tikal Futura, looms above the neighboring buildings in the nation's capital, Guatemala City. Named after the magnificent Mayan ruins at Tikal, whose architecture it mimics, the mall is much like malls anywhere. Behind the jade-toned tower and pyramid-like façade are stores like The Gap, McDonalds, Payless Shoes, and other shrines to modern consumerism. Tikal Futura references a national cultural treasure and a Mayan national identity but portends a homogenized nation. Figuratively speaking, Tikal Futura and the economic system it represents are "putting the Mayan in the mall."

This book tells the story of the making of modern Guatemala. A history of the construction of social space from the 1920s to the new millennium, it focuses on Guatemala City's poor neighborhoods, on the markets that provision them, and on their connections with the countryside and the greater world beyond. The history of modernism in the land that modernity forgot is a human history, as cultural and social as it is political and

economic. It is a story that ties together hemispheric development endeavors and the grass-roots everyday development that built neighborhoods and made them function. It encompasses the growing rural migration to Guatemala City, the exploding of the contemporary informal
economy, the descending of a nation into war, and the striving of ordinary
individuals to survive even as their efforts defined the life and feel and
texture of the land.[1]

Seemingly endless paradox and contrast are assimilated in the spatial
unfolding of Guatemala's distorted development. Grand Tikal Futura, harbinger of first-world consumerism though it is, sits at the epicenter of a
country in which roughly three-quarters of the economically active population works in the informal economy, slightly more live in poverty, and
well over half are illiterate.[2] The mall's neighbors include multistoried
transnational corporate offices at intersections where rag-clad urchins spit
fire for a tip. The Kama Sutra love motel and the Pentecostal temple are
nearby. Mayan vendors hawk tortillas next to Goodyear Tire shops and
cinderblock shacks where cockfight spurs and guns are sold.

All these installations are denizens of a highway known as the Calzada
Roosevelt, named after FDR. The Roosevelt is really part of the Pan-
American Highway—the part that runs through the city where gated enclaves of the wealthy rub elbows with shantytowns on open sewers. It
connects that city with the corn-terraced villages straight out of *National
Geographic*. A U.S.-built road network that links the Americas, the Pan-
American (called the Carretera Interamericana in Central America) is a
highway whose construction was the largest infrastructure and development project in contemporary Latin America. One of the great, globalizing
development schemes that this book explores, the Pan-American was the
stuff of imperialism and dreams. The section of the highway that lies in
Guatemala City, the Roosevelt, epitomizes Guatemala's contemporary di-
chotomies. The Roosevelt is the broken heart of the road network that ties
the nation together, a miracle mile on acid, an asphalt ribbon through a
manmade ruin.

That the ruin was manmade is an overarching premise of this book.
From the arrival of the Spanish, Guatemala has been marked by oligarchic
control, huge landholdings, coerced labor, and profound racial division.
Today, the nation is still not even remotely healed from the genocide that
its military committed against the Maya in the early 1980s or from decades
of generalized state terror. Its civil war, in which the United States was

intimately involved, began in the 1960s and did not end until 1996. A great deal has been written about racism, imperialism, and genocide in this small nation, but very little about the fabric of development that binds them together.[3]

A dialogical and complex process of development—one that pairs the plans and projects of national and international power brokers with the everyday actions and economic activities of the populace—serves as a connecting thread in Guatemala's tumultuous twentieth-century history. It reveals a basic continuity and coherence in a past most commonly characterized by a series of radical political upheavals. Once Guatemala can be understood as a fully, if tragically, developed nation, its history becomes one of a place where people not only killed, but created; not only died, but lived.

Chapter 1, " 'Like Sturdy Little Animals': Making the Modern Anti-Modern, 1920s–1944," tackles the paradox of Guatemalan modernity—namely, how anti-modern it looks. Detailing discourses that remain embedded in contemporary Guatemalan culture, the chapter traces a change from romantic modernism in the 1920s to "reactionary modernism" from the 1930s to the mid-1940s.[4] Colonialist racism, I argue, connects the seemingly disparate ideas of Pan-Americanism, development, progress, and identity seen throughout the period and beyond. Today's upper classes see not the Maya but the Mayan in the mall. So they build fortresses to hold back and hide the third world around them. Their racism, their U.S.-influenced vision, and even the shape of the social landscape they would love to transform but never do are all products of modernist, internationally influenced development as articulated through Guatemalan race, class, land, and labor relationships.[5]

From the 1920s to the mid-1940s Guatemalans vigorously propounded and contested modernist ideas, influencing the lives and worldview of generations to come. Consider, for example, Ramón González, the hero of a Guatemalan proletarian novel entitled *Camino de adolescente: La vida de Ramón en el barrio "El Gallito"* (1990), whose story—and whose neighborhood, El Gallito—I will revisit many times throughout this book.[6] The opening lines of the novel reflect the modernism of the 1920s, as does the very existence of El Gallito itself. Too, Ramón's attitudes about race, work, and even his own identity bespeak deep-seated attitudes filtered through and colored by the modernism of decades before his birth.

"*LIFE microscopic*," begins the novel, "*seed so fecund in your developing, in time you will be: A MAN—AN ANT—A FLOWER—A BUTTERFLY—A TREE; in the end, what you are in the essence of your being.*"[7] These words, written by Ramón's friend and biographer Cristobal Monzón Lemus (the author of the book, called Crimolém for short), evince the life philosophy of the 1920s, one element of the rich romantic modernism that characterized the decade. Life philosophy and theosophical mysticism, replete with fascination about the ancient Maya, were elements of romantic modernism that mixed with more political modernist expressions: anti-imperialist Pan-Americanism and vibrant, internationalist labor organizing. The labor unions of the 1920s pushed the government to form state-owned worker neighborhoods like the gritty El Gallito, where Ramón grew up.

In Guatemala City the workers' mission of forging proletarian consciousness where none had existed before was far from complete when the Great Depression hit. With the fall in world coffee prices and the election of President Jorge Ubico, romantic modernism fast gave way to reactionary modernism. Ubico assumed dictatorial power and crushed the unions. His rule, from 1931 to 1944, was quasi-fascist, statist, and paternalistic. His regime attempted to enforce an organic national unity even as it established a police state and resurrected forced labor, primarily Mayan, in the service of development and agrocapitalism. The "Indians" may have become the national mascot, but together with their brown-skinned mestizo relatives they suffered intense repression. That racist repression, based in labor relationships, modernized and cemented a "space-is-money" instead of an equally repressive "time-is-money" formula within the culture of development. It also carried forth into the age of modernization race-based relationships that made the Maya the symbol of Guatemala's skewed modernity—the modern anti-modern.

Ubico combined his racist and backward-looking "agromodernism" not only with modern technologies of public intrusion into the private sphere, but also with development, much of it led by the United States. U.S. Pan-Americanism overshadowed its Hispanic variety. Unionization stopped, but clubs and associations proliferated. Some of them, like Rotary, were headquartered in the United States. Many, though, like the Invencibles soccer club that Ramón helped to found in El Gallito, sprang from the most humble of neighborhoods.

Humble Guatemala City neighborhoods were either born or completely transformed during the decades of modernization. Chapter 2 turns to the formation and early years of El Gallito, Ramón's neighborhood. On one hand, it tells the heretofore unresearched story of the great land invasions of 1945–48 that turned the ravines surrounding El Gallito and other neighborhoods into shantytowns and backtracks into the 1930s to detail the neighborhood's formation. On the other hand, this chapter, "Chaos and Rationality: The Dialectic of the Guatemalan Ghetto," explores the melding of romantic modernism and reactionary modernism detailed in chapter 1 into the social democratic high modernism of the Revolution of 1944–54.

The Revolution, commonly referred to as the Ten Years of Spring, was brought to a head by military reformers in 1944. It was both a capitalist movement and a deep democratic opening. Revolutionary policies were economically nationalist. They promoted industry, infrastructure, education, and social welfare. Political parties bloomed. Grass-roots organizing exploded among workers, urban and rural alike. The Revolution also provided many citizens with their first and only empowering interaction with the state. However, as I argue, the Revolution's leaders were high modernists. They believed in top-down, plan-rational solutions to the nation's problems. Politicians ranging from presidents to petty municipal officials all propounded state-led development plans. These schemes, far from engaging in a gradual process of supporting, educating, and empowering the vast underclass, instead envisioned sterilizing and remaking the great unwashed. The profound nature of the social democratic opening in Guatemala, however, guaranteed that the workers and the poor—organized or not—continually pushed the state faster and further than it wished to go.

The story of the birth of the modern Guatemalan ghetto related in chapter 2 exemplifies the dialectic between chaos and rationality that to this day has characterized development in the nation. It was precisely this dialectic, which came to light at a time of rapid modernization and urban growth, that influenced the way politics and development tragically played out in the crucible of the Cold War. Just as citizens outpaced the state's ability and willingness to meet their demands, so did the nation, taken as a whole, venture beyond boundaries acceptable to the United States. After launching a comprehensive land reform, the government was overthrown in 1954 by an invasion of Ubico-era military men organized, funded, and supported by the Central Intelligence Agency (CIA). Until 1986, right-wing military governments followed in a string broken only from 1966 to 1970, and even then just nominally.

Though they could not have been more different from their predecessors, the anticommunist military governments appropriated a great deal from the Revolution of 1944–54. They adopted the revolutionary structure of state and brought its high-modern developmental plans to fruition. The astonishing and paradoxical continuity between the developmentalism of the social democratic Revolution and the repressive, military Cold War governments that followed is the subject of chapters 3, 4, and 5.

Chapter 3, "*Oficios de su Sexo*: Gender, the Informal Economy, and Anticommunist Development," examines the transition from the social democratic high modernism of 1944–54 to the anticommunist, authoritarian high modernism of 1954 to the early 1960s. The highly gendered discourses of Cold War–era development, I argue, open a window on how the right wing donned the mantle of the very Revolution it had thwarted, setting off to save a supposedly dissolving nuclear family, which I contend had broken apart long before, the government's social engineers unleashed feminized development endeavors with names such as Social Welfare and Integrated Community Development. In so doing, they continued the projects of the Revolution but stripped them of social democratic content.

The United States was a leader in this process. Up north, the project of development became increasingly intertwined with public relations, advertising, and espionage in the age of the communications revolution. Development became as much a part of the burgeoning culture industry in the United States as it was a conglomeration of institutions dedicated to creating infrastructure. These changes, too, were ushered in with biological, gendered language that focused on family and pushed Guatemalans to team their Ubico-esque, repressive "State-as-Father" with a giving "State-as-Mother" that was more aesthetic than effective.

The race-tinged turn to agromodernism explored in chapter 1 and the dynamic of chaos and rationality shown in chapter 2 conditioned the woes of modernization that the State-as-Mother confronted. Chapter 3 unearths these problems at the neighborhood and household levels. Drawing on life stories from petitions and the reports of social workers as well as on Ramón González's childhood in El Gallito, the chapter maps the neighborhood-based creation of economy and social safety net against the history of the state's attempt to do the same. It zooms in on single-parent families in hellish ghettoes and details the maturation of the modern informal economy. The informal economy still characterizes Guatemala, but, I contend, would be more appropriately called *the economy* itself, since it accounts for some three-quarters of all economic activity. It is no coincidence that this sector, relegated to secondary status despite its centrality, is epitomized by and was cocreated by women's labor.

Guatemala, like a child, would grow up to be like the United States, the dominant ideology held. Its informal economy would be subsumed by a formal economy. Its premodern social structures would give way to streamlined relationships with corporations and the state, and its new, liberal citizens would be individual worker–consumers free from the radical mess of popular organizing. None of this occurred. The very process of modernization fueled the informal economy and forged informal bonds of solidarity that only today are beginning to dissolve.

If social welfare programs and soft-edged plans like Integrated Community Development were the feminine side of development, infrastructure projects and war were the masculine side. Chapter 4, "Making the Immoral Metropolis: Infrastructure, Economics, and War," turns to the constructive developmentalism of the mid-twentieth century. Examining the period from 1959 to roughly 1970, it details how the anticommunist, authoritarian modernism that followed the invasion of 1954 emerged as unbridled military modernism in the wake of the Cuban Revolution. It examines this modernism at ground level, looking at the creation of a ghetto-speckled, gang-ridden, murderous city. Today, dangerous male *mareros*, or gangbangers, are held responsible for the immoral metropolis. Development and war, however, are the real culprits. In midcentury the government built new highways, transforming the economy. The main roads converged in Guatemala City in a cloverleaf called the Trébol, which neighbored La Terminal, a new, gargantuan wholesale market for foodstuffs. The Trébol and La Terminal fast devolved into cesspools of crime and violence. In the midst of what was already a period of rapid social change, civil war broke out. Chapter 4 examines the development-related growth of the Marxist guerrillas and the use of repression and terror on the part of the government, which the military completely took over in 1963. It contextualizes state-led development within the rubric of Cold War polarization, arguing that the problems development today looks to fix were themselves the product of development as it played out physically and politically in the 1960s and 1970s.

As Guatemala City mushroomed in the second half of the twentieth century, it became the immoral metropolis today symbolized by the hyper-macho marero. This tattooed tough, however, is himself an expression of development. The original "immorals," in state discourse, were the misguided youth who, inspired by Cuba and communist internationalism in general, turned to armed insurrection against the illegitimate state. The anticommunist military government, born of polarized politics, turned to death squads, torture, and scorched-earth tactics to defeat the rebels—helped by the United States, just as it was in unleashing its huge infrastructure development projects. In Guatemala City these projects had the effect of exacerbating the conditions that fed the insurgency and grass-roots resistance. They increased homelessness, crime, poverty, and delinquency of all sorts.

At the same time, proletarianization and poverty were spreading throughout the countryside. The new economic landscape convinced Ramón González to try his hand as an independent corn wholesaler. It ruined him and spurred him to migrate to Los Angeles, where he met Crimolém at work in the Metropolitan Car Wash. Had he stayed in Guatemala, Ramón might well have been caught up in the brutal war that culminated in the genocide of the 1980s. It was a war that had everything to do with development and that in part was fueled by the very forces that pushed Ramón to migrate.

Chapter 5, "Executing Capital: Green Revolution, Genocide, and the Transition to Neoliberalism," covers the developmental policies of the military elite from 1970 to 1985, a period in which the military modernism of the 1960s led to economic and social transformation through terror. Focusing particularly on Guatemala's peculiar participation in the worldwide phenomenon of increased agricultural production known as the Green Revolution, the chapter examines agrarian transformation policies developed in the 1960s and their confluence with acts of war in the years that followed. It maps the history of the military-led, blood-soaked Green Revolution against the story of Carlos Melgar Zamboni, a humble city beef retailer who lived an urban version of Guatemala's martial agrarian transformation. At heart, agrarian transformation sought to extend agrocapitalism by commercializing and diversifying agriculture, a project that had particular impact in the highlands. During the 1970s, military heads of state and technocratic, civilian cabinet members worked together to bring this project to fruition. In so doing they created a much more modern structure of state, triggered a nontraditional agroexport boom, caused near famine in the highlands, and teamed counterinsurgency with development in ways that came to a head in the killing fields of the early 1980s. The military, pairing unspeakable crimes against humanity with a program of "Inter-Institutional Coordination" and "Development Poles," brought the Green Revolution to the highlands in a final paroxysm of violence.

The Green Revolution, coinciding with genocide, bequeathed to civilian rule a nation firmly embedded in global discourses of developmentalism. From 1970 forward, both the public and private sectors created scores of institutions that would increasingly interface with a dispersed universe of nongovernmental organizations (NGOs) and transnational aid agencies —a conglomeration that itself congealed in the tumultuous seventies and eighties. Carlos Melgar and city butchers like him organized at the grass roots to participate in this process of modernization and win the Guatemalan small retailer a place at the table. As his story shows, state terror held them back until 1985. Meanwhile, the large enterprises in Guatemala's evolving agroexport sector continued to marginalize them. The chapter concludes with an epilogue that details the butchers' story from 1985 to the new millennium. Their dreams of retail development finally came true, only to be quashed by the sad realities of neoliberalism. While vast economic forces might keep creating small proprietors like Melgar, and while the development industry might putatively keep trying to incorporate them, the very logic of the system favors large capital enterprises.

The Guatemala of today became politically recognizable in 1986, when the first in a continuing string of civilian presidents took office. The period from that time to the present can be considered one of "postmodernism and return to democracy." The fragile, so-called democracy confronted immense challenges. The government negotiated peace with the still-extant guerrillas, a process that took until 1996, and meanwhile began to resettle tens of thousands of refugees.[8] National projects included returning the military to the barracks, establishing a culture of civilian rule, and simultaneously marginalizing and incorporating the diverse, widespread popular movement. A series of right-wing and center-right governments gradually and sometimes reluctantly instituted neoliberal policies as globalization transformed the face of Guatemala and social indicators failed to improve.[9] Crime, narco-trafficking, and massive migration to the United States were three of the most visible phenomena of the new era.

Not long after the generals returned the country to civilian rule the Cold War ended. It remained and still remains to be seen whether or not government repression and global corporate development have effectively killed popular democracy and installed individualistic, consumerist ideology in its place.[10] Chapters 6 and 7 take up this topic, looking at retail and development panoptically. The first focuses specifically on the Guatemala City municipal markets, showing how social and commercial formations ostensibly opaque to global, neoliberal capital are an inherent part of the new, postgenocidal landscape gradually made more transparent to that system. The second, covering developmental, political, and cultural trends in the age of globalization from 1985 to the new millennium, focuses on another dialectic: that between the concentration of power and the fragmentation of space. Together, these two chapters underscore the paradoxes and deadening aftereffects of Cold War development.

Chapter 6 is titled "A Society of Vendors: Contradictions and Everyday Life in the Guatemalan Market." Continuing the story of Carlos Melgar, it focuses on the development schemes of the previous chapters and examines where they converged, detailing infrastructure building and institutionalization in urban markets. Tracing the history of a vendors' advocacy group in the 1990s and 2000s and delving into everyday life, commerce, and politics in the markets, the chapter also looks back at the growth of municipal markets and informal, sidewalk satellite markets since the early 1970s. I argue that Guatemala, far from having the rationalized, engineered systems envisioned by the developers, remains in many ways a society of vendors—vendors who vie with each other and selectively contest the transnational corporate project as a whole and who also nearly single-handedly perform the life-sustaining task of keeping the population provisioned. The very existence of these people is paradoxical. On one hand, grass-roots retail bespeaks the incomplete success of the formal sector, that is, the supermarkets, malls, agroexporters, and large corporations, in structuring distribution and consumption according to its logic. On the other hand, the continued growth of both municipal and street markets is precisely the result of the trajectory of development. Development has modernized Guatemala. However, the starvation wages and exploitation of workers embedded in that modernization guarantee the expansion of the informal economy that development putatively seeks to incorporate and transform. The case studies in chapter 6 demonstrate that corporate capital is unintentionally reproducing the class of small business proprietors that is at the heart of its own mythic origins even as the logic of corporate capital seeks to destroy that very class and reincorporate it as low-paid wage labor.

Such contradictions are at the heart of chapter 7, "*Cuatro Gramos Norte*: Fragmentation and Concentration in the Wake of Victory," which examines the creation of space from 1986 to the middle of the first decade of the new millennium. It argues not only that this process embeds within it all the development of the previous century, but also that globalization is characterized by a dynamic that pairs the concentration of power with the fragmentation of social space. It contrasts government policies with the aims of NGOs, the waning of the left with the florescence of grass-roots movements, and evangelism with pop culture, pornography, and consumerism in an age marked by crime, corruption, and violence. The chapter also sketches the urban geography of globalized Guatemala, noting the rise of the maquiladora, the growth of land invasions, and the rapid spread of malls like Grand Tikal Futura and foreign franchises around the city. Like the book to which it serves as conclusion, this chapter takes its name from a play on words. *Cuatro Gramos Norte*, or Four Grams North, is what clever college kids call an upscale street mall and restaurant complex in Guatemala City whose real name is Cuatro Grados Norte (Four Degrees North). They are joking about cocaine. Not unlike the way Grand Tikal Futura symbolizes the Mayan in the Mall, Cuatro Grados stands as a sad example of globalized Guatemala. It is chic, it could be in Denmark, and it is an oasis ringed by unspeakable human misery. The book concludes by contrasting Cuatro Grados to the municipal dump near El Gallito. Here, under clouds of vultures, scores of starving paupers pick through garbage to stay alive.

The postmodern era is marked not only by intense social and political fragmentation, this book argues, but also by the concentration of political and economic power imposed upon Guatemala by decades of sustained violence. The results are lack of solidarity, increased division of wealth, spiraling crime, migration, and hopelessness.

Nothing in Guatemala's primal nature, Indian soul, or location in Latin America caused these problems to be inevitable. The problems were developed, quite literally. Perpetuating the myth that Guatemala is underdeveloped perpetuates the myth that development can solve the very problems it has created and continues to create.

Grand Tikal Futura is aptly named. It stands, paradigmatically, for all that development has achieved and for the shining future its promoters dream of creating. Whether or not the Maya themselves or their mestizo cousins ever get to enter the postmodern, global retail emporium as shoppers is immaterial. Either way, they lose. Development has put the Mayan in the mall.

Guatemalan modernity is paradoxical. The nation's landscape embraces malls like Grand Tikal Futura and mountain villages where no light bulb has ever shone. Its labor and wage structures are at once futuristic and anachronistic, showing where transnational corporate capital, if unchecked, is headed but simultaneously reproducing racist, colonial peonage. Guatemala, enigmatic, cutting-edge, and caught in time like a bug in amber, is the land of the modern anti-modern.

Even the busiest urban spaces can seem anti-modern in Guatemala. In part this is thanks to their chaotic organization. Mostly, though, it's due to race—to the presence of the ethnic other, the Maya, whose very bodies stand emblematically for the past. Consider La Sexta, or Sixth Avenue, the main commercial boulevard of zone 1, the city's historic center. In the early twentieth century, La Sexta was the city's most luxurious strip—a history that an urban remodeling project in 2010 and 2011 has tried to recapture. Before its facelift in the new millennium, La Sexta had been an iconic lowbrow street market for decades. Its sidewalks were lined with vendors' kiosks, each equipped with blasting boombox and offering cheap Asian Walkmans, fake Duracells, knockoff Nikes, bootlegged CDs, and maquiladora-made clothes. Only a footpath separated the stalls and the storefronts, and it overflowedwith humanity.

The stores, like the vendors, did a bustling business, even those that sold exactly the same *chafa* (junk) that those outside were hawking, their fluorescent interiors adding value in the form of distinction. Other commercial fixtures included Payless Shoes, McDonald's, and Burger King. The portal of Electra Stereo served as a shelter for homeless paupers addicted to sniffing glue. There were several *centros comerciales*, precursors to the mod-

ern mall, and cinemas with Hollywood's latest. One porn theater featured
B-grade Italian smut. Cantinas abounded, and in some of them the neighborhood drag queens could be heard bragging about how many of the
vending campesinos they had bagged. And rounding out the local commerce were retailers on foot: shoeshine boys, gum and candy sellers, and
men pushing Coke and ice cream carts as they hollered promotions for
their wares.

Before a team of Guatemalans had managed to "rescue" the historic
center and Sexta Avenida,[1] I asked one rich man what was so wrong with
the area. He gestured widely: "*Them.*" The street vendors. "Indians," the
gesture said. "They're why no one goes there," this man told me.

In fact, no one went there *at night*. When the vendors rolled their boxes
off on dollies toward the shantytowns at sundown, La Sexta died a sudden
death. Only the sounds of street fights and occasional pops of gunfire broke
the stillness. By day, however, the area provided entertainment and low-
cost shopping for thousands of lower- and middle-class families. Many of
the postmodern planners who were clamoring to remake the district and
who continue to opine on urban development overlook the culture and
commerce of the "popular class," envisioning instead a future exemplified
by Grand Tikal Futura. Theirs is a first-world future that effaces the local
and enshrines the global. They see the Mayan in the mall, a commercial
universe in which Sexta Avenida's brown-skinned "them" couldn't hope for
a better job, ever, than starvation-wage service work. Their racism, their
U.S.-influenced vision of the future, and even the shape of the social landscape they seek to transform are all elements of specific modernist, internationally influenced developments in Guatemala.

Race, just as much as Guatemala's adherence to its status as agroexporter, conditioned the nation's modernism and affected its culture of
development. Race serves as the thread that connects the national imaginary that emerged from the 1920s and the new labor movement, born in
the same decade, that has had cultural and political impact ever since.
Notions of race affected the nation's marketing of itself abroad, its relationship with other countries and international movements, and even its perceived position in a burgeoning hemispheric system dominated by the
United States. Finally, racial ideas, labor patterns, and demographics were
integral to Guatemala's institution-building and infrastructure-building
projects and help in part to illuminate the underlying continuity behind

the shocking swings in the style of modernism from the 1920s to the end of the Second World War.[2]

Sea changes in Guatemalan modernism were marked by outbreaks of violence. The years from 1920 to 1944, key in Guatemala's process of globalization, began and ended with democratic revolutions. Overall, these years show a trajectory from romantic to reactionary modernism. In 1920 a cross-class popular movement dating to devastating earthquakes in late 1917 and early 1918 overthrew the dictator Manuel Estrada Cabrera (1898–1920). This democratic movement heralded an era of ebullient and idealistic romantic modernism that lasted through the presidencies of Carlos Herrera (1920–21), José María Orellana (1921–26), and Lázaro Chacón (1926–30). Political chaos ensued when Chacón fell ill, and, ultimately, Jorge Ubico (1931–44) was elected. At the end of the first year of his term, Ubico began establishing himself as dictator. The nation moved into an age of "reactionary modernism," a term I borrow, as noted, from Jeffrey Herf's book on Germany during Weimar and the Third Reich. Herf argues that the Germans combined antimodernist "inwardness" with modernist "means-end rationality" and technology, a phenomenon also seen in Guatemala as the oppressive Ubico state appropriated and retooled the effervescent ideas and politics of the 1920s.[3]

The anti-modern—or the myriad ways in which the Guatemalan landscape, culture, material culture, society, and economy reference and look like the past—is in fact fully modern, and much of what gives daily life its seemingly anti-modern texture unfolded as part of the modernizing process itself. Pausing from time to time to contrast the present and the past, I want to turn back the clock to 1920. At that time La Sexta, until recently most notable for its Mayan street vendors, occupied a very different space in the national imaginary. So too did the country's indigenous citizens.

"La Patria Nueva": Romantic Modernism, Mysticism, and Marketing the Maya

La Sexta's architecture is charming. Largely rebuilt in the 1920s and 1930s after a series of earthquakes wrecked the city in 1917–18, its structures show an aesthetic of nostalgic colonial folkloricism mixed with arts-and-crafts and art-deco idioms. The buildings bespeak the romantic modernism of the cultural and commercial elite in the twenties and early thirties. *Sextear* was the verb they coined for strolling along the avenue. *Sexteando* meant enjoying luxury stores, hotels, and restaurants, watching foreign films in palatial theaters, and even showing off the nation's first automobiles in a low-speed cruise.

The romantic modernism of the long 1920s (ca. 1918–31) left sociopolitical traces that, like La Sexta's buildings, still grace the landscape today. For example, the era saw the maturation of an ideology of biological vitalism, the sort of life philosophy alluded to in Crimolém's introduction: "*LIFE microscopic, seed so fecund in your developing.*" Elite thinkers teamed their life philosophy with mystic spiritism, and politically with anti-imperialist Hispanic Pan-Americanism. Like their upper-class counterparts, workers were protagonists in this period of political opening. They organized the nation's first militant unions. In so doing they drew on numerous international discourses of social justice and working-class identity and solidarity.

All of these modernisms conditioned anti-modern Guatemala. All were imbued with notions of race, and all affected how different sectors, later to go to war, imagined the nation. The vitalism and spiritism of the generation of the 1920s, for example, later reappeared in the army high command's biological nationalism, a major contributing factor to its scorched-earth genocide against the Maya in the 1980s. Through the mechanisms of commerce and media, life force and spirit appeared in pop culture, in the marketing of the Maya, and in the commodifying of a national imaginary for the tourism industry. At the same time, anti-imperialism and Latin Pan-Americanism influenced two revolutionary generations, those of the 1940s and the 1960s, both of whom correctly identified the racism embedded in the imperial mission of the United States but failed to overcome its effects either in Guatemalan society or in their own organizations. Indeed, throughout the long haul of social space creation in the 1900s, modernist and progressive elites and workers alike consistently reproduced the great Guatemalan divide—Maya/Ladino—even when they sought specifically to erase it.

In the 1920s the elites drew on U.S. racist images of servitude even as they picked up on an image of Mayan glamour, itself created abroad. La Sexta's famous stores, both foreign-owned and national alike, used Sambo images in their ads. The National Tobacco Company depicted a boy in blackface carting a giant pack of cigarettes on his back, in an image strangely reminiscent of Mayan porters hauling firewood with tumplines.[4]

LA PATRIA NUEVA

Mayan flapper. The cover of this newspaper insert from 1925 illustrates the mutually reinforcing tropes of modernity and tradition in the vitalist years of the 1920s. Anonymous, "La Patria Nueva," *El Imparcial*, Guatemala, 14 September 1925. Courtesy of CIRMA Historical Archive.

During the same era, the international marketing invention of Guatemala as *Mundo Maya* was underway. Peasant Mayan themes were a hit as early as 1917, when Wanamaker's department store in New York City exhibited Mayan pyramids of yore and primitive huts of today together with purses and parasols for sale.[5] In Guatemala, meanwhile, both ancient Mayans and *indígenas*, or Indians barely associated with this glorious past, were the subject of much elite discussion. In the 1920s elite media, touting the Patria Nueva, or New Nation, often portrayed the Mayan woman as the harbinger of a modern era. She appeared in newspapers and magazines as a flapper, her traditional Mayan skirt and blouse, or *traje*, redrawn with Jazz Age flare.

Over time, part of the allure of the elite's imagined Maya would be their claim to an esoteric spirituality. Years later, in 1947, for example, *Acacia*, the magazine of the Great Masonic Lodge of Guatemala, would report that the Popul Vuh, the Mayan creation myth, was the basis of western Masonry.[6] By the end of the twentieth century the bond between Mayan spirituality and esoteric wisdom would be complete, and the whole discursive conglomeration would go down market. Tourists today can pay to become certified Mayan shamans, and no holiday in Guatemala is complete without a visit to a shrine of Maximón, a trickster saint who grants favors in return for liquor, cigars, and a tip. Maximón has accompanied the New Age into contemporary pop culture. In 2003 *El Globo*, a penny-press tabloid, featured a piece called "Maximón: The Most Unusual Saint." Also in its mix were articles on Jennifer Lopez's dreams, time–space travel, artificial intelligence and telepathy, and coverage of the capital's crime scene, including a feature on the discovery of a decapitated corpse.[7] In the same year, *Esotérika*, a paper devoted specifically to the New Age (the "t" in its title is drawn as an Egyptian ankh cross), went on sale. Besides providing numerology and horoscopes and interpreting dreams—of seeing pigs copulate or of eating excrement—the paper promoted Mayan seers like Don Miguel Sontay of El Quiché and Maximón alike.[8]

Esoteric spirituality was all the rage among the elite in the 1920s, but the highbrow romantic modernists still looked toward Europe, not to their own indigenous backyard. The decade saw a florescence of the theosophy movement, a mysticism teamed with modernist thinking but deeply rooted in centuries of spiritual tradition and decades of liberal discourse.[9] Theosophical lodges sprang up at a rapid clip, lodges like "Gnosis," founded in the capital in 1923. Their proponents, among them Carlos Wyld Ospina, the editor of the magazine *Brahma-Vidya*, billed the movement as both modernist and rooted in ancient wisdom and secret knowledge.[10]

The theosophy and spiritism of the 1920s crossed paths with European vitalist philosophy, popularizing a biological language of nationalism that within a generation would be found more in the military than in any other sector. Theosophical magazines like *Epoca*, published by Rodolfo Leiva and Ospina, made frequent reference to metaphysics and phenomenology. *Epoca*'s premiere issue credited Immanuel Kant with having opened the Western way to understanding hidden wisdom but lavished most of its attention on Arthur Schopenhauer. A piece entitled "Theosophical Attitude" quoted Schopenhauer's *The World as Will and Representation*, evoked the new and stylish Freudian psychology, and, through a series of illogical leaps, brought the reader from Schopenhauer's thesis (watered down such that knowledge equals representation) to the more advanced Cosmic Reality and Supreme Truth.[11] Like the new European—modernist, nationalist, and, in many circles, fascist—the new Guatemalan and the Patria Nueva were infused with spirit and endowed with a pulsing, biological energy. An article from 1929 in *El Imparcial*, "The New Guatemalan" by Fernando E. Sandoval, itself leading with a quotation from Schopenhauer, sums up the genre:

> Within Guatemalan social biology a new type has arisen, whose characteristics make him the sign that the environment is transforming. He has no more harmony with the past than that which a root has with the earth from which it draws its juice. The vital atmosphere that is the prevalent feature of his development will be adapted to his own modalities. Life in and of itself is no more than the double-dealing of a reciprocal adaptation: of beings to the environment and of the environment to beings. . . .
>
> The two poles around which the personality of the *new Guatemalan* revolves are: *dissatisfaction* and *creative will*. . . . Change with the times or perish, such is the formula. . . . [But] it is not this postulate nor any other that would make the force of the *new Guatemalan* focus . . . [rather,] it is the profound force that derives from instinct, and that whispers in the ear of the chosen, and the impulses, like a spur on a bridled beast—a force that crystallizes in the phrase "national survival."[12]

Creative will and *irrational force* were the buzzwords of a generation. Elite thinkers challenged the positivism of the last half century, even as they revitalized (pun intended) its liberalism. Throughout the decade and into the early 1930s public intellectuals followed European modernism with great interest. Pieces covered the life and ideas of Benito Mussolini, the futurism of Filippo Tommasio Marinetti, cubism, surrealism, and the writings of Jean Cocteau. In particular, David Vela, the once and future editor of *El Imparcial*, the nation's main newspaper for some fifty years, attempted to introduce a generation to high intellectualism. Besides promoting European thought, Vela espoused a Hispanic Pan-Americanism with a long history, its proponents ranging from Simón Bolívar to José Martí to the Uruguayan essayist José Enrique Rodó.[13] Rodó's enormously influential publication *Ariel* (1900), written in the wake of the Spanish-American War, used the characters Ariel and Caliban from Shakespeare's *The Tempest* to contrast the civilized, spiritual nature of Latin America (Ariel) with the brute mass capitalism of the United States (Caliban).[14]

Even as intellectual elites looking abroad espoused a biological Pan-Hispanic Americanism that included the indigenous in ways mostly imaginary, the United States, itself no stranger to racism, was promoting a different Pan-Americanism. Theirs was one of a business culture, made operational through the Pan-American Union (PAU) and promoted at the grass roots by organizations like Rotary International and the Lions Clubs. Early in the 1920s, the PAU initiated the Pan-American Highway project, promoted in propaganda as a vehicle for tourism, a road to international harmony, and a route to development. By 1927 Rotary had founded a tourist club in Guatemala City that advocated for highway construction and offered discounts on hotels and restaurants. Within a few years the club was making arrangements for Thomas Cook and American Express travelers' checks to be accepted. In 1930 the PAU was proudly reporting that Central American service workers could say "hotel," "baggage," and "I'm your man."[15]

The fact that all of this activity was simply a cover for highly racialized economic and cultural imperialism was not lost on Guatemalans. Just as in Europe, critics in Guatemala decried Americanization, and they wrote news magazines, formed clubs, and even founded a chapter of the Anti-Imperialist League.[16] It was in their crusade against the *Yanquis* that the elites found common ground with workers, who were busily organizing in the 1920s. La Patria Nueva emerged in the 1920s as a vibrant imaginary—its heroes arrayed against the imperialists to the north, its blood imbued with the cosmic spirit of pyramid builders, Egyptian and Mesoamerican alike. This cultural global modernism accompanied the growth of soft industry, the congealing of an urban working class, the spread of civic organizations, and the growth of urban neighborhoods. Together in their expanding city, workers, elites, and middle sectors envisioned a Patria Nueva of justice, progress, and growth, but somehow the Patria's mascot, the new indígena, failed to win a place at the table.[17]

Workers in the 1920s: Internationalism and Insularity

In the 1920s urban workers played an enormous role in defining the texture of Guatemalan modernism. They were protagonists in setting the political agenda and in resisting domination from abroad. Additionally, they looked internationally to draw on discourses of class justice, thereby contributing to the shape of the Guatemalan resistance for decades to come. Their nascent movement failed to incorporate the Maya, as would the later worker revolution of 1944–54. It did, however, begin to set the stage for the popular front of the 1970s and 1980s and establish the discourse that would lead many Maya to describe their race in terms of class: *de la clase indígena* —from the indigenous class.

Their workers' fight came to a head with the overthrow of a dictator. In 1920 a cross-class alliance led by the Unionista party ousted President Estrada Cabrera, during whose twenty-two-year despotic regime North American imperial enterprises, most notably Electric Bond and Share and the United Fruit Company (UFCO), made great strides in Guatemala.[18]

Urban workers made great strides as well, with Estrada Cabera's aid and to his detriment. In so doing, they drew on a centuries-old history. Hierarchical artisan organizations, guildlike structures that provided trades with internal organization and juridical existence within the colonial system, dated to the 1500s. Despite legislative changes in the early 1800s, trade-based identity, complete with a social geography (Street of the Blacksmiths, Street of the Bakers, and so on) and apprenticeship systems, continued to offer cohesion and continuity in the functioning of Guatemala's *gremios*, or trades. When liberal coffee growers took over the state in 1871, they gradually allowed workers to register their mutual aid societies and associations. These groups were not yet unions, but the foundation for their later birth was laid in the 1880s, when several of Guatemala's most famous factories opened—the match factory, the Cerveza Gallo plant, and Cementos Novella in the capital as well as Cantel Textiles in Quetzaltenango department.[19]

The urban labor sector was small but growing. Estrada Cabrera tried to turn the workers into a political bulwark, especially when he needed to be "reelected." He actively encouraged the formation of trade associations and their participation in or transformation into political clubs. However, the dictator could not control grass-roots organizing. The 1910s saw the nation's first salary strikes as well as the definitive creation of unions that were moving beyond mutualism. In 1919 the antidictatorial movement that would bring about Estrada Cabrera's downfall a year later began to flourish. Organized workers were at its heart.[20]

Generally speaking, the workers who overthrew Estrada Cabrera preserved the anti-modern mutualism of their gremios while participating ever more intensely in modernist labor internationalism. Internationalism had gradually begun to take root in Guatemala in the 1910s, mostly owing to the influences of the First World War, the Mexican Revolution, and the Russian Revolution.[21] Over the course of that globally tumultuous decade mutualism remained dominant in Guatemalan labor, but some groups became more militant and began to affiliate with international labor organizations. As a result, the union movement of the 1920s was vibrant but never unified. Divisions of ideology and affiliation gave rise to competing confederations and a marbled mix of mutualist gremios and larger unions representing railroad, port, UFCO, and factory workers.[22]

One of the most important influences going into the decade was the idea, fueled by the American Federation of Labor (AFL), of Pan-American labor solidarity, which Samuel Gompers promoted in the aftermath of the Russian Revolution and in the midst of the Mexican Revolution.[23] The antisocialist, antianarchist AFL–Pan-American line remained strong but was fast accompanied by the formation of the Communist Party, which was illegal and repressed but popular, along with dynamic organizing by anarcho-syndicalist and social democratic groups and, to a lesser extent, by organizations inspired by the Catholic Rerum Novarum. There was a short-lived Unificación Obrera Socialista in 1921.[24] Workers of the decade also participated with unions of the Congress of Industrial Organizations (CIO) in the United States. They demonstrated for the convicted anarchists Nicola Sacco and Bartolomeo Vanzetti and took to the streets to show support for Augusto Sandino's anti-imperialist, antidictatorial struggle in Nicaragua.[25] The more that less-than-worldly workers did the job of grass-roots organizing—albeit in a milieu still overwhelmingly urban, male, and Ladino—the more they became engaged with global labor discourses and organizations. In effect, they found the doorway to the world out there by building consciousness and solidarity in their very own neighborhoods and places of work.

Their organizing gave them power. There were regular strikes by workers at the International Railways of Central America (IRCA), the railroad owned by United Fruit, and by UFCO stevedores, along with actions by workers at the beer factory, bakers, telegraph workers, and barbers during the first five years of the 1920s, as artisan associations and unions continued to form at a rapid rate.[26] Interestingly, strikes on the part of the artisans, the gremios, brought matters to a head in 1925. Cobblers, bakers, and carpenters struck for nearly three weeks in the capital and in the cities of Escuintla and Antigua, demanding shorter work hours, better workplace conditions, and decent treatment. Tailors and trolley workers threatened to walk out as well. The bakers were particularly active, striking on and off again repeatedly over a period of three months. As soon as their struggle slowed, in November, coffee pickers, customs workers, and railroad workers were on the pickets. The year ended with a historic strike by the women workers at Casa Gerlach, a coffee concern. In response, the government created a National Labor Department as a division of the Development Ministry and signed a labor code that had been several years in the making.[27]

As 1926 began, textile and soap factory workers, transport workers, and bakers went on strike—a wave of activism that led to the splitting of one of the nation's main confederations into two groups, one communist and the other more reformist, or economist, in the words of its critics.[28] The union movement was growing, and it was growing in a variety of directions.[29] By decade's end, communist and anarchist groups were spreading. They vied both against each other and against the procapital, reformist unions. Internally, they broke into squabbling factions. Sectarianism weakened the labor movement even as its grass-roots base was expanding and its leaders were forging ties of solidarity around North, Central, and South America.[30] As we will see, labor suffered crushing blows in the 1930s, but by the beginning of the decade workers had created lasting cultural and political discourses that remained an integral part of society and the culture of development.

"One of the Most Important Branches of Society": Laboring of Culture in the 1920s

Antonio Obando Sánchez was a teenager when he fought against Estrada Cabrera. A recent urban arrival from nearby farmland, young Antonio, a dirt-poor servant, showed up at the Unionista party headquarters almost out of curiosity. They gave him a gun. The street fight lasted a week. Years later, in his memoirs, Obando Sánchez wrote about the *comedores populares* that the women of the city opened, cooking meals in their kitchens to feed the insurgents who were fighting the dictator's troops. Obando also wrote about a sniper. Up along Sixth Avenue, one can still walk by the site. A French mercenary picked off dozens of the idealistic generation of 1920 from a rooftop next to the Parque Centenario, now officially the Parque Gómez Carrillo but still known by its original name by all.[31] Today, the park is wedged between the army barracks (in the twenties also the officers' school), the palace of the National Police, and the army's glassy financial tower near the central square. The landscape itself bears witness to a near-constant history of dictatorship, and the uprising of April 1920 was the first spark in a struggle against it that would last until the middle of the 1980s.

For young men and women of the urban working class, including Obando Sánchez, the uprising heralded the beginning of an era heady with political possibility. It was Obando's first foray into politics, and it gave him a political perspective that was reinforced a year later when the first president of the new era, Carlos Herrera, fell to a military coup "headed by José María Orellana and brought about by Washington," which favored big-stick diplomacy and the imposition of a Kemmerer mission in Guatemala.[32]

Working in carpentry shops, the Electric Company, and even briefly in UFCO's Honduran banana plantations in the years ahead, Obando Sánchez braved government repression to become an organizer. By 1926 he was in a leadership position and helped to found the breakaway *central* (international), the Federación Regional Obrera de Guatemala (FROG), a champion of communism in the 1920s. He worked both with the Anti-Imperialist League of the Americas, which was affiliated with the American Popular Revolutionary Alliance, founded by Víctor Haya de la Torre in Peru, and with the Guatemalan branch of Socorro Rojo, the social service organization of the Communist International. Ultimately, he traveled to the Soviet Union several times, first in 1930, at the twilight of the presidency of Lázaro Chacón. A liberal, Chacón had taken office as first designate upon Orellana's death in 1926. Elected shortly thereafter, he led an administration that curried favor with the working class through quasi-populist discourses while oppressing and imprisoning radicals.[33]

From 1932 to 1944, during the Ubico dictatorship, Obando Sánchez was in prison. Later, he participated in the organizing explosion of the Revolution of 1944–54, only to end up in exile in Argentina after the CIA invasion of 1954. He ended his memoir with the story of a trip he took to the Soviet Union in 1963. Standing in Red Square before the Tomb of Lenin, he remembered his youth and Guatemalan labor's youth in 1924, the year of Lenin's death. "I couldn't even help it," he wrote. "There escaped from my lips, like an imperceptible whisper, a—¡*Gracias, camarada!*"[34]

That Obando Sánchez could whisper thanks to Lenin after living much of his life behind bars and in exile—and after having watched his move-

ment crushed, not once but twice—evidences not only his personal commitment but also the deep and lasting roots of labor organizing, the laboring of culture in the 1920s and beyond that he helped to make a reality.[35]
Besides organizing scores of workers and establishing internationalist and
proletarian discourses that remain very much alive in Guatemala to this
day, unionists shaped the national imaginary, the language of politics, and
the identity of the poor in ways that left their footprint all over Guatemalan
culture and society. They affected the way in which elite sectors dealt with
and spoke about the poor. They influenced the rise of the ubiquitous term
pueblo to refer to the masses as an organic, unified whole, a term that soon
took on the tone of a national folk identity.[36] They were leaders in forging a
political, public language in which this hardworking pueblo, with the
Maya–Ladino divide neatly erased from its contingency, became both the
motor and the object of all development. Ubico would play to the folk's
sentiment even as he crushed their unions. The leaders of the Revolution
of 1944–54 led the pueblo's movement even as they used the tactics of
high-modernist social engineering to improve the pueblo from the top
down. The post-1954 military state co-opted the Revolution's folk discourse and retooled it, forever claiming to work on behalf of the very
pueblo it was systematically oppressing.

The links between elite policy and discourse and the language of organized labor were forged in the romantic modernism of the long 1920s. By
bringing working-class issues to the fore, organizers completely transformed elite public discussion. One early effect was the rise of joint cultural
projects that teamed workers and intellectuals. For example, in 1922, when
the Popular University for workers was first proposed, both Fernando E.
Sandoval—later, as we have seen, to opine in Schopenhauer-inspired strains
on the new Guatemalan—and Carlos Wyld Ospina, offered their services as
educators for free.[37] After its foundation a year later, the Universidad
Popular remained a meeting ground both for poorly educated tradesmen
seeking instruction that would relate to their lives and livelihoods and for
elites hoping to transform society along the lines of progressivism and
modernism.[38]

The two groups weren't always a perfect fit, especially as the union
movement radicalized and became more internationalist. By 1925 Wyld
Ospina, while maintaining that the government should support unions,
was claiming in the pages of *El Imparcial* that "the idea of socialism" was "a
European import." The Guatemalan reality, he held, was one of "hundreds

of thousands of illiterate agricultural peons and a few thousand semi-literate artisans." The artisans were not a class but a "subgroup" manipulated by political leaders. Wyld Ospina, well intentioned and as dedicated to championing the Mayan campesino as he may have been, did not stop to note that he himself was borrowing freely from European thought. When he paraphrased Gustave Le Bon—"the masses are guided by feeling, not by reason"—he was engaging in a discourse prevalent in the Europe of the 1890s that combined a revision of Marxism and revolt against positivism with the ugly currents of social Darwinism and upper-class racism rooted in the thought of Arthur de Gobineau. In promoting a racialized, folk-Guatemalan approach to worker organizing, he sent intellectual taproots into the pool of European thought that nourished national socialism.[39] He also furthered the binary language of race that, while it had a basis in demographic realities and was intended to be pro-Indian, painted Mayans as an ethno-anthropological other, separate from the social needs of a working class, special and apart. Had the "semi-literate artisans" been allowed to keep organizing through the 1930s, they may well have forged urban–rural and Ladino–Maya solidarity, as their inheritors (both Ladino and Maya) attempted to do during the Revolution of 1944–54. During the 1920s they certainly kept organizing and opened not only a school for proletarian children in 1926, but also a Centro Obrero de Estudios Sociales a year later—the kind of grass-roots institution designed specifically to grapple with social realities at once global, national, and local.[40]

Beyond intersecting with the elite, the projects and public language of the unions spread through the lower class faster and more widely than did the organized unions themselves. In 1922 an unaffiliated group of about sixty workers in Guatemala City wrote to the government requesting a grant of suburban farmland. They were, they said, "notoriously poor workers who ought to receive their land for free ... proletarian workers and sons of labor, who win sustenance through the sweat of their brows." Rents were rising, the population was growing, and thus their request was surely just. These are difficult times, they noted, and "the majority of countries find themselves in political convulsions." This veiled threat they followed up with one not so veiled: "Lest we find ourselves in a situation like GER-MANY's." Street riots and chaos might be avoided by following the lead of postrevolutionary Mexico, where, the workers maintained, labor legislation was the order of the day. They also wrote internationalist, anti-Semitic doggerel in capital letters, charging that "THE PROPERTY OWNERS EX-

TORT US MERCILESSLY . . . THESE FOREIGN JEWS AND GUATEMA-
LANS." The sons of labor even used the language of Pan-Americanism:
"Farmland should belong to the State," they held, "as was established by
the Laws of the Incas of Peru. . . . Their system has been the wisest ever
registered in the history of the PUEBLOS AMERICANOS." The workers,
who never identified either their occupations or any established mutual aid
society or association to which they belonged, coupled their internationalism and Pan-Americanism with legal acumen. They attached a law that
they themselves had drafted, a law to regulate the expropriation of latifun-
dia by the state and its partition among the working class. Such was the
amplitude of consciousness and the depth of the search for a new identity
among the class that Wyld Ospina called semi-literate hordes.[41]

As organizers spread the union movement and gave it shape in the
middle years of the decade, workers were highly successful in pressing
urban land and housing claims. During Chacón's presidency, neighborhoods carved out of fincas purchased by the state as the capital grew sprang
up in Guatemala City in response to workers' demands. Created or billed
as being for the proletariat, these included Barrio El Gallito, La Palmita,
Barrio La Concordia, Colonia Roma, and others.[42]

The union-born spate of urban space creation inspired actions and
reactions by Guatemalans of all classes. Organized unions and mutual aid
societies established the template for winning land, housing, road access,
and infrastructure in the central valley. By the late 1920s cooperatives had
formed around the city and its fringes to demand the same. Some of these,
like the Unión Cultural y Auxilios Mutuos de Trabajadores in El Gallito,
were workers' groups; others were residents' associations formed by neighbors who had become conscious of the power of collective organization.[43]
Elite experts, beginning to adopt notions of social engineering, held forth
on the need for worker housing modeled on projects in postrevolutionary
Mexico and even as far away as Massachusetts.[44] Would-be businessmen
referenced unionism; in 1927–28 a trio of protodevelopers—an office
worker, an architect, and a bookbinder from Amatitlán—united as Grupo
Libre to win construction contracts in worker neighborhoods. "We come
from one of the most important branches of society," they wrote in making
their ultimately unsuccessful bid, "that which unites the Working Class
with Capital."[45]

Overall, both organized labor and ordinary individuals deploying labor's rhetoric had great reason to feel proud and little reason to anticipate

the repression that was soon to come. In 1931, just before Ubico's fierce crackdown, the Federación Obrero Regional, a breakaway from Obando Sánchez's FROG started that same year by Alfredo Toledo, the founder of the Communist Party and the general secretary of FROG, was busily organizing workers by neighborhood. They already had locals and womens' auxiliaries in each of the city's major worker barrios and were spreading into outlying, largely Mayan areas such as Mixco.[46] According to their statistics, Guatemala was still a city of artisans and *jornaleros*, or agricultural day laborers without regular employment. A full 25 percent of all workers were unemployed, they reported to Ubico, enclosing a detailed proposal for the creation of a state agency to support the urban unemployed, especially in housing.[47] The organized unemployed undoubtedly expected they would win. They had no idea of the horrors about to come.

"Our Guatemalan Hearts in Unison Beat":
From Incomplete Proletarian Unity to Incomplete Organic Unity

Some Guatemalans still whisper praise for Jorge Ubico, as if they are ashamed of holding such a political stance. Most, though, in remembering the epoch from 1931 to 1944, struggle to find words strong enough to describe just how evil the dictator was. Obando Sánchez calls Ubico, among other things, "la fiera sanguinaria," the bloodthirsty fiend. In the labor leader's language, it is as if Ubico and capital are conflated, and indeed the dictator's regime profoundly and paradoxically shaped modern Guatemalan capitalism and development.

The Great Depression and the dictator closed the door on the capacity of development to be a broad, socially inclusive project. Ubico's brutal crushing of the unions both reinforced a cult of secrecy and thwarted the wide range of possibility workers had to transform society democratically. The spiritualist, vitalist intellectuals who had influenced the modernism of the 1920s gave way to a new group concerned with purity of blood, eugenics, and racial superiority. These thinkers, say the historians Marta Causús Arzú and Teresa García Geráldez, contributed to a new, hegemonic discourse of racial domination and helped to create "a State without a nation."[48] Even as its racial perspective changed, romantic modernism among the elite ceded its leadership position to a practical, corporate-capitalist discourse closely in line with U.S. Pan-Americanism. In short, the Rotary Club picked up where the Theosophists left off. Ubico cooperated fully with U.S. businesses and the U.S. military. He embraced their notion of progress, even as his policies cemented coercive (many use the word *feudal*) land and labor relations on a landscape that had only just begun to change.

Under Ubico's rule, Guatemala turned to a reactionary modernism. Not unlike the reactionary modernism that Herf identified in Nazi Germany, Ubico's modernism spoke of infrastructure development in futuristic terms but was squarely rooted in the racist, colonial past.[49] The Ubico state was backward looking. It represented a planter class whose modern political cal rise had been cemented by the liberal revolution of 1871. The dictator combined age-old notions of patronage with the new worker discourse of the 1920s. He portrayed himself as a populist, as *tata*, or Father, in the city and countryside alike—championing campesinos' petty causes in far-flung villages and granting urban lots to "honorable" workers and "sons of labor." Ubico's regime was forward looking, too. Its propaganda was progress oriented, touting highways, industry, modern agriculture, and public works as the nation's pride. In this realm, too, Ubico was tata, presenting his vision of development within a cult of leadership in which he was praised as Caesar.[50]

In general, Ubico's policies furthered the expansion of the apparatus of state and of state surveillance into the private sphere.[51] They also marked the institutionalization of development led by agroexport and fed by systematically underpaid labor, something the unions of the 1920s had just barely begun to change. The long 1920s represented an opportunity for a different developmental path. During the long 1930s, ca. 1931–44, the state appropriated and reconfigured the modernist discourses of the 1920s, of worker pride and social justice, spiritual life force and progress, and racial exceptionalism. Too, the state advanced a model of progress and politics rooted in the coffee economy of the late nineteenth century. Ubico's government reinforced the roles of peonage, patronage, and authoritarianism in what, during the throes of the Depression, was coming to be known as development. Thus the 1930s underscore the spatially articulated contradictions with which modern capital built and rebuilt itself: New Deal, on the one hand, tata/fiera sanguinaria, on the other. Tying them together, well before the globalization watershed of Bretton Woods, would be an emerging banking system designed to benefit the great estates, a Pan-American Union apparatus on hand with development money and propaganda, a slowly emerging highway network that was really a web of ox-cart trails—carved through the mountains by the imprisoned poor, and an agricultural labor regime that likewise approximated slavery thanks to its use of anachronistic vagrancy laws in the Mayan highlands.[52]

For Ubico and the class he represented, the first step was to crush the unions. It was not long in coming. Only five unions were created during Ubico's thirteen-year rule. Of those, four formed in 1931. In fact, there was little sign during that first year that Ubico was planning to use the Policia de Investigación to infiltrate and destroy the nation's strongest unions.[53] The attack began in early 1932. Banging in doors, storming homes and meetings, police arrested scores of labor leaders and intellectuals (estimates range from two hundred to four hundred). No one was immune. Security forces dragged away reformist, mutualist, and even AFL-affiliated organizers with the same zeal that they arrested communists and anarchists. Ubico branded all organized labor communist in tones that prefigured the propaganda of the CIA-engineered invasion of 1954. Military tribunals tried the offenders. Some, they put against a wall and shot. Others they tortured.[54]

One of the best sources on Guatemalan labor history attributes the ferocity of the crackdown to the overall vibrancy of the labor and popular movement in Central America at the beginning of the 1930s. Ubico's pogrom against labor was part of a generalized reaction to organizing throughout the isthmus.[55] It was also a component in a hemispheric wave of organizing around the ideals of progress and development. While this Depression-era discourse emanated from the very heights of capital, it took quotidian form in Guatemala through workaday groups at the neighborhood level.

Given the extirpation of organized labor during the 1930s, the clamor at the grass roots for services of state found its only outlet to be neighborhood groups, associations, and clubs. The Ubico government promoted their formation, and in so doing participated with the U.S. culture industry to organize people for progress. Groups like Rotary International and the Boy Scouts both served this purpose and aided governments like Ubico's. State formation, the evolution of the development industry, and the spread of transnational corporate capitalism went hand in hand.

Clubs and associations predated the 1930s, but over the course of the decade they grew in numbers and took on new social and political importance. Many, like Rotary International and a wide variety of sporting and even aviation clubs, dated to the mid- to late 1920s, setting the stage for what was to become a widespread discourse of physical and moral fitness in the 1930s.[56] Young Ubico, long before he was dictator, spent his free time setting up Boy Scout troops, and scouting grew throughout the 1920s. It became a virtual craze in the 1930s, as the Ubico government not only promoted it, but also engineered the foundation of youth agricultural clubs (not unlike 4-H in the U.S.) and nationalist, antiunion organizations such as Juventud Obrera.[57]

Clubs and organizations occupied a middling position in a complex global project that is recognizable as such only in hindsight. On one hand, they filtered downward. They were meant to spread ideology among their members, channeling their energy and shaping their desires and visions. On the other, they filtered upward. Local groups, bound together through institutionalization, as seen in congresses, conferences, trade organizations, and the like, were meant to transform the landscape in the service of development as envisioned from on high.

For the various sectors attempting to engineer this situation, the challenge was dual: to create the conditions under which dominant ideology could be spread and to bring these artificially created social groups into contact with one another, with the state, and with capital. A recommendation of the U.S. Department of State and the PAU from 1936 held that nations should establish "National Committees of Intellectual Cooperation" that included "Committees of Moral Disarmament." The idea was for governments to "seek to promote cooperation between groups which form public opinion, such as labor organizations, youth societies, women's clubs, peace societies and social welfare organizations."[58]

In 1934 Ubico launched the Feria Nacional de Noviembre, an industrial exhibition and celebration of progress. Foreign and national capitalists would mingle with citizens organized by Rotary, the Boy Scouts, and the like. The Ferias de Noviembre had little to do with "the primitive economic concept behind the fairs of old." Instead, they were to be "expositions of living forces, syntheses of productive potential" (note the vitalism).[59] In Ubico's ferias, schoolgirls in marshal uniforms marched in formation with the flag. Streamlined Post Office and Electric Company floats rolled down asphalt streets. The ferias referenced an industrial future barely imagined by the agroexport emphasis of the regime. They also indulged in a monumental spectacle of state with the strains of futuristic nationalism that Richard Golsan has termed "Fascist Aesthetics."[60]

Similar aesthetics are seen in the Ubico regime's increasingly militarized schools.[61] The imposition of the cult of the dictator and of progress in the classroom dovetailed with PAU projects, and pro-Ubico tutelage combined with geopolitical rhetoric promoting what one PAU official would call "the New World's New Order."[62] The first Pan-American Day, in 1936, featured school activities throughout the Americas, coordinated by national governments, the Rotary Club, Chambers of Commerce, geographic societies, and similar groups.[63] Ultimately, it was U.S. business interests and U.S. business culture that events like Pan-American Day were meant to further, but the means aided the ends of tyrants, the *fieras sanguinarias*, as well.

In 1937 María Hilda Medina of Guatemala won the Highway Essay Contest held for Pan-American Day. "Progress, a heroic word that means life, that brings fame to the *Patria*, that carries the standards of civilization and culture to the vanguard," her essay began. "A pueblo's work in highway building is glory that conquers, well-being and greatness, wealth that labors and saves," she added, in near perfect Ubiquista language.[64] Indeed, Ubico's and the PAU's curricula fit together well. A magazine from 1938, its cover featuring marching girls—in iconography eerily like the Third Reich's—ran snippets of youngsters' essays comparing Ubico to Justo Rufino Barrios, the nation's first great Liberal dictator and the political progenitor of the series of coffee barons who ran the state until 1944.[65] "Let our Guatemalan hearts in unison beat," wrote one young woman, "for two beloved *patrios*; one represented by a glorious tomb, the other, by our *jefe*, legal, and leader of Progress and Liberty."[66]

Guatemalan hearts were not, however, beating in unison. First of all, many were beating in prison or in exile. More to the point, though, is the paradoxical reality that as the Ubico regime attempted to replace a nascent proletarian unity with an organic, nationalist unity, it strengthened already sharply drawn class and ethnic distinctions. The planter class would soon be pitted against new industrialists and the middle classes, who billed the Revolution of 1944 as antifeudal. As we will see, those same classes would find themselves swept up by the demands of the lower classes, the vast majority of the population. Far from being organically unified, however, the lower classes were themselves ever more divided. As a proletariat became historically recognizable as a class through the complex processes that make pueblos into mass societies, it also demonstrated evolved differentiation that resulted in innumerable conflicts. Some of these divisions were ideological and political. The biggest, however, was racial. To this day, the Guatemalan indígena resides in a different category from the Guatemalan *obrero*, or worker. Greg Grandin has demonstrated a key dynamic of modernization in Guatemala, namely, that "ethnic identity deepen[s] while state power increase[s]."[67] This process occurred, as Grandin demonstrates, concurrently with the marketing of the Maya, a discursive phenomenon at the heart of the Guatemalan modern anti-modern and an economic phenomenon driving both the tourist industry and the elite national imaginary today.

"Indians That I Have Drawn":
Tourism, *Indigenismo*, and the Mayan Anti-Modern

Over the course of the twentieth century, imagined Maya came to occupy a discursive space in which their ancient civilization was linked with modernism and progress and their contemporary society was equated with backwardness. Their folkloric charm, meanwhile, had money-making potential for Ladino and foreign developers of the tourism industry. The sectors controlling public discourse doubly negated the Maya, who was neither heir to a magnificent past nor participant in an unfolding future.

Business culture of the U.S. linked the ancient Maya and Aztec with modernity's march. Much of this hype centered at first around Mexico, positioned at the cutting edge during the institutionalization of the Revolution in the 1920s and 1930s. For example, *Modern Mexico/México Moderno*, a publication of the Mexican Chamber of Commerce of the United States, traced highway development to the Maya of the Yucatán, whose "Great White Ways," made of lime and white earth, once dazzled "under the tropical sun."[68] The same magazine headlined: "Aztecs and Mayas Our Architectural Ancestors, Masters of Form, Color and Ornament."[69] The U.S. media presented a commodified Latin America to the public at fairs and exhibitions. The American Republics exhibits at the New York World's Fair in 1939, for example, mixed modern art with folklore and industrialization with imperialism.[70]

Though their own culture industry was far less sophisticated, Guatemalans sensed the business potential in marketing the Maya. In 1939 Luis Fernando Flores, a Ladino painter, wrote to the government requesting art supplies. He wanted to promote tourism through a showing of Mayan-themed art at the Guatemalan Pavilion of the Golden Gate Exposition in San Francisco. His work had been well accepted by the *gringos* at both the Hotel Palace in Guatemala and at an expo in Dallas in 1938, where his paintings with "Mayan motifs" had been snapped up at "very good prices."[71]

Mayan motifs were marketable worldwide and at home alike. The historian Anne Rubenstein tells a story of tourism's early days in Chichicastenango, a highland market town that to this day is on the must-see list of every foreign visitor. In the 1930s a U.S. expatriate opened the Maya Inn hotel to accommodate the new trickle of anthropologists and tourists drawn by the colorful traje and ebullient market—a charm that Rubenstein demonstrates was based on the town's "reiteration of the old romance of pre-industrial long-distance trade." Voyeuristic foreigners were not, however, welcomed with open arms. Local Maya cursed their brethren who worked in the hotel. When a foreign film crew shooting a Tarzan movie kicked over some candles in the church, they rioted and beat up the local "hinge man" who was serving as the film company's liaison to the Mayan community.[72]

The same individual was working as an assistant to the anthropologist Sol Tax. Funded by the Carnegie Institute, the future University of Chicago professor was at work on the project that, though originally planned to be about Chichicastenango, became *Penny Capitalism*, which covered marketing practices among the Kaqchikeles of Panajachel.[73] Anthropology, like other disciplines, for example, psychology and sociology, that dated to the late nineteenth century and early twentieth, unwittingly contributed to vulgar popular language about people like the Maya and places like Latin America. Filtered through crass commercial thinking, academic output often provided a patina for racist drivel that promoted tourism and conditioned development initiatives in general.

An excellent example is found in the work of the artist and self-styled anthropologist Eben F. Comins, publicized by the PAU. Comins, for many years a professor of art at Wellesley, spent the late 1930s sketching Indians in Mexico, Guatemala, Peru, and Bolivia. His article "Indians That I Have Drawn" appeared in the PAU's *Bulletin* in July 1939, complete with a racial genealogy. "After studying the faces of thousands," Comins wrote, "I find three dominant color strains. . . . I. Red-Brown People (Pacific Islands, Indian Ocean); II. Blue-Black, Brown People (Hindu); III. Yellow-Brown People (Chinese and Mongolian)."[74] Comins did not think he was being racist. In fact, he idolized the Indian of yore. "Four hundred years have gone by since the Spanish invasion," he wrote, "and consequently there has been much interbreeding but still strands stand out . . . The one that struck me . . . was the red tone. The red tone is not mongrel blood. It is in the Indians who gave the highest civilization to our two continents, the Mayans and Incas." His admiration for their descendants had limits, however: "Their hands and feet are tiny but their stature has nothing to do with their strength. They are like powerful and sturdy little animals."[75]

Such pronouncements sum up the spirit that informed the tourist and crafts industries. However, they mask both the complexities of Mayas' relations with the greater state and society and the physical realities of land and labor in Guatemala's highly regional landscape.[76] Additionally, they hide another aspect of racism that is nested inside the contested field of capitalist development—serious indigenismo and genuine, if elitist, concern for the indigenous poor.[77]

The creation of the Instituto Indigenista Interamericana at the First Inter-American Congress on Indian Life in Pátzcuaro, Michoacán, Mexico, in April 1940 marked the institutionalization of indigenista discourse. The journalist Vela served on the institute's organizing committee. It resolved to study land distribution, protect small properties, extend rural credit, promote road building, improve public health and housing, and market and foment folk culture.[78] As a result of this congress the Instituto Indigenista Nacional was born in Guatemala. Headed by an anthropologist trained at the University of Chicago, the institute produced studies that, according to Jim Handy, "helped pave the way for the Agrarian Reform Law in 1952."[79]

Also helping to pave the way for agrarian reform was the agrarian situation itself. Ubico had maintained and promoted the grossly unequal division of land, power, and wealth in the countryside. For this reason his regime and the class it represented were as responsible as anyone for the Guatemalan modern anti-modern.

"What Would I Do for the Rest of the Day?":
Time, Space, and Money in Agromodernism

In 1931 Ubico decreed that in order to "contribute to the progress of agricultural industry," Juntas Departamentales and Comités Locales of Agriculture and Roads were to be established all over the country.[80] *Agriculture* and *roads* were the two words that marked the opening salvo in a campaign of development that mixed past and present and helped make the Guatemalan modern anti-modern. *Finqueros*, the finca owners who were

the political winners in the Ubico regime, directed virtually all road development.[81] Campesinos unwillingly provided unpaid labor to make it
happen. Adopting the discourses of futuristic agroindustry asserted by the
PAU, Guatemala's leaders reinforced retrograde finca agriculture while
simultaneously opening the nation for further foreign penetration. They
strengthened both the nation's agroexport and sub-subsistence *minifundia*
agricultural portfolios, putting Guatemala on the losing end of the global
commodity market and establishing much of the modern face of its
twentieth-century poverty, both national and local.

The John Deere tractor never replaced the machete in Guatemala, but
in homage to the dream of its doing so, fincas would have to be connected
by roads. Forced labor staffed both the farms and the road-building crews.
Ubico promulgated the Ley de Vialidad in 1933. It required either two
weeks of involuntary service per year or, to be exempted, a payment of one
quetzal a week.[82] Militias and conscript labor provided for legally by the
Ley de Vialidad mobilized around the nation on public works construction. It was a messy process. After three weeks of forced labor building
roads and telegraph lines in 1933, just after the passage of the law, campesinos in San José Pinula, not far from Guatemala City proper, fled the
worksite and went into hiding. The work could not be completed "without
the cooperation of the *gente de vialidad*," the Jefe Político wrote to the
development minister. He suggested either that military or paramilitary
personnel take up the slack or that funds be freed to pay local workers day
wages.[83]

During this era, a vagrancy law allowed finqueros to round up campesinos to perform forced labor in the fields. In his memoirs Carlos Manuel
Pellecer, a labor leader of the 1940s, tells the story of a U.S. magazine
reporter traveling in the Mayan highlands during the 1930s. The reporter
ran into a Mayan who was selling orchids and tried to buy them all. "No,"
the campesino told him, "I can only sell them one by one." The surprised
reporter asked him why. "If I sold them all," the campesino replied, "what
would I do for the rest of the day?"[84] Pellecer went on to describe the
reporter's excoriation of the lazy, backward Indian—a diatribe based in a
"time is money" attitude (he used English for this phrase) that Pellecer
viewed with disdain.[85] What the foreigner didn't understand, he explained,
was that, thanks to the vagrancy law, which forced campesinos to work 280
days a year or suffer one to two months in prison, people had to look busy
all the time. Without his armful of orchids, the Mayan man might be

subject to a sudden request: produce your *libreto de jornalero*—the little booklet in which workdays were recorded, often falsely, to extract even more labor from the poor—or go to jail.[86]

Agrarian labor and agrarian life have conditioned all development in Guatemala. Great plantations, besides dominating both land and investment resources and thus triggering unsustainable rural-to-urban migration, have from colonial times played a determining role in defining temporality and transhumance in the nation. The planting and harvesting of agroexport crops, just as of maize in the highlands, have structured seasonal migrations of labor, while lash- and gun-enforced starvation wages guaranteed the emergence of what is ironically known as the informal economy.

The reliance on agroexport fueled by underpaid, often Mayan, manual labor, reinforced in the Ubico era, has crystallized in myriad and lasting ways in the local culture of development. If in the first world temporality came to be defined by factors such as the speed of the assembly line, the hourly wage and yearly salary, the rate of return on investment—resulting in a now-naturalized formula of efficiency, speed, mechanization, and wage earning that links time intimately with money—in Guatemala, capitalist consumption of the hungry rural body as a valueless, timeless thing produced very different results. There is little to no cultural consensus that time equals money; but space does: a big plantation, a plot of corn, a stall in a market, a hut in a ravine. As Guatemala modernized, families, already conditioned to migrating, distributed themselves more widely over space —some in the village, some on the finca, some in the city, and, later, some in the United States—establishing ever more ephemeral households as sites of dispersed production. Wage labor was unavailable in sufficient quantities to support the population, and what wage labor there was paid only a pittance, forcing families to find other ways to survive. Meanwhile, Guatemalan capital enterprises from big to small developed within the context of labor exploitation, eschewing mechanization and efficiency: why get a washing machine when a servant will launder by hand for pennies? Why buy a forklift when workers will haul loads with tumplines?

Guatemalan underdevelopment, poverty, and chaos are not signs of the lack of modernization. They are the products of it. The Ubico state mobilized modernist discourses and fascist forms of corporate sociopolitical organization while promoting a racist lord and peon economy. In short, totalitarianism, the agroeconomy, the exploitation of Mayan and mestizo workers, and imperialism, itself steeped in racist ideology, all became written upon the landscape and embedded in the Guatemalan culture of development.

Imperialism and the Landscape:
Creating Space from Above and Below

Beyond finca agriculture, both U.S. and German imperialism structured the Guatemalan economy in the early to mid-1900s. German bankers and traders linked to houses in Bremen and Hamburg had been involved in the cultivation and commercialization of coffee since the 1880s. Over time they came to control as much as two-thirds of the trade and penetrated Guatemalan administrative and financial institutions.[87] The most significant U.S. enterprise on Guatemalan soil, meanwhile, was UFCO, which owned not only vast banana plantations, but also the nation's railroads. Electric Bond and Share owned the electric company, and a subsidiary of International Telephone & Telegraph, the telephone system. With the coming of the Second World War, U.S. imperialism defeated its German counterpart in Guatemala. Though pro-Nazi, Ubico bowed to U.S. pressure, expropriating German properties and cooperating with the Allied war effort.[88]

The Second World War and the increased role of the United States in Guatemala and in the hemisphere had a deep impact on the country. It is a commonplace in Guatemalan historical analysis that the war—the Allies' democratic discourse, the leaping to mass consciousness of the outside world in turmoil—was the biggest contributing factor to the Revolution of 1944 that overthrew Ubico.[89] This analysis also generally applies to the short-lived wave of democratization seen throughout Latin America in the mid-1940s, when growing middle-class and industrial working-class sectors seized upon a moment of political possibility to take power and fight for modern development, social welfare, and social democracy. These democracies, however, like Guatemala's in 1954, quickly gave way to renewed authoritarianism.[90]

Development is at the center of the story of this fast transition from dictatorship to democracy to dictatorship again. Modernization among growing populations gave rise to the classes and socioeconomic conditions that propelled the democratic generation of the 1940s to power and structured its programs and agendas. At the same time, the ideological battle over development that informed anticommunist, U.S. Cold War imperialism in Latin America quickly led to democracy's downfall. Bridging these historical, ideological periods is the physical infrastructure of development itself, the literal writing of economic power on the landscape.

During the Second World War the United States spearheaded a massive wartime propaganda and diplomatic effort in Latin America. It also invested heavily in infrastructure building. Concerned with hemispheric defense, access to the Panama Canal, and, above all, availability of strategic materials ranging from sisal to antimony, the U.S. War Department sent a team of engineers to Central America in 1942. Its mission was to finish the Inter-American Highway, the Mesoamerican leg of the Pan-American Highway that the PAU and the U.S. Bureau of Public Roads had been promoting piecemeal for nearly two decades.[91] By the mission's end in late 1943, the War Department had built a semipassable thoroughfare. While inadequate for modern transportation, it could at least facilitate the movement of materiel.[92]

The War Department temporarily renamed the Pan-American Highway the Ruta Militar de Emergencia (RUME) but called it, more popularly, the Pioneer Road. While the Bureau of Public Roads would later nix some route changes, the U.S. War Department nonetheless blazed the main trail of Guatemala's highway network. They did it with forced labor and entered into the task with extraordinary naiveté about the state of Central America's physical plant. On arrival in the isthmus, Col. Edward C. Kelton was amazed to discover that there were only two cement factories. There was almost no power equipment and no steel at all. Kelton also found that Washington was more concerned with shipping strategic materials to Europe and the Pacific than down to Central America. The Grace Line and UFCO contributed to transport, ripping up old railroad tracks for supplies. Trained labor was another problem. The U.S. Army provided the bulk of specialists, but locally peons were plentiful. They were unpaid campesinos rounded up by the fully militarized Guatemalan Highway Department. "Conscript labor was assigned to the RUME on the same basis as that customarily followed for the highway department," was how Kelton dryly described the process in his final report.[93]

This first step toward a modern highway network, in tandem with Ubico's trails, cumulatively began to remake Guatemala. Highways and points of production work together, and as points of production transform, so do the social and race relations that accompany them. The new sugar, cotton, and beef economy would soon follow the highways. As the agricultural situation changed, uprooted people followed the new highways as well. Many of them ended up in Guatemala City, where the new roads had contributed to a spate of industrial growth.[94] Highway development and the slow replacement of beasts of burden with motor vehicles increased mobility and economic possibility for all classes. Modernization came but written into it was the anti-modern—sets of class relations, economic structures, and, mostly, a chasm of racial divide. Still, new technology and communication brought with them a sense of impending change. That sense came to a head in 1944, when the elite, the workers, and the growing middle class alike unleashed a revolution that promised to make issues of progress its top priority.

In June 1944 teachers, professionals, students, and the populace at large took to the streets and protested against the dictator. By July, Ubico had gone into exile. In October a new generation of military officers overthrew his handpicked successor and made the democratic revolution—middle class, on the one hand, and rooted in a profound grass-roots activism, on the other—a reality. For the next ten years Guatemalans established the still-lasting structures of state, organized in urban and rural unions of historic proportions, and challenged the traditional agrarian power structure that Ubico had represented. Two presidents—Juan José Arévalo (1945–51) and Jacobo Arbenz (1951–54)—were charged by the people with modernizing the nation and balancing the needs and demands of an enormous and ethnically divided underclass, a leviathan union movement, the entrenched agroelite, the new and strengthening sectors of entrepreneurs and industrialists, and growing, white-collar middle cadres called bourgeois by the left. It was not an easy job.

In 1952 Arbenz launched an agrarian reform. This bold step was largely the result of dynamic campesino organizing. The Arbenz government expropriated some land from UFCO, and in 1954 the United States fomented an invasion and coup.[1] The years between 1945 and 1954, however, saw the birth of the modern Guatemalan state, the modern Guatemalan ghetto, and the modern Guatemalan articulation of justice and development.

The Revolution itself was deeply rooted in the popular sectors. The grass-roots organizing and mobilization that characterized it drew on the progressive discourses of the long 1920s, as political actors reworked notions of justice and progress within the context of the new internationalism of the mid-1940s.[2] Population growth, increased mobility and communications occasioned by infrastructure building, and even Ubico-era networks of political patronage along with clubs, associations, and the like all conditioned the explosion of a highly contested and exuberant discourse about the form the new democracy would take. Yet for all its locally articulated, ground-level complexity, the Revolution was led at the highest levels by high modernists and social engineers. Many of these political leaders, Arbenz among them, were children of the upper and middle classes, trained in Ubico's schools and in his army. Their social and economic engineering was top down and was designed to bring plan rationality, or systematicity, to the nation. On the one hand, they crafted policy in response to changing conditions on the ground in an era in which modernization was giving rise to highly visible social problems; on the other, their actions reflected the political pressures exerted by organizations from far left to far right. Nearly all of their plans, however, were constantly stymied by chaos at the ground level. Urban development schemes buckled under the weight of land invasions. Rural development faced the clamor of the landless and the depredations of those who would exploit them, and ultimately it was one of several factors that triggered a CIA invasion. Planning rationality is one thing, the revolutionary governments discovered, but implementing it is quite another.

The Maya may have become the symbol of Guatemala's backwardness, belying the nation's modernist currents, but the fact remains that Guatemalan modernization produced failure after failure. Why? The high modernism of the Revolution of 1944–54 provides multiple case studies of the problem: a dialectic of chaos and rationality that made the nation's ghettos and that also made the nation-as-ghetto.

Chaos is an all-pervasive feature of life and of development in Guatemala. Water systems and electricity, where they exist, don't work. Officials are corrupt, and the bureaucracy is torturous. Businesses open and close at random hours. Supply and distribution are incomplete and unreliable. Public transportation is disorganized and dangerous. The list is endless. And chaos hinders rationality at the ground level as well. One person opens a successful tomato stand, and suddenly there are dozens, and no one can make money. One poor worker saves up to buy some land and discovers she's been cheated on the deed, such scams being a veritable cottage industry. But chaos and rationality are dialectical, and taken together they explain much of historical change in Guatemala. Amidst the chaos is an alternative rationality, one built from the ground up with its own internal logic. Amidst the top-down rationality of the state is nested chaos—in the case of the revolutionary state, a chaos of social democracy that unleashed discourses of economic justice which threatened the capitalist power structure as it emerged from the Second World War into the era of the Cold War.

The story of Guatemalan development during the middle years of the twentieth century debunks a popular and pernicious notion, namely, that capitalist development left countries like Guatemala behind because there simply wasn't enough of it. In fact, the state liberally applied high-modern, rational planning. It didn't work, and it still doesn't work. Plan-rational social engineering is top down, and it fails to confront the economic and social realities that thwart it. Expanded to its logical conclusion, this argument suggests that capitalism simply cannot develop places like Guatemala because it also develops the poverty and need and chaos that stymie its very rationality. Capitalist development, then, should be reread: when unmitigated by socialist measures that redistribute wealth, it is not *against* third-world conditions, but a cocreator *with* and *of* third-world conditions. It is no coincidence that the United States overthrew the Guatemalan government precisely when it began to take steps in recognition of this inherent contradiction in capitalism.

This same inherent contradiction links the making of the urban ghetto and the making of the nation-as-ghetto. The story of the birth and growth of Barrio El Gallito, Ramón González's home in Crimolém's working-class novel, shows the genesis of what would later become the nation's most notorious slum. During the same period, the future of the nation as slum, as a third-world, supposedly underdeveloped, war-torn country, was cemented as well. The state, moving from Liberal dictatorship to revolutionary democracy to Cold War, anticommunist dictatorship, was caught within a web of evolving hemispheric and global economics and politics, all of which coalesced in one way or another in development. Yet development never seemed to work. A common "body politics" linked the evolution of capital, development of all stripes (agrarian, rural, infrastructural, and the like), and the lived experience of common citizens. Guatemala became ever poorer, its people ever more chaotic, and thus it needed ever more plan rationality, ever more development. This dynamic was acute by midcentury. At the local level it could all be seen in a single city neighborhood in the early years of the Revolution, El Gallito.

"To Make Patria": Saving El Gallito

In September of 1946 residents of Barrio El Gallito read in the newspaper about a plan to relocate them to the empty fields of the finca Bethania, raze their homes, rebuild their neighborhood, and return them years later as renters in modern apartment complexes. Furious, nearly seventy of them filed an *expediente* (legal brief) with the Ministry of Public Works to put an end to the scheme. They boasted that their hand-built homes surpassed those of the city center in standards of hygiene. Citing constitutional articles protecting workers, the residents noted the cynical timing of the plan—put through as congress was debating a labor code—and branded its author antirevolutionary.[3]

For the residents, space and proprietorship in El Gallito were intimately bound up with workers' rights. *They* were the laboring class; they had won the Revolution; they had settled the neighborhood explicitly created for workers nearly two decades earlier. To the engineer Enrique Prera, the director of Water and Sewers, former City Urbanization chief, and the plan's author, El Gallito represented little more than failure. And if the dwellers of El Gallito saw the Revolution as a time to take control, Prera saw it very differently. To him, the Revolution was a time to make the world anew and repair the devastated landscape. Far from empowering El Gallito's poor, he would remodel them through a remarkable project of high-modernist construction and social engineering.

Prera began his proposal with an analysis of a "theory of urbanism." Residents reflect their barrios, he explained. Clean, modern citizens live in neighborhoods of which the same could be said. To sanitize filth holes like El Gallito, he claimed, "is to make *patria*; to convert an enormous mass of humanity destined for vice and crime into citizens." That, the midlevel municipal employee maintained, is how "the urbanist becomes a moralist."[4]

To implement his moral vision, Prera advocated a cellular housing system in use in Britain and Russia. Three thousand modular dwellings would be accompanied by libraries, schools, play and sports facilities, dining and dance halls, and even an open-air theater. In planning his community, Prera reproduced the urban high modernism of Le Corbusier and the more quotidian midcentury currents of thought in urban planning that, in the United States, would give rise to both the projects and Levittown; but he bowed to the Guatemalan by making the Catholic Church the centerpiece of his circular design. The result would be the citizen, in a country where, since 20 October 1944, the masses "destined for crime and vice" had been using *ciudadano* as the preferred mode of addressing one another, assuming, perhaps naively, that they were citizens already—and citizens with honor at that.[5]

Honor was precisely Prera's point of attack. El Gallito was about as far from his sterile modernism as the human mind can imagine, and he set out with a camera to prove that point. People were building huts out of plywood and scrap metal. Pigs and dogs ran wild in the mud footpaths. Drunks snored in the gutter near illegal cantinas. Prera found a small boy defecating in a vacant lot, surrounded by watching vultures. What troubled him most about the scene was the shamelessness of the boy, who didn't bat an eyelash when Prera caught him in his lens. "¡Pobre Guatemala!," he lamented.[6]

Prera's supervisor, the engineer León Yela, the subdirector of Public Works, made the moral subtext more specific when he passed the proposal plan along to the director. El Gallito, he opined, was a place where people lived "in chaotic disorder and painful promiscuity." It would mean nothing, he said, to change the physical structure of the barrio if the population continued to be "uncultured, indolent, dirty and slovenly." His verdict: a profound moral change was needed. Prera's plan, combined with government extirpation of vice in general and an antialcohol campaign in particular, could be adequate. However, he noted wistfully, in this era "when we speak of liberty and democracy," one couldn't just displace the inhabitants to finca Bethania "as if to a concentration camp." The change would have to be gradual, and homeowners would have to be paid market price for their expropriated dwellings.[7]

Market price speaks to the heart of León's argument. The government's original sin, he claimed, was to have given away the lots in El Gallito for free when the neighborhood was legally formed in 1928–29. Instead of inculcating a work ethic, the state had promoted beggary. Instead of solving the problem of homelessness that dated all the way back to the city-wrecking earthquakes of late 1917 and early 1918—a problem that, together with worker activism, prompted the government to buy finca El Gallito a decade later—the state had compounded chaos by implying that it had the power to provide for the lazy who refused to provide for themselves.[8]

"A Thousand Bothers":
The Early Years of the Worker Neighborhoods

In fact, like other so-called worker neighborhoods in Guatemala City, such
as La Recolección and La Palmita, El Gallito had been born in a state of
chaos. The state formed these neighborhoods both as an emergency measure to relocate homeless families who had been sheltered in state *campamentos* for years and as an explicit response to labor organizing in Guatemala City in the 1920s. The original plan had been to sell the lots on the
newly purchased fincas to inhabitants for low monthly payments. In 1928,
after a brief trial period, however, the Lázaro Chacón government back-
tracked and began granting properties to the proletariat and to disadvan-
taged groups like single mothers and widows for free, by lottery. The
Ministry of Development (later renamed Public Works) administered the
neighborhoods, and in a confidential memo in 1942 its director admitted
that from the beginning, poor judgment, confusing regulations, and out-
right favoritism and corruption on the government's part had caused a
nightmare of chaos and "a thousand bothers."[9]

The rules, not the residents, caused the "thousand bothers." The government awarded the lots to the poorest of the poor but provided neither
aid nor services such as plumbing, sewers, electricity, or garbage collection.
Regulations required inhabitants to build a solid dwelling, not a *barraca*, or
hut, though this was allowed as a temporary measure, within five years,
although mortgages and loans were out of their reach. For ten years residents could not rent, sell, subdivide, or otherwise transfer or make money
from their property, which in the eyes of the law wasn't even really theirs
since the government failed to register it officially.[10] In short, penniless
people received naked dirt plots and were expected, collectively, to build a
city neighborhood.

Today El Gallito is in the very heart of Guatemala City. It forms a part of
zone 3, a narrow, north–south strip made up of densely populated work-
ing- and lower-class neighborhoods, bounded on the west and north by the
ravine of the La Barranca River, on the east by zone 1, the historic center,
and by the equally poor zone 8. At its southernmost point is the Trébol, the
city's major highway cloverleaf. Zone 3 is also home to the general cemetery and the municipal dump, one of the most notorious sites of poverty
and misery in the Western Hemisphere. But in 1930, when the populating
of the lots began, present-day zone 3 was only dotted with settlement, and

El Gallito was a remote rural property awaiting human transformation. Winners of the land lottery wandered onto this empty canvas with their families and their belongings and tried to figure out what to do. Lots were poorly marked, and numerous families quickly laid claim to the same spaces; residents had to petition the ministry to appoint an overseer.[11] Once the land was divided up, which was carried out so haphazardly that decades of confusing and conflicting claims would follow, families had to muster the resources to erect housing. They found it a daunting task. In 1931 a group of over twenty families requested access to mortgages. They even offered to sign legal documents forcing them to invest all the mortgage money in construction. The government turned them down.[12]

Faced with mismanagement and necessity, the poor created a complex mix of strategies related to acquiring, keeping, and developing land in neighborhoods like El Gallito. The creation of space in the neighborhood exemplifies chaotic elements that characterize contemporary Guatemalan development: mistrust, litigiousness, and competition; popular notions of justice; deliberate opacity and double-dealing to keep the state confused; and the forging of a geography of small enterprises that, like an underground constellation of points of production, sustains human life, however miserably. None of these strategies was either born in or caused by neighborhoods like El Gallito. Instead, El Gallito opens a window—politically, socially, and economically—on the making of modern culture in this particular corner of what would later be known as the third world.

Petitions for urban lots, stretching all the way from the 1930s to the 1960s, show rhetorical and political strategies. After the initial lotteries of the late 1920s, properties were awarded by petition, and petitioners soon overwhelmed the government's capacity to deal with them. A poor person's first choice was where to send the petition. Levels of authority overlapped within the bureaucracy, a source both of confusion and of opportunity to manipulate the system. Petitions sent as a personal appeal to the president sometimes proved more effective than those directed to Public Works; usually, the president's secretary forwarded them without comment to Public Works, but on occasion an executive directive would be attached. The narrative forms of these appeals for aid from on high reference a tradition of client–patron relations hundreds of years old that were at the heart of the Ubico state. Nearly all petitions for state-owned lots began with stories of hardship. "I am the father of six small children, and since my wife is ill, I have to feed and house them," wrote Manuel Alvarez, an unemployed, thirty-seven-year-old carpenter from Quetzaltenango living in the city's campamento in the Campo del Marte, built after the earthquake. "I do this so deficiently that I fear all of us will soon have to be hospitalized for malnutrition, because in truth there is no more than the little food we get from public charity to quiet the hunger, the thirst and the misery that flog us today without compassion." Alvarez also mobilized the two other most common lot-petitioning tropes: political affiliation ("we have always served in the ranks of the Partido Progresista") and the denunciation of unutilized lots. Indeed, the ministry investigated the fourteen lots in El Gallito that Alvarez named by number and found that, though undeveloped, they were already owned. Still loathe to expropriate, the bureaucracy turned down Alvarez's request.[13]

Alvarez's request, one that epitomizes thousands from the 1930s to the 1960s, mobilized a popular discourse of property rights based on use rather than ownership. While the government's rules required that lot recipients develop their land, the courts and cabinet ministers were nonetheless reluctant to expropriate private property. As early as 1932, with the government already swamped in requests for properties, the official in charge of the neighborhood commented that enforcing building codes would free up land. In practice, this rarely happened.[14] Instead, lots, as they became available, were granted through such opaque mechanisms as political favoritism, pure dumb luck, and vicious denunciations and legal maneuvering. Renters turned against the landlords who had illegally given them a home; lovers denounced their partners; and neighbors spied on one another, sending the government reports of money-making enterprises and demanding that justice be done. Most nefarious were political denunciations. In the mid-1930s the government began requiring police investigations of petitioners, a requirement that for the next decade served as a political background check. But the state got aid in its political oppression from the needy poor. During the Ubico dictatorship and again after the anticommunist invasion of 1954, many neighbors denounced lot owners' subversive political activities. Scarcity, poverty, and state policy pitted people against each other.

If feuds, surveillance, and mistrust were manifestations of Guatemala's growth pattern, so too were popular discourses of justice. As the state institutionalized random patronage, people came to demand that patronage within the context of the bureaucracy. Rosa Gómez Archila viuda de León wrote to the government in 1935, "But I'm truly poor, a widow with a family! And for this, no more, I burn for the right that you might with justice come to my aid! No, Señor! It cannot be! Me, I am alone in the World, my only shelter being, after God, nothing more than the justice based in the laws of the Supreme Government." In Rosa's case, the Supreme Government came through. She ended up being awarded a lot in El Gallito that a supposedly rich military man had abandoned.[15] Rosa's call for justice matched the government's political line, as would tens of thousands of such demands over the decades ahead.

After the problem of getting land from the government came the problem of using it, and the utilization of government-granted land was likewise an area of unceasing contestation, subterfuge, and chaos. From the very beginning, improvisational building in El Gallito, anticipating the massive land invasions later to come, proved to be a successful strategy, but only for a handful of people. Soledad Girón de Cardona, for example, won the title to lot 459-B (B because it previously hadn't existed on any plan) by filling in a precipitous gully with earth and building a hut on it.[16] Such stories encouraged similar actions, but most offenders were evicted, at least until the mid-1940s. More successful than improvisational building was finding and claiming a sliver of undistributed land, or *cuchilla*. Poor people became skilled at reading the landscape and untangling the intricacies of borders and ownership and would petition Public Works with hand-drawn maps. It became customary during the 1930s to create tiny B lots in response to their claims, even though it meant that government engineers had to do spot inspections and surveys to make sure access paths and future development plans for public facilities were taken into account.

Improvisational builders and cuchilla petitioners often chose sites destined for future streets, blocking access to interior lots. Another case, also from the early thirties, illustrates this sort of chaos in El Gallito space creation. A man named Antonio Méndez Paz extended his lot, blocking access to three things: other people's properties, an area of the ravine used for a dump, and a white sand deposit. Trash and dead animals began piling up in residential areas. Besides finding this situation objectionable, neighbors were also furious about the loss of a local raw material. Over one hundred of them, "from little children to little old people," had been excavating the sand and selling it for a few centavos a sack. How dare this man inhibit the working class's right "to take the white sand that gives them life to keep from dying of hunger?" they wrote. "It is justice that we ask." In the end, Méndez was forced to redraw his lot, but the neighbors didn't get their justice, as Public Works immediately took steps to block their access to the sand pit.[17] Despite state efforts, over a decade later—as Prera was planning to level the neighborhood, erect his monument to Le Corbusier, and turn lowlifes into citizens—Public Works was in the midst of another campaign to stop sand and stone excavation in El Gallito and La Palmita.[18] Inner-city dwellers were literally mining the peripheries of their neighborhoods.

Besides showing the use made of raw materials and underscoring the porous boundary between public and private space in the barrio, the case of Méndez Paz highlights another chaotic element: naming conventions. The neighbors investigated Méndez Paz and alleged that he had falsified his name to double-cross the state. An original lot recipient, he had sold his lot, illegally, and then approached lawyers named Paz y Paz to win the land back, duping his buyer. Méndez, neighbors claimed, had never been a Paz; he made up the last name to trick the lawyers into thinking he was a distant relative. Name confusion was so common and record keeping so poor, that Méndez Whoever(?) managed to slip between identities undetected.[19] Throughout the century, as today, popular naming conventions confounded authorities and afforded opportunities both for evading the state's gaze and for running scams like that of Méndez Paz. Partly, name confusion can be attributed to a largely illiterate or only functionally literate society; Mayan last names in particular tend to be spelled differently every time they appear in an expediente. It is also a custom among some Maya, however, to use a different first name from that appearing on their identification. Public Works officials trying to investigate Joaquín Chigüil Tecún (Chichil Tecum, Chigal Tegun, etc.), a K'iche' Maya from Totonicapán involved in a land dispute in the city, hunted for him for months, stymied because everyone knew him as Francisco. When they finally found him, they evicted him.[20]

In *Weapons of the Weak*, James Scott discusses strategies by which the oppressed class "flies below the radar" and resists authority passively.[21] Undecipherable naming conventions, even when they reflect culture and custom instead of a consciously designed plan to fool or defraud someone, fit into this category. But in neighborhoods like El Gallito, residents deliberately and continuously tested the limits of passive resistance with far more overt strategies. They weren't supposed to subdivide, sell, or rent, but they did so frequently. While most used their homes for legal businesses, such as washing laundry or making tortillas, some ran brothels and illegal cantinas. A few created whole prohibited business networks, like Pedro

Chinchilla, an absentee owner who in the early 1940s rented his lot to Victoriano Toc Marroquín. Toc, instead of living in the property's humble hut, sublet it to a third individual, who used it as a horse stable. This venture proved so successful that Toc cut up the remainder of the lot to use for pigsties, starting a thriving livestock business in relatively urban El Gallito.[22] The state put an end to it. In general, the government was hostile to city livestock and agriculture, and, afraid that poor residents would sow all the ravines, parks, and streets with corn, Public Works had worked hard during the mid-1930s to extirpate maize cultivation in its city neighborhoods.[23] Their success was only partial. Even today, especially in the metropolis's outer zones, *milpa* cornfields can be seen terraced into the near-vertical slopes of Guatemala City's ravines.

In 1946, then, the engineer Enrique Prera had a point. El Gallito was indeed chaotic, as were neighborhoods like it throughout the rapidly growing city. What he missed was the order within the chaos, and the root problems that had given rise to it. What he missed was the fact that the social and physical geography of the neighborhood reflected ingenuity and enterprise.

Prera's plan never stood a chance, even if the residents hadn't opposed it. When the director general of Public Works forwarded it to the minister, he attached a memo calling it utterly impractical. It would be wonderful to turn El Gallito into a middle-class neighborhood, he argued, but Prera's utopian scheme overlooked the fact that there were honorable people with good homes there who had no desire to go live in the mud while the neighborhood was being rebuilt. Constructing adequate lodging for them —some nineteen thousand people in three thousand families—in finca Bethania would be too costly. Why, he asked the minister, are we making grand plans while at the same time overlooking the main problem? Why are we tolerating illegal land occupations?[24]

"Because of Social Causes We Do Not Understand":
Land Invasions of the 1940s

The great Guatemala City ravine invasions of 1945–48 mark the birth of the modern Guatemalan ghetto. Propelled by a changing physical landscape, a tolerant political economy, and a heightened sense of possibility in the years following the Revolution and the end of the Second World War, migrants began to set their sights on the capital at a markedly increased rate. The city itself, meanwhile, was absorbing neighboring municipalities, transforming local networks of production as city-supplying farmland became part of the urban fabric, itself needing to be provisioned by farms farther abroad. Within the city's historic heart, citizens emboldened by new civil liberties and inspired by greater employment opportunities in construction, industry, and services began to migrate more intensively within the metropolis. In short, an always mobile populace became more so, and a city already lacking in infrastructure and housing became, slowly, the metropolis marked by the *asentamientos precarios* (precarious settlements, or shantytowns) that prevail today.

Urban invasions of state-owned land began in La Palmita and quickly spread to El Gallito. Both neighborhoods backed onto the vertiginous ravines that crisscross the Ermita Valley in which the capital is located. The landslide-prone ravines had never been inhabited. They couldn't be, or so city authorities thought.

Early in April 1945, just weeks after Arévalo's inauguration, Eduarda de Monzón and Isabel Hernández launched a two-couple land invasion in the La Palmita ravine. Poor, illiterate migrants from Santa Rosa, Eduarda and Isabel, the invasion's masterminds, were among the first to take advantage of the overlay of a new people's government upon a sloppy land tenancy system and a convoluted bureaucracy. In so doing, they not only won a home of their own, but also the distinction of being the first among thousands to demand economic justice from the new regime by simply taking it.

Humberto Zelaya discovered the invaders on the morning of 5 April. For years the government's point man for neighborhood affairs—technically, the *encargado de campamentos y colonias* of the Development Ministry's Dirección General de Obras Públicas (DGOP)—the straight-laced Zelaya was making his weekly rounds when he saw the couples driving stakes. Though he would write his report in the names of the men— Eduarda's husband, Antonio, and Isabel's partner, Pedro Monzón—it was the women who responded to his questioning. Countering his claim that their building was unauthorized and his mandate that they had a week to desist, they deployed a two-part strategy. First, they appealed to his sense of fairness: why should the poor go without when the land was standing empty? Second, they referred to technicalities. The land, Isabel maintained, was adjacent to lot 1069; a friend of hers had informed her that

1069's owner had illegally bought four lots from the encargado for twenty quetzales apiece (Isabel must not have known she was addressing the encargado when she made this claim). Thus apprised of his own misdeeds, Zelaya demanded the informant's name. Together, he and the women trooped through the neighborhood to find the rumor monger. After several stops, the group finally settled on naming María Leverón de Argueta as the source of information.[25]

Events unfolded rapidly. The next day the two couples and Leverón appeared to give testimony at the DGOP office, and within a week they did the same thing before a judge, the Juzgado 4° de Paz. When it turned out that 1069, a corner lot, was triangular and therefore larger than the norm and that Leverón had nothing to do with the matter, Isabel and Eduarda changed their story. They had never named Leverón, they claimed, but her sister Edelmira had, who, under questioning, conveniently turned out to be "in a state of dementia." Isabel and Eduarda admitted to building illegally but argued that necessity obliged them to proceed in this way, neither harming nor depriving anyone since nobody else would dare to make a home in such a dangerous place.[26]

Others, however, did dare. By the time the women were testifying, word had spread that there was land for the taking in the La Palmita ravine. Zelaya served several other groups with cease and desist orders; shacks were cropping up, including the ones that Isabel's and Eduarda's mates continued to build. Responding to Zelaya's urgent communiqués, the director of Public Works toured La Palmita on 12 April. He came too early. The following night saw the first full-scale invasion, with several dozen families staking claims at two o'clock in the morning. At sunrise the Guardia Civil, an oppressive force throughout the thirties but now tethered to the Revolution, arrested a handful of people, all of whom, before their quick release, swore that Zelaya himself had sold them the land. The case wound through the courts and ministries in the month ahead. Zelaya, an honest man, denied ever having been a "promoter of public disorder," as various judges and the *intendente municipal* ordered evictions that the squatters ignored. By mid-May there were over six hundred unauthorized residents in the La Palmita ravine. Warning his boss, the minister, of insoluble problems ahead if nothing were done, Zelaya spoke to the government's uncomfortable position as protector of the pueblo and enforcer of the law. "I figure it is now time for people to understand that the State is obliged to protect and provide for those who respect its laws," he wrote, "but we never have to tolerate abuses and disorder like that . . . in La Palmita."[27]

Zelaya was singing to the wind. The invasion of La Palmita was never brought under control. Invaders tested authority's willingness to evict them by force of arms and found authority unwilling. Invasions in El Gallito followed. A year and a half later, exactly as Prera's reurbanization plan was going public, Zelaya would declare the invaders in El Gallito to be in open rebellion. "If people criticize the urbanization of El Gallito today," he noted dryly, "imagine what they will say when the layout of the streets disappears and all public services become impossible."[28]

Zelaya had first reported invasions in El Gallito in June of 1946, not just in ravines but also in undeveloped lots. The minister, hardened by the failure to stop La Palmita invaders, had sent out the Guardia Civil, and for two to three months land seizures were quelled.[29] They began again with new force at the end of August, in El Gallito and La Palmita alike. Invaders ignored Zelaya, court-ordered eviction notices, and the Guardia Civil, prompting the Guardia to petition the government for permission to de-molish illegal dwellings—permission that was promptly denied.[30] The same new occupants who had burst out laughing and mocked Zelaya in September 1946 were still there, settled in huts, a year later.[31]

Readings of thirty-three years' worth of petitions and transactions in El Gallito and La Palmita as well as of the police and social worker reports that were often attached show conclusively that the vast majority of inhabitants, legal and illegal alike, were extremely poor. However, like the land lotteries before them, the land invasions presented opportunities for scams. While it was grossly exaggerated, there was a measure of truth in Subdirector Yela's statement that there were some squatters who owned homes in other locations and were building illegal huts to start a rental or other "productive business." Some, he said, insisted that "since they have four or five children they need four or five huts, even though those children are still nursing."[32]

By the middle of 1948 invaders in La Palmita were in a state of virtual warfare with the Guardia Civil, and two subinspectors set out to prove that the invaders were really speculators. They unearthed a number of infrac-tions on the part of about a half dozen squatters. Rosario Méndez already had a home in La Palmita; so too did Elena Fernández, whose husband was a well-paid railroad worker; Sofía Romero just sold her El Gallito house to come here to speculate, and so on.[33] More interesting than the officers' revelations, however, is the fact that they appear to have been tipped off by another combative invader, Cayetano Villalta García. What emerges is a tangled tale that, while short on certainties, illustrates the chaotic politics of the ravines.

Villalta García's dealings with the government dated back to 1946, when he, a relative named Flavio, and a few dozen other people had begun building huts on the banks of an open sewer in the La Palmita ravine. The Guardia ordered them to leave, and they filed an expediente requesting property rights. It was denied. Then Villalta unleashed a torrent of paperwork on the government that would not subside for two years. In 1946 alone he and the other settlers filed at least three allegations that the Guardia Civil was threatening them with violence. This proved an effective delay tactic, since the government investigated in every case. By the end of the year the building had become systematic, according to Public Works officials, who noted the degree of informal organization in the ravine with alarm. The colony had also grown. "There are now 400 families," an official wrote in December of 1946. "This is an incubator of disease."[34]

The incubator continued to swell throughout 1947, despite several rounds of official eviction notices that the occupiers ignored, always filing counterclaims.[35] In this year, however, political organizers arrived to seek support among the growing and complicated network of alliances in the ravine. The two most important groups on hand were the Partido Acción Revolucionaria (PAR) and the smaller Frente Popular Libertador (FPL), both revolutionary labor parties. While the PAR served briefly as an umbrella labor organization, for the most part it competed bitterly with the FPL and others, weakening the Revolution's working-class base.[36] Villalta García worked with the PAR and FPL, apparently playing them against each other and both against the government. By early 1948, in response to yet another attempted eviction, he warned President Arévalo that "we have our branch of the PAR here, and, as you know, the PAR has many adversaries."[37] At exactly the same time as Villalta was issuing this threat, the Guardia Civil was reporting that squatters, Villalta among them, had chased them away with machetes when they tried to serve eviction notices, screaming that they were "supported by the FPL, already having lots of meetings, and that nobody could force them to leave."[38]

What happened next is unclear. A good guess is that eviction appeared inevitable, and that Villalta García approached the local Guardia officers, whom by this time he must have known quite well, and offered them damning information on a few of the other squatters. Perhaps he thought that some sacrificial lambs would satisfy the government's need to impose order. Perhaps he had vendettas against the people he named. Perhaps he wasn't the informant at all but knew who was. Or perhaps he was aware that at this very time the Guardia officers, more than fed up, were compiling a personal case file on him, detailing the truly incredible extent of legal proceedings and correspondence to which he had subjected the government over the past two years. All that is known for sure is that Villalta's personal account of his neighbors' misdeeds appeared in President Arévalo's office, on official stamped paper, three days before the Guardia officers filed their own report with the same information.[39]

Two weeks after this last exchange, with eviction hanging in the balance, documents cease. Villalta's fate remains unknown. The compilation of his long-running battle is filled with Public Works' cover sheets, each of which has a space in which the *trámite*, or ordered proceeding, is supposed to be filled in. Most of these simply have a series of question marks. The majority were written by typewriter, but several say "?????" in crayon.

The ministry and Zelaya alike were overwhelmed. At the same time as the drama at La Palmita was unfolding, a similar invasion mushroomed out of control on the slopes bordering 3a Calle del Bosque in El Gallito. The settlers were represented by a group of women who wrote, "We understand perfectly that we have no right to ask you [for tenancy] based in any human laws, but in accordance with those of a higher order, those that come from on high, yes, because we are not at fault for being poor and because of social causes we do not understand, we find ourselves in this painful situation. Therefore," they continued, "we ask you in the name of the principles of universal ethics." The government rejected their petition, despite their claim that during the Revolution "the people offered their blood at the foot of the altar of the *Patria* . . . poor people, but valiant and suffering, who ask not for compensation but for justice."[40]

The individual land invaders drop out of sight, but it is known that their shantytowns suffered terribly when a storm ripped through Guatemala City in October 1949. It devastated many precarious neighborhoods, including those in the Palmita and El Gallito ravines. What had been an eviction and control problem became one of emergency relocation.

"Swarms of Women in Rags":
Two Modernist Neighborhood Dreams Are Dashed

The secretary of Public Works, Víctor Manuel Marroquín Gómez, was charged with the job of moving La Palmita's homeless to the area's new state property, Colonia Labor.[41] Colonia Labor was a neighborhood in formation, its every block highly contested. In general, goings-on in the colonia show the mixed spatial, social, and political geography of urban territory in midcentury Guatemala. The Life Insurance Society Pedro Molina Flores and the Public Works Employees' Union were petitioning for land for social centers near the Evangelical church. The Guardia Civil wanted a police station. Neighborhood administrators were trying to stop plans to put in an insane asylum and poorhouse, and a frustrated city planner, with support from the director of Public Works, was begging the unresponsive minister to prohibit hut building by people who "allege extreme poverty" but forget to mention their "laziness and vice-ridden habits" and the fact that they "reject all honest employment offered to them." The poor women, the director maintained, were no better than the alcoholic men. "There are swarms of women in rags in these neighborhoods who could well earn an honest living if they wanted to," he wrote.[42]

The director's dreams of social hygiene in Colonia Labor, never realizable in the first place, were shattered by the influx of storm refugees. A frustrated Marroquín Gómez was still trying to place families all through 1951. Touched by their misery, he petitioned his ministry for special dispensations for some of the worst hit but was told that it was out of Public Works' hands. In February of 1950 the government had attempted to rationalize the chaos by transferring management of Colonia Labor, along with another neighborhood, Colonia 20 de Octubre, to the Crédito Hipotecario Nacional (CHN), the national mortgage bank.[43] The result, however, was more chaos. Confusion and overlapping of authority made it harder for officials to place storm victims, many of whom waited for years for aid that often never came.

Those who did ultimately get housing were most likely to get it three years later, when the government opened the finca Bethania for settlement in 1952. Located to the northeast across the ravine behind El Gallito, Bethania is an excellent example of midcentury urban space formation. Today part of zone 7's archipelago of densely populated poor and working-class neighborhoods that run the ridge between the El Naranjo and La

Barranca rivers, Bethania began life as an isolated farm. Its story shows grass-roots revolutionary politics, modern housing solutions that failed utterly, institutional confusion, and urban planning thwarted by unforeseen disasters such as the storm, by unprecedented levels of poverty and need, and by chaos.

Although preliminary surveys were underway, the government had been publicly denying plans to urbanize the finca Bethania since the mid-1940s, when the FPL had kicked up a hornets' nest by promising evicted El Gallito land invaders spaces in the faraway farm. The PAR cried dirty politics, and the FPL continued to champion the cause of El Gallito and La Palmita invaders alike, getting plans for Bethania off to a chaotic start.[44]

Both grass-roots political organizing and engineering foul-ups complicated Bethania's birth. Before the storm added another layer of confusion, the government had already generated two conflicting lists of land beneficiaries.[45] Only the land set aside for the Sanatorio de Rehabilitación de Alcohólicos remained uncontested as unions and corporate entities vied for what remained. Their claims were complicated by the fact that the land itself remained completely illegible. A single engineer had begun surveying and measuring the finca in August of 1947, but the government was building the National Stadium at the same time, and, in the confusion, all the measurements got lost. The ministry started over, but personnel changes caused more documentation problems.[46] Before the state finally opened the finca in 1952, complete with rental units, construction snags had been considerable. They included a seven-month work stoppage for lack of funds, interminable delays in opening an entrance road, and difficulties in laying drains and water systems, which would later prove inadequate. Swamped with over 5,000 applications before a single home was rented, the government failed to keep its promises to numerous unions and groups.[47] The 620 worker dwellings, meanwhile, lacked basic services and had run nearly double the projected cost. Zelaya, defending the honor of the engineers and builders, attributed the cost overrun to "some unknown factor."[48]

Amidst the din, civil engineers continued to point out that roads to connect the finca both to the Pan-American Highway and to the city center would be of great utility. In 1961 there was still no bridge over the ravine to Bethania.[49] The neighborhood, by that time run not by Public Works but by the Instituto de Fomento de la Producción (INFOP), suffered chronic problems both with access and basic services such as light and electricity.

A city of shantytowns. This photograph shows Colonia La Limonada in 1960, some fifteen years after the first major land invasions in the Guatemala City ravines. Anonymous, "Colonia La Limonada, Zona 5," Guatemala City, May 1960. Archivo de fotografías de El Imparcial. Fototeca Guatemala, CIRMA (Reference Code: GT-FG-CIRMA-062–1960-Colonia).

Public health was also disastrous. According to the fifth-grade newspaper of Bethania's Escuela Experimental Indoamericana—a school linked with rural "fundamental education" trials—three children a day were dying in Bethania from parasites and malnutrition in 1953.[50] The situation would get no better under the anticommunist regimes after 1954.[51] By decade's end, government files on Bethania would be stuffed with *expedientes* from the hungry, desperate, ill, and unemployed.

"Land, Bread, and Industrialization": Revolutionary
Government and the "Global Biopolitical Economy"

In contemporary Guatemala, bodies are still riddled with parasites and wasting away from malnutrition. Like the *traje*-clad body, the rifle-bearing body in camouflage and war paint, the decaying body in a mass grave in a mountain village, the puffy body in suit and tie at Harvard Business School, this scarred, stunted, brown corpus is a symbol of corporate capitalist modernity and all it has brought to Guatemala and the globe.

In midcentury the geography of Guatemalan poverty emerged in its still-recognizable form. The cultural and socioeconomic realities of the lower classes both defined Guatemalan modernity and arose from the conditions of its modernization. That reciprocally formed modernization happened within a rapidly changing political economy that was locally, regionally, and globally conditioned.

In *A Finger in the Wound: Body Politics in Quincentennial Guatemala*, the anthropologist Diane Nelson explores modernity in transnational Guatemala. Underscoring the complexity, ambiguities, and slippages of the lived experience of modernity, Nelson uses the wounded body and body politic as a central metaphor for the Mayan movement's and the state's trajectory through the matrix of the "global biopolitical economy."[52] Nelson's body imagery gives a linguistic tool to situate the flows of twentieth-century development within a wide field of analysis that ranges from the unapproachable consciousness of the individual to the impossible-to-summarize process of globalization writ large. To borrow her metaphor, during the Revolution there was an elite reliance on plan-rational engineering that entailed transforming the body politic in ways that devolved upon the individual body. The elite's top-down plan-rationality, however, entailed policies and practices that both responded to and fomented widespread, grass-roots democracy, a social democracy that drew on and expanded the labor politics of the long 1920s and that reenvisioned the forms of state patronage promoted during the long 1930s. The leftward lean of this chaotic democracy contested control of the national body, angering powerful economic sectors. It also challenged the U.S. vision of the hemispheric body. This challenge prompted an international alliance of right-wing sectors to invade the nation and impose its ideology by force of arms—arms that included not only guns, but also, as we will see, exactly the same technologies of social engineering that revolutionary leaders had tried to use.

In short, during the age of rapid modernization, body, region, nation, and globe came to be linked in very specific ways. The historical interplay of chaos and rationality exposes how that happened. During the Revolution, Guatemalan national leaders drew on global technologies of modernization—a body of thought produced within a contested field of cultural production that in the global West was intimately related with the rise of corporate capitalism, as scholars like David Noble have demonstrated.[53] Over time, both popular pressure from below and discourses of development from above that challenged the corporate capitalist model influenced the revolutionary state to attempt to engineer a radical socioeconomic restructuring of the landscape.[54] The landscape ("chaos"), however, is not so easily transformed by social engineering ("rationality").

Guatemalan society was at a complex historical conjuncture in the 1940s. Campesinos, many of them newly organizing in rural unions that were themselves linked to national and international organizations, fed both themselves and the nation. They did so via a locally articulated, bottom-up network of markets. The markets were integral to regional cultures and were structured temporally and spatially by microclimates, by Mayan, agricultural, and Church calendars, by the available infrastructure, and by custom. Great landowners, meanwhile, included entrenched traditional elites, new modernizers attempting to pioneer something along the lines of agroindustry, and UFCO. Even as the modern, global economic system was congealing, forces ranging from state agencies to the PAU, which remained a promoter of agrarian education, modernization, and infrastructure development after its absorption into the Organization of American States (OAS) in 1948,[55] were endorsing variations of a capital intensive agricultural economy that would demand far greater monetary inputs than the Guatemalan state, not to mention the Guatemalan campesino, could hope to provide. All of these sectors, here greatly simplified, contested and shaped the landscape. They did so within the context of Cold War geopolitics that became more polarizing by the minute.

If there was a common definable goal of the contested Revolution, it was to get beyond the feudalism of the Ubico era. The ousting of Ubico ushered in a new age of reform designed to bring Guatemala into the modern world in the age of the United Nations and the highly influential Comisión Económica para América Latina (CEPAL). At the same time, at Bretton Woods the International Monetary Fund and World Bank were born, the U.S. dollar became the dominant international currency, and the context for future development in places like Guatemala was set.[56]

Within this context, with their body politic exploding into life, Guatemalans created or revamped virtually the entire landscape, society, and state. They created the modern banking system, the social security system, and the military structure. They gave rise to new, influential labor and cooperative movements and created scores of political parties. They built the basic commercial and public works infrastructure that lasts to this day. Their policies and development plans and even their use of the army in national development set the template for what would follow after the CIA-engineered invasion that overthrew the Revolution in 1954. Furthermore, those same plans went hand in hand with the gradual rise of heretofore unseen social classes and sectors: a new commercial and industrial elite; a diversified planter class; an expanding compendium of white-collar, service-sector, and government workers; an enormous urban underclass; and a ghettoized rural proletariat. Guatemalans of every political bent recognize the importance of their democratic Revolution. The new cadre of middle-class intellectuals, enjoying its first taste of power, inherited what its members saw as a broken body. Heady with theory, they would tackle the challenge of deciding how to give that body new life.

Democratization, development, and modernization were at the top of the agenda for both the Arévalo and Arbenz administrations. To their chagrin, the astronomical growth of the union movement both incurred the wrath of the United States and pushed them further than they wished to go.[57] The reforms witnessed under Arévalo were moderate but nonetheless lost the Revolution the support of the elite, who were threatened by the labor movement, especially its rural wing. Well before Arbenz took the oath of office in 1951, the elite,[58] terrified of the mobilized populace, had, with U.S. support, launched a major anticommunist offensive on the capitalist Revolution.[59]

Nothing in Arévalo's actual policies should have aroused such opposition. His plan was to stimulate agriculture, particularly nontraditional exports, through colonization, cooperatives, and experimental farms. A Department of Agricultural Mechanization was charged with transforming the countryside, along with a rural education program planned by the new Instituto Indígena Nacional. Industry would follow on agriculture's heels. Both were to be spurred by INFOP.[60] Arbenz sharpened the Revolution's focus on production. An economic nationalist, he was an ambitious developmentalist whose plans rested on extensive highway construction and high-modern public works projects, undertaken without U.S. aid.[61]

Pushed by the Confederación Nacional Campesina de Guatemala, a confederation of twenty-five rural unions formed in 1950, Arbenz launched a comprehensive agrarian reform in 1952. The idea of agrarian reform predated Arbenz's presidency.[62] It enjoyed advocacy not only from the labor movement and the Communist Party, but also from international finance and major, mainstream Guatemalan political parties as well. Yet campesinos and authorities had different goals for agrarian reform. The campesinos wanted land for their own purposes, and the authorities wanted to increase production. By increasing agroexport revenue, elites could foster a domestic market and build industry. Moreover, the backward campesino would learn high-technology farming and would be slowly drawn into the national sphere through education, social welfare, and highway construction.[63] Geography, systematicity, and space intersected in this thinking in a vision of widened exchange in the context of an economy stalled by uncommodified land, much of it fallow. The agrarian reform was a market- and value-oriented scheme based both on increasing private ownership of the means of production and on mechanizing and modernizing the inputs, process, and distribution of that production with fertilizers, irrigation, tractors, trucks, highways, and ports. It was part of a vast project that involved engineering not only the landscape but society as well.

Arbenz delivered his state-of-the-union address in March 1953 in the midst of a concerted and vocal anticommunist campaign. Reaffirming his policy of "land, bread, and industrialization," the president tried to appeal to sectors with widely divergent goals. He did so by appealing to their common need for infrastructure. The Atlantic Highway—linking the two oceans and later to join the Pan-American as the second axis of the nation's transportation network—was only partly paved, thanks to a lack of funds and equipment. However, Arbenz reported, work was underway to finish the project. He also planned to connect Guatemala City to all border crossings, ports, and departmental capitals by paved highways.[64] Only a few years later, after the CIA invasion, U.S. dollars and military rulers would bring Arbenz's developmentalist dreams to fruition. The bulk of the population, though, would find their dreams dashed. They would find that they were not to speak in a democracy, but to be spoken to by dictators. They were not to consume, but, as dispensable cheap laborers, to be consumed.

"Condemning Them to Perpetual Poverty":
Agrarian Reform and the Fight over Chaos and Rationality

The revolutionary state's vision of the Guatemalan national body devolved upon the body of the campesino. The untrained peon was, through rural education, to become a modernizing gentleman farmer. In general, the purpose of such an education was not just to teach reading, agronomy, and the like but to inculcate campesinos with modernist moral and political attitudes.[65]

As early as June 1945 the new Instituto Indigenista Nacional began training teachers to be sent to work in the highlands. The Revolution's Misiones Ambulantes de Cultura and rural education in general were projects designed both to foment state formation and loyalty to the Revolution and to conduct a frontal attack on illiteracy and "economic, hygienic, cultural and civic ignorance." A concept borrowed from the Mexicans, these cultural missions broadly aimed to assimilate the Maya into Ladino culture and to tie campesinos more closely to state institutions.[66]

The genealogy of rural education presented in a postinvasion propaganda tract, *Armas para ganar una nueva batalla* (Weapons to win a new battle), in 1957 illustrates how increasing ideological firepower came to be concentrated on the campesinos in a complex international evolutionary process. The roots of the rural education program, the piece claimed, were found in the efforts of Professor William Griffith of the United States and his work with the Interamerican Foundation in the mid- to late 1940s (the organization was extinct by 1957). Griffith worked for the formation of a Congreso Indigenista, which met in Cobán in 1948 and was to collaborate with the government in a widespread program of rural education. Meanwhile, the Servicio Cooperativo Interamericano de Educación (SCIDE) collaborated with the Ministry of Education to train one hundred teachers in the late 1940s. These teachers, in turn, established twenty *núcleos escolares campesinos* (campesino scholar centers) in the Kaqchikel-speaking highlands by decade's end, reportedly with little success or impact.[67] The agency withdrew from the country in 1950, when Arévalo, facing political pressure, refused to extend SCIDE's contract.[68] However, even without SCIDE's help, the incoming Arbenz administration revamped and expanded Arévalo's project of mobile cultural missions, just as the postinvasion dictatorships would revamp and expand Arbenz's.

The tensions between top-down rural education and bottom-up agrarian activism were seen clearly in the implementation of Arbenz's agrarian reform. The local agrarian reform committees, or Comités Agrarios Locales (CALS), formed in the 1950s to manage land expropriation and distribution, emerged as a ground of contestation. The CALS were sites of both profound grass-roots democracy and social control. On the one hand, they gave many campesinos their first voice in government, and consequently they have been hailed for their empowering effects. On the other, they linked those campesinos with vertically arranged state agencies.[69] That the Arbenz government was continuing to rely on top-down strategies, however, was confirmed with the creation in 1953 of the Instituto Nacional de Economía Indígena. The institute's stated aims were to break the closed economy, incorporate the Maya, regulate migrant labor, commercialize local crops, and introduce scientific fertilizers, seeds, tools, and techniques in the highlands.[70]

In early 1954 Robert Dillon, a UN agronomist who had been doing fieldwork for the institute since its inception, submitted a confidential memo to the government outlining his concerns. Dillon was passionate about agrarian reform. He wanted it, but he wanted a market-oriented plan, one that would be gradual, free from sudden expropriations (with tenant-workers buying lands), and supported by technical aid from state and international institutions. Not only was the government creating mayhem by expropriating lands before distributing its own property, it was giving lands to the wrong people. In effect, according to Dillon, unskilled finca laborers won the most territory, disadvantaging more skilled farmers found in the crowded Mayan highlands and causing a labor shortage. The plots were too small, and beneficiaries were tilling with hoes and machetes. Speculators would show up, wait for the Agrarian Bank's credits to be distributed, and during the ensuing party sell the drunken campesinos packages of the wrong fertilizers and useless tools. Awakening with a hangover, campesinos would discover that they were broke and on their own. "You are condemning them to perpetual poverty," Dillon told the government.[71]

Whether or not Dillon's assessment was correct will go unanswered. The United States and the Ubico-oriented wing of the Guatemalan military overthrew the revolutionary government and brought the experiment to a close.[72] A CIA-designed and -supported army under Col. Carlos Castillo Armas "invaded" the nation in June 1954. The Revolution was over, and the era of terror, violence, and dictatorship had begun. Huge numbers of agrarian reform beneficiaries lost their land, and in the barrios, as in the countryside, citizens like Eduarda de Monzón and Joaquín Chigüil Tecún found themselves without hope of being active participants in their government. However, while democracy, civil rights, and, needless to say, agrarian reform went by the wayside, much of the Revolution's program continued under a new guise. This is because the Revolution had brought to the nation the idea, if not the reality, of systematicity in keeping with global high modernism. That there ought to be such systematicity was never again at issue. But systematicity is neutral. The war was fought over its application.

The invasion of 1954 marked a tremendous change in politics, but less of one in the business of development. If the Revolution of 1944–54 was a period of social democratic high modernism, the decade or so that followed was one of anticommunist high modernism—a period in which the high modernism of the Revolution, stripped of its social democratic content, melded with the reactionary modernism of the Ubico days within the polarizing context of the Cold War.

The postinvasion state picked up its predecessor's structure of state, developmental projects, and public language. For this they were rewarded with dollars. As Arbenz's infrastructure-building plans began to come to fruition, the trends of urban growth and infrastructure development seen during the Revolution exploded, and in this milieu the contemporary informal economy took shape. Women, mostly of humble origins, were protagonists in forging this economy. And despite the propaganda of the counterrevolutionary state, it was they who provided a social safety net as well. They did so even as the institutionalizing, modernizing international development industry was working with the Guatemalan military governments to construct a State-as-Mother. The anticommunist modernists' first great social development project, it proved to be both fictitious and a failure.

I n 1933 or 1934 Antonia Alonzo Abá arrived in Guatemala City to work as a
nanny. She was twelve years old. Born in Santa Catarina Pinula—today
part of the Guatemalan Metropolitan Area but then a rural hinterland—the
girl came from a family already geographically separated by poverty. Her
mother was also away from home, working in the finca El Capulín in Villa
Canales. When she could, Antonia left the city to visit her. It was at the
finca that she met an older man, Luis García Chuni. She was thirteen and
unmarried when she gave birth to their first son, Francisco. The un-
schooled teenager lived with Luis for three more years, giving birth to
Justo, their second child, when she was sixteen. By then Luis had become
abusive, and Antonia, with her few belongings and a toddler and an infant
in tow, left the finca for the city.

Antonia needed a trade, and, living in Tívoli, a neighborhood later to
form part of zone 10, she found one, getting folk training as a *comadrona
empírica*, or midwife. Sometime around 1951 she found a post for herself
and her children as *guardianes*, live-in watchmen and caretakers, still a
commonly seen variation of peonage in Guatemala, in a house in zone 5.
During her five years there she lost track of her older son, Francisco, who
left home in search of work. Meanwhile, Justo, by then in his teens, got a
job locally as a blacksmith's apprentice, earning seventy-five centavos a day.
Perhaps this extra income convinced Antonia to take the risk of leaving the
guardian position, going back to midwifery, and investing in a home. The
risk was especially high since she made the investment at the very margins
of legality.

Over in Bethania, Agustín Sazo Ajú was offering a special deal. Agustín
was a single father caring for an infant. His wife had left him, taking their

older children with her. He was prepared to donate his home to Antonia for free, and all he wanted in return was a loan of fifty quetzales, which he said he would pay back "whenever he might be able to do so." He and Antonia made the deal and signed legal papers to this effect, making a typical end-run around restrictions on the selling of state housing. In October of 1956 Antonia and Justo moved in. It was to be a short-lived residency.

Jealous competitors for state housing quickly filed denunciations, claiming that sales prohibitions had been violated and that two working adults were occupying a home that was supposed to be occupied by poor people with dependents. The state sent Graciela Cabrera P., a social worker, to investigate. One of the army of women from the Ministry of Communications and Public Works who were charged with surveillance of households, Cabrera determined that rules were being broken. With Justo's seventy-five cents a day and the twenty quetzales that Antonia made monthly as a midwife, the mother and son could easily rent a place of their own. They were evicted, and the house was granted to a young, single mother with three babies.

Antonia didn't take this lying down. Aware that the whole social work bureaucracy dated to the Revolution, she accused Cabrera of having been a member of the revolutionary party. Cabrera, she claimed, was in league with two other Bethania dwellers who were really selling their house but who were also hiding their past revolutionary politics and who furthermore were railroad workers (the railroad union was among the nation's strongest at the time, and Antonia was subtly playing on the government's antiunion sentiments). She demanded not only an investigation of these irregularities, but also a visual inspection of her home to verify that she was truly poor and owned no luxury goods. Antonia signed her petition with a thumbprint. Government officials, quite accustomed to this kind of denunciation, dismissed her case, and in April of 1957 Antonia and Justo left Bethania to meet their unknown fate.[1]

Antonia's life certainly played out against a backdrop of radical political change. When she arrived in Guatemala City, Ubico had only recently cemented his dictatorial rule. She was still a resident when its citizens poured onto the streets and sparked the Revolution of 1944, and she wrote her cleverly anticommunist petition after that Revolution had been crushed. Assuming she lived into her fifties, one would think she witnessed the civil war that turned into genocide and, a decade later, the putative return to democracy and the coming of the postmodern age. One has a tendency to think of revolutions and dictatorships as tearing people's lives apart, yet Antonia and many like her lived lives that show more continuity and, to stretch the meaning of the word, stability than they do change. Development, both as visited on the population from above and as created by people like Antonia from below, helps explain why.

"The Revolution Charted the Course":
The Continuity Behind the Change

Perhaps when Antonia was working as a guardian in zone 5 during the invasion of 1954 she joined her neighbors at the *tienda* to gather around the radio and listen to the news. Guatemalans who tuned in at 9:00 P.M. on Sunday, 27 June, may well have been expecting to hear of battles. Primed by a CIA disinformation campaign and softened by bombing sorties on the capital, they believed that a large Army of Liberation had marched in from Honduras and was closing in on the National Palace. Instead, they heard their president's resignation speech. It wasn't live. Jacobo Arbenz had taped it several hours earlier, having decided to step down under circumstances debated to this day. With Arbenz's resignation, the Guatemalan Revolution came abruptly to an end. It had lasted nine years, eight months, and one week. What lay ahead was a thirty-two-year succession of coups, juntas, civilian–military pacts, and rigged elections as the country became ever more embroiled in civil war. From 1954 to 1986, only one president would hail from outside the army high command, and Guatemala would earn its reputation as a "garrison state."[2]

The first three of these governments, that of Carlos Castillo Armas, adopted and retooled the Revolution's public language, structure of state, and plan for national development. Ruling by decree, the Castillo Armas government (1954–57) crushed unions, burned books, drove leftists into exile, and institutionalized the Cold War anticommunist state that would keep the military at the center of national power.[3] After Castillo Armas was riddled with gunfire in 1957, a series of unstable juntas oversaw an election whose results were annulled by riots, and in a second election Gen. Miguel Ydígoras Fuentes (1958–63) prevailed. Ydígoras was slightly more politically open than Castillo. However, his corrupt regime saw increased cooperation with U.S. corporate and military powers and marked the further consolidation of military rule, especially after Marxist insurgency and pop-

ular insurrection broke out in the early 1960s. Minister of Defense Col.
Enrique Peralta Azurdia overthrew Ydígoras in 1963 and ruled by fiat until
1966. During these three years the Guatemalan army came to control the
executive, legislative, and judicial branches of government, and state terror—death squads, disappearances, and torture—became the norm. The
military elite continued to exercise power behind the scenes during the
civilian presidency of Julio César Méndez Montenegro (1966–70) and
returned to the National Palace in 1970, where they would remain until
1986, completing the so-called pacification of the countryside and returning the country to democracy via the elections of 1985.[4]

Beginning in 1954, these governments turned a Keynesian, social democratic political economy that was still in formation into an anticommunist,
authoritarian developmental state. Funded by the United States, they began to bring elements of the Revolution's nationalist development scheme
to fruition while simultaneously opening the door to foreign capital. They
also instituted state terror as a means of achieving change. In so doing, they
mimetically reproduced central tropes in Guatemalan body politics. From
the 1920s and 1930s they drew the *indigenismo*, organic *pueblo*, blended
Hispanic and U.S. Pan-Americanism, and agromodernism examined in
chapter 1. From the Revolution they tapped into discourses of "making
patria" and "land, bread and industrialization." In highly gendered ways,
leaders after 1954 teamed the Ubico-era State-as-Father with an aesthetic
State-as-Mother in their efforts to extend modern relations of exchange,
continuously referencing femininity and family in their public language
and institution building. The failure of development to provide opportunities for real families, however, guaranteed the growth of the on-the-
ground conditions that state-led development would need to fix, creating a
dialogical vicious circle that underpins Guatemala's convoluted political
history with a grim continuity.

In many ways Arbenz's resignation broadcast of 27 June 1954 serves as a
fulcrum. It separates Revolution from Counterrevolution, an open political
culture from a regime of virulent anticommunism. On another level, however, that day's dramatic events obscure larger continuities not only in the
everyday lives of citizens like Alonzo Abá, but between the democratic Ten
Years of Spring and the repressive governments that followed. As Jorge
Toriello, one of the national heroes of the Revolution of 1944, would note
on the thirtieth anniversary of the invasion in 1974, "The Bank of Guatemala and the banking system, the new Monetary Law ... social security, the

unions, workers' and employers' organizations, recreation centers, cooperatives, transportation companies, insurance companies," and many other facets of modern Guatemalan life dated to the revolutionary period. When asked by a reporter why the Revolution had "broken down" or "failed" in 1954, Toriello responded that it had done no such thing. "The Revolution charted the course for what was yet to come," the reporter from *El Imparcial* paraphrased him as saying. "It won socioeconomic and cultural victories that remain in effect and that have been increasing in scope for the benefit of the people."[5]

Toriello's observation, though overly sanguine about benefits flowing to the people, was correct in other ways. The Guatemalan state's bureaucratic structure, developmental policies, and its central, organizing myth could all be traced to the Revolution. So too could its productive, developmentalist army and its projects in agrarian, urban, industrial, and infrastructure development. How to explain this continuity? How could such similar projects and language of development underpin both an effervescent, polyvalent movement for social democracy and economic justice and the oppressive military state that followed?

In her study of Puerto Rico, *Reproducing Empire*, Laura Briggs conclusively demonstrates that discourses of sexuality, family, reproduction, and gender were absolutely central to the U.S. imperial project.[6] Guatemala was no exception. In broad strokes, by the 1960s the international backers of the development schemes of the country's military governments had come to espouse modernization theory, which posited a linear model of development in which the United States and Europe represented the future toward which more primitive regions were developing; they were reacting to the left's evolving, increasingly radical dependency theory, in which peripheral, underdeveloped societies needed to break free from dependency on the capitalist, imperialist core.[7] On one hand, gender ideology and gendered aesthetics helped to disguise this shift in ideological underpinning; on the other, the examining of gendered discourses reveals the slippages between transnational discourses of development and the ideological universe of the Guatemalan military and economic elite, which was far from homogenous and never totally in line with the United States. Gendered ideas and projects open a window on the workings of development-as-myth that came to characterize neoliberal globalization, and help to reveal subterranean mechanisms of continuity between revolution and counterrevolution in Guatemala. Gendered language appeared in everyday life, in political propaganda, in development, in institution building, and in social and economic thinking. As Joan Wallach Scott has pointed out, gender is not only "a constitutive element of social relationships based on perceived differences between the sexes," but also "a primary field within which or by means of which power is articulated."[8] In the first decade of counterrevolutionary Guatemala, anticommunist high modernism replaced social democratic high modernism. As part of the process, gender emerged as a wide field upon which political legitimacy, nation building, and development in general were partially enacted on a multiplicity of levels. The result was not equality but tragedy.

"Oficios de su Sexo":
The Gendered Myth of the Informal Economy

At the beginning of her petition, Antonia, or the notary who wrote the document for her, listed her occupation as *oficios domésticos*. Oficios domésticos and the synonymous and more commonly used *oficios de su sexo* were phrases that appeared again and again to describe women and women's work in twentieth-century Guatemalan bureaucratic paperwork. Reading these women's stories, however, one finds that sex offices, or trades, didn't end with cooking, cleaning, and child rearing. Government officials, notaries, and women themselves used the phrase even when the woman in question was making money by selling her labor. One of the most common professions eclipsed was that of the *tortillera*, or tortilla maker, whose labor provided Guatemalans with their staple food, just as it does today. Others included washerwoman, baker, day-care provider, midwife, paid housekeeper, and even chambermaid, shopkeeper, market vendor, and many others.

Oficios de su sexo is just a phrase, but it is a phrase located at the nexus of popular everyday discourse and the developmental projects that over time transformed society. As Guatemala modernized, its already separated families modernized, and its citizens gave rise to a widened informal economy that defines the nation to this day. Families were at the heart of this creation, and women were both at the heart of families, often as single heads of household, and at the heart of constructing this economy from below.

The phrase *oficios de su sexo* as well as the many feminized projects of developmentalists both national and international that I will shortly ex-

The economically active population window shopping. This shoeshine boy exemplifies a sector hidden by statistics and putatively given aid by "maternal" projects of state. Anonymous, "Niño lustrador en vitrina (Shoeshine Boy in Window)," Guatemala City. Archivo de fotografías de El Gráfico. Fototeca Guatemala, CIRMA (Reference Code: GT-FG-CIRMA-086-positivos asentamientos).

plore, evidence how a myth has been made of the economy itself. Since development, at its core, addresses the economy, debunking this myth is essential to understanding the real historical dynamics that shaped the making of modern Guatemala.

Putatively, the word *economy* refers to the collective activity of enterprises that produce growth. Guatemala's gross domestic product (GDP) grew steadily throughout the twentieth century, but the growth of misery far outpaced it. So too did the growth of the informal economy, a popularized version of the term *informal sector*, coined by the British economist Keith Hart and soon used by the International Labor Organization (ILO) in Africa in the early 1970s.[9] The informal economy refers to the world of people who vend on the streets without a license, make tortillas, wash clothes and clean homes, shine shoes, hawk snake oil, beg, or even sell their bodies in an attempt to survive in a world where growth excludes them. Around three-quarters of the Guatemalan population, excluding the significant percentage now in the United States, work in the informal economy.[10] The simple truth is that for most people the informal economy is *the* economy. It defines the financial reality in which they live. In fact, if the word *economy* were to be defined as the bulk of a population's financial and productive activities, it would refer not to Guatemala's formal sector, but to its informal sector. The rendering of these informal activities as *not* the economy is ideological, from their exclusion from the GDP to neoliberal institutions' efforts to incorporate these sectors.

The sheer size of the informal economy in the new millennium is astounding. According to statistics published by the Ministry of Economy in the "Encuesta nacional de empleo e ingresos" (National employment and income poll) for October 2002, (72 percent of Guatemala's economically active population was working in the informal sector at that time. It was probably an underestimate; the unions criticized the number, saying it didn't reflect the true extent of unemployment.[11] Of the Guatemalans laboring in this sector, just under a million were children—again, probably a serious underestimate.[12]

There was never a time when the majority of Guatemalans worked in formal situations marked by tax paying, the receipt of benefits and legal protections, and the like. Nevertheless, there are recognizable landmarks in the emergence of the informal economy as it exists today. First was the Revolution, when modernization and political liberty expanded the geographical boundaries within which families—many of them itinerant and separated—worked. The second and far more important landmark was the political economy in the decade after the anticommunist invasion of 1954, which crushed alternative models of politics and development and saw the rise of institutions built to fix the very problems that modernization had been and was still creating. Third and fourth, and the story yet to come, were the armed internal conflict, punctuated in 1976 by a devastating earthquake, and the coming age of neoliberal globalization. For present purposes, suffice to say that if the Revolution of 1944–54 saw the making of the modern Guatemalan ghetto, the anticommunist years from 1954 to the mid-1960s saw the maturation of Guatemala's contemporary informal economy.[13]

From the mid-1950s to the mid-1960s, infrastructure development, motor transportation, radio-wave communications, including the new but as yet barely distributed television, population growth, and increased contact of citizen and state hastened rural proletarianization and rural-to-urban migration. This national leap into third-world modernity had a personal side. Already structured by the migration involved in seasonal finca labor, domestic labor, and itinerant market vending, families split even further, especially as Guatemala City increasingly became a destination of choice and new residence alike. Paradoxically, even as families atomized further and further through space, they had to cling even more closely together for survival as they became more dependent on the money economy. It was families who constructed the modern Guatemalan economy, its function and its feel, and this explains in great measure why the Guatemalan present is so studded with remnants of the Guatemalan past.

The phrase *oficios de su sexo* hides two facts: women were at the center of both the family and the economy, and they were building economic structures that were not transparent to transnational business.[14] In the early 1970s, around the time Hart was giving the informal economy its name, a survey of over a thousand informal street vendors in Guatemala City showed that 80 percent of them were female single heads of household.[15] Then, as throughout the century, the most important businesses needed for survival in any city neighborhood tended to be owned by females. The case of Mercedes Chavarría de Moreno was typical. A middle-class woman living in El Gallito in the 1930s, she had opened a dress-making shop and a tienda in a rental property elsewhere in the city the decade before. She had built these enterprises alone; her husband worked in census taking and mechanical drawing. She did so while having a child nearly every year for eight years. By 1934 her children were in their teens and found employment in their mother's businesses.[16]

The family dynamic of the male partner working in some sort of wage-remitting job while the female built a business in the home was and still is quite common. Angela de Morales, for example, ran a butcher shop out of her family's adobe home in El Gallito in the 1930s, while her husband was out in the city working at his own occupation.[17] Businesses like these played an essential role in supplying city neighborhoods and are at the root of distribution networks as they have developed in Guatemala. In particular, tiendas and *carnicerías* (butcher shops) were normal economic routes of entry for women, just as market stalls were. Bernarda Cardona, to cite one example, moved from Retalhuleu to the capital in the 1930s and opened a pork shop, probably importing the meat from her hometown.

She supported six children through this enterprise; if there was an income-earning husband or partner in the picture, he never appeared in the documents.[18] While the phrase *oficios de su sexo* sometimes hid full-scale wage labor—as in the case of Bartola de Ibañez, who in 1943 was an absentee El Gallito lot owner employed as a cook in Zacapa while her sister-in-law cared for her makeshift hut back in the capital—it most often elided the constructive labor of women who made neighborhoods and communities function in the face of the formal economy's failure to do so.[19] These essential services are the sort of oficios de su sexo that historically conditioned the nature of the Guatemalan economy and its murky mix of formal and informal sectors.

Guatemalan governments, responding both to that murky on-the-ground mix and to global pressures and discourses, tried to manage or alleviate the situation (or both) with a feminized apparatus of state. Starting during the Revolution, the government introduced female social workers and charity-like programs (day-care centers, sewing machine handouts, and the like) run by women and often propagandized by the first lady. Preservation of the dissolving family was at the heart of these feminized programs' mission. "Oficios de su sexo" are located at the center of the contemporary informal economy, at the center of the astonishing and contradictory dynamic of breakdown and preservation of family and culture in Guatemala, and at the center of the institutionalization of the modernizing state.[20]

Manufacturing the State-as-Mother: Applied Propaganda and Applied Sociology

Arbenz's decision to step down, made public in his resignation speech of 27 June 1954, was a betrayal of the army and of the Revolution and it needed to be explained. Propagandists stepped in to do the job. They did it by emasculating the president and blaming his wife, María Vilanova de Arbenz. According to their mythology, Vilanova convinced her husband to flee instead of fight on that fateful day. A manipulator and seductress, Vilanova had not only turned her husband Communist but had pushed him to participate in the Revolution of 1944 in the first place.[21] The gendered story built around the rise and fall of Arbenz serves as an entry point for an examination of how gender discourse linked the U.S. culture industry—specifically, public relations—with military actions in Guatemala.

The invasion of Guatemala in 1954 was shrouded in secrecy and lies. Manufactured by the CIA, it was as much a public relations and disinformation campaign as it was a military action.[22] By late 1953–early 1954 the CIA was actively orchestrating Castillo Armas's invasion. It was also collaborating with the so-called liberator in the preparation of death and exile lists, deciding who would live, die, or be deported after the anticommunist victory. The CIA and State Department brought the play to its final act in early July 1954, when U.S. Ambassador John E. "Pistol-Packing" Peurifoy personally flew Castillo Armas into Guatemala City in the embassy plane after the colonel's manufactured victory in the field.[23]

Much of the original evidence about Communism in Guatemala that the CIA would later deploy had come directly from the U.S. public relations industry. Not long after the Revolution, UFCO had contracted Edward Bernays to convince the U.S. Congress and mainstream press that Guatemala had fallen into the Soviet sphere. The author of *Crystallizing Public Opinion* (1923), *Propaganda* (1928), and *Public Relations* (1945), Bernays, who had helped to launch the Columbia Broadcasting System and had devised marketing strategies for such companies as Procter & Gamble and Crisco, was widely regarded as the founder of public relations in its modern form.[24]

Efforts to convince U.S. lawmakers and businessmen that Guatemala had fallen were successful. In December 1953, the U.S. National Planning Association (NPA), in a publication entitled *Communism Versus Progress in Guatemala*, declared that the small Central American nation was "for all practical purposes dominated by the Communists."[25] The NPA, "an independent, nonpolitical, nonprofit organization established in 1934.... where leaders of agriculture, business, labor, and the professions join in programs to maintain and strengthen private initiative and enterprise," was chaired by Frank Atschul, the chairman of the board of General American Investors. Signing members included John F. Chapman, the associate editor of the *Harvard Business Review*; Michael Ross, the director of international affairs of the NPA; and Walter H. Wheeler, the president of Pitney-Bowes, Inc.[26] When the Guatemalan government attempted to defend itself against such charges at the United Nations, it was referred to the OAS, a U.S. mouthpiece.[27]

Gender discourse quickly became an arrow in the quiver of propagandists and political apologists attempting to justify invading Guatemala and overthrowing a democratically elected government. In the U.S. House of

Representatives in September 1954, three months after the CIA-led invasion, a member of Guatemala's National Committee of Defense Against
the Communists made the charge that Vilanova de Arbenz had turned her
man Communist. She had so unmanned him that she had to buy him six
books as his government was teetering in early June: *Letters to a Mother,
Modern Matrimony, The Education of Parents, Impotency in the Male, Ona-
nism and Homosexuality,* and *Nervous States.*[28] This testimony summed up
a wide body of literature produced by CIA operatives, who had culled their
information from the fertile world of Guatemalan political rumor.[29] Politically, the problem was that Jacobo Arbenz had been a leader and hero
within the very Guatemalan army that overthrew him. Emasculating Arbenz served the purposes of U.S. propagandists and Guatemalan right-
wing politicians alike.[30]

Silly as the propaganda is, the Vilanova story is important. It shows
discourses that helped to condition future first lady programs and state
aesthetics, giving a good example of how, in the words of Joan Scott,
"politics constructs gender and gender constructs politics."[31] Far from
being constrained to the world of political rumor and propaganda, gender
was at the center of political efforts to organize and reach women as the
war between left and right intensified.[32]

Immediately after the invasion, the office of the first lady took on new
prominence and importance in Guatemalan politics. As one hand of the
rightist propaganda machine painted the Arbenzes as evil, the other portrayed Castillo Armas and his wife, Odilia Palomo Paíz, as Guatemalans
extraordinaire. While the newspapers charged that the Arbenzes had
sacked the national treasury before going into exile and that Jacobo had
murdered his ex-army compatriot and fellow revolutionary junta member
Francisco Arana, they also plastered doña Odilia's face onto the Guatemalan national consciousness, well before her husband had managed to
jockey himself from junta member into the position of *presidente.*[33] Odilia
was ever visible on the front page of *El Imparcial,* out promoting hospitals
and public health programs for children.[34] María Teresa Laparra de Ydígoras, the wife of Gen. Ydígoras and first lady from 1958 to 1963, followed
suit. Very active in the Oficina de Asuntos Sociales de la Presidencia (President's Office for Social Affairs), she most notably handed out free sewing
machines to women in a sort of charitable cottage industry promotion.[35]
This gesture bespoke the historical transformation in the role of the first
lady in general and of the social welfare apparatus in specific.

Beginning in the Castillo Armas administration, the anticommunist state built on and expanded the feminized social services bureaucracy first introduced during the Revolution. In effect, they built an aesthetic State-as-Mother. If during the Revolution the original idea had been to provide a minimum level of social security—a social safety net—in keeping with the economics of Keynes and in response to the demands put forth in the major union platforms, under anticommunists, the idea of "social welfare" (*bienestar social*) took on the tinge of motherly, state-based charity. The Castillo Armas government created a new ministry, the Ministerio del Trabajo y Previsión Social (Work and Social Welfare), and founded the Consejo Nacional de Bienestar Social (National Council of Social Welfare), which held its first national conference in 1958, during the presidency of Ydígoras Fuentes.[36] Into the 1960s the Secretaría de Bienestar Social (SBS, Secretariat of Social Welfare) coordinated aid to families, albeit to only a tiny percentage of the families actually in need. The Secretaría de Asuntos Sociales de la Presidencia (Presidential Secretariat of Social Affairs) had largely absorbed the SBS's functions by decade's end and remained a charity-giving platform for the public performance of the first lady.[37]

Guatemalan social welfare, as it crystallized after 1954, encapsulated within its anticommunist bent a long history of right-wing, feminized applied sociology in Latin America and the Western Hemisphere. This history can be traced to the 1920s, when strong capitalist states spearheaded an international diplomatic effort to proselytize government-run social services and state social work. Such programs would counter the appeal of organized labor and left-wing mass political movements in the Americas, they claimed. By 1948 there were fifty-one schools of applied sociology in Latin America, the vast majority of which admitted only women.[38]

As Latin America emerged from the Depression into the Second World War and postwar years ridden with the social woes of urbanization, rapid population growth, modernization, and structural inequalities of income distribution, the PAU grew more devoted to this special women's wing of government work.[39] This happened as the development industry was maturing and mushrooming. In the burgeoning Cold War, development was increasingly deployed as a weapon of counterinsurgency, and in the United States its constituents became a part of the global north's culture industry, a phrase typically reserved for media, advertising, and other mass-culture businesses. The development industry, dovetailing with the media and communications revolution, was as dedicated to creating symbols, representations, and beliefs and individualistic capitalist consumers as it was to building roads and sewers.[40] In dialogue with this transformation, the post-1954 anticommunist regimes in Guatemala drew on sophisticated technologies of propaganda and social engineering as part of their development programs. Women and families became a key focal point of policy intervention even as new institutions promised maternal comfort to the poor. The State-as-Mother failed miserably. Real mothers, though, and real families coped with modernization, helped to create the economy and weave the social safety net, and were protagonists in defining the texture and structure of survival that endure in Guatemala to this day.

"Dios se lo Pague":
Women, Families, and Real Nets and Networks

Antonia Alonzo Abá's life story evokes common themes in twentieth-century Guatemala, both new ones and old ones. Economically, it shows the daily struggle to eat and stave off homelessness. It reveals diverse worlds of employment, ranging from peonage situations—including finca, nanny, and caretaker work—to folk employment as midwife and the son's modernized artisanship as an apprentice blacksmith and metalworker. It gives a glimpse at the interface of the family and the state, both in its Cold War politics and in the presence of Graciela Cabrera, the social worker. More intimately, Antonia's life bears witness to the ties between country and city and the *machismo* that made the single mother a social icon and teenage pregnancy unremarkably common. Her teenage pregnancy also brings one face to face with criminal demons of sexual desire (read: statutory rape). On a wider scale, however, Antonia's biography underscores the economic realities that kept couples and families geographically separated. In short, it exemplifies the dynamic of family dissolution commonly associated with the modernization of presumptively traditional societies.

When, however, did the Guatemalan family dissolve? Readings of thousands of *expedientes* from the 1920s to the 1960s indicate that the nuclear family—understood as a married, monogamous man and woman living and caring for their children together—was not a social norm in Guatemala. Marriage, often at a very young age, was common, but fidelity and stable cohabitation were not. The predominance of migrant labor in agriculture, domestic service, and food and crafts distribution that kept vendors moving around the country undoubtedly contributed to the rise of alternative models of sexual behavior, assuming, probably incorrectly, that the monogamous, geographically rooted couple had ever historically been a model in the first place.[41]

As far back as the 1920s expedientes to the government reveal that people made no effort to hide their single parentage, their relationships with *concubinas*, or the status of their children born out of wedlock. When Ubico's government began investigating petitioners' morals in the 1930s, variation from the model of the monogamous nuclear family was never taken as a reason to doubt a person's honor; the police were only looking for subversive political activity.[42] As social workers—that is, women like Cabrera, who came to investigate Antonia's case—began to pick up where police investigators left off, a concern for the preservation of a nuclear family model that had never existed in the first place became steadily more prevalent. The power of the myth, however, aided in the construction of the anticommunist state and its ideology of development, even as that anticommunist state built on the structures of the democratic Revolution that preceded it.

Gendered mythology was at the heart of process. To review, first, a generally accepted idea I have summed up under the rubric of oficios de su sexo made and has continued to make a myth of the economy itself, relegating the vast majority of productive economic labor, much of it conducted by women, to an informal sphere. Second, at precisely the moment when the Cold War military state needed to appropriate development for its own political purposes, it expanded a feminized bureaucracy over which the first lady presided as national Mother. The role of the U.S. public relations industry in the Adam and Eve–like demonization of Jacobo and Maria Vilanova de Arbenz speaks to the high-level connections through which myths were woven and coups were justified. Third, those same powers used the State-as-Mother in a purely aesthetic attempt to save a mythological monogamous family. The idea was to create a social safety net, even as the Cold War state was dismantling the Revolution's Keynesian potential to provide such a net to the nation.

Just as el pueblo stepped in to give Guatemala an economy that development failed to produce, so too did it provide a social safety net . . . of sorts. Home businesses did more than just structure supply and distribution lines in Guatemala. They also provided the credit and bartered services that served as social glue and that made both basic survival and further productive enterprises possible. In Monzón Lemus's novelistic re-telling of Ramón's life in El Gallito, this dynamic appears everywhere. Don Tomás, Ramón's and Antonio's father, rented half the family's shack to doña Tencha, a tortillera whose business fed the whole section of the neighborhood. At the end of the month Tomás would collect only a few centavos in rent because doña Tencha paid them largely in tortillas and beans. She was there each midday when the kids came home for school. Besides feeding them a hot lunch, she functioned as an additional care-taker, making sure they were staying out of trouble while their father was off earning a pittance for sweeping the city streets. The reader can feel the author's warmth for doña Tencha throughout the book, drawn though she is as a busybody and a gossip. After wolfing down their meal, the boys would run off to school, regaling her with "¡Dios se lo pague, doña Ten-cha!" This traditional underclass thank you, translating roughly as "May God pay you back," speaks directly to a history of neighborhood-run mu-tual aid and reciprocity.

The boys were surrounded by businesses run by women. Their deceased mother, the original winner of the lot in El Gallito, had managed a little, probably illegal cantina on the property. Their aunt had a stall in the central market, where she sold jars, jugs, and cornhusks for making tamales. But most important to the family was doña Naya's tienda because doña Naya sold to don Tomás on credit. She would write down daily in his little notebook what he owed for bread, coffee, sugar, candles, and matches. Together with doña Tencha's tortillas and beans and some secondhand clothes, these were the sum total of the family's commodities. Had he been unable to wait until payday to settle at the tienda or unable to occasionally defer some basic living expenses in order to afford, for example, a pair of new shoes, don Tomás simply could not have supported his children.[43] Bank credit did not define the Guatemalan landscape; personal credit did. And by participating as equal members or even as leaders in the establish-ment of the businesses that feed Guatemala and provide it with credit, women were at the heart of weaving the nation's real social safety net. So too were they at the heart of the real economy: the economy that ties together the corn and bean fields, the trucking business, the wholesale market, the retail market, and the tortillería.[44]

No doubt, just as the economy failed to provide general prosperity, the social safety net could easily fall apart. Often, families and communities ended up having to deal with the state when the web of credit relations and underground commerce led to disputes. Such was the case of Lina Díaz. In the mid-1950s Lina, an undocumented, single, forty-five-year-old El Salvadoran woman with no education, was living in the Bethania house of a man named Manuel López who was away working on the finca La Máquina in Puerto San José, Escuintla. Lina ran a tienda out of this informally occupied home. She was doing well until six neighbors, led by a minor-aged girl, Marta Polanco, denounced her as an illegal alien and, even though she was not the homeowner of record, requested that she be evicted. Lina counterclaimed that they were denouncing her because they owed her money for credit extended at the tienda, a situation that had gotten so bad she was taking them to court. As the eviction case unfolded, the ownership of the home proved ever more mysterious. The title appeared in the name of a woman no one had ever heard of and whom no one could find, and the home had previously belonged to another man with the last name of López (a relative of Manuel's?), at the time residing in zone 5. This second López testified that he got possession of the home in 1952 but within a couple of months was stripped of the property by Raymundo Álvarez Ixcop, the local PAR boss, because he wouldn't join the party. At the end of it all and despite an eloquent defense, Lina was evicted. The documents indicate that more trouble was coming for everyone involved with this piece of Bethania property, and doubtless the neighbors ended up regretting the loss of the tienda. It could be a long hike to buy matches and coffee and sugar without one nearby and a pointless hike at that if neighborly credit was not forthcoming.[45]

Informal credit, home businesses, and shady rental deals conducted outside the state's gaze played a huge part in ensuring survival, and they informed how people created the Guatemalan landscape. While this web of homespun economy functioned and continues to function, it could not prevent poverty-borne disaster. At midcentury the state became involved with a very few of the hardest-hit cases, through its growing and uncoordinated web of social workers, found in the Instituto Guatemalteco de Seguridad Social (IGSS) and in various government ministries and dependencies. The case files of these social workers give a glimpse into poor households and how they functioned.

Emeteria Varela grew up in Oratoria, Santa Rosa, and married Eleuterio González, a local boy. They had seven children, a family they found themselves unable to support. Like so many other families whose numbers

outpaced their collective earning potential, they decided to move to Guatemala City. Eleuterio did well, finding a maintenance job at the Neuro-
Psychiatric Hospital, but in 1953 he dropped dead of a heart attack when he
fell while boarding a city bus. Fortunately, poor, dead Eleuterio had been
affiliated with the IGSS, and that agency's social services division took on
his thirty-six-year-old widow's case. IGSS awarded Emeteria eighty quetzales per month, ten for each child and ten for her. The agency also
arranged for a home in Bethania. Once there, she became romantically
involved with a neighbor, Javier González, no relation to her deceased
husband of the same last name. Javier was a single father of one whose
work in construction was taking him far afield, to Uspantán, Quiché. Emeteria and her children moved in with Javier. When the couple had a baby
together, the household would have totaled eleven people, except that
Alfonso, Emeteria's eldest, disliked his stepfather so much that he refused
to live at home. The young man got a job as a sales assistant in the shop at
the Señor de las Misericordias chapel that provided him with room, board,
and fifteen quetzales a month. But his night classes at the Academia Prác-
tica Comercial cost twenty quetzales a month, so to help him out his
mother gave him the monthly allowance of ten quetzales that was his
portion of the IGSS allotment.

Emeteria was a very giving woman. In fact, when she no longer needed
her own Bethania home, having moved in with Javier, she decided to sell it
but found out that it was illegal. At about the same time, Rosa Amelia Roca
de Morán appeared on the scene. Rosa was thirty-one, married, and the
mother of four children. Though she was from Emeteria's hometown of
Oratorio, Santa Rosa, the two women were probably not old friends, given
that Rosa had left with her family for the capital at a very early age. When
the women met, Rosa was in trouble. Her husband had always provided the
bulk of the family income, but he had gone deeply into debt when he lost
his job—a debt that in 1957 he was trying to pay off by working odd jobs
that paid only 1.25 quetzales a day. To contribute, Rosa, a self-described
fashion designer, bought a Singer sewing machine with state-sponsored
credit. She also arranged for the Public Health Ministry's Department of
Social Services to give her an advance for fabric. Despite selling some
dresses, she couldn't make ends meet and missed her sewing machine
payments. The Singer was repossessed. It must have seemed like a godsend
when, in 1957, Emeteria gave Rosa and her family a Bethania home for free,
even arranging the paperwork so that the transaction was entirely legal.[46]

A look at the budgets of these two families sheds some light on the economy. Incomes were far too low to support human life. Emeteria's family was making 110 quetzales a month, 80 from IGSS and 30 from her *conviviente*, Javier. Having a free house and a budget of 68 quetzales for food, 20 for clothing, 10 for her son Alfonso, and 12 for utilities and other expenses, she was exactly breaking even. Rosa and her husband, meanwhile, with their four children, were making 37.50 quetzales a month from the father's work at 1.25 per day. With a bare-bones budget of 60.60 quetzales, their monthly shortfall was 23.10 quetzales. Food budgets could provide only tortillas and beans as daily staples. Education, medical expenses, and the like did not appear in either budget. Entertainment was out of the question. On a macro level, job creation through consumer commodity and service industries was stunted by this sort of base poverty. On a micro level, meanwhile, families like Rosa's, which received no financial aid from social services, confronted an endless slide into debt and possible homelessness.[47]

Given the precariousness of life, the support of family could be absolutely essential, but families grew so fast they could barely keep up. Teenagers finally in a position to help their parents and siblings started having children of their own. The case of Lucía Morataya Chichón is an example. Lucía was a forty-one-year-old woman who had migrated to the city center from Amatitlán sometime in the 1940s. The death of her husband had left her with scant resources, and, like many women, she managed to earn a living to support her small children by taking in laundry. When her first son, Alberto, came of age, he might have been able to help, but the boy, barely sprouting whiskers, already had children of his own. The fifty centavos a day he earned in the Beneficio de Café Progreso wasn't nearly enough to keep his own family from starvation. Lucía's case is known because Guardia Judicial officers, so often seen as a plague upon the people, were truly touched by her situation. In 1946 she was too ill to work regularly and still was trying to build a makeshift shelter on illegal La Palmita land. The officers wanted an exception made for her, but it was not forthcoming.[48]

Family members needed each other to survive. The starvation wages that confronted people, many of them coming from a fading life of semi-self-sufficiency in the country, paradoxically reinforced family structures even as they exacerbated the woe of family dissolution. Problems were especially acute when families were composed of single mothers with lots

of babies. In such instances, child labor could be key to family survival, and
many single mothers depended on their youngsters to earn the daily bread
when there were infants to care for, such as a family of five living on the
income of a thirteen-year-old shoeshine boy in La Florida in 1963.[49] It is a
situation still seen in Guatemala today.

What is life like in a world where labor is worth nothing? It might
arguably be tolerable when people manage to cluster in mutually supporting social formations, family or otherwise, but the catch-22 of starvation-
wage labor is that the social conditions it engenders tend to break families
and communities apart. As we have seen, women played a critical role in
weaving Guatemala's real social safety net. They and the children were also
the most likely to fall through it.

The social worker reports from the welfare agency lack the narrative
introduction that, in an expediente, eases the reader into the world of
misery and pain therein contained. "Teresa Vásquez Mendoza, 25 años de
edad, nacida en El Progreso, soltera abandonada, domiciliada en 6a calle
4–22 zona 3, analfabeta de ocupación tortillera," began one in 1963, reveal-
ing right away that the subject is an abandoned twenty-five-year-old single
mother, born in the countryside, illiterate, a tortillera, living at an address
that a few lines down on the form is revealed to be, despite its official
numeration, a shack at the bottom of the zone 3 ravine at the edge of an
open sewer. By the age of twenty-five, Teresa had given birth to six children,
four of whom survived. In early 1963 the youngest was ten months old, and
the second eldest was four. The oldest living child was never found by the
social worker. Neither was the father. Fifteen years older than Teresa, never
married to her, and also hailing from El Progreso, he had simply disappeared. When she had last seen him, he had been working as a street
cleaner for the municipality of Guatemala.

Teresa's children were ill. Their daily diet consisted of tortillas, beans,
and some coffee or *atol* (corn-mush soup). Their hut had a dirt floor and
was flea-ridden and filthy. The social worker, well accustomed to the city's
marginal neighborhoods, noted that this place was especially shocking.
Teresa found it difficult to earn money by making tortillas because though
she could clamber up the ravine's steep bank alone she couldn't do it
carrying children. When Teresa checked the children in at the social services center (Guardería y Sala Cuna No. 1), one was suffering from severe
malnutrition. But she left them there for only about three months. For
unknown reasons, and to the social worker's dismay, Teresa picked up her

children one day and fell out of both the state's gaze and its small social safety net.[50]

The case of Teresa Vásquez Mendoza and her missing partner, Antonio Orellana Barillas, leaves many questions unanswered. It is the sort of horror-ridden narrative that could serve as the germ for a TV movie-of-the-week, with creative fiction woven around the few hard facts. Teresa and Antonio were both from El Progreso. Did they meet there? Did they decide to flee to the city because she was a pregnant teenager and he was in his late thirties? Did they meet in the city, either through the informal networks that recreated hometown clusters inside the connection-driven market for affordable residential space, or because their families had migrated there when they were very young? Finally, what happened to Teresa and her children? Did Antonio suddenly show up, repentant, perhaps with a few quetzales in his pocket? Did she leave for El Progreso? There are no answers to these questions.

Cases like Teresa's do, however, disclose the level of misery that could end up confronting the illiterate poor in Guatemala City's huge underground economy, especially if they lacked extensive family connections within the city limits. They disclose that women had it worse than men, and that children had it worst of all.

"To Make a Woman Literate Is to Create a Teacher": Ideology and Integrated Community Development

Mental health reports on children at the Guardería No. 3 in Guatemala City show the effects of broken homes and poverty and even contain classic signs of sexual and other physical abuse that social workers were either not trained to recognize or did not wish to. For example, one six-year-old boy still couldn't name his colors. He was unable to concentrate and was completely insecure. He lived with his father, who wouldn't allow his mother to visit because he maintained she was a freeloader and a parasite. The child had suffered from measles, chickenpox, and chronic tonsillitis. A five-year-old girl caught the director's eye because she had deficient language skills and was uncoordinated, inhibited, and scared of other people. She wet herself day and night, smelled of urine, and never came to school in clean clothes. According to social workers, her father had died some time before, leaving the mother alone with eight children. For her part, the mother "manifested anomalous behavior and complete irresponsibility," engaged in short and wild love affairs, and had once been jailed for contributing to the delinquency of minors. Her teenage sons were in trouble with the law; several had been locked up in the Ciudad de los Niños, from which they had promptly escaped. Another five-year-old, a boy, was inhibited and passive. He suffered constantly from panic attacks and occasionally from convulsions and was unable to tie his shoes or dress himself. His diarrhea and other recurring rectal problems seem to have alerted the social workers to possible rape, but the worst, they said, was that "the father is addicted to alcohol . . . [and] presents scandalous behavior." If sexual abuse was intimated in the case above, it seems astonishingly unmentioned in that of a six-year-old girl who was described as "ashamed of herself." The child was a sleepwalker who moved awkwardly, didn't use verbs in speech, and constantly covered her genitals as if to protect them. Diagnosis: "Severe emotional problems."[51]

In twentieth-century Guatemala, misery bred chaos, established it as order, and reproduced it in an evolving social landscape. Split families, street crime, begging, constant migration, child labor, passed-out-on-the-sidewalk drunkenness: these were not the result of people's values but manifestations of necessity and pain. Like values, however, they became historically embedded as customs: having a slew of children to increase the family income; hitting the cantina until blindness sets in on payday; and, in a later era, organizing the street kids in gangs; hiring the *coyote* and fleeing north. Here the dialectic of chaos and rationality I explored in chapter two intersects with the themes of gender and development. The revolutionary state, informed by John Maynard Keynes, Franklin Roosevelt, and the early strains of dependency theory, deployed social welfare and social work as one way to rationalize chaos, while simultaneously attempting to change the structures of poverty by fomenting industry, diversifying agriculture, and ultimately by redistributing land. The counterrevolutionary state, with its U.S. backers informed by anticommunism and modernization theory, adopted and expanded its predecessor's social welfare bureaucracy, even as its economic policies, intentionally or not, exacerbated the causes of on-the-ground poverty. In this transition lies the gendered rise of the State-as-Mother and of the first lady and social welfare in general as political cover—as gendered political aesthetics. Also visible, however, is an increased interest on the part of the state in sexual behaviors and moral norms. This voyeuristic aspect of social work first arose in Guatemala during the Revolution. In the years after, conditioned by geopolitics, state politics, and gender ideologies, it came to characterize ever more sophisticated campaigns of social engineering that were at the heart of development and counterinsurgency alike. In short, the same forces that made a myth of the invasion, a myth of the real economy, a myth of women's labor, and even a myth of the family came to use gendered development programs in the service of war.

The military high command was fully aware that development was a weapon. As we saw in chapter 2, in 1957 the book *Armas para ganar una nueva batalla* celebrated Castillo Armas's rural "cultural commissions" and his creation of the Dirección General del Desarrollo Socio-Educativo Rural (Department of Rural Socio-Educational Development).[52] The new weapons fit the new battle's aims: to crush alternative projects fostered by the political opening of the Revolution; to keep the rural population docile; to create the impression that a middle class was being produced; to foment tribal anticommunism; and to penetrate rural areas and separate as many individuals as possible from the means of production, that is, the land, and tie them to a global marketplace. The Dirección General del Desarrollo Socio-Educativo Rural speaks not to the backward condition of rural Guatemalans, but to their location at the crossroads of the most powerful and important forces of modernization of the day.

Starting with such initiatives, the Guatemalan state gradually unfolded a strategy known as Integrated Community Development (ICD) that over time represented the maturation of the feminized state practice of social work and the recognition of the social embeddedness of modern problems. The ICD strategy sought exactly what its name implied—to address communities as organic wholes—and it teamed bureaucratic efforts to apply once disparate development and welfare initiatives in tandem. Such programs included infrastructure building and economic projects, education of all types, including civic, moral, hygienic, and political, and family welfare and public health campaigns. When the government formalized ICD in 1964 after years of experimentation, it was run by the SBS. At first it was largely a rural program, though under its later guises leaders extended its scope into city projects as well. It was also a program deeply involved with counterinsurgency. Informed by strategies and programs of the UN, OAS, and the U.S. Agency for International Development (USAID) this development scheme drew on a growing concern both with stitching together communities that the process of modernization was tearing apart and with modernizing communities that hadn't yet been torn.[53]

The history of the idea of integration under Guatemala's anticommunist regimes is one that references the broken national family just as much as it does the broken everyday family. In the absence of meaningful agrarian reform or democracy, the Castillo Armas government and its backers promoted ethnic integration as the way to fix the backward highlands. An international conference held in Guatemala City in 1956, reportedly pushed through by U.S. advisors, focused on "all aspects of the fusion of Indians and *ladinos*" and was sponsored by the Seminario de Integración Social, an "autonomous cultural institution" founded in 1954.[54]

Years later the Guatemalan historian Carlos Guzmán Böckler would savage the Seminar on Guatemalan Social Integration of 1956 both for being in line with the dominant bourgeois ideology and for informing programs like ICD and army civic action. He correctly noted that the program's "very name denotes a program." The seminar's participants, Guzmán Böckler said, falsely painted a bifurcated Guatemala, one of Indian and one of Ladino, arguing that the traditional Indian was becoming Ladino in a two-generation process. If Guzmán Böckler's assessment of foreign anthropologists was a bit harsh and knowledge of indigenous society a bit thin, his point that the Maya were growing both in absolute numbers and in percentage of the population remains well taken. The Maya were not an ethic, but a sociological minority, he argued, and the state, supported by social scientists, launched an attack on the people, their culture, and their languages—an attack that Mayan persistence and resistance made an ultimate failure.[55]

The ICD strategy was the nonviolent side of that attack. Drawing on revolutionary-era rural education technologies, it had evolved piecemeal under Castillo Armas and Ydígoras Fuentes. Supported by foreign capital and international institutions, it flowered fully under the military dictatorship of Col. Enrique Peralta Azurdia, who deposed Ydígoras by coup in 1963 and ruled as dictator until 1966. Appropriating the educational bent of revolutionary policy and assigning the poor the responsibility for their own poverty, ICD combined existing infrastructure and public works programs with literacy campaigns, housewife clubs to promote home economics, hygienic model homes (never built), and new farming ventures—raising ducks, for example. Women, Castillo's propaganda claimed, were the keys to the program's success. Claiming that "to make a woman literate is to create a teacher," the anticommunist state touted the program's similarity to "the celebrated *Nai Talin*, or 'new education' of Mahatma Gandhi."[56]

The ICD strategy evidenced an ideological process of ordering society biologically that devolved in a series of repeating patterns upon the individual body: the New World as an anticommunist alliance; Central America as a defense bloc and common market; Guatemala as an agroexporter open to foreign capital; the community as a bounded group of obeisant laborers; the family as a gendered site of ideological reproduction; and the individual as a unit in organized mechanisms of state and corporate power. More simply put, ICD's proponents decided that they needed to address organic units of people (communities) and surgically modify their entire way of being, from their habits to their deepest thoughts. By carrying this project to fruition, the social engineers maintained, they would ensure a stable workforce and enforce acceptable social norms. In effect, however, their programs served mostly to provide motherly political aesthetics that worked to conceal such physical and economic violence as the crushing of unions, paying of starvation wages, and so forth. Development would come swooping into the village, breaking up informal economic ties and teaching the inhabitants venture capitalism, for example, duck farming, building them housing, training them in home economics, and integrating them into the national and international family through education or indoctrination that would erase their folk knowledge and sense of ethnic difference with carefully crafted lessons in civic virtue. The very idea of ICD—informed as it was by the development-culture industry that helped to create it—reproduced the ideology of private ownership of the means of production. Corporate capitalist systems have historically confronted individuals with groups: individual workers who deal with the company, for example, or individual citizens who deal with the state. But because humans always work in groups, this type of capitalism institutionalizes itself to deal with groups—hence ICD, the real goal of which can only be to atomize the community.

In his discussion of the production of space, the philosopher Henri Lefebvre points out that the developmental expansion of space in the capitalist mode of production is accompanied by *"a reproduction of the relations of production."*[57] In this thinking, Lefebvre follows Marx directly. His point implies that all the superstructure that goes reciprocally along with relationships of production is embedded, too. Values, morals, dreams, aesthetics, gender and sex norms, spirituality, customs, social practices: all of these accompany the invisible forces of production relationships into the making and meaning of any given space, not deterministically but in myriad complex ways. It is precisely this complexity that makes gender emerge as a "useful category of historical analysis," to quote Joan Scott. Gender reveals one aspect of a contested field of meaning, power, and lived experience that lies behind diverse stories: Antonia Alonzo Abá's odyssey as a teenage mother and urban migrant; María Vilanova de Arbenz's vilification; Lina Díaz's eviction; and Graciela Cabrera's toils as a social worker in barrios and state institutions alike.[58]

"The whole of space is increasingly modeled after private enterprise, private property and the family—after a reproduction of production relations paralleling biological reproduction and genitality," writes Lefebvre.[59] From the mid-1950s to the mid-1960s Guatemalan state officials and their foreign partners used globally discussed practices and technologies to bend development to help achieve their political goals. If only people could be made to think of themselves as individual citizens interacting with a benevolent state directing them paternally toward prosperity while caring for them maternally through charity and aid, perhaps their Communist tendencies could be held in check.

State-led development from 1954 to the mid-1960s certainly failed completely in deterring Communist tendencies. Guatemala came alive with Marxist and popular-left resistance that drew on notions of class and justice with roots not only in international Communism and liberation theology, but also in the politics of the Guatemalan 1920s and the Revolution of 1944–54. In countering this movement, the Guatemalan military drew extensively on biological, vitalist ideas of progress and nation—ideas born in the late 1800s but strengthened and popularized during the long 1920s and 1930s. At the same time, the military worked with the U.S. government to bring more and more of the Revolution's infrastructure demands to fruition, even as it amplified the gendered sphere of State-as-Mother through military civic action.

Given the complete failure to produce hegemony and prevent war in Guatemala, it is easy to lose sight of the successes of the development-culture industry. Yet successes there have been. To this day people clamor for development, even though state-led and global development projects have done little but increase poverty and cloak violence from above. If the idea of development has enjoyed widespread acceptance, so too has the gendered notion of a broken, inferior informal economy, even though this phrase masks the fact that this economy is largely responsible for sustaining human life, while the formal economy is arguably responsible for taking or exploiting that life. Finally, gender continues to be a powerful element in constructing a language of good and evil that both veils reality and informs the construction of social and physical space.

From roughly the late 1950s to the early 1970s development's masculine side—modernization, infrastructure building, highway construction, and the like—unleashed tremendous demographic changes even as economics and politics, both local and global, impelled a population to war. These factors combined to shape the contemporary landscape of Guatemala City. Besides structuring the city's already evolving geography, events also conspired to create a highly contested map of good and evil. Today, Guatemala City is an exemplar of what I call an immoral metropolis. The blame for the city's immorality ultimately devolved not upon empowered economic and political actors, but on poor and powerless adolescent males. Half-naked, tattooed, and dangerous, these young men—like the women of oficios de su sexo—bear witness to the complex workings of gender, power, and myth.

Development and war combined during the long 1960s to give Guatemala City its modern face and make it a modern immoral metropolis. Depending on one's perspective, the capital was riddled with social undesirables and terrorist rebels or prowled by right-wing assassins and kept in economic misery by imperial capital. Common to both outlooks was a simple fact: Guatemala City was becoming a very, very dangerous place.

Central America in the new millennium is ostensibly pacified. Death squads, torture chambers, massacres, and the economic totality of globalization seem to have effectively nipped resistance in the bud. In Guatemala, as in neighboring nations, evil's mascot is no longer a Marxist guerrilla or, from the other side, a fat, rich capitalist. Instead, that mascot is a teenage boy. His brown skin riddled with tattoos, his teeth banded with gold, his hair hidden beneath what people from another land would call a ski cap, he is a natural born killer, a *marero*, a gangbanger. The gang members, who trace their organizational roots to the streets of Los Angeles, seem to rule. They rape and rob and kill.

"¡Mareros hacen ritos satánicos!" (Gangbangers worship Satan!) trumpeted a headline from 2003 on *Extra*, one of Guatemala's rich crop of new-millennium tabloids. The story inside didn't substantiate the claim but added an extra spice of horror to the issue, whose cover otherwise featured a mutilated corpse and a topless woman.[1] At around the same time, the respectable *Prensa Libre* published a spread on the growing *mara* problem. "They're Taking Control of the Streets," ran the headline to a map of Guatemala City gangland. Alongside the map was a picture of a naked, tattooed male chest and stomach. Its rippling muscles, bulging veins, and visible pubic hair bespoke the explicit link between the infected city and raw male sexuality. The sidebar beside the map was titled, "On the Hunt for the Antisocial."[2]

How have poor teenagers—especially young men—come to be the emblem of all a society's and city's problems? The answer is as simple as it is commonsensical: via a dynamic of downward moral displacement in which the dominant logic makes it imperative to impose punishment, social engineering, and repression on the victims of the system's very nature by shifting the blame for the badness onto them and thereby avoiding a substantive discussion of the problems' real origin. Downward moral displacement is seen in virtually all societies. U.S. citizens, for example, need only think of the public language that justifies imprisoning enormous percentages of young African American men. Downward moral displacement works both because the culture industry promotes it and because people buy it. Its formula is seductively simple: bad neighborhoods with bad cultures, revolving around bad drugs, produce bad people who do bad things. Downward moral displacement taps into the baser part of human nature—fears, prejudices, and the quite understandable desire not to be robbed or stabbed or otherwise disturbed by the ever-growing underclass that capitalist modernization produces. If we could just fix *them*, people think, the world would be near perfect.

So insidious, so hegemonic is downward moral displacement that contemporary discourse has endowed even spaces with the magical ability to generate evil. The inner city, for example, emerges as a generator of social ill: Prera, the engineer who was going to save El Gallito, described its denizens as "destined for crime and vice." To speak of "mean streets" is to speak the language of a fetishism that ignores the social relations of production and endows neighborhoods and alleys and even sylvan hideaways —the mountain grottoes where subversive *compañeros* speak in whispers with the gullible rural poor—with the power to make sin happen. The social leftovers spat out by these living spots of sin haunt the world like phantoms. They are the pathological, the incapable, the incurable. They are, in a word, the problem.

What makes Guatemala unique in this regard—downward moral displacement being seen all over—is the history of war that conditions its language, attitudes, and conceptions concerning good and evil. Even as developers were building highways and other infrastructure that brought the nation fully into the automobile age and forever transformed its economic and social reality, that same reality occasioned the outbreak of civil war. The city, expanding exponentially with the fervor and insecurity of a poor population in tremendous flux, not only sprouted new neighborhoods and markets and byways. It also came to encompass a geography— both spoken and physical—of good and evil, of safety and danger, and of public and private upon which life and death depended. Death squads, torture chambers, army barracks, safe houses, hidden arsenals; places where bombs might go off or where relatives were last seen alive; neighborhoods taken by *el pueblo* or occupied by *los militares*: these became very real features on the city's moral map. Over time, the war conditioned the culture of development. It brought a secrecy, a hopelessness, and deep levels of mistrust. Finally, the dynamic of good and evil in Guatemala has contributed to the fragile cohesion of consensus in this nation where capitalist hegemony has never taken root. If there is agreement about nothing else, there is at least widespread acceptance of the fact that the *mareros* are bad.

Just as gender ideology underpins community development and social welfare, so it informs the myth that male teenagers are somehow responsible for Guatemala's woes. Quite obviously the mareros are a product of development gone wrong. So too is the immoral metropolis. From the 1960s through the 1980s the production of urban space occurred within the context of a morally charged war within which all morals went by the wayside. The immoral metropolis didn't just happen. It was made.

"This Great Adaptive Deficiency":
Modernity and the Inadequate Conduct of the Poor

One day in 1964 Pedro Gonzalo Bor Chacón turned a corner in a Guatemala City market and ran into his runaway son. Pedro the second, his namesake, had been missing for weeks. The boy had fled home because he was hungry. He was so hungry, in fact, that he traded his labor, free, for food at one of the market's *comedores*, keeping himself alive and entering adult independence in the dim rows of cubicle kitchens with their woodfire stoves and oil drums full of water. He probably squatted somewhere in the market, too, maybe in a stall, maybe in a nearby hut, or maybe in one of the homeless colonies that formed outside around the mounds of trash. What Pedro Senior said to Pedro Junior that day is lost forever. He must have been glad to see his son alive. All that's certain is that little Pedro stayed at the market and big Pedro left without him. The kid had just turned twelve.

The story of the Bor family is the story of a house of cards collapsing. Not long before, the family—consisting of the parents and six children living in Colonia 3 de Julio in zone 12—had been getting by. Pedro had a decent job at a company called Viviendas, S.A., where he'd been an *albañil* (mason and construction worker) for years. His wife helped keep the family in money and food with her labor as a *tortillera*, mother, and care-taker. The couple had managed to get electricity into their one-room house and were saving up to install running water and a bathroom. But in March of 1963 the wife died of cancer. Not long after, Pedro got laid off. From that time forward he would begin to lose his health, his house, and his children.

The funeral for Pedro's wife cost seventy quetzales, and Pedro was already behind in his house payments. Jobless, he was supporting the whole family by selling two liters of cream a day for fifteen centavos apiece. Desperate, he went to social services, requesting clothes, food for the children, and money to start a vegetable stand in a market. Pedro's plan was typical, and, as we have seen, stories like his were at the heart of the construction of the everyday economy that feeds the capital. The social worker gave Pedro food, soap, and a bit of advice. Better to sell grains, she said, because vegetables go bad so quickly.

Pedro never launched a career as a food merchant because he landed a temporary job laying cinderblocks for a new Esso filling station. It paid forty-five quetzales a month. Meanwhile, his eldest son, Miguel Angel, thirteen, began to work as an apprentice at an auto mechanic's, contribut-ing a few welcome coins to the family pot. But the family was still depen-dent upon food aid from social services, and social services threatened to cut this off unless the children (Miguel Angel excepted) continued to attend school at the Centro Educativo Asistencial. All illiterate, they were absent almost continuously, probably out working odd jobs. Just as social services was beginning to lose patience, Pedro got hit by a car as he was leaving work at the Esso station. Once again he was unemployed, this time on crutches. His children were expelled from school for poor attendance. One of his little girls had to be hospitalized, but he couldn't pay, and his five-year-old son was going blind with a degenerative eye condition that could be easily fixed with an operation he couldn't afford. The state, deem-ing Pedro irresponsible, stepped in and took four of the six children into

temporary custody, housing them in the Hogar Temporal. They might
have taken five, but at this time little Pedro ran away. It was early 1964.

At this moment another branch of the state began to initiate eviction
proceedings. Pedro owed the mortgage bank, the Crédito Hipotecario, 174
quetzales. The social worker bent over backward to help. She arranged for
the five-year-old to have his eye operation. She located every one of Pedro
Bor's numerous relatives in the city and begged them to pitch in, managing
to get one cousin to contribute a modest sum for a short period of time.
She met with the chief of urban colonias and pled for leniency on the house
payments, brokering a deal in which Pedro would avoid eviction if he
started making double payments. But Pedro, his foot now healed, was
unable to find or hold down a steady job. He was laid off again and
ultimately evicted. He couldn't even send his son to meetings of the Committee for the Blind that would have helped the boy learn to live with
impaired vision because he failed to buy the child glasses.

By the end of 1964 the family was broken, with three of the children in
permanent state custody and eviction underway. Pedro, the social service
psychiatrist wrote, "does not suffer from mental illness, but one does note
in him a marked psychological anomaly that entails the inadequacy of his
socioeconomic conduct. It is very possible that the poverty of his intellectual resources influences this great adaptive deficiency. . . . His conduct
depends not only on his low mental level, but also on his apathetic charac-
ter and his tendency toward hypochondria. . . . Bor is an individual incapable of taking charge of his family obligations."[3]

"Great adaptive deficiency." Such were the words that summed up the
failure of a father to deal with tragedy in the context of an economy in
which it was literally impossible for him to make ends meet. Perhaps they
are words—uttered tongue-in-cheek, of course—that sum up an era. From
the end of the fifties forward, Guatemala City exploded in size and, as part
of that dynamic, exploded in misery. From the beginning of the sixties it
erupted in violence. New Marxist movements began to wage war against
the dominant system and the dominant classes. Eventually the war engulfed countryside and city alike, structuring the development of both.

As Greg Grandin argues, the war in Guatemala exemplified the polar
politics of the Cold War. The state lost any sense of true democratic values
and, with U.S. support, unleashed brutal repression that came to its horri-
ble conclusion in genocide. The new guerrillas, meanwhile, represented a
militant turn in Guatemalan Communism. They were inspired by the

revolution in Cuba and other Communist struggles around the globe and were disillusioned with the broader-based, social-democratic Communism of the revolutionary era. These guerrillas did not want to transform the state from within: they wanted to overthrow it.[4] Inseparable from this tragic conflict were the social realities of what the developmentalists would insist on calling the great adaptive deficiency of a people in the throes of experiencing modernity for the first time as an infrastructure grid spread across the nation.

"The Bloodstream of the Physical Body":
Connecting Space, Linking Bodies

During the Cold War, transnational and national developers connected spaces small and large and expanded the commercial flows that make their economic system work. At all levels these developers created institutions and built highways and other infrastructure, and the basic logic of liberal transnational capitalism is reflected in these creations. It was not a logic that benefited either ordinary Guatemalans or the Guatemalan capitalist class as a whole.

The seemingly mundane task of installing a modern communications network not only in Guatemala but around the world involved the rise of huge industries and business networks, few to none of which were located in Guatemala itself. By the early 1960s the nation's Ministry of Public Works was inundated by proposals from highway contractors and consultancies like Highways of the World (HOTW) of Mount Prospect, Illinois. Newly formed, HOTW teamed seventeen professors, engineers, and construction professionals dedicated to helping the third world "keep up with the needs of this automotive age." Well-planned highways, they argued, not only benefited capitalism and capitalists but humanity as well. "We recognize, of course, that many other factors than highway facilities enter into economic and social development," wrote the managing director, George F. Noble, recently back from a highway consultancy in Thailand and a veteran of projects in Illinois, Pennsylvania, and Saudi Arabia, "but we repeat our belief that highways constitute the bloodstream of the physical body of the economic structure just as telecommunication facilities constitute the controlling nerve system of that body."[5]

Companies like HOTW bespeak the epochal remaking and standardization of the world's landscape that had been ongoing since the turn of the

century but that peaked in the first decades of the Cold War—a project
often described in the same sort of bodily language that HOTW deployed.
The roster of services of HOTW shows the complexity and centrality of
highway planning and construction. Their calculus was to include current
and potential population centers; agriculture, waterway access, irrigation,
timber, livestock, and fisheries—both current and potentially exploitable;
mining and raw materials; power; possible industrial development, with
special attention to plastics; tourism; telecommunications; and ports, air-
ports, railroads, pipelines, and existing highways with traffic volumes.

Guatemala never contracted HOTW, but the nation's corporeal transformation went forward nonetheless. By and large, the United States funded
the project. In October 1954 the United States and Guatemala signed a
contract to finish the Pan-American Highway from the central highlands to
the Mexican border, with the U.S. Bureau of Public Roads paying most of
the bill.[6] The contract marked the beginning of a road-construction spree
that, if it were a ballet, might be entitled "Dance of the Caterpillar Tractors." From 1954 onward, work continued steadily on the Pan-American
and numerous secondary and feeder roads. These included the Atlantic
and Pacific highways, completed by 1962, along with a variety of agrarian
access routes. Funding came from the World Bank and various U.S. government dependencies, including the International Cooperation Administration (ICA), which also worked with the Agrarian Bank in providing super-
vised agricultural credits.[7]

The postinvasion rush of funds brought work to numerous contractors.[8]
U.S.-based Thompson Cornwall was chief among them, tackling, among
other projects, the blasting of the Pan-American Highway's El Tapón pass
in Huehuetenango, near the Mexican border. It was a colossal engineering
challenge.[9] Guatemalan highway workers like don Ossiel, a Huehuetenango native living and working as a taxi driver in Antigua at the time of
this writing, remember the blasting of El Tapón as a heroic, exciting feat, as
laced with legend as John Henry of U.S. fame. Don Ossiel liked working for
Thompson Cornwall. They paid better than the Guatemalan state or
smaller contractors, and they allowed ambitious youngsters like him to
prove their mettle with big sticks of dynamite and win promotions. He
remembers craft pride and a sense of purpose forged around open fires in
mountain campsites. Don Ossiel may never be able to retire, but from
humble roots as a marimba maker's son he managed to send his children to
college. Today, they work around the country as low-paid but respectable

professionals: a bilingual secretary, an accountant. The proud patriarch still loves to make the drive up the Pan-American toward Mexico, waxing nostalgic about the challenges and sheer explosiveness of dominating the mountains. It was not an easy job. As don Ossiel puts it, "You can't just let the *chavos* [guys] throw some dynamite in a hole, and BOOM!"[10]

By the end of 1958, four years after the original contract, the leg to Mexico remained uncompleted, and only 134 of the 511 kilometers in the Guatemalan section of the Pan-American Highway were paved.[11] There were just under 37,000 vehicles in the nation, a tiny number. Few families owned cars. Outside of major population centers, dirt trails and mule and oxen trains still defined the landscape. Even where there were roads, travel was complicated. Local construction was so disorganized that the roads didn't meet up at municipal borders.[12]

Municipalities were on their own amidst the global construction din, and within them there was a great clamor to get a piece of the action. In 1958 villagers in Michicoy, Huehuetenango, petitioned Ydígoras for a tractor and aid. "We are delighted to see that cars are coming close to us, and we are struggling to see if this little branch road [*ramalito*] might reach our little market [*mercadito*]," they wrote, expressing their wish to market their coffee more widely, "but God desired us to be poor and we aren't wholesalers."[13] The petition exemplifies the entrepreneurial spirit of Guatemalan campesinos seen in thousands of such requests. The Michicoy farmers wanted so badly to participate in the growing market economy that they had hacked out their own road with hoes and shovels. An inadequate, four-kilometer stretch, the campesinos' road didn't even reach the Pan-American directly but instead cut to another improvised access road—a road that, according to them, had been built not by the state or by the municipality but by the *finquero* Olivio Chávez to service his plantations.[14]

It was to rationalize these sorts of situations that in 1958, ICA/International Development Services launched a one-million-dollar Project Access Roads in Guatemala as the latest chapter in the ongoing Rural Development Program fashioned after the invasion of 1954 (the progenitor, as we have seen, of ICA).[15] At the same time, the government was explaining to outraged communities that Pan-American Highway contractors were under no obligation to build feeder roads into towns along the route.[16] At all levels, then, from the Pan-American to the municipal, everyone wanted to figure out how to tie the system together. On high, the tying together occasioned the rise of contracting companies, equipment industries, and

scores of institutions, all working in service of agroexport-led development. Down below, it involved the activities of rich *finqueros*, who built
their own roads, and poor villagers, who did the same thing or demanded
aid, all accomplished under the auspices of Guatemalan relations of production, namely, through the backbreaking labor of the underpaid poor.

Guatemalan road workers of the 1960s and 1970s were ambulatory
bands of low-paid *peones*. They worked in a military-like structure under
the direction of *caporales*, perhaps best compared to chain-gang bosses.
Away from home and grouped in all-male clusters, the peones had a tendency to get out of hand. Like a general (and he usually was a general), the
minister of public works could order their summary arrest. Mostly, peones
fell afoul for getting drunk. Many, however, ended up in jail for crashing or
"borrowing" equipment, failing to show up for work, and even, especially
in remote areas, for rape. Despite these problems, the road crews were in
high demand. Municipal governments frequently got tired of awaiting their
arrival and assembled the town's *principales* (political leaders) to drum up
volunteer labor. The public works ministry often responded positively to
this initiative—a money-saver—and would lend the town equipment. Not
surprisingly, the poor local so-called volunteers, like their underpaid peón
counterparts, would throw down their shovels and walk off the job when
the work got too onerous.[17]

The chaotic mess of everyday road building in Guatemala formed the
bottom level of ambitious integration plans. In 1962 functionaries of
CEPAL, the Banco Centroamericano de Integración Económica (BCIE),
and the Secretaria de Integración Económica Centroamericana (SIECA)
inaugurated the Programa Regional de Carreteras Centroamericanas, designed not only to add new highways throughout Central America but also
to modernize existing ones, less than a third of which were passable year-
round.[18] The program established, with little variation and much World
Bank financing, the present-day Central American road network. Construction, in Guatemala as throughout Central America, would continue in
the decades ahead. Into the 1970s Guatemala's governments were still
gradually opening new areas of the country, such as Alta and Baja Verapaz,
to motor travel, gradually bringing "economic blood" to the highland
body—the same body that, as we will see, suffered bloody army repression
and massacres.[19]

The purpose of these road-building efforts was to facilitate the expansion of capital. The BCIE/SIECA plan of 1962, a key factor in determining

future public works, came into being for one reason only: to bolster the Central American Common Market (CACM). The CACM—according to the left an invention of U.S. imperialism—was one step in the series of corporate capital's spatial orderings as it ever more integrally linked infrastructure building with engineering plans to "future-scape" society and culture in order to create atomized, individualistic, and most certainly not Communist workers and consumers.[20] Formed in 1961, the CACM recycled the dream of Central American unity within the political economy of the Cold War.[21] According to its propaganda, the CACM was to bring the consumer age to Central America through (what else?) development— roads and industrialization and trade that would bring the banana republics up to par with the United States. Not unlike the free-trade blocs of the 1990s and the new millennium, the CACM did little to provide prosperity to the underclass. Instead, it enriched transnational corporations without either challenging Guatemala's low-wage base or stimulating the growth of economic linkages that would foster employment or economic stability. Interestingly, statistics show that the CACM also failed to enrich a significant portion of the Guatemalan and Central American upper class. By the end of the 1960s U.S. capital, not national enterprises, had largely absorbed the boom that the CACM unleashed.[22]

Grass-roots economic expansion in Guatemala came through the labor of tortilleras, *tienda* owners, tiny coffee farmers who built their own roads, and other pioneers of the modern informal sector. At the upper levels, it came through the devouring of the economic landscape by transnational capital. This was not what the Guatemalan educated elite had dreamed of during the Revolution of 1944–54, a time when economic nationalism had run high. The Arévalo government's Industrial Development Law and creation of INFOP, the production institute, had produced slow increases in cement, electrical energy, and general production, though the artisan sector remained by far the industrial economy's most important.[23] But Guatemala's real boom came after the Industrial Development Law of 1959. Written, paradoxically, during a period in which Guatemala's new (sugar, cotton, industry) and old (coffee) economic elite alike were creating a fractious constellation of business associations to promote their interests, the Development Law allowed 100 percent foreign ownership of firms and "encouraged the establishment of multinational subsidiaries that only assembled or packaged imported components." From 1959 to 1969, U.S. investment in the region increased by 120 percent.[24] At least thirty-four U.S.-based businesses acquired or opened firms in Guatemala, including General Mills, Cargill Central Soy, Beatrice Foods, Coca-Cola, and Pillsbury.[25]

By the late 1970s foreign penetration of the Guatemalan economy had become so intense that watchdog groups and the left began publishing lists of transnationals in the nation. Their lists were so long and the companies so dwarfed Guatemalan-owned enterprises that even without accompanying diatribes they made their point quite eloquently.[26] A hand-done list reproduced here in its original form (see appendix) shows exactly who was reaping the benefits of Guatemala's modernization.

Economic statistics—in wages and in business ownership alike—reveal that the Guatemalan "body" was being consumed. High-level planners quite specifically thought of the New World as a body, using locutions like "bloodstream," "nerve system," and "economic blood." By their logic, the body's flesh would be fed by the circulatory system of highways and enlivened by the nervous system of telecommunications. Like children, its underdeveloped economies and societies would grow from third to first world. As we saw in chapter 3, mythological discourse played a hand in rationalizing high-level political and economic policy. Body imagery, synchronizing as it did with notions of "production relations [that paralleled] biological reproduction and genitality" (to revisit Lefebvre), seemed to make sense. It appeared as natural, and no doubt many of the development industry's promoters believed, just as they continue to believe, that their projects and efforts would improve the human condition and aid the growth process of supposedly underdeveloped societies.

The proponents of a capitalism based on age-old patterns of wage exploitation forged and modernized on the plantation ruled Guatemala after the invasion of 1954. They equated nationalism with tribal anticommunism and worked to keep labor cheap and beaten. But, perhaps through some great adaptive deficiency, the class that fed itself on the nation's poor found itself consumed by forces higher up the food chain.

"The Idiosyncrasies of a Certain Class":
Markets, Material Culture, and Morality

Guatemala City would serve well as a monument to the tragedies of twentieth-century development. Modernization, third-world style, concentrated on the capital and forged a veritable hellhole, the hellhole for which tattooed teenagers are today held responsible. Tracing the highways discussed above out of the countryside and into the city—the center of the grid—sheds light on the genesis of this jumble of urban space.

The year 1959 marked a watershed in Guatemala City's growth process. From below came the greatest paroxysm of homelessness to date, as a new wave of land occupations marked the arrival of some 11,700 people in 2,470 families around the finca La Palma, the area where La Palmita was located.[27] The overwhelmed Ydígoras government legalized land occupation in La Palmita and El Gallito the same year, granting rights to families who had constructed dwellings and who had "good customs."[28] The government also launched high-modernist initiatives in 1959 that profoundly impacted the city. They inaugurated El Trébol—Guatemala City's biggest highway cloverleaf, linking the Pan-American Highway and the Atlantic Highway. Nearby they built La Terminal, a national bus terminal and a wholesale outlet that would supply goods to the expanding city's network of municipal markets.

Today, El Trébol is ground zero in a perpetual traffic jam. Lined with vending stalls, stripper bars, and brothels, it is not only a transportation disaster, but also one of the city's most notoriously dangerous nexuses. Not even the fast food franchises that have invaded the banks of the Pan-American along the rest of its urban run will get near El Trébol. La Terminal is worse. Jammed with humanity, many of them transmigrating or newly arrived Mayan wholesalers who live in their windowless stalls, the wholesale market is pestilent and perilous. Crawling with rats and vermin, choking on its own garbage, the greater La Terminal area is a focal point of theft, drug and gun running, homelessness, glue sniffing, misery, and crime of every variety. Both El Trébol and La Terminal contribute significantly to the city's stunning daily death toll. And while these problems became more acute around the turn of the millennium, they are nothing new. They were there from the two projects' inception.

El Trébol, officially Project 13-B of the Pan-American Highway plan, was billed as a monumental work that would solve traffic problems, open economic frontiers, and, thanks to the hundreds of housing units built around it, ease overcrowding and set the template for solving urban overcrowding. Three years in the making, the cloverleaf cost over $5.2 million, involved scores of property expropriations and drainage problems, and accompanied a general overhaul or creation of key city avenues.[29] The creation of El Trébol symbolizes the connection of the city to the countryside via the new highway network. It was a visible coming-of-age of the automobile economy sketched in asphalt by an international apparatus over the course of decades.

La Terminal, El Trébol's sister project, shows the content of that coming-of-age. The reconfiguring of the landscape by highway development in the United States had been and would continue to be accompanied by the rise of the trucking industry, fast food franchises, the dispersion of industry outside of union-heavy cities to more rural locales, suburbanization—in short, by a constellation of capital creation in heavy, light, and agro industries alike, which would ultimately be concentrated in the hands of a relatively few huge multinational corporations.[30] Not so in Guatemala. The perseverance of development led by agroexport along with light investment in manufacturing, concentrated landownership, starvation wages, the attempted crushing of the union movement, and the poverty of public services such as education brought a very different set of effects. On one hand, capture of wealth by enormous corporations is similar. On the other, however, there arose a paradoxical dispersion of points of production as citizens appropriated new infrastructure and continued to fashion their own economy.

La Terminal and by extension El Trébol and the highway network are a prime example of how such dispersion worked. A large complex opened in stages between 1959 and the early 1960s, La Terminal had two functions. First, it would be a transportation nerve center, connecting extraurban bus routes to a single nexus. Second, it would supply the city with food. The high-modern, two-level installation ultimately boasted a dedicated grain market, a garbage dump, a police station, a medical clinic, a school, and a nursery.[31] In its early stages the project was characterized mostly by government hype and popular resistance; bus companies and vendors alike preferred to remain in their traditional locales. The vendors vowed in a town meeting that the transfer to La Terminal would happen over their dead bodies.[32]

Despite resistance, La Terminal was fully functioning by the mid-1960s, but in a chaotic way not anticipated by authorities and with profound social effects. The market represented income opportunity, and, utilizing the adjacent bus station, the desperate rural poor poured into the area, invading nearby land (all were evicted except those along the railroad line).[33] Would-be vendors from far-flung points arrived to peddle in the streets or hallways, even as the established vendors undermined the system by selling retail. Far from the systematized network of production, distribution, and sales the modernists had in mind, what resulted was a free-for-all of selling and underselling fueled by the busses and centered on La Terminal.

Given the terrible conditions of the physical plant and the loss of profit brought on by the flood of informal sellers, both La Terminal's paying vendors and those who wanted to avoid forced transfer to the facility began to protest as early as 1963. Begging for understanding, city hall ran a full-page ad in *El Imparcial*, picturing the modern market surrounded by rickety, hand-built huts. "Given the idiosyncrasies of a certain class of people," the caption read, in a classic of downward moral displacement, "they think they have the right to protest when one tries to lift them out of filth."[34]

The market was born a dump, and it would remain a dump. But it was an important dump. By the end of the 1960s the Ministry of Agriculture correctly noted that La Terminal had become the nation's epicenter of nonexport commercial agriculture. Food from the east, where the highway network was better (and where the population was Ladino), had begun to arrive in wooden crates instead of bundled up in nets. Still, at least 20 percent of all produce came to the wholesale center not in trucks but in pickups and busses, causing mayhem in the unloading areas and encouraging illicit retail activity. People walked and slept on their bundles, contaminating the goods. So much food rotted that there was a booming business in pig slop. What was needed, the ministry said, was better education in the Mayan highlands, farmland now tied to the city wholesale market by roads and trucks and busses.[35]

It didn't happen. As the civil war intensified, the government spent its greatest energies not on education in the highlands but on conducting counterinsurgency campaigns. And as the countryside became ever more dangerous, so too did the city in general and La Terminal in particular. Indeed, rot and crime and danger still exist today around La Terminal. Crime is nothing new to the market. In one of the earliest references to gangs in Guatemala City, 110 vendors at La Terminal petitioned the government for extra security in 1973, decrying "*pandillas* [gangs] of thugs, thieves, and criminals" who "are well known characters armed with pistols and knives." No one would confront them for fear of reprisal.[36]

Besides becoming a focal point of urban misery, La Terminal's wholesale market occasioned social and economic changes in the countryside, giving rise to a bottom-up and locally articulated, yet still modernized, system of transmigration, distribution, and agriculture that remains little understood. For example, many Terminal vendors in 2003 were K'iche' Maya from Totonicapán and El Quiché departments—men who travel back and forth in a transformed but generations-old tradition of salesmanship.[37] Though further study is needed to document the changes, the opening of La Terminal also affected crop strategies in the countryside; onions and avocados tend to come to the city from the department of Sololá, tomatoes from Santa María de Jesús, and so forth. Crop specialization would change food supply lines and production patterns throughout the network of rural markets, or at least those linked to the city, even as the putative agrarian transformation was strengthening large estates and generating a rural proletariat.[38]

The agrarian transformation of the Guatemalan countryside after the invasion of 1954 was aimed at producing more wealth for agroexporters and resulted in more rural proletarianization and poverty. At the same time, the most productive activity in the city was the business of producing more city. The two phenomena are intimately related. Nearby municipalities that were essential metropolitan food suppliers, like San José Pinula, found themselves in competition with faraway farmers, a key factor in preparing the way for their urbanization.[39] Meanwhile, the agricultural economy outside the city could not sustain the rural population. Families like that of Juan Gámez and Carmen Muñoz, landless agricultural workers from Chinique, El Quiché, spent a lifetime moving from finca to finca all over the highlands. The couple finally ended up in the city, and after her husband's death, Carmen, a destitute, fifty-one-year-old widow, petitioned the government for housing.[40] They were not unique. From 1950 to 1964 the population of the municipality of Guatemala grew from about 290,000 to about 572,000. In 1950 just under 10,000 of its inhabitants lived in areas still considered rural. By 1964, none did.[41]

The city was growing from without and from within. As more and more migrants poured into the urban area, many living as *palomares*, that is, visiting or subletting a friend's or relative's dwelling, the city began to absorb the farmland and villages around it. The majority of the migrants, though by no means all, came from the Ladino, eastern reaches of the nation. Unable to find work in industry, they ended up either in commerce, the service sector, or self-employed in the growing informal economy.[42] Though employment statistics for the period are either unreliable or unavailable, the expansion of the city to the south and west—to present-day zones 10, 13, and 14—as well as the urbanization of outlying municipalities

Material culture, immoral metropolis. Here an indigenous youth confronts a one-armed bandit. The contemporary equivalent is the video game, which is said to lead to delinquency and vice. Anonymous, "Máquinas tragamonedas (Slot Machines)," Guatemala, c. 1970. Archivo de fotografías del Comité Holandés de Solidaridad con el Pueblo de Guatemala. Fototeca Guatemala, CIRMA (Reference Code: GT-FG-CIRMA-117–010–113).

certainly offered work in construction, domestic labor, and such retail services as waiting tables and tending shops.[43] There was work, but not nearly enough to employ the bulk of the economically active population. And what work there was didn't pay enough for the worker to get ahead.

The process of urbanization and suburbanization gave Guatemala City a more modern face, a texture of districts and neighborhoods and businesses that penetrated down into the city's smallest corners. One of the biggest activities of the SBS in the 1960s was the trafficking of slot machines into the growing web of urban discos and restaurants. Ordered by the Division of Child and Family Welfare of the SBS, one-armed bandits like the Mills Bells-o-Matic "Aces Wild" found their way into leisure-time Guatemala. They appeared in Eduardo Alberto Lam's "Toy San" Chinese restaurant across from the Cine Tropical on Avenida Bolívar in gritty zone 3, in Ana María Chang's "Discoteca Tijuana" and "Discoteque Playboy" on the swank Avenida Las Américas in zone 13, and in María Ramírez's little watering hole "El Portalito" in La Terminal.[44]

The *traganíqueles*, or nickel-chuggers, are one of those insignificant appurtenances that, like the jukebox (named *rocola*, after rock music), mark space as twentieth-century modern. They recall the quotidian transformation of material culture that accompanied highways, cars, and airplanes into everyday life. Just as the dynamic of downward moral displacement prompted cultural critics and the media to lay the blame for modern problems on delinquents and rebels, so it occasioned the rise of a discourse that endowed devices with the power of evil. (A pool table, as everybody knows, is the sign of misspent youth.) In Guatemala, the traganíqueles were the progenitors of a type of material culture that would remain a scapegoat in this society where value judgments remain notably instant and extreme.

Where once the one-armed bandits stood, today's immoral metropolis sports banks of video games, or *maquinitas*. According to the kids I interviewed in zone 1's labyrinth of *centros comerciales*—precursors to the modern mall where unemployed teenage dropouts hang out and engage in a murky, disorganized commerce of drug running and petty crime—the "little machines" are a preteen's entry into the urban underworld. Just as pot leads to harder drugs, maquinitas lead to delinquency. Feinting like boxers, boys dance in front of them, slowly making the business connections that will help put some money in their pockets in any way other than through seventy-two hours a week (six days, twelve hours each) of wage labor for pay that won't support a hovel and a diet of tortillas and beans. "Those guys will all be mareros," one teenager tells me, pausing to add, "They're already hustlers," using a local slang word for male sex workers. "Me," he adds, fingering his eyebrow piercing, "I'm neither."

This informal interview occurs in an all-male space. Girls wander by the periphery but never enter, except occasionally in the crook of a boyfriend's arm. The maquinita emerges as a gender-coded piece of material culture that, like the pool table, references a masculine social initiation tinged with delinquency that revisits society in the hypermacho icon of the tattooed marero.[45]

Whether it's a one-armed bandit in a barroom, a barrio by the ravine, a slum-studded cloverleaf, or an entire urban zone doesn't matter. The space reflects the social relations of production, hidden by nothing except the myth of downward moral displacement. The reality of those relations runs right up the food chain, from the devoured worker to the devoured national capitalists. The miracle is that Guatemalans, even confronted with this stark reality, have managed to create spaces that also reflect joy, ingenuity, and bottom-up social relations of production. Despite terrible hardships, Guatemalans continue to insert inherent human goodness into the weave of the informal economy, of the immoral metropolis, and of the ravaged countryside.

Planning the Metropolis: Urban Liberty, Urban Chaos

Those human spaces—spaces in which, despite the poverty, people are quite *alegre*, know each other, help each other, and joke and laugh—remained interwoven with the impoverished landscapes of the city as it unfolded from the end of the 1950s to the early 1970s. In economic terms, what that urban expansion reveals is a based-on-nothing, self-referential development that, far from distributing wealth, encouraged ever more acute spatial divisions of class. Guatemala City represents another aspect of the same dynamics that turned places like boomtown, multiethnic Detroit into a graveyard ghetto during the same era.[46] Its evolution shows the logic of a system of extraction based on private ownership, private enterprise, and private space.

Given the nature of the system of production in Guatemala, the city as behemoth became an end in itself, its own expansion supplying the basis of economic motion without firm or sustainable foundations. Guatemala City, sopping up the rural poor, expanded along two basic axes: luxury and poverty. Luxury would go south along the Avenida Reforma, as the rich fled the city center. Poverty would get much of what remained. In the center and surrounding areas, ghetto making proceeded at a rapid clip. In the outlying municipalities, meanwhile, farm economies were torn asunder as the land was cut into *lotificaciones* and urbanized.

There are seventeen municipalities in the department of Guatemala, and today all of them have some degree of urbanization, forming the área metropolitana de Guatemala (AMG).[47] The process of urbanization became notable during the revolutionary decade and accelerated during the 1960s and 1970s. The urban specialist Silvia García Vettorazzi maintains that "the processes of production of space in the city have been determined by the logic, strategies, and practices of private actors faced with the lack of effective regulation and control on the part of the public sector . . . [such that] spatial expansion happens in a disorderly, chaotic manner, giving rise to an ever more dispersed and fragmented city."[48] Lack of control stemmed from municipalities acting on their own, from low interest in urban planning, and from spiraling necessity that kept the city in a constant state of emergency.

This is not to say the public sector did nothing. Throughout the third quarter of the century, the *municipalidad* divided the city into zones, established a workable address system, and even installed timed stoplights on some streets.[49] There had been several preliminary urban planning laws and proposals, but Guatemala City never had a master urbanization plan until 1972.[50] Entitled *Esquema director de ordenamiento metropolitano* (EDOM), the plan called for new housing, preferential development axes, new busses and mass transit routes, better highway and road organization, and intermunicipal cooperation.[51] It never came to fruition, thanks partly to the devastation of the earthquake of 1976 and largely to disfavor on the part of the ruling military cadres.[52]

Noting the chaos and congestion in the area, EDOM called for getting rid of La Terminal and constructing a new wholesale market away from the city center. Municipal markets, meanwhile, were the city's most important food distribution centers and tended to be randomly and inconveniently located. At the time the plan was published there were twenty-one markets in the municipality of Guatemala, fourteen of which had been built since 1955. Large *mercados ambulantes*, or informal street markets—clusters of unlicensed vendors—had sprung up in zones 1, 3, 5, 6, 7, and 8.[53] Recognizing the importance of the economy built from below, the plan sought to rationalize the situation over the course of decades. Philosophically, it would uphold the right of city dwellers "to satisfy their need to live, to work, to be educated, to recreate, and to be instructed. This socioeconomic goal," the plan continued, "is called 'Urban Liberty,' [and] in and of itself is a momentous objective that must be pursued by means of correcting and developing our social structure."[54]

Given the administration's failure to translate EDOM into reality, Urban Liberty continued to be much the same thing it had always been—a free-for-all of unregulated space creation driven both from above and from below. Indeed, much of the contemporary city, including its complex ethnic geography, had taken shape in a fairly improvisational manner during the third quarter of the twentieth century. By 1964 the government considered the municipalities of Villa Nueva, Petapa, and Mixco to be part of the AMG.[55] Mixco, a neighboring valley where wheat had been grown in colonial times, today is the nation's second city, the capital's Brooklyn, if you will. Mixco is part of the northwest corridor, whose main arteries are the

Mayan maquilas. Maquilas and maquila-supplying workshops, many of them Mayan-owned, proliferated in San Juan Sacatepéquez as the city grew. Anonymous, "Taller de sastrería para maquilas (Tailor Shop for Maquilas)," San Juan Sacatepéquez, Guatemala, n.d. Archivo de fotografías del Ejército Guerrillero de los Pobres, EGP. Fototeca Guatemala, CIRMA (Reference Code: GT-FG-CIRMA-060–004–195).

Pan-American Highway and the Calzada de San Juan, which runs to San Juan and San Pedro Sacatepéquez. Until midcentury Mixco was a village surrounded by a patchwork of large estates and tiny, Kaqchikel Mayan hamlets. Unlike Mixco, which is visually inseparable from the city proper, San Juan Sacatepéquez and San Pedro Sacatepéquez still feel geographically distinct, thanks to their mountain location high above the city and to the perseverance of *milpa* corn agriculture. Also Kaqchikel, these municipalities, home to poor farmers in the 1950s, are now best known for Mayan-owned textile maquiladoras, some of which manufacture highly prized *traje* and many of which supply the gray market with counterfeit brand name apparel. This Kaqchikel industrial cluster, unique in Guatemala, was born in 1959 when Cornelio Xuyá, a city textile worker, opened his own shop in San Pedro. The looms were run by pedals. San Pedro Sacatepéquez had yet to be wired with electricity.[56]

Mixco was and is the epicenter of the northwest corridor. In 1958 Mixco lost La Florida to the municipality of Guatemala; it became zone 19 of the city. La Florida, heavily Mayan demographically and in the early 2000s the

city's most densely populated lower-class neighborhood, had been a finca
whose anxious owners parceled it into lots during the agrarian reform.
Remote but by the late 1950s becoming urbanized and serviced by busses,
La Florida was a nexus of migration both for rural workers seeking a
foothold in the city and for city workers fleeing high rents in the center.[57]
Neighboring La Florida was Colonia Belén, populated in 1958 by settlers
who immediately began petitioning for churches, schools, drains, and access roads to both the Pan-American and the highway to San Juan and San
Pedro Sacatepéquez.[58] La Brigada, another contiguous Mixco neighborhood, dates to the same period, and was settled by the overflow from San
Juan and San Pedro. Today afflicted with gang violence, La Brigada is a
neighborhood where textile maquiladoras (not Mayan owned) and other
industries continue to attract Guatemalans seeking work. The neighborhood and the shantytowns that ring it retain a heavily Kaqchikel demographic, supplemented by Maya from Baja Verapaz, El Quiché, and San
Marcos.[59]

La Brigada is also notable for its historically high percentage of *albañiles*,
masons and construction workers, who built much of the city and its
periphery. According to Manuela Camus, nearly half the male heads of
household in La Brigada work in construction.[60] La Brigada is a metaphor
of the city at large: its local tradition of building reflects both the main
economic activity of midcentury metropolitan spill and the ongoing tradition of regional specializations; its demographic reflects the nation's ethnic
complexity as well as the failures of development in the countryside; its
factories and its gangs and drug runners, the crowds on its streets—a mix
that in Camus's words includes Mormon proselytizers, Mayan women in
traje, stumbling drunks, and transvestites—sum up, as does the chaotic
urban fabric of Guatemala City as a whole, the pain, paradoxes, and surprises of globalization in this corner of the third world.[61]

"Angels Without Glory":
Geographies of Deprivation and Death

From the 1960s forward, agrarian transformation and the proliferation of
agroexport enterprises, population growth, and economic restructuring
had been resulting in huge rural-to-urban migrations. By 1968 hellish
ghettoes were home to about 60,000 families in Guatemala City.[62] As the
center of agroexport shifted from the Atlantic to the Pacific lowlands,

migratory flows changed, bringing greater numbers of Mayans from the land-exhausted highlands into the city as the 1970s began.[63] By the mid-1970s the city's resources were stretched far beyond their limits. In 1974 Mayor Leonel Ponciano León declared that the population of the capital had reached 800,000, with 1.2 million living in the AMG. Within a quarter century Guatemala City had doubled its number of residents. It had also become a city of slums.[64]

"They look like angels without glory," wrote Marco Antonio Cacao, a reporter for *El Imparcial*, describing Guatemala City's street children in 1974. Not even lucky enough to enjoy the shelter of makeshift huts in the city's gorges and ravines, the angels were "scattered on the sidewalks, barefoot," haggard and pale from the cold.[65] To survive, some begged and some shined shoes, Cacao reported, earning next to nothing for their work since 90 percent of shoeshine earnings had to be remitted to cat's-paws who controlled the trade. None of the children interviewed knew who their parents were.[66] The city's homeless youth, ranging from hapless rural arrivals to hopeless runaways like Pedro Bor's son, in many ways epitomized the new Guatemala that emerged in the 1960s and 1970s. They were also a harbinger of the horrors that lay ahead, as a devastating earthquake in 1976 and genocidal massacres in the highlands in the 1980s created new waves of homelessness and orphans.

The angels without glory would later join the ranks of the mareros without mercy. As a social group their history references the failure of state-led development, the effects of high-modernist planning, and the third layer in this story of the making of the immoral metropolis—civil war. The violence that engulfed the countryside and city, ultimately escalating into what was the most brutal example of the right wing's capacity to use torture, terror, and mass murder in all of the Americas, left a society scarred by pathologies, produced thousands of orphans, and imposed an untenable economic system that continues to generate misery at an astonishing rate.

Years later, Chiqui Ramírez, a guerrilla, would discuss the street kids in her memoirs. "They lived in the street, they grew up in the street," she wrote, "they sold their bodies in the street, they procreated in the street, and they got hooked on drugs in the street. Many of these children, pushed by hunger, loneliness, lack of family and home, grouped themselves into bands [*pandillas*], later forming the gangs [*maras*]. We see a lot of them now, adults subsumed in drugs, prostitution, and robbery, and we morbidly celebrate when they get lynched for their thieving, just because we've been convinced that the problem is their *lifestyle*. We don't really try to analyze the origin of their existence. The State, with its repression, and Guatemalan society, with its complicit silence, also gave rise to these native sons."[67]

Ramírez dedicated her life to fighting against such conditions. Born to the owners of a bar and pool hall in Guatemala City, she grew up not far from El Gallito. She classifies her family as "petit bourgeoisie," but she remembers the scent of labor on the body of an uncle who was a railroad man and union member.[68] As a child, she and her friends used to hang out at the Jacobo Sánchez Communist school on Avenida Centro América and 17th Street, in the heart of zone 3. The comrades would let the kids use the school supplies, read the books, fiddle with the mimeograph machine, and, most of all, talk. It was early in the 1950s. Arbenz was president, and politics were polarized. Ramírez was in the school one day when a mob attacked. Poor folk, street vendors, and orphans worked up by rightist agitators, they bombed the building, caving in the roof. They were about to lynch a comrade, but the police intervened and saved the day.[69]

By 1962 Ramírez was a student representative of the Frente Unido del Estudiantado Guatemalteco Organizado (United Front of Organized Guatemalan Students), or FUEGO, meaning "fire."[70] Formed in 1958, FUEGO was the secondary-school equivalent of the politically active University Students' Association. Its officers were well-dressed high school students who followed the civil rights struggle in the United States, listened to Radio Havana, held roundtables, and put on plays and art shows. They were kids who danced to rock and roll.[71]

And they were doomed. Ramírez spent most of her life in Guatemala City in hiding, watching her friends die. She was ready to adhere to the rule that, if arrested, you had to endure torture for twenty-four hours before you said anything, delaying the inevitable imparting of information so that the compañeros would have time to move. Later, she hid with the guerrilla cadres in the jungle. In 2001, when her memoirs were published, she was living in Canada, having been in exile in Cuba and Nicaragua before then. Along the line, she had separated from her three children. Her husband was dead. So were most of her friends. So was her dream.

The guerrillas trace their dream to November of 1960, when word leaked out that the United States was training exiled Cuban troops in Retalhuleu (for what would later be the Bay of Pigs invasion). On 13

November nationalistic junior officers at Fort Matamoros in the capital and at the Zacapa garrison staged a revolt that took over a week for the army to crush. Several conspirators, among them Lt. Marco Antonio Yon Sosa and 2d Lt. Luís Turcios Lima, twenty-two and nineteen years old, respectively, managed to escape. They would soon return and spark Guatemala's organized Marxist insurgency.[72]

The insurgency was not a surprise. Politically torn apart by the U.S.–Castillo Armas invasion, socially rent by rapid modernization, and awed, like everyone, by events in Cuba, Guatemalans had been awaiting the left's new rise. "Terrorist" bombings had become common in the capital starting in July 1959; that month the targets included the Palace of the Archbishopric and the U.S. embassy; in September the target was the headquarters of the far-right party, the fascist Movimiento Democrático Nacional, soon renamed the Movimiento de Liberación Nacional (MLN). Exactly one year later, bombings had become so common that the Ydígoras government, itself under constant threat of military coup, instituted martial law and a curfew.[73]

Yon Sosa's and Turcios Lima's Movimiento Revolucionario 13 de Noviembre (MR-13) announced its belligerency only months after the rising of 1960, and by the following summer the government declared the rebels defeated.[74] Despite continuing military defeats and setbacks, as the U.S.-supported Guatemalan army launched counterinsurgency training and operations, the guerrillas rallied. The MR-13 formed the first fronts in early 1962 in Izabal, working in tandem with the Partido Guatemalteco del Trabajo (PGT, Guatemalan Workers Party), the remnants of Guatemala's Communist Party, whose own fronts were located in Baja Verapaz.[75] The same year saw the creation of the Fuerzas Armadas Rebeldes (FAR), one of the major combatants in the years ahead.[76]

As guerrillas were spreading through the hills, young Chiqui Ramírez was getting involved in Guatemala City. Like the rest of FUEGO's leaders, she joined the Juventud Patriótica del Trabajo, Patriotic Worker Youth, the PGT's wing for young people. The leftist resistance was as much an urban movement and a youth movement as it was a rural guerrilla insurgency. It is impossible to understand Guatemala City (or anyplace in Guatemala, for that matter) without understanding its overlay of politics and war, an overlay grounded in the agrarian economy and a critical element in defining the geography of the immoral metropolis.

"I Cleaned My Colt 45 and Looked Around":
Militarization, Modernization, and Murder

No sooner had Ramírez joined the party than Guatemala City experienced
a popular revolution. In early 1962 Ydígoras was under attack from all sides.
The students, the left, and the urban lower class in general struck and
demonstrated. Job actions paralyzed the nation. Despite efforts by the
AFL's Inter-American anticommunist wing, Organización Regional Interamericana de Trabajadores (ORIT), and the government to turn them into
yellow-dog shops and a Catholic movement alike, the unions had lived to
fight another day.[77] The conflagration started when dissatisfaction with the
municipal elections of 1961—supposedly engineered by Ydígoras's Reden-
ción party—erupted into protests and wildcat strikes early in 1962. The
government, claiming that "both Guatemalan and foreign elements of
recognized Communist affiliation have been maintaining a climate of agi-
tation in the country," imposed a state of siege in late January.[78]

Demonstrations and strikes continued despite the crackdown. As students and the popular movement filled the streets with protesters, unions
stepped up their walkouts, closing the schools, the courts, many of the
banks, and all urban mass transit. By 15 March all public services in every
sector affected by strikes were militarized. The government instituted martial law, judgment by court martial, and official censorship.[79] Meanwhile,
the students, including Ramírez's comrades, had been organizing in the
barrios. In March and April *capitalinos* took to the streets and called for
Ydígoras's resignation. Civilians skirmished with soldiers in the streets. In
zone 5, thanks to heavy organizing in places like La Limonada, the collection of shantytowns around La Palmita, residents threw up barricades and
declared their neighborhoods "liberated territory."[80]

"We were furious," remembers Carlos Ramos, today a wizened don who
owns a modest bar. As a returned migrant from the United States, he shares
his wisdom about *el norte* with young men drinking beer and plotting the
exodus to come. During the uprising of 1962, Carlos was sixteen years old
and living with his parents and seven siblings in a two-room house in zone
5, helping out by pushing a knife- and scissor-sharpening cart around the
streets. "Why were we so angry? Who knows?" he says. "It was everything.
The poor are always angry." Carlos's father, a landless migrant from Chi-
quimula some five years in the city, begged his son to stay out of trouble.
"But I was *muy güiro, pues*" (wet behind the ears). "People were every-

where, saying 'the government this, the rich people that, *a la lucha*' and who knows what else. Who knew? We threw rocks and bottles. It was *impresionante*" (something to see).[81]

Don Carlos remembers the uprising of 1962 as an uncorking of pent-up popular rage, leaderless and lacking a coherent political message. Yet a political message and political leaders there were—some experienced union and party activists and many uninitiated youngsters like Ramírez. The grass-roots uprising they helped foment soon spread to fourteen of the nation's twenty-two departments. The Ydígoras administration and the army quickly crushed the protestors. Yet even in the face of being forcibly pacified by military repression, students and workers kept clamoring for a change of government. Meanwhile, riding the wave of mass public disgust, guerrilla groups gained momentum. In Guatemala City, the Resistencia Rebelde Secreta wing of the MR-13 guerrillas (RRS-MR-13), formed and readied itself for action.[82]

Eleven months after the uprising, Ydígoras fell to a military coup. Minister of Defense Col. Enrique Peralta Azurdia (1963–66) was now the head of state.[83] Peralta had climbed to this position through his work in agriculture—work that put him at the center of agrarian transformation in the post-1954 period and that, along with infrastructure development, formed the backdrop of the making of the immoral metropolis.

An Ubico-era military man with a Pan-American perspective, Peralta had served Ydígoras as head of the Department of Agrarian Affairs and minister of agriculture. More than any other one person, Peralta masterminded Guatemala's counterinsurgent Green Revolution (see chapter 5). Peralta felt that the private sector and the middle class should be the object of rural development and that agriculture should be commercialized and industrialized. With help from U.S. advisors from the ICA, he concentrated resources along the Pacific, where sugar, beef, and cotton industries were expanding, and started a development zone in Izabal. By 1959 Ydígoras could boast of fifteen agrarian development zones and twelve new colonization programs, most of them Peralta's work.[84]

Agrarian transformation was institutionalized with the creation in 1962 of the Instituto de Transformación Agraria (INTA), which formalized post-1954 agrarian policy.[85] Peralta drafted the law that created the INTA and wove it together with another new program, military civic action. Through civic action programs and agrarian transformation the military became directly and indirectly inserted into relations of production and exchange throughout the country. Civic action grew steadily in Guatemala, fueled by the Alliance for Progress and increasingly inspired by U.S. tactics in Vietnam.[86] A military initiative, it brought schools and clinics to a handful of hamlets and, importantly, lavished attention on the troops. Drawing on the revolutionary rural education system, the high command established literacy programs, sports teams, and professional development courses in transmission technology, nursing, cooking, construction, and other trades.[87] The plans of INTA, meanwhile, used campesinos in two ways. First, they were to spearhead colonization to open new areas where large estates would later follow. Second, they would be settler–laborers near large fincas and would receive grants of tiny plots that could serve them as provision grounds. At the same time civic action and INTA were transforming the countryside, rural military commissioners and antigovernment members of the fascist MLN party were organizing rural, proplanter vigilante and paramilitary groups.[88] In tandem, these forces paved the way for the Green Revolution in Guatemala, a militarized, violent process that came to a head between 1970 and 1985.

The Peralta administration "braided" war, development, and military control of the state together, transforming the anticommunist, authoritarian modernism that had been dominant since 1954 into a pure, military modernism. It became difficult to distinguish where the military ended and the ministry of education or agriculture, to pick two examples, began.[89] The Guatemalan army became the government itself, filling executive, legislative, and judicial functions. Peralta was not president, but Jefe del Gobierno, or chief of government. As soon as he took power, a spate of decree-laws validated oppression in the Orwellian language of downward moral displacement. The *Carta Fundamental de Gobierno* (Government Charter) established army rule, to be headed by Peralta and a council of ministers, while the chilling Defense of Democratic Institutions Law forbade all forms of association to *comunistas*; the Ministry of National Defense was to begin compiling a registry of Communists immediately. The law established prison terms or capital punishment for subversive offenses, such as making bombs or distributing pamphlets, and decreed that all such crimes would be tried by military tribunals. Soon thereafter, the government decreed that anyone suspected of disturbing the public order could be detained without any judicial order for up to a month, a period that could be extended at will. Furthermore, it gave official blessing to all security measures against groups and associations.[90] The military also unleashed a full-scale campaign of repression against students. It occupied a number of secondary schools; they were to be temporarily reorganized to function as "civic-military centers." Begging the cooperation of all concerned parents, the army explained that "cruel illusions" were leading the nation's young "toward totalitarianism."[91]

Chiqui Ramírez remembers the era as one of cruel illusions as well—as the time when she and her friends forged a clandestine existence. "I cleaned my Colt 45 and looked around," she writes of her arrival at a safe house on the highway to San Juan Sacatepéquez in the northwest corridor. "Slumped on a cold mattress with no sheets, breathing in the smoke of a cigarette, I let my mind go blank. Clandestine life had soaked me up. An emptiness took root in my heart, preparing me for the imminence of death. My sadness for this generation that was being mutilated—this generation I was a part of— became chronic."[92]

Violence, too, became chronic. Political polarization became chronic, and so did military rule. Torture became commonplace. Guatemala City's streets reflected a geography of murder and war overlaid upon a geography of poverty and privation—a geography that embedded families like Pedro Bor's and idealistic kids like Chiqui Ramírez within a rubric of contested relations of production that ran from rioting street vendors to the highest levels of the vying Cold War heads of state.

As early as 1964 the guerrillas, inspired not only by Cuba but also by events in Vietnam, Zanzibar, the Congo, Algiers, and Brazil, began hit-and-run hostilities.[93] Typical attacks were lightning fast and more terrifying than lethal, but by mid-1965 they had put the guerrillas at center stage in the national discourse. In May of that year unknown assassins showered the vice minister of defense with machine-gun fire as he was driving home for lunch. By year's end the guerrillas were suspected to be so prevalent in the capital that military and civilian authorities staged nighttime sweeps of the city. While the terror inflicted by jackbooted soldiers kicking in doors by dead of night continues to infect society with dread pathologies, these raids reportedly captured reams of subversive material. Such raids escalated in 1966, as the government reported new guerrilla fronts in Baja Verapaz and suffered further urban guerrilla victories, including the kidnapping of the vice president of Congress in June, less than a month before Julio César Méndez Montenegro, the new president, took power.[94]

Both Méndez and his vice president, Clemente Marroquín Rojas, had progressive backgrounds with roots in the Revolution of 1944–54.[95] In fact,

Peralta's military let Méndez and Marroquín take office only after they had signed a secret pact with the high command. The pact allowed military rule to continue unchecked behind the facade of civilian government.[96] In 1966, the first year of Méndez's presidency, the army launched a new civic action program in the country's eastern zone, the same area where scorched-earth tactics were underway. In this endeavor the army cooperated with the Ministries of Education and Agriculture and Public Health, the Secretariat of Social Welfare, and the Food and Agriculture Organization of the United Nations.[97] From 1966 to 1968 army civic action publicized its digging of wells and building of hospitals, as well as its dispatching of military medical missions, around Zacapa. This is the same area where the future head of state Col. Carlos Manuel Arana Osorio was earning his reputation as "the Jackal of Zacapa," spearheading village-to-village liquidation of subversives in a project conducted, as was civic action, with the assistance of USAID.[98] Meanwhile, on the city streets and in the countryside the civil war intensified.[99] In 1970 Guatemala returned to military hands and would remain under their rule until 1986.

In the 1960s military rule meant murder. At the end of 1965 a U.S. force arrived in Guatemala, soon leading security forces in "Operation Cleanup," which "conducted over eighty raids and multiple extrajudicial assassinations, including an action that during four days in March [1966] captured, tortured, and executed more than thirty prominent left opposition leaders."[100] In addition, death squads arose during Peralta's regime, such as Mano Blanca (White Hand), whose leaflets appeared in Guatemala City in June of 1966. Within eighteen months twenty right-wing terror groups were in action.[101] The death squads were officially sanctioned, notably by the MLN party. They had direct ties to the military and in some cases to the police.[102]

Over the years the death squads disappeared thousands of victims, often dumping their tortured bodies in public places weeks or months later. Events in mid-1967 convey a sense of Guatemala City's waves of terror. On 25 May three bombs detonated within the space of five minutes in the central city. The next morning seven mutilated corpses were discovered in and around the capital. About a week later a leaflet entitled "Junio Rojo" (Red June) began circulating in huge numbers. Published by a group called the Consejo Anticomunista de Guatemala (CADEG), it listed the names of ninety alleged Communists and called upon death squads, including Mano Blanca and the Defense Council of the National

Police (the existence of which the police denied), to act swiftly on the information. Soon CADEG was spreading terror on a national scale.[103]

The slaughter continued in the years ahead. By 1974, when *El Imparcial* was highlighting the "angels without glory," Guatemala City, like the rest of the country, was prowled by death squads and covered with clandestine cemeteries and dumping grounds for tortured bodies. Rape had become commonplace. Women's cadavers bore the marks of unspeakable sexual violation. On some, the breasts had been hacked off. Like the corpses, the street children were a testament to the system's depravity. The disappearance of over fifteen thousand civilians left nearly twenty-eight thousand children parentless between 1970 and 1973 alone.[104] For the moment, they were capitalism's "angels," while Chiqui Ramírez and her cohort were the devils. Later, once the resisters had been snuffed, a new beast would arise from the urban entrails—the marero, the penniless, pubescent mascot of the immoral metropolis.

C arlos Melgar Zamboni was born in San Lucas Tolimán, Sololá, on Lake Atitlán and the skirts of Tolimán volcano. He was one of seven children, and the family was poor. His mother was a rural schoolteacher, and his father worked as an administrator on a finca in Patulul. Like so many other families of the era, the Melgars couldn't make ends meet. In 1957 they left the countryside and moved to Guatemala City.

The family located in La Florida, the fast-growing blue collar neighborhood in zone 19. There, young Carlos began his working life, earning by day and studying by night. For a while he worked as a mason's assistant, then as a bicycle repairman. Meanwhile, his uncle and his older brother had opened a butcher shop in Mercado Cervantes, a quiet market in zone 3 located in Llano de Palomo, a neighborhood bordering El Gallito. Taking advantage of the family connection, Carlos set up shop as a beef butcher in La Terminal, the wholesale outlet in zone 4. He dealt, as did his relatives, in beef alone; Guatemalan *expendedores*, or market and neighborhood meat vendors, typically sell the meat of only one animal. Later in life Carlos would move to Llano de Palomo and take over his relatives' stall in Mercado Cervantes. He would also become a key figure in Guatemalan grassroots retail, located at the very nexus of Guatemala's Green Revolution and its transition to neoliberalism. His story in retail brings together the events in the countryside, the politics of terror, and the final turn toward transnational, neoliberal capital that the military rulers of Guatemala executed in the 1970s and 1980s.

From 1970 to the elections of 1985 the military high command built a complex structure of state that, by the end of the period, was institutionalized both to look like a modern democracy and to interact with the transnational governmental and nongovernmental institutions that characterized late capitalism. Drawing on decades of agrarian development, the generals also completed Guatemala's Green Revolution, achieving wide success in commercializing agriculture. Guatemala emerged from its years of military rule with a greatly diversified agricultural portfolio, a bureaucratic-rational state, and a public and private sector alike characterized by training institutes, trade associations, and similar institutions that were able to plug in to the new universe of NGOs and other development organizations that had also taken form in the 1970s and 1980s. This epoch of intense modernization in Guatemala culminated in genocide. The period from 1970 to 1985 was one of transformation through terror.

Counterinsurgency and development, the army's two missions, are not analytically separate. Indeed, the very fact that they were paired explains much of what happened. The Guatemalan military high command was not a natural group to institute a neoliberal regime; it was split into ideological factions with rival class alliances and espoused developmental policies that showed a marbled mix of modernization theory, dependency theory, and a Volkish nationalism reminiscent of the 1930s. Leaders spoke of protectionist import substituting industrialization (ISI) yet appointed foreign-trained technocrats to key ministries. They built bridges to transnational capital even as they worked to make the military itself a major capital actor in the nation's economy. While these contradictions and slippages always need to be borne in mind, one fact remains clear about the officers' relation to transnational neoliberal capital: they were its chosen executioners.

Carlos Melgar was no stranger to these trends. With other beef vendors he began organizing a commercial association in the late 1960s. However, it wasn't until 1985 that the group's members felt they could go public without getting murdered by the state. Just as their organizing took place at a dangerous crossroads of politics and commerce, so the commodity they sold bespoke an agrarian economy in the throes of change.

"Malnutrition Is a Way of Life": The Green Revolution, Nontraditional Exports, and Hunger in the Highlands

A central figure in engineering agricultural change, as we have seen, was Col. Enrique Peralta Azurdia. As minister of agriculture, he masterminded the INTA, and then, as head of state from 1963 to 1966, he "braided" the military and the state together, a process that continued during the Méndez Montengro presidency. Under the rule of the generals who followed, rural Guatemala experienced a tremendous crisis and sea change in its agrarian regime—its own version of the Green Revolution. Carlos Manuel Arana Osorio (1970–74), Kjell Eugenio Laugerud García (1974–78), Romeo Lucas García (1978–82), Efraín Ríos Montt (1982–83), and Oscar Humberto Mejía Víctores (1983–86) not only oversaw the so-called pacification of the countryside; they also brought decades of agricultural commercialization to fruition.

With the inauguration of General Arana on 1 July 1970, a new party was formed that would control the executive branch until 1978. Its unanimity, however, went only as far as a desire for law and order. Arana favored military participation in directing the country's economic development, yet appointed a number of U.S.-educated technocrats to prominent ministries. His agricultural allies favored protectionism, while his industrialist backers pushed for neoliberal policies. The result, both under Arana and his successor, General Laugerud, was a new, institutionalized, technocratic state transparent to capital and led by a messianic military that envisioned itself as savior of the nation. It was a deadly mix, especially in the countryside.[1]

The Arana administration, like that of Laugerud to come, refined and extended the already intertwined strands of economic and social policy, developmentalism, and counterinsurgency.[2] Most notable was a "vast development plan" to be fueled by a twenty-three-million-dollar loan from USAID. The new law established agrarian development zones around the country, but particularly in what would later be called the Franja Transversal del Norte (FTN) (the entire department of Izabal was made a zone, for example). *Terrenos baldíos*, uncultivated lands, were to be "inscribed in favor of the nation" by the INTA, which administered the program. The plan's stated goals were to aid campesinos as well as small and medium-sized farmers to further colonize the northern territories and diversify national production. Significantly, the plan also emphasized the commercialization of agriculture in the western Mayan highlands.[3] Near the end of 1970 the government launched a new Agricultural Development Bank (BANDESA).[4] Not capitalized until early 1972, BANDESA, was to distribute loans to small- and medium-scale farmers. Meanwhile, the Instituto Nacional de Comercialización Agrícola (INDECA), the bank's sister institute, was most importantly charged with stabilizing the price of basic grains. INDECA was also to handle supplies, rationalize storage systems, and in general institute market economics in the highlands.[5] In what became a three-pronged strategy, the agricultural picture was rounded out with the creation in 1972 of the Instituto de Ciencia y Tecnología Agrícola (ICTA), which set up centers and experiment stations piecemeal throughout the nation in the 1970s, and promoted not only foreign manufactures such as fertilizers and pesticides, but also foreign markets (by promoting soy cultivation, for example). These agencies expanded steadily throughout Arana's and Laugerud's presidencies, and INDECA passed to military leadership in 1975.[6]

The purpose of these agencies was to promote and modernize agroexport—the same sector that was causing all the problems for butchers like Melgar. The foundation in 1971 of the Centro Nacional de Promoción de Exportaciones (GUATEXPRO), both reflected and accelerated changes in the countryside. The agency was charged with providing technical aid to agroexport enterprises.[7] By mid-1972, the Interamerican Export Center of the OAS proclaimed that Guatemala was on the verge of converting itself into an exporter of nontraditional crops, producing 521 unspecified new products.[8] Tensions resulted, and less than a year later the Asociación General de Agricultores (AGA), which had represented the landed elite since 1920, split ranks. Traditional finqueros remained in the AGA, while the modernizing, export- and diversification-oriented sector formed the Cámera del Agro, whose members had close ties to the governing military elite.[9]

Agrarian transformation and diversification turned Guatemala into an exporter of nontraditional crops over the course of the 1970s and 1980s. The background to the "vast development plan" that spurred this process in the early to mid-1970s was an ongoing crisis in basic grains. Time and again, the country was on the brink of famine.

In 1970 corn and beans, the campesinos' staples, were already so scarce that the government prohibited their export. In early 1973 the government again forbade the export of grains, meat, and medicines. In Guatemala City, industrial workers protested and denounced rising bread prices in the headquarters of the Autonomous Federation of Guatemalan Unions (FASGUA), a trade union federation.[10] By the last months of Arana's presidency food prices were spiraling upward. The leaders of INDECA promised that the agency would stockpile additional grains in the face of dwindling reserves. Within a year the commercialization institute had provoked open resistance on the part of highland rice, bean, and corn cultivators. The agency was charged with the task of buying all basic grain harvests, but growers bitterly charged that INDECA was forcing them to sell at too low a price.[11]

In 1982, at the height of violence, the FAR noted that "malnutrition is a way of life for the *pueblo guatemalteco*."[12] Setting out to explain the phenomenon, the guerrillas traced the history of hunger to the Alliance for Progress and the transnational attempt to bring the Green Revolution to Guatemala. They bitingly criticized the numerous USAID-funded state institutions like INDECA and BANDESA. In 1965, they claimed, 45 percent of the rural population had been unable to cover their basic food needs; after just ten years of Green Revolution policies, by 1975 some 70 percent could not. While government policies and transnational capital caused the basic grains crisis, meat was also in ever shorter supply, the FAR said.

The Clandestine Slaughterhouse:
Living through Agroexport in Guatemala City

Guatemala had also become a meat exporter from the 1960s to the 1980s, meaning that many dairy herds were replaced with beef cattle. Special slaughterhouses and packing plants shipped out the bulk of Guatemalan beef in accordance with U.S. Department of Agriculture (USDA) standards, while what was left for the *pueblo* came from inferior facilities and sick animals. Many of these beeves were poisoned with DDT, which had become popular during Guatemala's cotton boom.[13]

The post-1954 military governments worked closely with international institutions and corporations to promote agribusiness and in particular sales of fertilizers and pesticides. The meat industry evolved in tandem with these phenomena. It was pushed by the military's opening up of ranchland in the Petén and the FTN, where many generals invested, as well as in in the *oriente* and Costa Sur through highway development. By the end of the 1970s there were 117,596 cattle ranches in Guatemala, with a total of over two million head.[14]

Carlos Melgar tells the history of the meat business from a city butcher's perspective. Up to the early 1970s, he says, sides of beef arrived in the capital from a central slaughterhouse in Escuintla, the Rastro de Ganado Mayor. Unloaded from trucks at a distribution center near La Terminal, meat got chopped up by "cada quien," whomever. They took the heads and guts off to a viscera market, while flesh went into a foul and disorderly distribution network that ferried it to the municipal markets and local

butcher shops. "They came from every market, by every means of transport," Melgar explains. "They hauled it in pickups, they hauled it in panel
vans, they hauled it in trucks, but, almost always, they hauled in heaps. Just
tossed around . . . *Brrm, brrm, brrm*! Just piles of meat."[15]

Melgar recalls the situation changing in the early 1970s, when the city
opened *rastros municipales* that took over much of the capital's slaughtering
business from the Escuintla facility, which not long after disappeared.[16] At
the same time, he explains, there appeared a profusion of *rastros clandestinos*—clandestine slaughterhouses. "They showed up in San José Pinula, in
Palín, in Mixco," he says, evoking with his words the interior patios of
typical Guatemalan homes bathed in blood and strewn with carcasses livid
with flies. I imagine children squatting around a pile of viscera to sort them.
Melgar and I share a look of mutual understanding about the magnitude of
the public health nightmare. The clandestine slaughterhouses were not run
by experienced butchers, but by campesinos-turned-urbanites. They set on
sickly animals with machetes when the opportunity arose by pure chance.
How were the rastros clandestinos founded? "¡Mirá, vos—there's a cow!"[17]

Agroexporters were largely to blame for this situation, just as the FAR
guerrillas would later report. As the Guatemalan beef industry took on its
modern face, it systematically denied a supply of clean, fresh meat to the
populace in favor of selling every ounce it could abroad. The exporting
rastros, Melgar explains, by regulation were supposed to put 60 percent of
their output into the domestic market, but they never complied. It was a
problem that continued in the decades ahead; by 1998 these rastros themselves were in the midst of an economic downturn, and the municipal
slaughterhouses remained unregulated and filthy.[18]

Besides being a prime example of agroexport, beef is emblematic of the
highly contested world of Guatemalan retail. In 1959 a company named La
Fragua opened its first supermarket, entering into competition with Guatemala's municipal market vendors. Disgusted with the unregulated and
unsanitary Rastro de Ganado Mayor, La Fragua teamed up with the producers, whose exports had to meet USDA standards, to create a vertically
integrated supply chain.[19] The beef in the supermarket and the beef in the
market, with its halo of flies, lost life under very different circumstances.

It was to address disparities in quality and supply and injustices in
pricing that Melgar got involved in organizing in La Terminal late in the
1960s. It was not easy to make a living in the meat business. Wholesale
prices kept rising, distribution was chaotic and far from hygienic, and, in

general conditions of poverty, meat was a luxury consumer item. By the early 1970s the butchers had amassed dozens of supporters and were hoping both to form a mutual aid society and to put pressure on the government to control meat prices. It was an informal movement, with no paperwork, under the nominal leadership of Rogelio Pérez. "Inside the group, I wanted to be secretary," Melgar remembers, "but it wasn't as if there were elections or anything. It was more like, 'Hey you, go there; hey you, come here.' That was how it was run. And nobody wanted to call attention to himself."[20]

Despite its informality, the nameless butchers' group caught the attention of the Asociación de Estudiantes Universitarios (AEU), who sent some *asesores* (technical consultants) to help in planning strategies and actions. The first action came in 1972, when butchers demonstrated in front of the National Palace. The police drove them away with tear gas, so they went over to the Congress to press their claims to the deputies. Melgar remembers that after they were inside, a truck pulled up in plain sight. It was the "pájaro azul," the blue bird—a vehicle of state security forces that carried you away to a different sort of clandestine slaughterhouse: the kind of vehicle you'd be seen getting into and might never be seen again. And as the butchers clamored to be heard on the not-too-political topic of the wholesale price of beef, armed guards began pouring into the building and clouds of tear gas filled the chamber. Melgar escaped, but he saw some of his compañeros being shoved into the pájaro azul.

Not long after, Melgar saw the name of Rogelio Pérez appear on the ticket of the mayoral candidate Leonel Ponciano León, who at the time was the municipalidad's director of public services and in charge of the municipal markets. Ponciano, who would later be mayor from 1974 to 1978, had been working on polling and licensing informal vendors in La Terminal, La Florida, and in La Asunción market in zone 5, bringing him into contact with grass-roots leaders like Pérez. Young Carlos Melgar was completely disillusioned by Pérez's betrayal of the trade for the power of politics. This sort of disillusionment would dog him for the length of his career.[21]

Melgar's attitude about politics has everything to do with the Guatemalan culture of development, just as his recounting of the vendors' early days has much to say about historical memory. Politics during his youth meant war, danger, and death. Under the Guatemalan military state, a structure of feeling around politics matured in which anything political was seen as hopelessly corrupt and manipulative. Meanwhile, alternative politics of any variety could be deadly.

According to Melgar, even as some of the meat vendors were betraying their brothers by working with the "muni" (as the municipalidad, or city hall, is called), others were joining the guerrillas. As I press him on the events of 1972 and the organizing in the late sixties that led up to it, he dodges my questions. Even though I explain that I am simply trying to get a feel for the political atmosphere inside the markets and barrios, this is *not* what he wants to talk about, and it certainly is not what he wants me to write about. If I do write about it, he wants me to make it clear that he had nothing to do with politics—not with the guerrilla left, the death squad right, or anything in between. I believe this, actually. But, I point out, it is impossible that he didn't know such things were going on. Students and guerrillas like Chiqui Ramírez were organizing in the very markets and neighborhoods where he lived, I point out. There was a war on.

Well, that event in 1972 . . . we circle back around. The asesores who came from the AEU hadn't been just technical advisors. They invited the meat vendors to a meeting in La Florida. Melgar went along. "We went to meet . . . well, I didn't know exactly what it was supposed to be about, but whatever, there I was, along with them, and we went to meet with some guerrillas," he says. "Well, they were inciting us, '¡a lucha!,' and really they had a better understanding with our university compañeros."[22]

He continued, "Entonces, eso no muy me gustó [well, I didn't like that a whole lot]. Because I didn't know anything about all that and besides, I'd had some experiences when I first started to work." He tells of being young—*patojos*, just kids—in La Terminal, and of how two members of the trade got involved. The story he relates is clipped, but the silences are full of unspoken violence. "They got themselves into the whole question, then we didn't see them again; we knew so little about the guerrilla. And when it all happened—the meeting with the group of *carniceros* and all that—well, I already knew what had happened to the families of these friends, so it made me a little bit afraid." After that, "if I knew we were going to the Economy Ministry, 'OK, let's go.' But if it was just, "eh, muchá, let's go to some meeting,' then it was better I didn't go." Melgar's career as a commercial organizer was structured and limited by terror. He was far from alone in that condition.

"So They Could Later Be Killed Off":
Campesinos and Cooperatives in the 1970s

Just weeks after the debut of the army's vast plan to remake agriculture in
1970, the Movimiento Campesino Independiente (MCI) celebrated its
fourth annual congress in the headquarters of the Central de Trabajadores
Federados. The MCI declared that the function of the Guatemalan campesino was to be an "agricultural motor." On this point, the government
agreed. But the campesinos did not trumpet the triumphs of the recently
penned agrarian legislation, the likes of which they had seen for two decades. Instead, they called for genuine agrarian reform, better access to
credit, a rural minimum wage, improved health services, schools, malnutrition relief, and the freedom to associate without fear of deadly reprisal.
Laugerud García, the next head of state, took great pains to give the
impression that he was meeting these demands. In reality, however, his
government's plans, like Arana's, failed to mitigate poverty. They increased
hunger, extended state surveillance and control, and aided the military in
conducting brutal counterinsurgency campaigns in the highlands.[23]

Laugerud represented the "civic action" wing of the military elite. They
were "tough love" thinkers inspired by "guns and butter" and similar failed
strategies in Vietnam. The idea was to use development as the soft arm of
war. The process of development would be led by the military, which not
only ran the state, but, as an autonomous institution, participated in the
national economy. The productive military of the 1970s opened its own
bank. The Banco del Ejército, or Army Bank, was set up to act as a combination commercial, credit, and development bank. Among other things, it
offered credits for cattle ranches and real estate investments.[24] This was not
surprising, since the army had made the Petén—where many of the new
ranches and fincas ended up—a virtual showcase of military-led development. The Petén Economic Development Agency (FYDEP) had passed to
direct military control in 1962 and drew on a history of modernization
schemes dating back to the 1940s. As civic action gained currency in the
years following the triumph of the Cuban Revolution, the Petén increasingly became a showpiece of modern projects: agricultural schools, land
colonization schemes, crop diversification, and even highway building.[25]

In keeping with this tradition, Laugerud in 1975 announced that the
army was mainly an "agent of social change."[26] He launched an army
cultural magazine, Revista Militar, and a military television station to pro-

mote programs like civic action, which, he said, epitomized the philosophy of the army as a social institution.[27] The army magazine would later claim that the military was responsible for assuring "subsistence, even in the farthest-flung places in which human life exists," and that the army was leading a "movement of salvation."[28] Through civic action the army would build both infrastructure and social structure, saving the nation's youth from Communism. And youth were vulnerable, held an article in *Revista Militar* in 1975, which called for the Central American Defense Council to establish youth-oriented civic action programs. For many young men, the author noted, the army itself was their first school, an education that came too late.[29]

Laugerud teamed his concern for the young with spectacular public gestures showing his fondness for the campesinos. In 1974 the new president shocked capital city politicians when he invited fifteen hundred farmers from the cooperative movement to lunch in the National Palace. Laugerud's supporters in the far-right MLN party, already alienated by his program of price controls, began to resign from government positions in protest. Nonetheless, viewing cooperatives as a vehicle for maintaining government control and for channeling government and aid funds (from USAID and the Inter-American Development Bank, among other sources), the Laugerud administration provided both money and equipment to cooperativists, whose numbers soared to some ninety thousand by the end of 1975.[30]

State support of the growing movement was cloaked in the language of social justice. Cooperatives spurred democracy, fair distribution of wealth, and agrarian reform, the government held. The real agenda, however, was very different. Social engineers came to view cooperatives, both agrarian and savings and credit, as an excellent vehicle for spreading modern relationships of exchange and state control throughout the countryside. Counterinsurgency experts, meanwhile, worked both to reclaim the movement from the left and to extend tentacles of surveillance and control among the population.[31]

The problem with cooperatives, from the government's point of view, was that they were inherently a form of popular organization. They continually emerged as fields of contestation. In the 1950s cooperatives had been largely associated with agrarian reform and explicitly anticapitalist organizations. In the 1960s many had worked with the Catholic Church, Catholic Action, and the Christian Democrats. It is no surprise that militarists suspected them of subversive tendencies and supported the move-ment only when it provided cover for other activities, such as controlling a population or bringing cheap labor to underpopulated areas. According to Michael McClintock, the Laugerud government regularly arrested, mur-dered, or disappeared cooperative leaders. Laugerud's outward support for the movement, some speculated, made "potential leaders among the peas-antry . . . show themselves . . . so they could later be killed off."[32]

The food shortages and development schemes combined with the co-operative movement to give the nation, especially the highlands, a tense, simmering feel during the first half of the 1970s. For ground-level economic actors like Melgar, meanwhile, state terror continued to be a major factor in decision making. By the end of 1975 Guatemala was ripe for the crisis to explode. The coming of the worst natural disaster of the century did not make the situation any better.

"An Earthquake That Never Ends": February 1976 and
the Formation of the Comité de Reconstrucción Nacional

The ground began to shake just after 3:00 A.M. on Wednesday, 4 February 1976. The earthquake registered 7.5 on the Richter scale. The epicenter was Gualán, a small town fifty miles northeast of the capital. The quake began with motion in the two faults that cut east–west across Guatemala's chain of mountains and volcanoes and run into the Caribbean. The first slippage triggered a web of smaller faults throughout the indigenous northwest, devastating the highlands.

In the days that followed, at least six hundred aftershocks hit the coun-try, including a major second quake, itself nearly 6.0 on the Richter scale. In the weeks ahead, Guatemalans began to tally the losses. Over twenty-two thousand people were dead, and more than three times that number were maimed or injured. Over a million were left homeless.[33]

Many towns in and around Chimaltenango department were left in shambles. Some 25 percent of Zaragoza's population of 8,000 perished. In San Martín Jilotopeque, only 856 of the town's 3,760 residents remained alive. They were so weary that they demanded payment to continue bury-ing the dead. Around the highlands, residents formed mutual aid groups, pooling food, resources, and labor, and brigades of student volunteers arrived to lend assistance. Despite these efforts, many communities re-ported starvation. Typhoid began to spread, and serum was scarce.[34]

Despite the capital's proximity to the epicenter, stone structures and steel buildings survived. Wealthy suburbs were more or less unaffected. The poor, however, were not as lucky. Weaker adobe homes and the makeshift huts of the shantytowns collapsed. Some two hundred thousand homeless *capitalinos* pitched homemade tents in the streets, parks, and ravines; they clawed through the ruins to find survivors. The wounded flooded hospitals, which began caring for patients on the sidewalks and in nearby offices. One hospital set up operating rooms in a Jeep dealership. Authorities dispatched squadrons to bury as many of the dead as possible with the greatest haste, anxious to quell outbreaks of typhoid and cholera. The city had no running water, and huge sections were left without electric power.[35]

Aid workers from around the world rushed to Guatemala City. Father Ramón Adán Stürtze, a Spanish Carmelite priest working in Malawi, left his post and came to Bethania. For two years he lived in the neighborhood in a handmade hut, finally managing to open a clinic. Stürtze never left, and by 2002 he had built a school, an old-age home, and a facility for alcoholics.[36] In 1976 another Catholic priest, Adrián Bastiansen, led a land invasion of the state-owned finca Santa Cristina in the urban municipality of Chinautla. Called Tierra Nueva, this postquake settlement was supported by various parishes, by an NGO called the Instituto de Desarrollo Social en América Central (IDESAC, Central American Social Development Institute) and by the Movimiento Nacional de Pobladores (MONAP, National Settlers' Movement). Soon the United Nations Children's Fund (UNICEF), the Lions Club, and numerous state and military agencies appeared on the scene as well.[37] Even as efforts such as these were underway, death squads were reportedly taking advantage of the tragedy, claiming at least two hundred victims just after the quake.[38]

"Guatemala lives in an earthquake that never ends," commented *De Sol a Sol.* A Marxist campesino magazine, its title, *From Sun to Sun,* evoked the constant labor of the poor. The magazine charged that factories were firing scores of union organizers and that banks offering reconstruction loans and construction industry firms were profiteering. In towns like Chajul, an Ixil-speaking hamlet in the K'iche' highlands, in the 1980s the scene of some of the worst army depravities, they wrote, the military availed itself of the chaos to murder anyone "who fights for the people."[39]

This charge was credible. The military state also responded to the chaos with institution building. By mid-March the Laugerud administration had reconstituted a defunct agency, the Comité de Reconstrucción Nacional (CRN), to coordinate relief efforts and manage aid funds. With millions of dollars flowing in from governments and NGOs around the world, the monetary stakes were high. A firestorm of political warfare, especially between Laugerud and ex-president Arana, prompted the resurrection of the CRN.[40]

The CRN is an agency of great importance in the history of Guatemalan militarism. As reconstituted in the wake of the earthquake of 1976, the CRN was placed under the directorship of a general and was given wide-ranging interinstitutional powers. Increasingly typical of Guatemala's governmental solutions, interinstitutional cooperation meant that "all government dependencies as well as decentralized entities" were compelled to lend assistance and expertise to the agency. In July 1976 the CRN created departmental, municipal, and local committees to identify problems and organize relief. Each departmental committee was headed by the governor and included in its leadership the army's corresponding brigade commander. The CRN and this structure lay dormant through the administration of Gen. Romeo Lucas García (1978–82), but governments in the early to mid-1980s resurrected it as part of a master plan to bring the Guatemalan populace fully under military control.[41]

The CRN, argues the political scientist Jennifer Schirmer, was the epitome and model of civilian–military cooperation in highland development in the 1970s. Interinstitutional coordination helped the state penetrate where previously it could not reach. Calling the CRN an "'integration of a group of Army officers, civil functionaries, and civilians from the private sector, the business sector, workers, students, and cooperatives,'" the one-time director Gen. Ricardo Peralta Méndez described for Schirmer how the CRN worked at the local level to promote "broad popular participation" in reconstruction and development.[42]

The CRN encapsulates Guatemala's transformation through terror in the seventies and eighties. "Broad popular participation" was not the goal; instead, the agency served to extend both state control and commercial relationships of exchange through military conquest. Laugerud's minister of defense, General Lucas García, dismantled the local CRN committees upon becoming head of state in 1978. Unlike his predecessors, Lucas believed not in civic action but in pure counterinsurgency. The genocide he began in the highlands by the end of his term paved the way for the return of the CRN and the interinstitutional model, but with a much more ambitious goal: the total transformation of society. By 1985 Guatemala would be a very different and very wounded nation.

The People Fight Back: Politics and Political Economy, 1976–82

The earthquake of 1976 ravaged a country already torn by civil war and suffering economic downturn. These were the years of the oil crisis, when investments by the Organization of Petroleum Exporting Countries filled the coffers of the financial world with Eurodollars. They were years of the visible realignment of the global economic regime, prompting scholars to hail the dawn of a new era. The geographer David Harvey calls this new age one of "flexible accumulation" following a period of high-modern "Fordist accumulation."[43] The words that mark this transition loom large in macroeconomic and geopolitical histories: the dirty wars in places like Argentina and Chile; the stagflation that prompted Richard Nixon to unlink the dollar's exchange from fixed-rate gold; the related explosion of third-world debt; the deep-rooted but newly noted predominance of the multinational corporation; the formation of the nonaligned movement. Guatemala was no stranger to these flows. Laugerud, following in Arana's footsteps, had appointed numerous technocrats. His civilian economy minister, for example, had represented Guatemala in the trade talks that led to the General Agreement on Tariffs and Trade (GATT) and in the UN Conference on Trade and Development created by the efforts of the nonaligned movement to keep the trends in global trade, like GATT, from steamrolling the developing world into endless poverty.[44] Multinational capital would win this battle, just as it won the on-the-ground battle in Guatemala. The earthquake was a key moment in the fight.

After the quake, the government fine-tuned its mechanisms of control to confront a resurgent left, even as it rejected U.S. military aid: in 1977 the military refused to bow to the human rights demands of the Carter administration, and the short-term lack of arms and materiel fed army panic and ferocity, though Israel quickly picked up as an arms supplier.[45] At the same time, the thousands of displaced migrants transformed the dynamics and the urgency of popular organizing around the nation. Guerrilla cadres swelled. Labor unions launched the largest actions of the century. Grassroots movements and popular organizations transformed Guatemala's political landscape.

In August of 1976 the government announced that Marxist forces were invading El Quiché, Sololá, and Huehuetenango departments and that they were sending in the Kaibiles, the army's equivalent of Green Berets.[46] The growth of the guerrilla force and government repression continued in the years ahead. In May 1977 the Ejército Guerrillero de los Pobres (EGP, Guerrilla Army of the Poor) captured the Salvadoran ambassador during an assembly of the Inter-American Development Bank and managed to have a manifesto published in *El Imparcial.*[47] During the next two months security forces killed two professors (one in a wheelchair) and two student leaders, Robin García and Leonel Caballeros, at the University of San Carlos. Soon thereafter the university campus became a focal point for government surveillance and a favored dumping ground of death squads.[48]

Labor organization also intensified immediately after the earthquake of 1976. In April of that year leaders of numerous organizations formed the Comité Nacional de Unidad Sindical (CNUS). The event followed a solidarity movement for 152 workers who were fired at the Coca-Cola bottling plant; the union had occupied the facility, and a dozen workers were wounded and fourteen were jailed when the police invaded. The wider purpose of the CNUS was to coordinate mass protests against the growing militarization of the countryside. A cross-class alliance that included bankers, municipal workers, teachers, and university students along with blue-collar industrial and rural farmworkers, the CNUS bespeaks years of organizing in the face of severe oppression. As part of its antiunion killing spree, the right murdered CNUS's first leader, Luis Ernesto de la Rosa, before year's end. In June of 1977 the killing of another CNUS leader sparked a demonstration of over twenty thousand in Guatemala City.[49]

Unions launched more job actions in 1977 than in any other year in the nation's history.[50] Most notably, the year ended with a huge strike and march led by the Mam-speaking miners of Ixtahuacán in Huehuetenango. The Mayan strikers led a 351-kilometer march down the Pan-American Highway from the northwestern province, ultimately gathering a crowd of over one hundred thousand as it reached the capital. A high-water mark in Guatemalan unionism, the Glorious March, as it came to be called, also showed growing campesino–worker and interethnic solidarity.[51]

Activism and violence continued into 1978, an election year. The year began with the EGP's capture on New Year's Eve of the ex–foreign minister and right-wing luminary Roberto Herrera Ibargüen, whom the guerrillas accused of complicity in the death squads. They won $2.5 million in ransom. Bloodshed increased through the March elections. In the north, guerrillas battled the army in the Ixcán, while actions on the Pacific water-shed in Suchitepéquez prompted the government to dispatch 800 police to the area. In Guatemala City death squads murdered with impunity.[52] In the first quarter of the year 1,200 hydroelectric dam workers marched out of the countryside and camped in the city's central park. No sooner were their demands met than a stunning 150,000 state workers struck. Through paralyzing work stoppages and massive demonstrations in February and March, they managed both to win significant raises and to force the army to promise publicly not to cancel the elections.[53]

Such was the backdrop to the fraud-ridden polling of 1978, which began with an indecisive vote on 5 March. Bombings and demonstrations fol-lowed when Congress declared General Lucas García and his running mate, Francisco Villagrán Kramer, elected after a runoff election decried as foul by left and right alike. Nonetheless, Lucas García's inauguration went forth on 1 July as planned.[54]

In the meantime, mass murder opened a Pandora's box of public fury and augured the horrors to come. On 29 May 1978 the army opened fire on unarmed civilians in the small town of Panzós in Alta Verapaz. Almost immediately outrage at this massacre of over 150 Q'eqchi' Mayan campesi-nos boiled over. In Guatemala City some 80,000 citizens demonstrated in protest, and the army began running advertisements showing soldiers building and helping in emergencies. "The Army of Guatemala: In Service to Its People," one headline read. Meanwhile, according to the left, the demonstration's organizers began to disappear and within days SWAT teams took over La Terminal. Supposedly they were there to "capture delinquents."[55] The massacre itself was symptomatic of a countryside in agony and chaos, not only because of increasing warfare, but also because a growing population was confronting growing agroexport acreage as the Green Revolution marched forward.[56]

Referring to Panzós as "The Last Colonial Massacre," the historian Greg Grandin writes that "it was part of a larger epic assault on the private fiefdoms of social control that simultaneously came under siege and were emboldened with the spread of commodified social relations and the extension of state power throughout Latin America."[57] The same development-born spread of agrocapitalism and the state contributed to the conditions prompting the foundation of the Comité de Unidad Campesino (CUC), which went public later in 1978. Rigoberta Menchú, the Mayan activist who later won the Nobel Peace Prize, was involved with this organization, which strove to unite the unarmed grass-roots movements—including agricultural unions and campesino leagues—into a multiethnic, multisector coalition.[58]

Protest continued. Less than a month after Lucas García took office, a series of crippling mass transit strikes broke out. In October a government-approved doubling of bus fares led to wildcat strikes and a week of turbulent riots; citizens threw up barricades and burned busses. Out of the maelstrom emerged a new right-wing death squad, the Ejército Secreto Anti-Comunista, or Secret Anti-Communist Army.[59] In June of 1979 headlines were made on the anniversary of the Panzós massacre when the Frente Democrático Contra la Represión publicly blamed the massacre on the army. The FDR explicitly referenced the Green Revolution, claiming that "all the land in the country has been appropriated by large landowners and big capital." The same month saw the kidnapping of the leader of the bank employees' union and the assassination of the military chief Gen. David Cancinos Barrios.[60]

In early July 1979, as Anastasio Somoza's days as Nicaragua's despot began to appear numbered, the CIA released a report claiming that Cuba was "intensifying its subversive efforts in Guatemala and El Salvador, to provoke a revolutionary uprising in all of Central America."[61] The Guatemalan military, along with the associated death squads, intensified counter-insurgency tactics against this eventuality. By September Amnesty International (AI) had launched a campaign denouncing Guatemala's "political assassinations, torture and kidnapping." Government forces, AI claimed, were responsible for a minimum of two thousand deaths since Lucas's inauguration.[62]

The guerrillas made great advances in 1979, as a new organization, the Organización del Pueblo en Armas (ORPA), became public. The EGP, meanwhile, was operating effectively and continued to kidnap elite rightists. By the end of the year the Christian Democrats were referring to 1979 as a "year of unprecedented political violence." Even ex-president Arana Osorio was proposing a "great national alliance" to achieve orderly and peaceful change.[63]

No national alliance arose to save the day. The events of 1980 further plunged Guatemala into violence and chaos. In February a group of activists led by the CUC occupied the Spanish embassy in Guatemala City to call attention to the government's oppressive activities in the highlands. Flouting international law, Guatemalan security forces stormed the embassy, and thirty-nine people died in a fire that started in the fray. Spain immediately severed diplomatic ties, and Guatemala faced the ire of the international community.[64]

The Spanish embassy tragedy was followed by massive agricultural strikes on the Pacific coast. The workers forced the government to raise the agricultural minimum wage to 3.20 quetzales per day in March. Not long after, numbers over fifty thousand strong swelled the Workers' Day parade in Guatemala City on 1 May, as opposition organizations called for citizens to "join the struggle for a popular, democratic, and revolutionary government." Umbrella groups formed on the left and right alike. Death squads worked overtime, and dozens of mutilated corpses would be found in the days ahead. The situation was so horrific in May of 1980 that even the MLN—the ultraright party with links to the death squads—called for social reform legislation that would provide low-cost housing and other benefits to the poor.[65]

Order in Guatemala had broken down completely. Vice President Villagrán Kramer, for one, had had enough. He resigned on 1 September 1980, bitterly denouncing the government's rightist elements and lack of decent reform policies. In the same month, another Christian Democrat, future president Vinicio Cerezo, was in Washington excoriating his government's role in political assassinations. Guatemala was coming apart at the seams, and the world was hearing about it.[66]

In January 1982 the guerrillas at long last announced a unifying body to direct their efforts. The Unidad Revolucionaria Nacional Guatemalteca (URNG), however, never managed to marshal the guerrillas to victory. In 1981 the military had already begun the infamous Guatemalan genocide, unleashing a vicious scorched-earth counterinsurgency campaign that over time would bring the war's death toll to over two hundred thousand and cause thousands more to flee to refugee camps or remain internally displaced. The army wiped out twenty-seven ORPA strongholds in the summer of 1981. Despite these setbacks the guerrillas continued to fight and gained strength and numbers throughout the last year of Lucas's term.[67]

"Thank You, God, for You Have Put Me Here":
Ríos Montt—Planning Security, Planning Development

Following in Lucas García's footsteps, Guatemala's last two military rulers, Generals Efraín Ríos Montt (1982–83) and Oscar Mejía Víctores (1983–86), oversaw both Guatemala's genocide and its putative return to democracy. In the highlands, army units went from town to town, often slaughtering every single inhabitant. Some, they put in buildings and burned alive; others, they threw in pits, doused them with gasoline, and burned them. They tortured suspected subversives, often from a location right in town so the screams could be heard by all. They stabbed pregnant women in the belly with bayonets. The other women, they raped.[68]

The military beat the guerrillas. They also brought the nation a shallow model of Western democracy that, as Grandin demonstrates, is "a product of terror."[69] From the elections of 1985 onward, Guatemalans have chosen their leaders at the polls, and the military has increasingly taken a back seat to elected civilian leaders. It was a victory won at enormous cost.

The process began on 23 March 1982, when over nine hundred officers, most of them lieutenants and captains, took over military bases around the country. By noon Lucas García had stepped down. The young officers' leader, Ríos Montt, was remembered as the Christian Democrat who had won the elections of 1974 and was scurrilously robbed of office. He originally headed a three-man junta. On 9 June 1982, however, he was able to declare himself the president of the Republic and the comandante general of the army and personally assumed all executive and legislative powers. In his acceptance speech, Ríos Montt, a devout Evangelist, offered a prayer. "Thank you, God," he intoned, "for you have put me here."[70]

The Ríos Montt regime continued its predecessor's terror tactics in the highlands, most notably in the Ixcán—and was militaristic in the extreme. The junta's National Plan for Security and Development, promulgated within weeks of the *golpe*, or coup, "veered Guatemala from a military-controlled 'national-security state' to a national-security civilian government, managed by the military," writes Tom Barry. It was a plan that drew on and distilled the technocratic institutionalization and modernization schemes that had characterized the 1970s. The four-point plan called for political stability in the form of return to civilian rule and for economic stability, to be achieved by easing the country's economic recession and aiding the rural poor. Guerrilla advances were to be subverted by engendering psychosocial stability, while the enemy's ultimate defeat would spring from military stability. Civic action, rural development, and agricultural diversity schemes, longtime hallmarks of Guatemalan state policy, remained central in the national development plan.[71]

Hunger, however, remained a way of life. In mid-July the order came down that INDECA was to release all its excess stored basic grains to the army, which would distribute it to highlanders of modest means. The Instituto Nacional de Cooperativas (INACOP) was strengthened when Ríos eliminated two other agencies and transferred their functions to INACOP control. Between August and September the army began to sketch out and implement its Programa de Asistencia a las Areas en Conflicto (PAAC). This plan—the hallmark of both the Ríos regime and the Mejía presidency to follow—resurrected the CRN. As PAAC operatives began a food-for-work plan, the CRN began pressing for an increase in its one-million-dollar budget, claiming that this was barely enough to deal with the flood of displaced persons in the highlands.[72]

Despite the violence of his regime, the messianic Ríos Montt managed to cultivate a populist image that to some extent persists to the present time. In one of his Sunday sermons to the nation, he accused the private sector of causing the country's problems. He singled out south-coast finqueros for paying only half the minimum wage. "In this country there are only exploiters and the exploited," Ríos raged.[73] While his analysis was on the mark, it did little to endear him to the oligarchy. He lost its support and the military high command's within a year of his coup.

Ríos Montt fell from power on 8 August 1983 the same way he had come in, namely, as a result of a coup. Ironically, it was rumored just before the coup that Ríos Montt was contemplating land transformation, or agrarian reform.[74] Probably, although it is difficult to determine, the golpe was in the planning stages well before these agrarian whisperings shocked the nation. The land transformation that Guatemala was to experience was the one that had been in the making since 1954 and that took its contemporary form with the vast development plan of 1970. The PAAC, picking up where the genocide left off, teamed state surveillance and control with agrarian transformation in a program of naked violence.

The *Superorganismo* Defeats the Pueblo: Development Poles, Model Villages, and the Institutional Dragnet, 1983–85

Minister of National Defense Brig. Gen. Oscar Humberto Mejía Víctores did not wrest power from Ríos Montt's hands without a struggle. At least a dozen soldiers died in shootouts at the various military bases around the country, where young Ríos loyalists proved the *caudillo* still had currency in the ranks. As soon as he had officially deposed Ríos, Mejía let it be known that he opposed agrarian reform.[75]

Mejía made two promises. First, he reaffirmed the government's absolute commitment to eradicate Marxist-Leninist subversion. While this goal
was not definitively achieved during the Mejía years, it was certainly not for
lack of trying. Second, Mejía vowed to oversee a return to civilian rule.
Polls duly held at the end of 1985 elected a nonmilitary president.[76]

Before the high command could bestow civilian rule upon the nation,
the insurgency had to be quelled. Mejía's military government followed on
the same trajectory as that of Ríos before it. "Victory '82" would defeat the
guerrillas militarily, while "Firmness '83" was to bring the countryside
under military control. "Institutional Reencounter '84" would stabilize
politics and begin the process of writing a new constitution, a return to
civilian rule to be completed by "National Stability '85."[77]

PAAC remained at the heart of the plan. The army's PAAC plan was the
culmination—the logical conclusion—of political policies and economic
realities that had been evolving since 1954. At its heart were the concepts of
development poles and model villages. The development poles were target
areas for intensive civic action campaigns. Model villages, meanwhile, were
garrisoned towns constructed by the army to be the new homes of Guatemala's growing displaced population. Counterinsurgency campaigns often
involved razing and burning villages and summarily slaughtering all their
inhabitants. Not surprisingly, entire townships had fled into the mountains, where some remained throughout the 1990s. The model villages
would serve both as quasi prisons and emergency housing for those who
chose or were forced to return. The Patrullas de Autodefensa Civil (PAC)
program of civilian patrols, meanwhile, first started late in Lucas García's
term, would cement the system. Civilian patrols brought virtually all males
of an age to fight under direct daily army supervision and turned them
against the insurgents at the same time. The PACs were not done away with
until the Peace Accords of 1996.[78]

The legislation detailing the administrative structure of the highland
efforts shows considerable continuity in intent and action overlaid by
bureaucratic fits and starts. In October 1983 the government established a
National Development Commission in El Quiché department, one of the
nation's most war-torn areas. The commander of the Quiché military zone
was to preside, while the Playa Grande zone commander would serve as
second in command. Scores of state agencies were to participate, clear evidence of how forces that had been evolving throughout the post-1954
period came together in a final, ultimate paroxysm of civic-military-

government action.[79] In the same month legislation established a variety of Interinstitutional Coordinating Councils to micromanage the highland projects at the departmental, municipal, and local levels.[80]

The laws of 1983 began to codify what was already a plan in action; in 1984 the government wiped the bureaucratic slate clean and institutionalized their efforts in lasting administrative structures. Legislation in spring and early summer included directives to build model villages, which would house over thirteen thousand individuals, and put forth a "maximum priority action plan" that established Polos de Desarrollo (Development Poles) around the country. It was not until November, however, that the government established the bureaucracy that would coordinate the final militarization of the highlands.[81]

At the nucleus of the new National System of Interinstitutional Coordination (IIC) was the CRN. The legislation of November 1984 created four layers of management structures, each called Coordinadoras Interinstitucionales: the CIN (national), the CID (departmental), the CIM (municipal), and the CDL (Local Development Coordinator). The Defense Department chief of staff directed the effort at the national level. In the field, army civic action and intelligence officers assisted zone commanders. The plan marshaled the expertise of Guatemala's various post-1954 state institutions into a military master plan and focused that expertise on the populace in beams so concentrated that they were effective at the level of individual citizens. The army began to win the war.[82]

The PGT (the Communist Party, marginalized by the 1980s) reported that the IIC system worked to "decide all aspects of community life, acting as a body" that combined military personnel with low-level state officials such as "doctors and paramedics, teachers, agricultural extension workers, cooperative consultants" and the like, all selected by the military. "The rest of the people at work in the community, who might be the pastor of some fundamentalist Evangelical sect, the North American 'volunteer' from some institution apparently dedicated to aid and development, etc., are, without being public employees per se, also people in the army's confidence."[83]

In the final analysis, violence was probably more effective as a counterinsurgency technique than interinstitutional coordination. As is true of every initiative in Guatemala, the IIC program has to be taken with a grain of salt. Nowhere did the PAAC function on the ground exactly as it was designed on paper. Further studies of particular communities and development poles will undoubtedly reveal that local conditions—the agricultural regime, the personalities and decisions of leaders of various social and political groups, the presence or absence of various NGOs and other transnational entities, the lived experience of the campesinos, and so forth— were far more important determining factors than plans from on high. Diane Nelson, for example, conducted a study of the Chisec and Cobán development poles in Alta Verapaz in the late 1980s and found that the interinstitutional coordinators were fairly unimportant.[84]

As it penetrated the towns and villages of the highlands, the army also promoted export-oriented agriculture based on nontraditional crops. Mayan citizens, for whom agriculture in basic grains was at the heart of their culture and the key to their survival, were herded into food-for-work programs. Loosely modeled on the kibbutz—Israel was by this time Guatemala's biggest military supporter—these farm programs produced such fare as Chinese cabbage, cardamom, and broccoli. "Without tampering with the existing pattern of landownership," one report commented, "the army intends to turn the Indian highlands into a vast factory farm."[85]

"National Stability '85," then, was anything but. The Green Revolution and the genocide had torn the countryside to pieces; despite continuing guerrilla actions and popular unrest, the army had decisively won the war.[86] That is how Guatemala returned to having civilian heads of state. In a popular runoff election on 8 December 1985, the Christian Democrat Vinicio Cerezo won the presidency. Behind him, the military was to remain an ever-present *éminence grise*. None of the army's mechanisms of social control were dismantled, and Cerezo was well aware he could be deposed at any moment. Nevertheless, Guatemala had returned to civilian rule. Thirty-one years of counterrevolution, war, and development had come to fruition.

Epilogue: The Clandestine Slaughterhouse and Neoliberalism

As Guatemala modernized and institutionalized in the 1970s and 1980s, small businessmen like Carlos Melgar and the city butchers wanted to participate in the process. They couldn't, however, for fear of being killed. Awaiting them at the end of the period was a complex, overlapping network of national, international, and local institutions that sought to help incorporate them into a commercial universe from whose creation they had been violently excluded. That network, like the evolving and increasingly neoliberal commercial world it represented, had taken form broadly during the Cold War and particularly during the violent years of Guatemala's transformation through terror, 1970–85.

Among Melgar's collection of paperwork is a book called *Elaboración de productos cárnicos*. A food science manual from 1982, its genealogy portended things to come: it was produced by a project of International Technical Cooperation between Mexico's Dirección General de Educación Tecnológica Agropecuaria and Secretaría de Educación Pública, the UN's Food and Agriculture Organization and Program for Development, and the governments of Switzerland and the Netherlands. For a young man dreaming of achieving success in the meat business, trapped in the filthy markets of Guatemala City, denied clean products by wholesalers, and living in fear of his government, the vision the book spelled out must have seemed an otherworldly dream.[87]

In 1985 the *carne* (meat) organizers began chasing that dream, finally filing legal papers and beginning to interface with the government. By 1992 they had become the Asociación de Expendedores de Carne (ASEC). Melgar was president. Just prior, the butchers had joined a Programa de Mejoramiento de la Carne (PROMECA, Program for Meat Improvement) sponsored by the government and a German organization called GTZ. Numerous public and private institutions were involved with PROMECA, including various ministries, the Instituto Nacional de Capacitación y Productividad (INTECAP, National Institute for Training and Productivity), and trade associations of meat producers, wholesalers, and retailers. Over the remainder of the 1990s, ASEC would receive hundreds of thousands of quetzales from GTZ, destined to improve the physical plant in the *expendedores* and to make equipment available at better wholesale prices.[88]

Conflicts and obstacles arose from the beginning. The wholesalers and government technocrats were most interested in teaching consumers to buy clean meat. This threatened to destroy ASEC's members unless market vendors were educated first. Melgar found himself debating marketing tactics with, among others, Víctor Arturo Monasterio Palacios of Vam Marketing, whose clients included the Guatemalan divisions of Bayer, Procter and Gamble, Texaco, Colgate Palmolive, and seventy-one other corporations, national and transnational alike. As Melgar was embroiled in this debate he was approached by the Liga del Consumidor (LIDECON, Consumer Defense League). They offered to serve as quality control assessor for ASEC butchers. Melgar smelled trouble and promptly declined.[89]

Melgar had become a hinge-man, linking the butchers' humble world with the state, private enterprise, and international institutions. He won some victories. With PROMECA funding, ASEC conducted a modern public relations campaign and gave butchers aprons, boots, and hardhats. They launched a newsletter and held workshops covering quality control, sanitation, finance, elementary marketing, and taxation.[90] By 1994, however, Melgar was on the verge of quitting ASEC. "We have had a bad past, but maybe we can improve the present," he wrote in an open letter to the organization that he entitled "Nostalgia."[91] Internal conflicts in ASEC were one challenge, but an even greater one was trying to make the grass-roots organization fit, in PROMECA, with the bigger capital interests. PROMECA had recently accused ASEC of being apathetic and disinterested in public education. The butchers countered that PROMECA treated them with disrespect and had never acknowledged their importance from the very beginning of the relationship.[92]

PROMECA, though, was only one way in which ASEC and the wider world participated in joint projects in the 1990s.[93] In a particularly bold move, with advice from the Ministry of the Economy and a loan from the National Development Program for Small and Medium-Sized Businesses, ASEC started a Programa de Auto-Abastecimiento (Self-Supply Program) in 1998. Prices were spiking because of wholesalers' speculation. The plan was to buy live cattle directly from the finca, slaughter them, and distribute the meat to participating members. Such a program would cut out middlemen and pressure wholesalers to cut prices in response.

About two years later the government shut the program down and wrote a report on its failures. ASEC used buyers with "neither knowledge nor experience in the purchase of cattle on the hoof," and they returned with meat the vendors didn't want but were obligated to purchase. Many didn't pay. Mistrust of ASEC spread, compounding doubts about its ability to bring in a steady supply of meat. As a result, ASEC became desperate to sell and signed up known deadbeats who had already "sent various wholesalers into bankruptcy." Meanwhile, its officers had no idea how to administer a program of this magnitude, much less keep its books. Assessors tried offering them courses in a sort of improvised night school. However, "the low level of scholarship of the people involved, along with irresponsible attitudes" rendered the measure ineffective. The self-supply project failed. Nevertheless, the assessors opined, it had indeed forced the giant meat wholesalers to lower their prices. "ASEC has continued making financial sacrifices," they wrote, "to maintain stable prices . . . for the consumer.

[The] socioeconomic benefits generated in one year of operations were far superior to the investment made." Unfortunately, the program was simply not sustainable.[94]

Melgar was frustrated, and his frustration came as much from within the butchers' ranks as from without. Just like social planners and engineers, he learned that changing people's habits is no easy task. Most meat vendors simply refused to attend training seminars. Those who had been trained often went right back to their old ways, neglecting to clean and saving money by eschewing refrigeration, disinfectants, and aprons. "They would only clean things up when the authorities were around," he says. If they got caught handling meat improperly, they would cry, "But how am I supposed to do it? You have to give me some training!" Melgar makes multiple gestures of frustration. "Then," he explains, "they would get together with the politicians to defend their rights. They defend things that make no sense."

By the new millennium, Melgar says, ASEC was impotent. None of the globally funded schemes were working. He slowly withdrew from the organization and today has nothing more to do with it. "Go to CETEC," he says, referring to the Centro de Tecnología de la Carne erected as part of PROMECA and run by the meat wholesalers' trade organization. "They have classes, but attendance is low. All you'll see is people playing poker." He pauses. "There comes a moment," he adds, "when there just isn't much stimulus to be a leader any more."[95]

As Melgar learned, organizing and training small producers to compete and survive in a world of big producers is an extremely difficult task, especially in conditions like those found in Guatemala. Scores of groups and institutions, of which ASEC is only one example, continue to try to help people figure out how to keep up, how to compete, how to exist within the system of relations of production as it has been developed over the twentieth century and into the twenty-first. This is a laudable goal, but the problem for these institutions is that the logic of big producers tends to exclude the participation of small producers, even when the small producers have the necessary education, training, and commercial expertise to be competitive.

Many of the institutions that seek to train, incorporate, or tame the lower sectors were born from Cold War initiatives. INTECAP, the training institute that works with groups like ASEC and many NGOs, for example, was a technocratic invention of 1972.[96] *Solidarismo*, in which workers and bosses form a happy family, came to Guatemala in 1982 with the foundation of the Unión Solidarista Guatemalteca. By 2002 over 20,000 workers in more than 4,560 Guatemalan businesses were affiliated with this fastest growing union in the nation, which had first been organized in Costa Rica in 1950. Affiliated workers enjoyed access to loans, *tiendas* with low-priced goods, credits for buying appliances, medical services, and sporting clubs.[97]

Guatemala's contemporary culture of development is characterized by the marginalization of the unions and the socialist left, teamed with the curtailing of state protectionism and social services. Within this landscape, new movements seek to empower the disenfranchised. The 1990s saw the florescence of the Central American *microempresa* (small business) movement, a reflection of more sophisticated and humane thinking in postmodern development. The Coordinadora Nacional de Microempresas de Guatemala (CONMIGUAT) had its first conference in 1997. CONMIGUAT's goal, like that of its pan-isthmian parent organization, was to "promote the commercial development of the sector, widen channels of commercialization, open new markets and confront the challenges of globalization of national, regional and international markets." Members included street vendors who sell seasonally, at Christmastime; weavers from Tecpán and other small regional associations of crafts artisans; the Asociación Nacional de Artesanos de Guatemala; and the Coordinadora de Desarrollo Integral de Mujeres Indígenas (Coordinators for Integrated Development of Indigenous Women).[98]

The microempresa movement stands up for the rights and dignity of Central America's largest sector of workers, many of whom are in the informal sector. It pushes for loans, technical training, pensions, social security, and vacation benefits from the various states and, most important, for the simple recognition of the small and family-run business as the backbone of the economy and the cornerstone of real economic growth. It seeks to educate its members about globalization and teach them how to make their voices heard. Ambitious and admirable, yet ambiguous, it advocates for a sector whose members the dominant economic system tends to relegate to unskilled jobs, not to the world of self-employment.[99]

The trajectory of ASEC through the worlds of *capacitación*, foreign aid, and institutional support, including from the microempresa sector, shows both the possibilities and the shortcomings of postmodern development schemes. According to the Comité Coordinador de Empresarios de la Microempresa de la Región Central de América (COCEMI, the Coordinating Committee of Small Business Owners of the Central American Region), CONMIGUAT's parent organization, "To begin to compete on a level playing field with other types of businesses, only one road is open to the microempresa: **to organize**."[100] It is a powerful verb they put in boldface type. By "organize," COCEMI's leaders did not mean to form a union or even necessarily to raise consciousness about greater economic processes that confront poor workers. What they meant was for the lower sectors to advocate within a system that by its very logic tends to eliminate them as independent proprietors.

ASEC organizes but does not Organize. Its proponents are not going out and engaging in consciousness raising among butchers. Death squads, massacres, and fifty years of abhorrent government have left their mark. Not only are the one-time idealistic youth who faced down the pájaro azul full of torturers loathe to consider themselves organizers, their compatriots are loathe to be organized, especially by an entity that smacks of school and state. Still, the meat vendors paradoxically reflect both Guatemala's union culture and capital's finest values; they'll strike at a moment's notice, but why, they think, should they stop grinding their rotten leftovers into the hamburger when they can make an extra quetzal or two that way? In the one-for-one and all-for-nobody atmosphere of contemporary commerce, conditioned by terror, leaders of ASEC face a grim choice, one that sums up what is happening through much of Guatemalan society. They can either start to raise consciousness—which means questioning the neoliberal system, a Sisyphean, hopeless, and indeed dangerous task—or they can push for laws and inspections that will get their less "capacitated" compañeros fined and arrested, and then what have they become? Like other organizers-not-organizers—people throughout the postmodern capitalist world who work on forming associations without challenging the dominant system of power—ASEC leaders find themselves, like the bucolic Mayan farmers of Guatemala's highlands, in an impossible position: in a space constructed by neoliberalism that promotes and negates them at the same time. Call it the clandestine slaughterhouse.

No sector of Guatemala's population is more promoted and negated by neoliberalism than its vendors. The nation's development coalesces, paradoxically, in its markets, where Carlos Melgar has spent his life. During the transformation through terror of the 1970s and 1980s, Guatemala's private sector and military governments made the nation more transparent to transnational, neoliberal capital. Just like each previous phase of development, though, this one reproduced within its ambit all the baggage of the past, so what emerged from the killing fields was an "opaque transparency" typical of so-called underdeveloped nations in general and a hallmark of neoliberalism as it has been constructed over the course of the century. A defining characteristic of globalization is how it strengthens the local, the pockets it cannot seem to penetrate, the falsely named premodern: the penniless, the peons, and the petty proprietors. Guatemala's markets, as opaque as they are to global capital, are an inherent element of the nation's new, transparent landscape. They are also a monument to development as it has played out in the nation since the dawn of the automobile age.

The markets are an odd but perfect symbol for late capitalism, hearkening as they do back to a precapitalist past. Their aisles are jammed with stray dogs and barefoot children who ought to be in school. Food is not in packages but in piles. Municipal markets occupy a vibrant liminal zone between past and present and good and bad. They look like a quaint and antiquated indigenous tradition but in fact are at the cutting edge of Guatemalan retail, serving as the nation's main supplier of food and consumer goods. They reference poverty, to be sure, but at the grass roots they also represent a chance for independent proprietorship and a good employment alternative to their fellow symbols of third-world modernity, the sweatshop (*maquiladora*) and the global service sector. Selling in the markets may not be a great life, but it's better than being drugged and sexually abused in a factory or laboring away for nothing stocking shelves in an international chain store.

Guatemalan markets are essentially homemade, and they look like it. In Guatemala City, as in the countryside, they preserve an open-air feel despite the roofs that cover them. The *puestos*, or selling spots, are usually either plywood stalls, rough wooden tables, or simply woven reed mats laid on the ground. These spaces, human, humble, and built from the bottom up, outsell the supermarkets. As of 2010 most Guatemalans, even those in the big city, shop in the municipal and street markets. The force of consumers' demand generates employment opportunity in supply, making Guatemala in many ways a society of vendors.

Markets perform as important a social and cultural function as they do an economic one. They are the main site of interaction for distinct and geographically disperse ethnic groups—a forum in which people coexist in ways sometimes ugly and sometimes peaceful.[1] Guatemala's markets are nexuses of social, cultural, and economic change. They are venues in which much of the culture of development is enacted, articulated, negotiated, and transformed. Contestation simmers at an everyday level, occasionally boiling over into open social conflict. Contestation also has its organizational side, with unions, informal alliances, and political manipulations. Melgar has been a protagonist in this story for four decades.

The butchers' organization, ASEC, was only the first of three market-born organizations that Melgar helped to found. The other two were the Asociación de Inquilinos de Mercados Municipales (ASIMEM, Municipal Market Vendors' Association) and the Comité del Mercado Cervantes (Comecer), both created in 1993. The point of ASIMEM was to protect the interests of fee-paying, licensed vendors against those of the informal sellers who filled the streets outside the markets and undersold them. For ASIMEM to work, each municipal market had to have an elected body of representatives and leaders who could represent its *inquilinos* (market tenants) to the whole. In his market, Melgar created Comecer to fill this need. By the mid-1990s he was president of both of these organizations and of ASEC as well.

Following on the heels of Melgar's disillusionment with ASEC, ASIMEM fell apart in 2001. In both of these organizations, his goal was to rationalize and modernize the world of retail. In his analysis, recalcitrant vendors and corrupt politicians have made the task impossible. The vendors are attached to their unhygienic ways and unwilling to spend any money for their own improvement, and the crooked politicians, multiplying like flies, act only in their self-interest. Indeed, these are very real problems in Guatemalan society. Teamed with an inefficient, absurd bureaucratic culture, the elites' unwillingness to institute a reasonable system of taxation, and the "space-is-money" attitude born in a world of endless cheap labor, they make a toxic mix.

While Melgar's bitterness is understandable, it obscures very real accomplishments. ASEC managed to keep wholesale meat prices somewhat under control and also made inroads, however slight, in making meat retail less smelly and more hygienic. ASIMEM, by 2005 a fragment of its former self, won many victories between 1993 and 2001, when it split apart in a battle between Melgar, who wanted to defend formal vendors against their informal counterparts, and Mario Alvizúrez, who brought street vendors into the fold. In ASIMEM's heyday, its officers worked with the Ministry of Education and the Programa Educativo para el Niño–Niña y Adolescente Trabajador (PENNAT), the market education organization, to improve the number and quality of schools in the markets. They reached out to medical laboratories to bring in medicines and cosponsored vaccination campaigns, including one against hepatitis B. Operating out of their own educational facility in Mercado Sur 2, they gave classes to hundreds, if not thousands, of vendors, Maya and Ladino alike, on subjects ranging from public health and hygiene to better business management. Finally, they gave inquilinos their first concerted political voice. They wrote position papers on the most pressing issues of the day and kept their finger on the pulse of the community, representing it before a wide body of national and international institutions. On a more quotidian level, they fought for police protection, battled corruption, clamored for garbage collection, and handled countless other workaday yet crucial issues. Time and again the volunteers who ran ASIMEM pressed cases through a tangled and infuriating bureaucracy, and most of the time they won.[2] Given the sociocultural realities of the markets themselves, their victories were as surprising as they were savored at the grass roots.

"Where Women Rule":
A Meeting with Mercado Cervantes's Core Community

Beatriz Cux López's life in Mercado Cervantes began when she was three months old. Her mother had a puesto by the front door. During the 1960s and 1970s Beatriz would come to the market after school and on weekends. She finished high school, qualifying as an accountant, and then studied five semesters at university. But there was no work for accountants, so she settled into the market, which effectively has been her second home since 1962. Today, she has a large puesto that overflows with fruit. It's a good life, I think, as I contemplate the iridescent wares. It's not poverty, but proprietorship. The market is pleasant, the environment is human, and the work, while doubtless hard and never will a millionaire make, is free from a boss's surveillance and unstructured by soulless technologies of ergonomics and productivity.

Favorably located in the corner near the meat stalls, Beatriz is within calling distance of Melgar. Her sister Zoila is not far away; she has sold fruit on their mother's old spot for the past dozen years or so. Catty-corner is Blanca Alicia González Farfán in the pork stall; the other women call her Helenita. She handles the meat with an intensity I will soon experience one on one. After the interviews, Blanca will bring us steaming cutlets in an orange-colored sauce, the biggest one for me. Julia in the juice stall gets one too, as does Siriaca Subuyuj, a Mayan vegetable vendor from San Juan Sacatepéquez who has a twenty-six-year history in Cervantes. I struggle to spell her name correctly—an awkward moment since it becomes clear she doesn't read or write. Beatriz kibitzes and tells me to put a *j* at the end. "What a beautiful name," I comment. Beatriz laughs. "She doesn't like it," she says. "¡Se pone 'Julia!'"[3]

Siriaca is in *traje* but contrary to the stereotype of total racial division, she is friends with the Ladina women with whom she works. Like that of many established market vendors, Siriaca's family is moving up in class: her son is well on his way to getting an architecture degree at the University of San Carlos (USAC). "It pains me," she says. Architecture means spending a lot of time in school, time that produces no income. "I wanted him to be a mechanic." In solidarity with her son, I share a bit about the economic illogic of studying history. She looks at me as if I were mad.[4]

As always seems to happen when I speak with Guatemalans, the conversation shifts to the United States. Like many Guatemalans, Siriaca has family in Los Angeles and in Chicago, where, she's heard, the cold is epic. She has no intention of going north. "This is my place," she states with finality. A widow, Siriaca has no desire to discuss *la violencia*. Every time our talk turns that way, she suddenly spots a customer and hurries off.

These women are leaders in the Mercado Cervantes. As market elders and members of Comecer and once of ASIMEM, they have participated in a grass-roots struggle to wrest support from City Hall. Though they would not put it this way, they have also worked to bring modern technologies and benefits into their ambit selectively. In effect, they have fought to control and fight back globalization and corporatization, letting in the good and keeping out the bad. For a time, Zoila was ASIMEM's treasurer and Comecer's secretary, and the written history of these organizations is largely in her handwriting, in spiral notebooks that Melgar keeps in boxes in his zone 3 home. Zoila is not a big talker, but she writes perceptively, pausing in the meetings to add some thick description to the minutes, capturing the emotions and tensions in the room.

Of Comecer's thirteen members, twelve are women. And then there is Carlos Melgar. "Where women rule," Blanca informs me, "men don't want to get in the way."[5] Punctuating her words with slashes at the pork, the knife-wielding Blanca is far more willing than Melgar to discuss this subject. I tried to tease a gender analysis from him in several interviews. My notes read, "Gender: won't go there."

"Cuidado con nosotros [watch out for us]," Blanca says. "Luchamos mucho [we fight a lot]. We're activists. We like it when they get it, *fast*. That way you get something done." Zoila speaks with a ferocity that makes it easy to draw her as a comic figure ("She exaggerates a little," Carlos whispers to me later), yet she is anything but. A pillar of her community and a Cervantes vendor for a quarter century ("veinticuatro años de servirle al pueblo [twenty-four years serving the people]," she says), Blanca brings cohesive energy and clarity to the market's social core. A migrant to the city, she was born in Jutiapa and raised in Escuintla. She got married in 1978 and came to the capital with her husband. He worked wage labor, and she started the pork business, drawing on hometown connections to do so.[6]

Blanca personally led the fight to get the *municipalidad*, or *muni* for short, to put a parking lot out front, an important project that had gotten hung up in endless red tape. "We were an all-woman group," she recalls, relating the story of going down to City Hall to sort out the mess. "They left us sitting all day, and by 3:00, we were *bored*." Finally, an official gave them a five-minute hearing and a lukewarm promise to look into the situation. "We put our arms out like this"—she flings them wide and grabs the cordage draped along the puesto's upper rim—"so that no one, no one, could get through the doors of the muni. ¡Escúchenos! [We will be heard!]" She laughs, imitating the municipal official frantically rifling the file cabinet for the Mercado Cervantes papers. "It took them five minutes! That was that."

Blanca is speaking not just to me but also for a gathering crowd that the gringo's visit has drawn. I hear murmurs of agreement. It is a good memory, this everyday yet hard-won victory. Through it all, Melgar is watching out of the corner of his eye from his beef stall. He nods at me; the meeting is going well. After all, he was the one who brought me here. "So Carlos is the only man. How is he as Comecer's president?" I ask Blanca, who has witnessed our silent exchange. At this point Beatriz jumps in. Is she afraid that Helenita is going to question, quite publicly, exactly who is leading whom? "He's a good leader," Beatriz affirms. "He never was a *mafioso*."

"To Fight for Integrated Development":
Grass-roots Institutional Space Creation

Not being a mafioso is at the core of how Melgar speaks about ASIMEM. Mafiosos include not only true criminals—and there had been corrupt financial dealings at the heart of the organization until he became its president[7]—but also anyone who would politicize what he sees as an apolitical entity devoted solely to protecting its members' commercial interests. It was an ambitious project.

At the time of its birth in 1993, ASIMEM was also known by the informal name of Nuevo Amanecer, or New Dawn. Its president and vice president were Josué Enríquez Dardón and Jesús Saloj Pantoj, respectively. Of the eighty founding members, thirty-one were women and twenty-two had at least one Mayan last name, not always an indication of cultural identification, as in the case of the Cux López sisters. Their listed professions ranged from student to farmer and weaver, and their identification cards showed they came from Totonicapán, Sololá, various villages in El Quiché, and San Juan Sacatepéquez. In short, it was a diverse and representative group of Guatemala City market vendors.[8]

The members of ASIMEM specifically referenced the developmental discourses of integrated community development and rural education as they had come down over the decades, giving a good indication that such language had made an impact among the populace. First among the stated goals: "To fight for the integrated development of the Community, based in . . . projects of professional training and communal development." The founding statute also promised that the group would collect statistics, conduct studies, foster urban–rural ties, work for the benefit of children in poor areas, hold courses and seminars, and the like.[9] The vendors, in forming their association, articulated development in very traditional terms, terms that had been crafted by the capitalist culture industry over the course of a century.

Regurgitated legal and developmental language and the laudable goals behind it aside, the real motivation for ASIMEM's foundation, Melgar says, was fear—fear of privatization. Vendors pay a rent far below market value for their puestos, a fact of which both they and municipal governments are keenly aware.[10] In 1993 privatization rumors were flying, and vendor demonstrations were frequent.[11] Confronting this threat was ASIMEM's principal mission.

Interestingly, fear of privatization resulted in institution making that in many ways reproduced the logic of the very system that would seek to privatize markets. The florescence of private interest groups, in this case, vendor associations, either unaffiliated or only nominally affiliated with a larger struggle for social justice is another apt example of Lefebvre's point about how the logic and social relations of private enterprise are reproduced in social space. Embedded in a wave of grass-roots institution building was an inherent contradiction, one summed up by an oxymoron: trade association versus private capital. It was a contradiction that would soon tear the group apart, but in 1993, when ASIMEM's founders articulated their hopes and high ideals, no one saw the problem coming.

The founding of ASIMEM, along with municipal politics in the 1990s, sparked institution making in municipal markets. Comecer, for example, formalized what had always been a loose conglomeration of market leaders, the "gente adulta," the grownups, as Blanca González put it.[12] The same thing happened in many markets, since the existence of a *junta directiva* (governing board) was a prerequisite for membership in ASIMEM. Indeed, ASIMEM's minutes from the last third of the 1990s and the first third of the 2000s show that all around Guatemala City groups like Comecer were in the making, with municipal encouragement and support. It wasn't always clear to market vendors exactly why they needed to elect a governing board and pay dues to be affiliated with ASIMEM. In a general meeting at Cervantes, leaders "talked to [the vendors] about the importance of being affiliated, because who knows what surprises new *gobernantes* will have in store for us."[13] The juntas directivas gave vendors a regularized means to plug in to ASIMEM and a way of dealing directly with the much-hated gobernantes.

The founding of ASIMEM and Comecer reflected a general trend toward formalization as economic actors at the lower end of the power spectrum confronted the so-called new world order of globalization and neoliberalism. For them, this corporate regime was represented at the local level by the municipal government. Too, Comecer's and ASIMEM's emergence evidenced the fragmentation of social sectors into interest groups in the age of the NGO, when promoters of a popular front for social justice, though still active, found themselves effectively defeated by international capital.

Both ASIMEM and Comecer preserved much of the informality of their social base, especially for the first three or four years of their existence. In its early years ASIMEM was plagued with bad record keeping and bookkeeping and chronic absenteeism, even up to the level of its various presidents, who had a tendency not to show up for meetings. In mid-1999, after stints as both vice president and provisional president, Melgar was elected to be ASIMEM's leader.[14] He held the post for just under two years, when Comecer, like many other markets to follow, dropped out of ASIMEM, and Alvizúrez assumed its presidency.[15] The Melgar–Alvizúrez split and the ensuing fragmentation of ASIMEM arose both from tensions inherent in Guatemala's market situation as it had evolved over decades and from the inherent contradiction at its heart. For Melgar, the rise and fall of ASIMEM is the story of mafiosos beating *comerciantes*, of politicians focused not on helping small businesspeople but on manipulating votes. While he has an extremely valid point, the real situation was somewhat more complex.

"They Need to Earn Their Centavos":
Vendor versus Vendor in the Making of Markets

Guatemala City's markets not only keep the population alive, but also reflect all the troubles in the capital's urban development over the course of decades. According to city officials, in 2003 there were twenty-three markets under municipal auspices, in which eighteen thousand inquilinos had legal recognition. Somewhere between 60 and 70 percent of the inquilinos registered with identification cards showing an origin outside the city, from all over the country but most notably from Sacatepéquez, Totonicapán, and Quetzaltenango. Municipal markets ranged in size from La Terminal, the largest, with four thousand inquilinos, to Justo Rufino Barrios in zone 21, the smallest, with ninety. The government's new and still greatly rejected wholesale market, the Centro de Mayoreo (CENMA), located outside the city center in Villa Lobos, had fifteen hundred inquilinos. Additionally—and here the muni was no doubt underestimating—another four to five thousand unlicensed vendors worked in some twenty *mercados satélites* in the street.[16]

Guatemala City's network of markets had expanded rapidly over the past four decades. In the years after 1970, the already significant flow of migrants from the countryside into the markets increased substantially. Reasons for the influx included the earthquake of 1976, violence in the countryside, and trends in agrarian development that made life untenable for large percentages of the rural population. Added to all these hardships was the economic pull of the city's severe shortage of municipal markets, which, of course, was a related phenomenon; all those new migrants had to buy food somewhere.[17] The so-called informal economy would step up to solve these problems, however imperfectly, in ways that restructured urban–rural ties and that profoundly influenced the everyday lived experience of all city residents, inside the markets and out. Beatriz Cux Lópex remembers an explosion of vendors in the Mercado Cervantes between 1982 and 1985. It was an ethnically coded explosion; she gestures at a passing woman in traje—the woman is Siriaca "Julia" Subuyuj, as I will learn later—as she makes the point. "There's more chaos [*bulla*] now," Beatriz tells me, "but it's nice, the way we live together [*es buena la convivencia*]."[18]

The municipality, meanwhile, overwhelmed by the earthquake, continued to float high-modernist plans in the face of problems that officials could barely quantify or keep abreast of, much less solve. The quake severely damaged the Mercado Central, for example, ground zero for rural–urban commerce for well over a century. It was going to have to be replaced, and the muni already had plans in hand for doing so. Just before the quake, Mayor Leonel Ponciano León had announced a scheme to raze the building and erect a modernist central market with a twenty-two-story hotel attached, much like Grand Tikal Futura and its Grand Hyatt of a later day. The new complex would make an aesthetic change in the city's universe of humble markets, and it would be a monument to the metropolis's bicentennial as well. The state of emergency after the earthquake damp-ened such ambitions. Though prompt demolition was slated and alterna-tive sites were set up for displaced vendors, the new Mercado Central didn't open until 1983. It was a grim, cement block gallery reminiscent of La Terminal. Vendors criticized it for being cramped and humid and reflecting an "anthill mentality."[19]

Problems stemming from the earthquake and the highland massacres exacerbated already severe tensions between market inquilinos and un-licensed street vendors. Over the last quarter of the twentieth century, informal or satellite markets sprang up not only in the twenty locations that city officials could pinpoint on a map, but also in the blocks around virtually every municipal market, including Cervantes. Itinerant vendors, or *vendedores ambulantes*, spread throughout the urban fabric. As we saw in chapter 4, the construction of La Terminal and the growth of bus transpor-tation had, by the early 1960s, marked a sea change in Guatemala City's culture and landscape of informal vending. From its inception, the capital had relied for its sustenance in part upon *vendedores pendulares*—pendu-lum vendors, a perfect term—who went back and forth between the coun-tryside and the city. Scholars write of this system of supply in terms of agricultural and ethnic geography, connecting the city with its evolving rural hinterland. Public history, though, tends to remember it in bucolic prose, focusing on the colors and quaintness of the mule trains pouring in on market days through the city's four *guardas* that gave access to the mountains beyond.[20]

Lines of Blue Bird busses spewing diesel fumes and disgorging hordes of impoverished rural proletarians and their wares onto crowded and dan-gerous city sidewalks failed to provide the same charm. As early as 1963 inquilinos in the Mercado Central were protesting against street vendors, who stole all their business and paid no taxes or fees. In return, the street vendors invaded the Central Market, where they stayed until police hauled them out.[21] A few years later, vendors all over the city threatened a strike if the muni didn't do something, prompting City Hall to turn to the national police for aid in conducting sweeps and raids against informal vendors. Success was partial, to say the least. According to *Prensa Libre*, three police officers refused to help municipal inspectors who were trying to dislodge a group in zone 3, telling the inspectors that the street vendors "need to earn their *centavos* and you have your salary assured." Emboldened, the vendors drew machetes and drove the inspectors away.[22]

Skateboards for sale. In this undated photo, the street vendor's wares bespeak both imported tastes and the spread of so-called informal market activity through Christmastime vending in the 1970s. Anonymous, "Venta callejera de patinetas (Skateboards for Sale on Street)," Guatemala City. Archivo de fotografías de El Gráfico. Fototeca Guatemala, CIRMA (Reference Code: GT-FG-CIRMA-086-positivos asentamientos).

In general, the 1960s marked the emergence of much of central Guatemala City's contemporary geography of street sales. The decades ahead saw its maturation. By the mid-1960s, zone 1 had become a true lowbrow commercial district. The enormous street market that spread up 18 Calle and crossed Sexta Avenida had taken form, and rich residents began to flee to the city's southern reaches.[23] During the 1970s the battle between vendors inside and vendors outside continued, as street sellers multiplied. Despite numerous municipal plans and sweeps conducted in response to inquilino pressure, spontaneous markets, satellite markets, and groups of vendedores ambulantes continued occupying space in every city zone, especially in the vicinity of markets and butcher shops, where shoppers were to be found.[24]

Street markets were seasonal. Much of the bulla today on Sexta Avenida dates to the coming of the Christmas vendors in the early 1970s. In reporting on the phenomenon, *El Imparcial* hailed, with trepidation, a "new commercial modality"—the arrival of commercial culture among the Gua-

A day in the life of La Sexta, or Sixth Avenue. The avenue was the city's most posh boulevard in the 1920s. By 1970, as can be seen in this photograph, it had become a packed lowbrow commercial district but was not yet lined with street vendors' stalls. Around 2010 La Sexta was being restored and the vendors were being removed. Anonymous, "Sexta Avenida de la zona 1 (Sixth Avenue in Zone 1)," Guatemala City, c. 1970. Archivo de fotografías del Comité Holandés de Solidaridad con el Pueblo de Guatemala. Fototeca Guatemala, CIRMA (Reference Code: GT-FG-CIRMA-117-010-093).

temalan poor. Yuletide peddlers filled the sidewalks and streets, offering clothes, plastic goods, and Ladino and Mayan *artesanía*. They blocked traffic and caused chaos, the reporter noted, but the Christmas vendors— like their cohorts who would establish year-round informal markets—were there to stay.[25] Two decades later, in 1992, the muni tried banning the Christmas sellers of Sexta Avenida. In response they affiliated as a union with the Central de Trabajadores del Campo y la Ciudad. Within five years they had a membership of seven hundred and belonged to CONMIGUAT, a group that represented small businesses.[26]

A Clash of Ideologies: Cervantes and ASIMEM Part Ways

Informal vendors and the threat they represented were constant topics of conversation in Comecer and ASIMEM alike. In 2000, for example, representatives of Cervantes told ASIMEM they had heard rumors that the street vendors of 19 Calle were planning to invade the territory around the market.

Mercado Bethania joined ASIMEM specifically because of problems with the informal sector. Street sellers were coming into the market and getting violent. Apparently, the deejay of the market radio station was giving inflammatory speeches on the air to whip up their rage. ASIMEM did the best it could, sending representatives to complain to municipal officials.[27]

At around the same time, ASIMEM officials were working on a white paper covering the so-called complementary economy. They argued that all ambulatory vendors should be licensed and registered with the tax agency and that they should pay a fee of ten quetzales a month. Additionally, ASIMEM said, all vendors should be able to prove ownership of the goods they were selling or pay a steep fine.[28] Although the municipality had been slowly tagging established street vendors for decades in an attempt to make them official and would keep doing so, it had no way of enforcing the widespread measures ASIMEM proposed. Even if it had, no mayor would have wanted to face the wrath of thousands of vendors who were not reluctant to demonstrate and riot. When the muni did pass its complementary economy law, ASIMEM protested, calling it toothless and saying that their representatives were never even allowed to speak at the planning meetings.[29]

Melgar had participated in founding ASIMEM specifically because it was going to represent vendors inside the markets.[30] But during his time as president a conflict was brewing within the association. Alvizúrez, at that time affiliated with the Frente Republicano Gualtemalteco (FRG), the right-wing party headed by Ríos Montt, wanted to grow both the organization and, according to Melgar, his political base. He talks about Alvizúrez's exploits as if they were sheer madness. "The union of Sexta Avenida vendedores ambulantes had some kind of problem," he explains, "and he [Alvizúrez] went and got himself into the middle of it, and then he brought them to ASIMEM so we'd take them in and fight for them. I told them, 'I'm sorry, you have a union to defend you . . . we can't mix one thing with another.' They got annoyed, and [Alvizúrez] made me out to look like I was against the people." Another time, says Melgar, Alvizúrez came to a meeting with "something like three hundred shoe salesmen—who knows where they worked? They were going to join the association, and I told them, no, they couldn't. They got quite mad, and left, and Alvizúrez, he got mad too, you know?" It happened again and again. Melgar remembers the arrival of Chiclet and trinket sellers from the *pasarelas*, the metal footbridges that let pedestrians cross the street, around El Guarda. "Pasarelas are for passing, not selling," he tells me emphatically. "It's *illegal*."[31]

The conflict between Alvizúrez and Melgar ultimately broke ASIMEM apart. "It sounds like a clash of ideologies," I say to Melgar, having in my heart some sympathy for the poor street vendors. "Exactly," he answers but immediately turns the discussion back to Alvizúrez's political aspirations.

I believe Melgar had already left ASIMEM on an emotional level before the split came. When it did, it happened over a different issue. Melgar hadn't run for reelection, and Alvizúrez became president in March of 2001. In the following month there were two strikes, neither of which Melgar or Mercado Cervantes supported. First was a municipal employees' strike, which ASIMEM voted to back. "They wanted us to defend them and demonstrate and all of that," he says. "But the problem with the municipality is *exactly* the personnel. They are responsible in the first degree for the disorder that you see in every market."[32] The second strike was a general market shutdown in response to yet another wave of privatization rumors. In an emergency meeting, Cervantes vendors decided not to participate.[33] ASIMEM voted to sanction Cervantes for six months and, according to Zoila Cux López's notes, had no shortage of malicious things to say about Cervantes's officers.[34] Melgar and other ex-members of ASIMEM's junta directiva wrote a letter to the new directors requesting a meeting and a peaceful resolution to the acrimony.[35] It was to no avail. After an emotional general meeting in Mercado Cervantes, the members decided the calumny and sanction were too much to take. They formally resigned, voicing their support for ASIMEM's existence and goals but not for its junta.[36]

Months later the ASIMEM junta would write to Melgar inviting him to make peace and attend the Día del Inquilino ceremonies—the Day of the Vendor was an original ASIMEM creation. But Melgar refused to go. The event, he says, was crawling with politicians from the FRG and was a publicity stunt designed to make it seem like the markets were behind Ríos Montt. A number of markets irritated by the FRG link, he says, dropped out of the organization as well. When Melgar was president of ASIMEM, there had been about 150 members. Two years later, when I interviewed him, there were tens of thousands. Most, he tells me, are informal vendors and sellers at the mercados satélites. The rest of the markets are represented either by themselves, like Cervantes, or by a handful of fledgling and powerless groups attempting to pick up where the ASIMEM of yore left off.[37] The vendor movement has fragmented and weakened even as it has grown. The reasons behind its failure are nothing grand. They are, instead, quotidian.

"Qué Buena la Marimba":
Everyday Life in the World of the Market

The markets are a world unto themselves. Children grow up in them; people grow old and die in them; vendors commune and squabble within their walls. They are kitchen, living room, and bathroom, and sometimes— as in La Terminal—even bedroom.[38] These *micro-mundos* are polyethnic and diverse. They include old-time Ladinos, middle-class vendors like Melgar, and even older Ladino market denizens, many of whom supported the right wing back to the invasion of 1954, when they organized on behalf of Castillo Armas.[39] Other vendors, by the new millennium also well established with a history of decades, sought refuge in the markets during the violence. They used the markets both as a hiding place from the death squads and as a means for one family member or *compañero* to make money and get food to supply a safe house.[40] There are also pendulares, most of them Mayan, and a constant flow of new arrivals. Some of the newcomers are in family units, placing one or two members inside the market and the rest selling on the street. A high percentage of new migrants to the markets are teenagers. Lots of these kids are dedicated more than anything to playing pickup *fútbol* games or to exploring the possibilities both licit and illicit available in a big city. Others show a tenacious, single-minded focus on commerce that keeps them working around the clock in a trade unlikely ever to lift them out of poverty. Beyond this array of social groups, each defined by its resident or hometown community and complex family situations, there are migrants from El Salvador, Honduras, and Nicaragua, many en route to the United States; loan sharks, drug dealers, and other underworld characters; evangelizers, missionaries, and street preachers; and the neighbors, who, as regular shoppers, are also a part of market life.[41]

All of this takes place within a space. It is no surprise that everyday physical concerns dominated ASIMEM's and Comecer's agendas. Security, garbage, parking, routine maintenance, telephones—all were subjects that came up repeatedly. So too behavior: liquor-selling stalls occasioned boorish and scandalous comportment in one market; in another, police were sleeping, drinking, and playing *fút* while their supervisor looked the other way.[42] Inside Mercado Cervantes, bathrooms were a particular area of concern. In municipal markets, as in all Guatemalan public space, a bathroom is a concession; it costs a coin to get in, more for paper. The *señora de los baños* played a role in everyone's life, and when inquilinos took to cursing at her, Comecer passed along a request for a bit of manners: "que mantengan un vocabulario—poco más o menos—con un poco de educación."[43]

Education, and not just in terms of keeping one's vocabulary polite, is an issue of primary importance inside the market. Numerous markets have elementary schools within their walls, schools that since 1995 have been run by PENNAT.[44] Some also have nurseries and in-house radio stations, La Voz de La Terminal, for example. In La Terminal the nursery is under the auspices of the first lady and Social Welfare.[45] In 1999 PENNAT and the Procuraduría de los Derechos Humanos (Federal Office of Human Rights) invited ASIMEM to attend an educational series on human rights in Mercado Sur 2.[46] While the agencies may have had the human rights of the children workers uppermost on their minds, ASIMEM members and vendors in general began to frame any number of their requests in human rights terms, even when the relation wasn't clear at face value. For example, when the committee for the saint's festival at Mercado San Martín got awarded only two days' worth of permits instead of the traditional three, they petitioned the human rights agency to protect their "tradition of forty-six years."[47]

Sex is also a part of everyday life in the markets. These commercial and residential centers are meeting places for people from far-flung villages. The larger markets, like La Terminal and La Florida, are surrounded by cantinas, brothels, and rent-by-the-hour hotels. I myself have witnessed open prostitution—both "plain vanilla" and transvestite—in and around numerous city (and country) markets. A volunteer with the Organización de Apoyo a una Sexualidad Integral frente al SIDA (OASIS, the Organization to Support an Integral Sexuality to Confront AIDS), the city's oldest gay rights group, told me that the majority of Guatemala City's lower-class, same-sex couples that she has worked with, both male and female, had met each other in the markets.[48] Markets are nexuses where liaisons of all types occur. Governmental and nongovernmental organizations pass through with vaccinations and medicines, holding talks on sexually transmitted diseases (STDs), AIDS, and family planning.[49]

Markets are located at the forefront of economic development and cultural cross-communication—between Maya and Ladino and between Guatemalan person and foreign merchandise. Taken as a whole, the markets show the same paradoxical mix of social dissolution and strengthened tradition that I noted in the institution of the Guatemalan family. For example, while prostitution and STDs are commonplace, so too is religion and its socially binding rich body of ritual. Near Christmastime in 2004 I was interviewing a street vendor who was a *marero* over a Coke in the hellish tangle behind Mercado Sur 2 on Fifth Avenue in zone 1. A young guy from Mazatenango, he was telling me the story of his initiation into mugging ("so I pulled a knife on him, pues") when suddenly we heard the sounds of carols coming from a marimba inside the market. The clouds and the scowl fell from his face, and for a moment he looked like the child he was. "Qué buena la marimba," he smiled. "Qué buena."

ASIMEM's Christmas plans included marimba and mariachi and were as much an everyday focus of the organization as any economic issue.[50] Such traditions are ongoing. Besides the shared holidays like Christmas and Holy Week, each market has festivals dedicated to its patron saint. Juntas directivas invite one another and ASIMEM as well.[51] Markets also cooperate with their home parishes. On Corpus Christi, the Parroquia de la Santísima Trinidad leads its procession through the Mercado Cervantes. They coordinate the event with the junta directiva beforehand. It's important that the vendors stop vending, that they attend, and that they clear an appropriate spot for the entry and exit of the Holy Altar.[52]

The patron of Mercado Cervantes is María Auxiliadora, whose day is the twenty-fourth of May. Blanca González runs the market's religious committee.[53] "Here we're very Catholic," she tells me—a common refrain in a country now rife with religious division in the wake of the Evangelical revolution. They celebrate Mass inside the market and sometimes put on marimba. The Virgin's *capilla* is a few yards away from Blanca's pork stall, just beyond Beatriz's fruit. After I explore the chapel, I try to ask Blanca some questions about the ceremonies and ritual. "There's Jesus," she lectures me, annoyed. "He's the son of God. Then there's Mary, His mother, who was a Virgin." I have become the Heathen. "I'm sorry, señora," I say. "I'm not Catholic. I'm not Evangelical either. But I'm on God's side."

Religious ritual, identity, and ceremony play a tremendously important role in imparting a sense of community, belonging, and stability in a world rent by modern problems. Among these problems, leaking roofs, harried bathroom attendants, and the need for vaccinations and a condom handout are the stuff of everyday life. But nothing is more commonplace than crime, and its proportions are epidemic.

Some snippets from the minutes read as follows: "In San José Mercantil they attacked last week and the police were tending to some other problems, and there is the president, wounded, they shot him in the leg"; "Customers aren't arriving in Mercado de Villa since they rob all the cars"; "Mercado Colón: a person asked special permission to leave at 9:00 at night. But there was a problem: she, along with some thieves, wanted to kill a señora."[54] In a single week in 2000 six markets were robbed, and this just among ASIMEM members.[55]

Sometimes the scams can be quite clever. In Mercado Colón a man rushed in and told an inquilina that her son was being robbed outside. The vendors ran out of their stalls to help, and the *ladrones* cleaned out their puestos in their absence.[56] In virtually every meeting with the muni over the course of its history, ASIMEM took up the issue of crime. The police were a particular problem. On the one hand, there weren't enough. On the other, the officers tended either to be lazy and worthless or to be criminals themselves. In 2000 a group of officers assigned to Mercado Reformita stole from some vendors. Through ASIMEM, the vendors complained to the muni, and in the end the police were forced to pay for what they had taken.[57] Not long before, a group of Mercado Roosevelt members had marched into the municipal police station, telling the man in charge that if a certain thieving officer ever set foot in the door of their market again they would lynch him on sight. "He was replaced immediately," they bragged.[58]

"The Muni Is Full of Con Men": Everyday Politics in the Markets

Inside the market itself, it is the job of the vendors' elected junta directiva to deal with day-to-day problems. The junta is often a site of contestation. As we saw in the formation of Comecer, city markets traditionally tended to be informally represented by their elders. The process of institutionalization sometimes exacerbated deep-rooted tensions.

In June of 2000 vendors from the Mercado Santa Luisa in Chinautla showed up at ASIMEM with a problem. Two committees had formed inside their market—one of Ladinos and the other of Maya. The conflict had gotten so ugly that a city market official referred them to ASIMEM for help. Santa Luisa, being an informal market, couldn't join, but Melgar went and gave them a *plática*, or pedagogical talk, on how and why to form an integrated committee and work together. They managed to do it, he tells me, though not without suffering through some rough patches. Melgar is always careful to speak respectfully of the Maya. He deploys the term *compañero indígena* with regularity. Still, he has a Ladino perspective. "The indígena want to do things their way," he says. "They don't want anyone telling them what to do or how to behave, and bueno, why should they, with the history they have? So they throw the trash in the street right there where they sell, for example. That's okay for them. But the Ladinos don't like it. Instead of working it out, they start to insult each other. And things go downhill from there. It's one thing to be in your little village," he says, "but it's another when you come to a city, and a market within a city, and there are other people there whom you have to respect."[59]

Everyday politics inside the city markets take place within a complex web. A multilayered series of negotiations either manages to keep the peace or, at best, directs energies into a semicoherent and statement-making demonstration or job action when rage boils over into potential violence. Indeed, the overall feeling of Guatemala City's markets is of a world at once steeped in tradition and hypermodern, deeply rooted but barely held together and ready to explode at any moment.

The fabric of relations of production is at the heart of the paradox. Even in a small market like Cervantes a great deal goes into day-to-day functioning. The market has meat, vegetable, and flower stalls and a constellation of tiendas, outlets that sell hardware, homeware, miscellaneous items, and candle and spice stores. There are very few of the clothing stores seen in other markets, though a few can be found on the sidewalk puestos outside. Larger markets offer everything from electric and electronic goods to car parts and accessories to recorded music and musical instruments. Some, like the Mercado Central, also have large *típica* sections where Mayan traje and weavings are sold. All have *comedores*, restaurant stalls, many with charcoal-fired stoves and most with picnic tables. Usually, these are arranged in an open gallery, so one comedor seems to melt into the next.

Overall, the commercial landscape evidences a system of distribution and supply generated and managed from below yet tied into the economy from above. Vendors are responsible for keeping their own puestos stocked. Beatriz Cux López, for example, gets fruit both from La Terminal and from an import distributor in zone 1, from whom she buys imported grapes, apples, nectarines, plums, kiwi fruit, Anjou pears, and oranges, when they are out of season in Guatemala.[60] Tiendas get their basic run of groceries, including canned goods, dry pastas, catsup and mayonnaise, toilet paper, soap, and the like, from a variety of distributors who come directly into the market; they all tend to carry the exact same goods. Plastics come from the capital's plants: Guateplast, Lacoplas, and Mayaplast, to name a few. Beer and soft drinks—Coke, Pepsi, Crush—arrive in trucks, as do drinkable Agua Salvavidas and milk, mostly from Foremost. Ceramics hail from less corporate suppliers who come from time to time in vans. For the comedores, homemade *carbón*, or charcoal, is even more informal, though pollution and deforestation have prompted its sale to be regulated. At Cervantes it comes via itinerant Mayan vendors from Patzún in the highlands. The women who run the comedores haul staple menu items like *atol* (corn mush soup) and the *masa* from which the ubiquitous tortillas are made by car or bus from their home kitchens.[61]

All of this commerce occasions businesses in trucking and supply, but it also gives rise to a social division of labor within the market itself. Beatriz, for example, shares in the employing of an assistant who helps carry things —Julio, a Mayan man with a campesino hat and a tumpline. All around any Guatemalan market are scores of kids with bikes who run goods to restaurants and hotels and even more *carteros*, or men with carts—flat, four-wheeled wooden vessels something akin to a wheelbarrow.[62] They are there for hire, to haul things from trucks to puestos or from puesto to puesto. Abelardo is a cartero at the new CENMA wholesale market. Thirty years old, he looks closer to fifty. His face is cragged, and some of his teeth are missing; one is a yellow and black mass banded in gold. Abelardo is a native of Chinandega, Nicaragua, which he fled in the early 1990s, tired of the years of war brought on by the U.S.-funded Contras. Now married to a Guatemalan and father of two, Abelardo makes 10 quetzales (US$1.30) as we speak, hauling a load of three thousand oranges for a Tzutuhil man, Diego, a pendulum wholesaler who travels back and forth from Santiago Atitlán.[63] While by Guatemalan standards it's not a bad take for half an hour's work, Abelardo sits for hours between such jobs and lives, in a word, in poverty.

Peripheral workers like Abelardo and Beatriz's helper, Julio, often have nothing officially to do with the municipality, unlike the licensed vendors. Neither do the many children who sell, clean, haul, watch stalls, babysit, and otherwise labor—not to mention the shoeshine boys and Chiclet vendors and others. The very fabric of the economy, of relations of production and exchange, within the markets belies the binary logic of vendors inside versus vendors outside, no matter how much business sense Melgar's approach may make.

Paradoxically, even though the informal sector is integral to life in the market and is beyond the muni's control, politically the muni has to deal with the entire array of interests, while the vendors' junta directiva, where there is one, represents the renters. It is no wonder that so many markets, like La Florida in zone 19, have two entirely separate committees, one for inside and one for outside.[64] Each has the mission of pressing its constituents' demands before City Hall officials.

Early in the new millennium, the job of day-to-day municipal interface fell to the muni's delegates, on assignment inside the markets themselves. In 2003 Cervantes's *delegada* was Marcia Yunixa Laz Cienfuegos, who had also served within the past two and a half years at Mercados Central, El Guarda, and El Gallito. Her job, as she put it, was to "deal with problems." She collected money from delinquent payers and heard and trafficked complaints about maintenance and other routine matters, dealing directly with the junta directiva. It was her thankless job to ask informal vendors to leave the premises. She also oversaw transactions such as the selling of puestos. Until not long before our interview, such sales had been both wholly illegal and incredibly common; the muni, as part of its effort to regularize the world of the markets, reformed the code and made the process more professional and transparent. However, as Laz Cienfuegos pointed out, since puesto sales often involve the transfer not only of the spot but also of all the merchandise it contains, she made a special effort to ensure that the vendors were keeping accurate inventories and accounts.[65]

Laz Cienfuegos, unlike the members of Comecer, had no real investment in the Mercado Cervantes per se, as her whirlwind of assignments throughout the markets attests. Neither did she have a real tie to the municipality of Guatemala. As a career politician, her fate was tied directly to that of then-Mayor Fritz García-Gallont (2000–4), who launched an unsuccessful presidential bid in 2003. She occupied a space detested by nearly everybody, though the vendors of Cervantes seemed to like her and get along with her personally. Besides being a politician and a transient, she had the added stigma of working for "Fritz," one of the most activist mayors, from the vendors' point of view, in city history.

The transfer from the La Terminal wholesale market to CENMA became a leading issue during García-Gallont's term, sometimes resulting in physical battles between municipal authorities and La Terminal vendors who refused to move.[66] The Terminal/CENMA affair added another layer of violence to the already simmering situation concerning urban transport, market vendor rents, and market privatization rumors. In April of 2000, as García-Gallont's term as mayor was just beginning, the city broke out in demonstrations, riots, and vandalism. The trigger was a proposed bus fare hike, which was never instituted. Students at USAC went on a hunger strike in front of the muni. Mobs attacked twenty-three busses and sacked several stores, killing five people and wounding seventeen. In the Mercado de Villa Nueva demonstrators burned tires. Amidst the mayhem, looters tore the neighborhood apart. Vendors, meanwhile, were up in arms about rumored rent raises. They joined the bus fare demonstrators with their own peaceful protest march.[67] The mayor would later claim that no one had planned to increase the rates and that the rumor to that effect had been just an act of "political manipulation."[68]

Only months later La Terminal broke out in riots over vendor displacement to CENMA. The *tomateros* were particularly defiant. In the end, one person was dead, two were wounded, and dozens had been beaten.[69] After the turbulence ended, the president of La Terminal's vendor committee wrote an open letter decrying the violence and denying that the committee had had a hand in it. "We are pacific people, lovers of peace," he said. All the major human rights organizations could vouch for them, the committee members held. Describing the hardships in La Terminal's various sections, they explained that "only GOD can know how much our people are suffering." Perhaps to atone to God, they promised that there would be no more riots and planned two enormous prayer meetings, one for Catholics and one for Evangelicals.[70] Despite this gesture, demonstrations, violence between vendors themselves and between the vendors and the muni, and overall resistance to CENMA continued in the years ahead. As late as 2005 the transfer of the wholesale market was still incomplete.

Besides attempting to make CENMA a success, the García-Gallont administration presided over a process of municipal decentralization that affected life in the markets. City Hall divided the municipality into fourteen districts, each with its *mini-muni*, or City Hall branch office. Vendors could now pay their rent in an office nearer where they worked, and in some cases at a bank branch within their market itself.[71]

One of the hallmarks of the municipal decentralization plan, on paper, at least, was to make the *alcaldes auxiliares*, or auxiliary mayors, who func-

tioned at the neighborhood level, get more involved in the interface between muni and market.[72] The alcaldes auxiliares had for some time been a
target of the vendors' rage. ASIMEM members encouraged their organization's secretary to resign in 1997 after he became an alcalde auxiliar: "It is
not permitted, mixing politics with our association," the minutes read.[73] A
year later a spokesperson for the Mercado presidenta told ASIMEM that
"the alcaldes auxiliares are just liars and politicians, and what's more,
they've written a report saying that the markets owe [the muni] 885,000
quetzales."[74] Grand plans aside, I found no evidence that the alcaldes
auxiliares were any more systematically involved in actual market life in the
2000s than they had been in the 1990s. Beyond dealing with the muni's
assigned delegate, most interface came through the periodic visits of officers from Desarrollo Social (Social Development), a branch created in
early 2000 and from the older Servicios Públicos. Servicios Públicos is the
outreach arm of the division of the muni that deals with the markets and
putatively addresses their maintenance and other concerns. Social Development, meanwhile, was to address community issues. "They're in
charge of the bathrooms," Melgar said, but without any bite, so perhaps his
sardonic dismissal was unintentional.[75]

Despite or perhaps because of all the bureaucracy, distrust between the
vendors and the muni is rampant. When City Hall wanted to conduct a
market census in 2000, alarm bells rang. ASIMEM, its meetings already
taking on a more combative tone, held an emergency general session.
Seeing it as prelude to a rent hike, inquilinos voted to oppose the measure.[76]
The census remained an issue in the weeks and months ahead, as the muni
began approaching the juntas directivas of markets individually. "The muni
is full of con men, and they try to keep us divided," one member charged.[77]
ASIMEM chose to press their case with Julio Eduardo Arango Escobar, the
procurador de derechos humanos, or human rights ombudsman. "The only
thing they [the muni] want is that inquilinos pay more, and they are
practically legalizing disorder," they wrote. "The chief of markets has tried
to slander the members of our junta directiva with the aim of dividing us
and irresponsibly provoking conflicts between inquilinos."[78]

Finally, ASIMEM and the muni reached a consensus on how to gather
statistics without raising rents, with procedures all agreed were fair. The
process did not go smoothly, and the results are not to be trusted. There
were demonstrations and lockouts of census takers, and one municipal
policeman was killed when the polling turned violent. Finally, the census

exacerbated tensions within ASIMEM, since Melgar and Mercado Cervantes made peace with the muni before Alvizúrez and his bloc did.[79] In the political universe of Guatemala City markets, conflict is the only constant.

Mercados del Nuevo Milenio:
Selective Modernization in the Markets

Early in 1999 a group of compañeras from Mercado Roosevelt, led by doña Anita, came to a series of ASIMEM meetings looking for support in their crusade against Pollo Rey, the Chicken King. The Pollo Rey brand, processed and distributed by Avícola Villalobos—wanted to put a wholesale *depósito* in the market to serve as an in-house supply for the market's chicken retailers. "None of us are going to let these Pollo Rey companies put their bodegas in," compañero Alejandro from La Palmita market assured the women, and the group voted to write to the company and send representatives to have a meeting with them as well.[80]

When ASIMEM took up the subject for the last time, the compañeras reported that the situation was even worse. Pollo Rey/Avícola Villalobos was supposed to be providing only some cleanup services to its retailers and bringing the chicken trailer around periodically, but now they were talking about coming in and remodeling the whole market. In fact, Roosevelt representatives told the group, they had heard that Pollo Rey was going to take over Mercado Cervantes and turn it into a "mercado Modelo."[81] Apparently the muni had made a backroom deal with Pollo Rey: the muni got fix-up money in return for letting the company "sponsor" markets and install its *depósitos*.[82] It didn't happen. The ASIMEM reps who had gone to Avícola Villalobos announced that the meeting had been a total success. Company executives had promised they would never open any such facilities, and they had provided tasty meat snacks as well. The victory must have been a relief to doña Anita and company since they were also grappling with an absence of police in the market, which was "crawling with thieves and completely without any authorities after 3:00 in the afternoon."[83] Faced with relative powerlessness to change unpleasant circumstances, beating back a big agroindustry concern must have tasted sweet.

When I followed the story of this triumph as it unwound in minutes taken over a three-month period, I was certain I had stumbled onto a defense of *pollos criollos*—backyard chickens, worm-eaters. These are a widely available delicacy in Guatemalan markets, and they provide family income. The market vendors, I thought, were standing up for the local agrarian cottage industries and keeping agroindustry out. I was wrong. The vendors didn't care about Pollo Rey. Most of them carried the product already, Melgar told me. The problem was that where the Chicken King *had* opened depósitos in markets, its staff had sold retail on the sly, underselling the legitimate vendors. In using ASIMEM to stop the plan, the vendors protected their pocketbooks and thwarted the dread prospect of privatization, snuck in though it was through the back door of marketing schemes and corporate sponsorship.[84]

Later, in 2002, the organization would make its position on concessions in markets clear. They were not welcome, and they were not constitutional. "We seek the common good and not the good of just a few," Alvizúrez, by then president of ASIMEM, was quoted in the press as saying. "Giving away the markets in concessions only benefits the municipal corporation and corporations who win them.[85]

For people without a great deal of formal education, Guatemalan vendors show an acute understanding of how corporate capital seeks to get the better of them. In 2000 they faced another aspect of globalization—patent protection. The United States was working with the Alfonso Portillo government to pass an Industrial Property Law aimed at putting an end to the abundance of counterfeit, copied, and pirated goods that range from clothes to compact discs to perfumes. Vendors, especially street vendors, realized that this could mean the end of their livelihood. "They're coming into the market," Arcemio Velásquez Santos stood up and warned ASIMEM. "They're coming, wanting tax receipts. . . . Brands like Lee, Tomy [Tommy Hilfiger], Levis, you'll have to change the tag. Let's recognize terror, compañeros, it's necessary that we do."[86]

What U.S. business interests perceived as protection of their legitimate interests, Guatemala City street vendors saw as a terrorist attack on their already tenuous means of survival. As the Guatemalan Congress was working on the Industrial Property Law, vendors, though not ASIMEM per se, threatened to begin peaceful resistance actions, prompting the minister of economy to explain in as popular a language as he could muster that if Guatemala didn't sign it might miss out on numerous "commercial benefits" that "the U.S. gives to poor countries."[87] Vendors made good on their threat, and, as Congress debated, a group of four thousand protestors gathered, some of them burning piñatas that looked suspiciously like the delegates inside. It was a massive action that won them a voice.[88]

Still under Melgar's leadership at that time, ASIMEM got only margin-
ally involved in the Ley de Propiedad Industrial affray. When nervous
representatives of Guarda Quinta Avenida—a good place to shop if you're
in the market for pirated goods—came in saying that "they [the powers
that be] were going to put an end to imitation brand names" and that "the
informal sector was going to be turned into the formal sector," Melgar,
according to Zoila's minutes, told the members, "You don't have to get
frightened about any taxes, because if that's what the law requires you have
to respect it."[89] Even without ASIMEM's support, vendors made their influence felt, as Ríos Montt, the head of Congress and a leader in the FRG
party (to which Alfonso Portillo also belonged), managed to attach
enough amendments to the law to provoke U.S. ambassador Prudence
Bushnell to call it completely unacceptable.[90] After Portillo vetoed the law
several times, in the end, a revised version passed.[91] In 2005, law or no law,
counterfeit *chafa* is still available all over Guatemala, just as it is in the cities
of the United States. Try though the corporate system may, it cannot
simply relegate people to starve to death with passivity.

Corporate capitalist technologies and techniques, however, are not
wholly without appeal among groups like the Guatemala City vendors. In
some of their projects the vendors experimented with a kind of advertising-
age commercialization. In 2001 Cervantes, like other markets, tried a
modern media and marketing event in an attempt to compete with supermarkets. In June Comecer got a talk from Juan Noriega, the city's coordinator of markets, who had a plan to save the markets. He urged the group to
take part in a cross-promotional event with private companies. Popular
brands such as Ana Belly (jellies, etc.), Regio (packaged foodstuffs), and
Pollo Rey were willing to pay to sponsor a special sales day in the markets,
the same kind of special the supermarkets always had. The companies
would even help clean and paint the markets and, to make sure all went
smoothly, would provide on-site paramedics and USAC medical students.
The idea intrigued Comecer members, and the meeting turned to excited
future casting. One day, they fantasized, the market would have an in-house
pharmacy service, a Cred-O-Matic ATM, and vendors would be able to take
credit cards. The campaign was to be called Mercados del Nuevo Milenio,
and for a few futuristic months Cervantes vendors dreamed in millennial
scope, envisioning themselves as proprietors in a market with all the
trappings of electronic and commercial modernity.[92]

The spirit continued at Comecer's next meetings, as members mulled over Noriega's ideas. "The projects [of our committee] should be that we have new ideas like Hygiene," the minutes read. "People should be more hygienic and there should be quality control. Cleaning the aisles." Repeating the refrain that so much more could be done if the muni would only reinvest more funds in the markets, Comecer leaders went on to plan the music and decor for the new millennium sales event.[93]

Over the next month or so the group approved page proofs for posters and flyers designed as a newspaper insert—just like those gringos might associate with the A&P—and in August the event occurred without unpleasant incidents. Comecer did an informal poll and found that, for the most part, the inquilinos were in favor of trying it again. Lots of customers had shown up, and even more would next time, they opined, if someone spent the money to turn the posters into actual newspaper advertisements. The only misgiving was the looming presence of Pollo Rey, who, as a major sponsor, had put in a sound system and hung globes with their logo all over the market. Some vendors were suspicious of a backdoor takeover. Still, Cervantes's vendors had become merchandisers and were willing to do it again. Given the complexities of funding, cross-promoting, and staging such events, however, it turned out to be (at least at the time of this writing) a one-time trial not to be repeated.[94]

At the moment, the mercados don't need to make themselves over as supermercados to win customers. Though you still cannot use a credit card to buy goods in the municipal markets, they remain the retail venue of choice for the population at large. According to research on consumer preferences done in 2003, markets and tiendas both beat supermarkets. Noting markets' attractiveness for their lower prices, the ability to haggle, and fresher produce, *Prensa Libre*, reporting on the data, commented that "markets still constitute a cultural aspect of life for Guatemalans."[95] This was true despite four decades of market penetration by modern supermarkets. Carlos Paiz Ayala, president of the La Fragua company, had opened his first supermarket in 1959, starting a concern later to be linked with the Costa Rican–Nicaraguan Corporación de Supermercados Unidos via their joint association with the Dutch Royal Ahold group. In 2004 La Fragua, headquartered in Guatemala, had over 150 franchise outlets, not only in its home country but also in El Salvador and Honduras: supermarkets like the high-class Hiper Paiz and Supertiendas Paiz (with their connected Super Gas stations) and the more down-market Despensa Familiar and Surtitiendas Paico. From Chips Ahoy cookies to Kraft cheese and Doritos tortilla chips, U.S. shoppers could find familiar fare in Paiz stores but not fresh fruit and vegetables; this market was still cornered by the traditional street vendors and mercados municipales.[96]

In Guatemala City's markets, the threads of national existence come together. They are tied to agroindustry and to tiny farm communities, to politics local and global, to distributors whose headquarters might be in gleaming first-world towers or in humble homes in a mountain Mayan village. They show every growing pain of a society torn apart by war and forcibly structured by neoliberal corporate capital. They are people's homes, and they keep other people's homes supplied with food. And they are paradoxical.

Markets of all varieties show the historical perpetuation of petit retail as a means of survival. From ambulatory candy and cigarette sellers to Mayan handcrafts dealers to Sexta Avenida's purveyors of clothes and light consumer durables to independent inquilinos and tienda owners, vendors are a vital sector of the economy and of the informal economy in Guatemala. Such development is a cultural phenomenon as well as an economic one; proprietorship, no matter how humbly defined, and the ability to sell are not only money making strategies of first resort, but also articulated as *rights* worthy of government subsidy to protect. People fight for those rights, and hence the multifaceted paradoxes: enterprising small businessmen and women rally for subsidies for themselves and organize to prevent subsidies from reaching their compatriots on the streets; government officials, many lining their pockets, debate modernizing the system all the time knowing that a jump in food prices would cause mass starvation and thus are doubly pressured from below; and globalizing corporate capital seeks to replace this whole universe, so dear to its discursive enshrinement of free enterprise and independent proprietorship, with a web of franchises. Corporate capital is unintentionally reproducing the small business class that was at the heart of its own mythic origins and destroying it at the same time.

"Guatemala is a nation of producers," Melgar told me. He spoke of cottage industries, homes where *cuxa* corn liquor and *quesadillas* and *tamales* are made. He spoke of "a people who take advantage of this earth, this earth you drop a seed into and it grows."[97] I see what he sees—little strips of land resplendent with crops, onion sorting on the beach, potato harvest day, beans growing around stalks of corn. But I think we both see the selling: the selling-as-begging of the hungry children on the streets; the selling of the handmade goods on every corner, public and private alike;

the universe of stalls; the call of selling that brings *them* out of the country and into the city in search of a better life. Markets both formal and informal are the point of entry and the site of social reproduction in Guatemala, a country of producers, to be sure, but a society of vendors. Within their ambit lies, contested, much of what the nation has in store.

The interviews with the vendors are over and we have said our good-byes. I am done with Mercado Cervantes, and tomorrow will try to extract whatever data I can from the less friendly warren of offices inside the muni. My stomach full of Blanca's pork and my arms laden with mangoes and apples that Beatriz and Zoila have given me, I think of how much I have learned and how little I know as I make my way through Cervantes's aisles to start the dangerous walk back home, where I live in luxury and have a view of Sexta Avenida's street sellers and glue sniffers. I pause to greet and thank the many vendors who shared their insights over the months in which I conducted my informal polls during many hauntings of the halls. Just as I am about to leave, one calls out to me. It is Juan Manuel from Sololá, motioning me back to the tienda he runs with his brothers. Leaning over the counter and supporting his weight on a sack of corn, he has a final question for me. "Gringo," he says, "can you help me get to the United States?"

Juan Manuel from Sololá and other young vendors like him are heirs to a century of modernist development. They move through a globalized Guatemala, a postmodern landscape—a social space that still has embedded within it the colonialism and racism of the 1920s, just as it does a far-from-united but still discursively powerful *pueblo* acutely aware of its exclusion from the good life that consumerism promises to bring. Exactly how Juan Manuel, a Kaqchikel-speaking tienda worker in a zone 3 municipal market, fits into Guatemala's new commodity culture as a consumer is entirely unclear. He is poor, Mayan, and unlikely to be in the mall.

What is clear, however, is that multiple layers of historical development built into the fabric of present-day life have crushed this youngster's possibilities: the inefficient, racist, space-is-money agromodernism updated by Ubico's state in the 1930s that relies on dirt-cheap labor, causing an endless cycle of chaos and rationality that colors all further development; the gendered aesthetics of state that strip modernizing projects of social democratic content, providing a patina of legitimacy while eschewing social welfare and responsible redistribution of wealth; an authoritarianism writ large across society that prefers murder to debate; and a technocratic state and export-oriented agrarian economy that does nothing for those who work in the agrarian sector except expel them totally unprepared into a marketplace glutted with unskilled labor.

Juan Manuel and the many young people who share his circumstances are surrounded by commodities that shimmer forth from a world without borders. For those who are, like him, poor, though, there are borders with a capital B, to the north and just around the corner, where a kaleidoscopic map of gates and guards exists to shun his ilk. Too, there are borders less visible: the social barriers that face the copper-skinned, the *lengua*-speakers, the functionally illiterate provided no education by their state, given no social safety net, and prevented from organizing in any way that threatens to bring about a real change. The creation of this last border was the greatest accomplishment of the Guatemalan genocide—the final piece of the puzzle needed to make it fallow ground for neoliberal globalization, a process with which it worked in tandem. As world politics changed, so changed Guatemala, all its contention turned inward, a nation ready to acquiesce to the dominant economic system without the direct and daily application of state terror. The result of Guatemala's development, beyond ever-escalating poverty, has been a widespread fragmentation. The left is fragmented, the universe of institutions that putatively develop is fragmented, and space itself is fragmented. Fragmentation plays a major role in making Guatemala feel and function like a shattered place, a nation both broken and lost.

As many scholars have noted, Guatemala's long history of racial exclusion and uneven distribution of land and wealth go a long way to explain this fragmentation. These factors have been embedded in the U.S.-led process of development from the 1920s forward. The making of the "modern anti-modern" intensified and took a drastic, violent turn during the period of the armed internal conflict, when the military came to execute development and statecraft alike. In the countryside, the rise of automotive-fueled marketing of local crops, subdivision of land, the loss of basic grain cultivation in favor of nontraditional exports, the growth of a rural proletariat, and, most of all, the mass murder and massive displacement of the internal population disrupted and transformed cargo systems and marketing networks that dated back centuries. Urban industrial expansion, though limited, had given rise to what the historian Paul Dosal calls a "new industrial oligarchy," which had a tenuous relationship with the ruling military. Foreign-owned or subsidiary concerns in textiles, foods, and soft consumer goods expanded in tandem with agricultural business (meat, fertilizers and pesticides, cotton, sugar, nontraditional exports) and illusory booms in raw materials: tin, nickel and oil.[1] The Guatemala City metropolitan area, with a population of about 112,000 in the early 1920s, had exploded in waves of population growth to roughly 285,000 in 1950; 590,000 in 1964; 910,000 in 1973; 1,076,000 in 1981; and 1,256,000 in 1994.[2]

With the defeat of the insurgency and the left in general came further fragmentation, as the stories of the municipal market vendors and butchers show. On an institutional level, there appeared a growing and ever-shifting array of transnational agencies, development consortiums, state aid institutions both national and foreign, NGOs, and the like.[3] Political parties, grass-roots movements, and special interest groups also multiplied in number. Evangelical Protestantism, spreading at lightning speed, redefined religious affiliation among all classes. Transnational capital—the lion's share based in the United States, to be sure, but perhaps best exemplified by Korean-owned sweatshops—swept into the country at unprecedented levels. Its presence helped to sharpen already acute divisions of space, further marbling the landscape between *have* territory and *have not* territory. Postmodern shopping malls, U.S. franchises, and upscale pedestrian streets and tourist facilities sprang up nearly overnight in moneyed areas. Meanwhile, the *asentamientos precarios*, the gullies and the slums, the urban nightmares and the rural backwaters, became more miserable, more dangerous, and even more unfit for human life than ever. In Guatemala, both the marginalization of the political left wing and neoliberal economics have contributed to a central paradox of contemporary life: the more concentrated that power becomes in the corporate capitalist world system, the more fragmented the landscape becomes. The two dynamics are inseparable.

The dynamic of post-1986 concentration–fragmentation has its emotional side. Guatemalans are disillusioned. Those survivors who believed in Communist victory have had to reconfigure their dreams and their lives;[4] those who believed in capitalist progress have had to accept that it is, at the very least, extremely slow in coming; and everyone has had to adjust to everyday life and politics in a country riddled with the sorts of social pathologies that follow extended civil wars and that the dominant economic regime tends to exacerbate. Civil society has proved hard to develop. Crime and migration steal away the nation's youth. Infrastructure is still lacking, but it remains unclear how postmodern development will fill in for high-modern development, which has been resoundingly pronounced a failure. Indeed, in the shattered landscape left behind by decades of war, narratives of failure are the one factor that unifies a fragmented body politic.

The Quest for Civil Society: Politics, Institutions, and Poverty

The first political task that faced the nation in 1986 was to engineer the transition to civilian rule. It did not prove simple. In an age still dominated by the military, Guatemalan politicians, intellectuals, and citizens at large

Urban development. City landscapes like this one surround gated oases of luxury in the contemporary Guatemalan landscape. Anonymous, "Panorámica de asentamientos (Panorama of Shantytowns)," Guatemala City. Archivo de fotografías de El Gráfico. Fototeca Guatemala, CIRMA (Reference Code: GT-FG-CIRMA-086-positivos asentamientos).

debated the mechanisms through which a stable and multifaceted civil society could be constructed.[5] Much of the thinking and writing surrounding the topic of civil society in the decade or so after the elections of 1985 was rich and sophisticated. Some of its varied strands drew on the best intellectual and popular movement output of the day—output that attempted to go beyond the evolutionist doctrines that had led modernist development for decades. Nonetheless, the fact remained that Guatemala had few of the ingredients needed for genuine bourgeois rule. There was no middle class to speak of; instead, there were *capas medias*, or middle sectors, too demographically weak and dispersed to be called a class. There was no widespread system or culture of formal education, meaning that the middle sectors, by and large, grew not by social reproduction but by the luck of any given individual's or family's financial ventures. There were few of the elements of a truly mixed economy, such as dynamic industries with linked support businesses. Ladino rule continued, although a burgeoning pan-Maya movement would challenge it and expand the definition of what civil society really meant. Finally, the population was impoverished, traumatized by decades of war, and heavily armed. While at its headiest the quest for civil society was also the quest for a postmodern way to conduct the modernist project of reengineering society in its totality, at the bottom line its challenge was simpler: how to keep the military in the barracks and out of the National Palace.

Though the military remained an *éminence grise* from 1986 to the new millennium, Guatemalans succeeded in keeping the executive civilian and signed peace accords with the URNG in 1996, ending the civil war. Parties in power through 2007 were all right-wing, ranging from the Christian Democrats to the modernizing, neoliberal, and technocratic Partido de Avanzada Nacional (PAN). Ríos Montt, the head of Congress for the bulk of the period and would-be candidate in every election until the courts finally let him run in 2003 (he lost), formed the FRG in 1988. By most accounts Alfonso Portillo Cabrera, an FRG man and president from 2000 to 2004, was the nation's worst and most corrupt leader since the return to democracy. This was not an easy title to hold given that the second president of the period, Jorge Serrano Elías (1991–93), had dissolved Congress, fired judges, and assumed dictatorial power in an ill-advised "self-coup" that lasted five days before he was forced into exile and ultimately replaced by his own human rights ombudsman. President Oscar Berger Perdomo (2004–8) had a daunting inheritance: rampant corruption, increasing poverty, skyrocketing crime, a heterogeneous mix of often-opposed popular movements on the brink of violence, and a sick economy. By the end of his term he was embroiled in political conflict and weathering heavy criticism but was praised by many for his anticorruption and forward-thinking politics.[6]

Anticorruption in Guatemala has gone hand in hand with reducing the power of the military. Leaving aside the twists of Guatemalan politics since 1986, the army high command remained a least common denominator on the stage of national power. In 1995 the Washington Office on Latin America (WOLA) published a policy brief that condemned the Guatemalan military for ongoing human rights abuses. The report highlighted El Archivo, an intelligence cluster with CIA ties that, among other activities, conducted assassinations in the manner of the death squads. El Archivo was found within the Estado Mayor Presidencial (EMP), a group of over five hundred officers that not only served the president, but also coordinated intelligence and political oppression.[7]

In March 2002 special criminal investigators from the Guatemalan National Police set an ambush in Guatemala City. Their mission was to intercept a ransom payoff for a kidnapped businesswoman. A white Toyota van pulled up to collect the booty, and when the police surprised them the occupants opened fire. In the end, one police investigator was left a paraplegic, and two of the supposed kidnappers were dead. They turned out to be G-2 agents, members of the Guatemalan army's elite intelligence corps. Officials scrambled to describe the bloody mess as a joint operation gone bad, but the Mission of the United Nations in Guatemala and the U.S. embassy investigated. Over a year later they warned of criminal clandestine groups linked with public security forces. In its reportage the newspaper *Siglo Veintiuno* showed the restraint of self-censorship (journalists are killed in Guatemala) but illustrated its article with arrows linking the police, various mafias, and the army.[8] Another newspaper described Guatemala as home to an army "structured for war in times of peace." In 2002 the nation had 20 military bases, 60 barracks, and 32,500 troops.[9]

There were also about five hundred NGOs, prompting some in the early years of the new millennium to denounce a parallel power structure free of government supervision and ripe for corruption and abuse. According to a report from 2004, various individuals and political parties—the FRG of ex-president Portillo chief among them—had used NGOs to enrich their relatives and supporters, pilfer or misdirect funds, and launder money.[10] Around the same time, a website published a report of unknown quality and veracity that savaged the proliferating NGOs. Beyond listing the reasons cited above, it took NGOs to task for being unaccountable and for filling in for a deficient state. It also held that NGOs served as vehicles for foreign human rights zealots who corrupted the judicial process in a single-minded, unsophisticated crusade to get the military without regard for complexity or truth. NGOs, it said, promoted a culture of "victimismo."[11]

Most people tend to view the NGOs as heroic. Taken as a whole, they promote civic participation and undertake countless infrastructure, micro-economic, public health, and education projects that directly benefit the population. They serve as watchdogs in what remains a nation with an abominable human rights record, protect the environment, and, as a friend commented to me, "actually get things done, unlike the government." Given their vast numbers, it is unsurprising that a few should run afoul of corruption, a problem that hardly diminishes the accomplishments of the whole. The NGOs are one of the most prevalent features of the late capitalist landscape in Guatemala, and, with the passage of time, history will tell what their impact was. For present purposes, suffice it to say that their very profusion is itself a direct result of development's trajectory.

No one is exactly sure how many NGOs there are in Guatemala (though 500–550 was probably an accurate figure for early 2005) since no current directory is kept and everyone differs as to what should be counted. NGOS form a diverse constellation: human rights and humanitarian aid groups that emerged out of the left–Catholic tradition; "suit and uniform" groups: neoliberal business organizations and development concerns financed by USAID, with military ties lurking in their gene pool; "sandals and peace sign" collectives: wildlife and environmental organizations; and many that give succor to the poor. Joining their ranks are fundamentalist Evangelical groups involved not only in spreading the faith but also in charity, aid, education, and health; parastatal groups founded with government support yet operating autonomously; relatively independent development associations, many with Canadian, European, and, more recently, Japanese funding; and a growing consortium of perhaps the most promising of all, local associations organized around common issues at the grass roots. Together, yet with very different agendas, these organizations pressure the government and provide many citizens with a chance for meaningful political participation, if only at the neighborhood level.[12]

For all their good works, NGOs in their various guises evidence the erosion of a popular front. They bespeak a new kind of colonialism, progress based on charity, and the fragmentation of popular movements in the face of concentrated corporate power. Perhaps today (and through the 1990s) more than ever, it is possible for citizens to organize within a structure that helps them to achieve their goals and pursue a better future. Those structures, however, are lost in a tangled web of groups, each tacking in its own direction. As NGOs have multiplied, hopes for fundamental change have dimmed. Such groups are not only a permanent feature of the Guatemalan political landscape. They are also the manifestation of a new culture of development forged during the Cold War. Its ingredients were many: popular resistance and liberation theology; the imperialist culture industry and its development-as-counterinsurgency schemes; identity politics in the North that go together with the undermining of the labor movement; the rise of the New South in the United States and the spread of Evangelism;[13] and the long, historio-geographical switch from Fordist to flexible accumulation. Holding hope and providing help as they do, NGOS underscore a central paradox of late capitalism: concentrated power and a profusion of organizations in civil society can easily go hand in hand.

"Dependency, Poverty and Degradation":
Fragments of a Fragmented Struggle

At the beginning of the 1980s Guatemala had a strong, diverse popular movement. It included unions, groups inspired by liberation theology, campesino and human rights advocates, and the guerrillas and their numerous foreign supporters in a broad though not fully united front. The decades ahead would see its fragmentation. Early in the new millennium union membership nationwide was only around 5 percent overall. The campesinos were well aware that their protests were in vain. The national left was all but politically powerless, and the most vibrant religious movement was Evangelical Protestantism.

Most promising was the pan-Mayan movement. Steadily gaining ground late in the 1990s and early in the 2000s, this political groundswell is far too complex to analyze here. Arguably the most important element of the new Guatemalan civil society, this movement has resulted in a popularly articulated identity of Maya and Mayanness hitherto unseen in Guatemala.[14] Virtually no one used the term *Maya*, except to refer to the ancient, extinct variety, when I conducted my first investigations in 1991 and 1992; today, it is a commonplace, above all among the young. Phrases like "mi cultura maya" and "hablo k'iche'-maya" have all but replaced "cultura indígena" and ethnic identifiers such as "K'iche'," which denote a group but not the whole.

As a new generation of young men and women comes up with no lived experience of the violence, their pan-Mayan identity melds with reminted historical memories of the civil war itself. Dozens of Maya young adults have told me that the war was a pan-Mayan uprising against the Ladinos and the rich. Most seem thoroughly unaware that the guerrilla leaders were nearly all Ladinos, many of whom blamed Mayan insularity and conservatism for their inability to get the countryside properly organized. As the historical literature on Guatemala grows, a new crop of rich histories of the conflict at the local level will no doubt begin to plumb the depths of how different generations in different localities identified and identify themselves with the war. In the meantime, suffice it to say that the popularized discourse of the pan-Mayan movement—not among its organizers but among the Mayan populace at large—has imbued a new generation both with a sense of ethnic solidarity and with a vaguer, but still real, inkling that they are tied into a larger global struggle for social and economic justice.

If the Guatemalan resistance, Mayan and otherwise, of the 1990s to 2010 has had a common thread, it is opposition to globalization. In October 2002 the Coordinadora Nacional de Organizaciones Campesinas closed three border crossings—two with Mexico and one with El Salvador. They were protesting the Free Trade Area of the Americas (FTAA), the Free Trade Agreement between the United States and Central America (CAFTA), and the Plan Puebla–Panamá (PPP).[15] Unlike FTAA and CAFTA, which fall within the domain of free trade agreements in general, the PPP combines infrastructure development with rhetoric about social advancement. Attributed to the former president of Mexico Vicente Fox but reportedly the brainchild of the OAS, the PPP is billed by its developers as being dedicated to the regional integration and social and economic development of some sixty-four million people in Mesoamerica, that is, southern Mexico to Panama. It seeks to link the nations with new superhighways—a Pan-American Highway plan remade for postmodern consumption with rhetoric eerily familiar from the original highway initiative. Though the planners have invited indigenous representatives to sit at the table, the PPP is widely criticized not only for its potential ecological impact, but also for its total lack of consideration for businesses both national and regional, down to the level of informal economy workers.[16]

Grass-roots groups tried to respond and began publishing easy-to-read educational materials around the country—for example, local newsletters like ¡Alerta!, which in 2002 warned Petén residents about "The Plan Puebla–Panamá: Dependency, Poverty and Degradation."[17] Not surprisingly, PPP plans were unfazed by this resistance. The immensity and complexity of neoliberal global economics occasion a dynamic of thwarted protest that repeats itself over and over. Though educational lore reduces the phenomenon to one forged in the GATT rounds of the 1980s, Latin America's conflict- and debt-ridden so-called lost decade, and unleashed in the 1990s with the formation of the World Trade Organization and the signing of the North American Free Trade Agreement, it remains unclear, even thus simplified, exactly who is causing the problems and how those problems ought to be confronted. All organizations seem clear that organizing a unified popular opposition front is crucial, yet such organizations keep multiplying and splitting and morphing every day.

Early in 2003 Guatemalan teachers, students, unions, campesinos, and transport workers lit up the nation with protests. They were acting together to protest globalization, push the claims of the teachers' union, and even demand justice for war victims. The actions ranged from highway closings to tire burnings in cities around the nation and managed both to paralyze transportation and commerce as well as give a hint of the disruptive power of concerted protest. Finally, the teachers took over both the national airport and the airport in the Petén, while others stopped all traffic on the Pan-American Highway at strategic points around the country. They also blocked customs at the borders. Despite paralyzing the national economy, no one managed to exact concessions, although the teachers did win a slight salary increase.[18] The popular movements were experiencing a common phenomenon of globalization. They could effectively shut down all transportation in the nation, strike, or do whatever they wanted: it didn't matter. Ultimately, the national government, even if it had been amenable, was powerless to do anything about the groups' substantive demands.

Meanwhile, the progressives were not the only sectors protesting. In the same time period, some five to six thousand ex-PAC members were periodically blocking the highways in confrontations that left dozens wounded and several dead. Members of the forced civil patrols during the civil war, largely those associated with the right wing after the passage of the years, had pressed claims for monetary compensation to the government. In response, President Portillo of the FRG promised them payments without budgeting or allocating funds or consulting either Congress or the judiciary. To no one's surprise, the ex-PAC members remained unpaid well into the Berger presidency, in late 2005. Not the least of the obstacles to this plan was the insistence of all sectors but the right wing that many of the PACs had violated human rights and committed crimes against humanity.[19]

As fragmented popular sectors have increased their protests, so too have ordinary citizens unaffiliated with any organized group. Tight state budgets and crumbling infrastructure have combined to drive people into a fury. Into the new millennium, tire burnings and riots over treacherous roads, dangerous bridges, and expensive but shoddy services such as electricity have been near-weekly events. In most municipalities outside the capital, electric power goes out four or five times on an average day, and sometimes for days at a time. Every now and then, for reasons unknown, the 110-volt lines surge with 220-volt current, exploding everything electric. Running water and sewer systems are likewise either unreliable or nonexistent. The pueblo is understandably less than amused. But inferior physical infrastructure is only one source of outrage. The lack of a reliable law enforcement mechanism has caused citizens to take justice into their own hands. Vigilante bands abound. On a single day in October of 2002, for example, a mob stormed the police station in Panzós, demanding that a prisoner accused of murder be released to them, while in San Marcos villagers from several communities stung by high electric rates closed the highways and sacked the commercial agency of Deocsa, the Distribuidora de Energía de Occidente. They added that they were opposed to the PPP.[20]

"The Maquila Depends on Poverty": Manufacturing, Commerce, and Marketing after the Return to Democracy

No economic sector more eloquently expresses the kind of on-the-ground conditions that drive people to rage and desperation than the maquiladoras. A catch-all word used in Spanish and now English, the maquiladora or maquila is an export reassembly plant, the sort of industrial enterprise that erupted late in the twentieth century like a pox on the poor side of the Mexico–U.S. border. In Guatemala the word *maquiladora* is practically synonymous with *textile plant*. The best translation, if a translation were even needed, would be "sweatshop."

In 1984 half a dozen maquilas employing about two thousand workers were operating in Guatemala, but most sources trace the harbinger of the coming boom to the opening in 1985 of Inexport, a pants-making plant in Guatemala City owned by a U.S. citizen, Henry Robbins Cohen. It was one of the few maquiladoras in which a union managed to gain a foothold.[21] The real explosion in the maquila sector, however, came at the very beginning of the 1990s. Responding in part to the pressure of Ronald Reagan's Caribbean Basin Initiative to promote the sector, the Guatemalans followed up a series of investor-friendly laws in 1989 with the passage of legislation that granted investors ten-year tax and customs exemptions. Export reassembly, meanwhile, was also being pushed by USAID; in 1990 it was providing over 80 percent of the funding for the Asociación Gremial de Exportadores de Productos No Tradicionales (AGEXPRONT, Trade Association of Exporters of Nontraditional Products).[22] By 1992 there were 275 maquilas in Guatemala, exporting about $350 million worth of clothing to the United States and employing over 50,000 workers.[23] Less than a decade later, early in the new millennium, nearly three times that number of people were working in maquilas, with dips and peaks in the sector along the way, mostly due to the volatility of the Asian economies over that period.[24] Though the clothing produced was overwhelmingly headed to the U.S. market—for companies such as Target, The Limited, Wal-Mart, GEAR for Sports, Liz Claiborne, and Lee Jeans—U.S. direct investment in the maquila sector itself remained relatively low. Koreans owned some 60 percent of the sweatshops.[25]

Early in the maquila boom, in 1991, a consortium of international unions petitioned the U.S. trade representative for a review of Guatemala's status under the worker rights provisions of the Generalized System of Preferences. The maquila sector was the problem. Noting that although some 8 percent of the workforce in general was unionized, the petition maintained that in the maquila sector the figure fell to under one-tenth of 1 percent.[26] In only one of the more than 225 factories, Pindu S.A., had workers been able to organize a union. Even there, however, the employer refused to bargain collectively with them. Inexport continued to fire organized workers and through intimidation managed to drive membership down to about 32 workers. The petition detailed the existence throughout the sector of one-on-one boss meetings, blacklisting of union workers, payoffs to quit or be fired, and other intimidating actions,[27] perhaps soft-handed tactics compared with the death threats regularly visited upon organizers, reportedly made credible by kidnapping, torture, and murder.[28]

In the United States and Mesoamerica alike, the evisceration of the union movement is one of the hallmarks of the neoliberal age. Union-free maquilas are futuristic. They reflect an industry that encapsulates a historic transformation, much as the slave-fueled sugar plantations of the New World did in the colonial era. In Guatemala the vast majority of maquila employees are young, often underage single women. They earn starvation wages (between $96 and $150 a month) and receive no social security benefits. They work up to seventeen hours a day, and their employers deny them bathroom breaks. They suffer sexual abuse at astonishing rates and often turn to drugs—according to many reports, amphetamines provided by the employers themselves—to keep their exhausted bodies laboring. Most maquilas are located in an archipelago of misery around Guatemala City, drawing on and feeding the multiplying shantytowns, which serve not only as permanent residence to many of the city's poorest families, but also as a way station for locals and rural-to-urban migrants alike on the perilous journey to the United States.[29] As poor Guatemalans flee their nation, economists worry that the maquilas might flee Guatemala. In 2004 all signs were pointing to China as the next great destination for the highly mobile export reassembly plants. As Alejandro Ceballos, the director of the Comisión de Vestuario y Textiles, or Vestex, of the nontraditional exporting association AGEXPRONT, pointed out in an interview in a pro-business newspaper, "The maquila depends on poverty."[30]

Maquiladoras are one part of the new geography of neoliberalism in Guatemala and Guatemala City—a geography defined not only by the proliferation of shantytowns and the movement of people to the north, but also by the sudden spread of U.S. franchises across the landscape, the most visible denizens of newly arrived businesses ranging from marketing firms to media and telecommunication companies. The franchises are often located in postmodern shopping malls that began to appear in force in the 1990s. Besides the ubiquitous Texaco stations, replete with StarMart facilities, McDonald's is probably the most commonly seen. The burger chain opened its first franchise in Guatemala in 1974 and by 2002 had thirty-eight restaurants with twenty-five hundred employees in the nation.[31] Burger King christened its twenty-second restaurant in 2000, and the next year Blockbuster Video arrived, spreading all over the city in the years ahead.[32] By late 2004 Domino's Pizza had thirty-six outlets in Guatemala,[33] and a drive through the city's commercial centers reveals similarly high numbers of Quizno's, Subway, and Wendy's chains. Guatemalan food franchises have followed suit, Pollo Campero fried chicken most successfully of all.

From the Calzada Roosevelt—the leg of the Pan-American Highway running through Mixco and into the center of the capital—the two most dominant logos on the Grand Tikal Futura hotel and mall are McDonald's and Payless Shoes, another franchise now speckling the city after a rapid turn-of-the-millennium rise. Occupied mostly by car repair shops and executive offices of transnationals like Merck and Nestlé throughout the 1980s, the Calzada Roosevelt has become a major retail and commercial center in the decade and a half since. The first of the enormous *centros comerciales* was Comercial Megacentro, built in the mid-1980s, and it was quickly followed by PeriRoosevelt. The full-service supermarket Hiper Paiz (now Wal-Mart) appeared in the early 1990s, and Grand Tikal Futura was erected right near it in 1996.[34]

Malls continued to proliferate in the years ahead, and by 2004 retail outlets included Price Smart, Office Depot, Club Co., Sears, and upscale consumer electronics and home furnishings outlets such as El Importador, FPK, and Max Distela. Around the rest of the city and particularly on the other end of the Pan-American Highway where it exits toward El Salvador malls became a common feature of the landscape. One of the nation's largest mall developers is Grupo Roble, founded in San Salvador in 1962 and by 2003 the owner of seventeen malls around the isthmus. Grupo Roble is a division of Grupo Poma, a Salvadoran business founded in 1919 as a distributor of Hudson and Essex automobiles, later becoming involved with General Motors and Toyota.

Marshaling the inexorable logic of class-based branding, Grupo Roble has created four styles of commercial space. The *multiplaza* is an upper-middle-class environment devoted mostly to sales of imported consumer goods. The *paseo* is for the rich, designed to impart an air of luxury and exclusivity. The *metrocentro* is for the middle class, "characterized by substituting for the traditional places of purchase in each city." Finally, the *unicentro* is "directed at the midde to low and popular sector, located principally in peripheral zones of the capital that have high potential for urban development," and offers "all the alternatives in commerce, services, and entertainment."[35] A Guatemalan friend joked with me about this sort of niche marketing, making up his own scale:

A. *Agroexportadores*
B. *Burguesía* (bourgeoisie)
C. *Corbata, comemierda* (wears tie, kisses ass [eats shit])
D. *Deprimido, delincuente* (depressed, delinquent)

While the above perfectly exemplifies Guatemalan black humor, and the joke itself captures the commercial essence of the new millennium, such market mechanisms are nothing new. In fact, the distinction-laden web of transnational commerce was woven into Guatemalan consumer culture over the course of the twentieth century, as we saw in chapter 1. A sample of transnational media and advertising and marketing firms founded in Guatemala from 1958 to 2004 gives a sense of the corporations at play and of the results of decades of commercial and cultural development (see table below).

Sample of Major U.S. Advertising, Marketing, and Public Relations Firms Operating in Guatemala, 2004

FOREIGN FIRM[a]	DATE FOUNDED IN GUATEMALA	SAMPLE TRANSNATIONAL CLIENTS IN 2004
J. Walter Thompson	1958	Best Foods (Naturas, Knorr, Continental, Lipton), Kimberly Clark, Shell, Kraft, Warner Lambert
McCann Erickson	1963	American Airlines, Coca-Cola, Esso Central America, Ginsa (Goodyear Tires, Kelly Tires), Hewlett-Packard, Mattel Toys, Microsoft, Nestlé, Sprint, UPS
Creación Saatchi & Saatchi	1976	Allsteel, Compaq, DuPont, Payless ShoeSource, Procter & Gamble
Leo Burnett	1977	Delta Airlines, Kellogg's, Mercosa (Max Factor), Pillsbury, Procter & Gamble
Eco Young & Rubicam	1987	AT&T, Colgate Palmolive, Dannon, Ray-o-Vac, Sony Corporation, Texaco
BBDO Guatemala	1989	Bayer Centroamérica, Bacardi, Blockbuster, FedEx, Pizza Hut, Western Union
Ogilvy	1994	Mitsubishi, American Express, T.G.I. Friday's, Sears, Kimberly Clark Guatemala, SmithKline Beecham, Telecomunicaciones de Guatemala (brands including Comtech, Direct TV, and PCS Digital)
Jotabequ (Grey Worldwide)	1997	British American Tobacco Guatemala, GlaxoSmithKline Beecham, Procter & Gamble Interamericas, 3M, Quaker Oats Company

Source: The November 2004 edition of the website of the Unión Guatemalteca de Agencias de Publicidad: http://www.ugap.com.

[a]This list of "Madison Avenue" agencies and some representative transnational corporate clients from 2004 gives a good indication of the commercial forces at play in Guatemala. There are numerous Latin American and other firms engaged in the same business, along with many corporate clients with no direct ties to the United States. Clients' particular brands are not indicated unless the parent company (or distributor) would be unfamiliar to U.S. readers.

Pentecostals, Porn, and Pop Culture:
Contested Consumption, Bodies, and Souls

Marketing and advertising are one element of the media and communications revolution responsible for what Néstor García Canclini calls cultural
hybridization in Latin America.[36] Guatemalan society shows in nearly all of
its various subgroups, divided as they are by ethnicity, class, language, and
geography, less a blending of traditional cultural expressions and new-
fangled, often imported ones than a marbling: wearing Nike *tenis* to the
saint's procession; loving marimba and Michael Jackson; putting candles
on the shrine and coins in the video game, and so forth. This is a country
with a consumer culture but few consumers, in the sense of having a mass
market with regular disposable income; with fads and fashions but no real
generation gap to speak of; with family dissolution and alleged moral
breakdown of the most pornographic varieties yet with more family and
traditional moral and religious structure than most gringos find familiar. It
is a country of paradoxes.

A newsstand in Guatemala City, circa 2003, will serve as a jumping-off
point. Religious magazines and a single porn publication sit side by side.
There are respectable newspapers and lurid tabloids designed ingeniously
with art that makes them readable even by the illiterate. For the young,
there are outreach publications promoting nationalism and morality along
with lowbrow pop culture rags. The tabletop on which all this literature is
arrayed invariably sports stereo equipment turned up ear-piercingly loud.
The music might be Mexican *ranchera*, Latin or U.S. bubble-gum pop, or,
ubiquitously, the Eagles' "Hotel California." It might, however, also be the
equally popular refrains of national *rockeros* turned international—most
notably Ricardo Arjona, who has lived in Mexico since hitting it big with
tunes like "Si el Norte Fuera el Sur (If the North Were the South)," one of
whose lyrics is, "Reagan would be Somoza." If the proprietor is young and
hip, the blaring music might even be *rock nacional*, a beat growing in
popularity. A garage band genre, Guatemalan rock has its roots in the sixties
but is largely attributed to the now-defunct group Alux Nahual, which first
performed publicly in 1979 and gained a following in the decade after.[37] To
the varied strains of this music one can select from penny-press titles like
Expresión Juvenil, whose message runs, we'll save you, lost youth, from your
drug-addled ways by showing you pictures of the republic's founders, and
Lucha 3000, a wrestling magazine in which fans can follow the careers of

Slayer, Ciclón Negro, El Momosteco Jr., and Black Boy. *El Globo* has cheesecake pictures, police beat, and the Guatemalan syncretic folk saint, Maximón. The tabloid *Extra* teams women's bare breasts with stories of crime and disaster: a woman with a slit throat, a tortured cadaver, a grisly car accident, pus-filled wounds from spider bites.[38] But the biggest contrast on the table, one that evidences the tensions and contestations of globalization and its cultures, is easily between the Evangelical magazines and *Sexo Libre*, Guatemala's only porn publication.

The Evangelical explosion from the 1980s to the present is the single most visible phenomenon of globalization in contemporary Guatemala.[39] Popular history dates organized Protestantism in Guatemala to the coming of John Clark Hill, a Presbyterian minister from the United States, in 1882, during the anticlerical regime of the liberal Justo Rufino Barrios. The handful of denominations grew slowly through the mid-1940s, although their spread was aided by a severe shortage of Catholic priests in the countryside. After the earthquake of 1976, the arrival of numerous U.S. missionaries, especially from neo-Pentecostal denominations, produced the first notable spike in a religious movement that had been steadily growing since the time of the Revolution. The year 1982 and the coup d'état of the Evangelical Efraín Ríos Montt saw the next wave of Protestants arrive from the North. Missionary television shows and radio programming and ads from U.S. groups like Club 700 and PTL complemented the on-the-ground efforts of Evangelical proselytizers who set the goal of converting half the population by 1990. They came close. According to some estimates, about 24 percent of Guatemalans were Protestant by that date, and by 1992, during the presidency of the Evangelical Jorge Serrano Elías, some put the number as high as 30 percent.[40] According to the U.S. Department of State, 40 percent of the Guatemalan population was Protestant (Evangelical and otherwise) in late 2004.[41]

Critiques of the Evangelicals vary. On the street the most common complaint is that they play highly amplified music and sing and clap, often until 1:00 or 2:00 in the morning. "It's the damned Indians," a Ladino neighbor grumbled to me during one sleepless night of hallelujah. "They have nothing, and this is their revenge."[42] More sophisticated analyses underscore the links between Protestant, especially Evangelical Protestant, religiosity and the political right.[43] Such critique is often partisan and tends to ignore the complexities of the issue, such as the grass-roots populism of Ríos Montt, the aid and community activities of the churches, the associated growth of charismatic Catholicism and the Catholic lay movement, and the like. Nevertheless, it correctly identifies not only the strong U.S. cultural influence and systematic persecution of Catholics in Guatemala who have been inspired by liberation theology, but also an ideology of individualism, anticommunism, and antiunionism seen in general throughout the Evangelical universe.[44]

In 1992, visiting a tourist town in the highlands, I staked out a luxury hotel in order to interview the workers. Most were penniless Maya from outlying villages, paid less than half the minimum wage plus tortillas, beans, and a place to sleep. One, a skeletal young man of seventeen named Jorge, was so malnourished he broke into spontaneous nosebleeds. He told me of working eighty-four hours a week, of suffering blows and verbal abuse from his boss, of women in the washroom forced to give sexual favors to their overseers. "Have you thought about a union?" I asked. "Oh, no," he replied. "Never. I'm Evangelical. Almost all of us who work here are. It's hard, yes, but you earn a living with the sweat of your brow. And after, there is Paradise. You have to be patient, pues." This, I thought, is a worldview the bosses can live with.

One of the most interesting aspects of Evangelism is how it ties together the extremely rich and the extremely poor in a social and architectural geography that mimetically reproduces capitalist divisions of wealth and space while at the same time discursively dissolving those ever more acute divisions in an ideological elixir of Rapture and Salvation to come. The tin-roofed shack with the electric guitar, the open-air baptism in a polluted river, the palatial and postmodern megachurches, the seventy-five-dollar-a-head conferences in Grand Tikal Futura—to a gringo, the contrasts are reminiscent of the Republican Party base in the United States, in which multimillionaires shake ideological hands with the working poor struggling to keep a sense of meaning in their lives.

By about 2005, one of the largest Evangelical business associations in Guatemala was the *Fraternidad Internacional de Hombres de Negocios del Evangelio Completo*, or Fihnec. Founded in the United States in 1952, Fihnec came to Guatemala around 1980, and by early in the 2000s it was active in over 150 nations. In Guatemala the group holds daily breakfasts, lunches, and dinners to present testimonial about the power of the Holy Spirit, along with annual conferences for its members, highly placed executives throughout the business world.[45] This is not a religious movement short of money. The Evangelical newsmagazine *La Palabra* (The Word) is a high-

budget publication, printed in full color throughout and featuring advertisements from companies like Regia (condiments), Del Monte, and La
Curacao (housewares). In 2003 it announced that Guatemala had eighteen
thousand Evangelical churches located in every corner of the nation.[46]
Most of the worshipers in those churches were far from the suit-and-tie set.

Part of what binds this disparate community together is an intense focus
on individual morality and purity. Sermons regularly cover marital fidelity,
and sobriety is a must. For youth, there are sports events, talks on the Bible
and sex, and even pop music concerts in celebration of Jesus, not unlike the
pop culture phenomenon seen in U.S. Evangelism.[47] In the wake of the
legalization of gay marriage in various parts of the world, La Palabra
reiterated the pulpit teaching that homosexuality is a grave sin, repeating
the story of Sodom and Gomorrah and avowing that the disorder was not
genetic and could be cured.[48] Infidelity and homosexuality are not the only
two sexual demons in the Evangelical world. "Masturbation is a resounding
NO to life," headlined La Palabra. The accompanying sidebar covered
temptations: the Internet, pornography.[49]

The Evangelicals' Devil is in fact at large in Guatemalan pop culture. At
the same city newsstands where La Palabra is for sale there are copies of
Sexo Libre, thinly veiled from the underage eye by translucent white plastic.
A very Guatemalan mix of porn and sex education, this first national foray
into public prurience prints Article 35 of the Constitution—Libertad de
Emisión del Pensamiento, or free speech—on the back cover of every issue.
The pictures inside are graphic but almost ashamedly so. The issues I
bought highlighted only white-skinned and often blonde-haired models
that bore not the slightest resemblance to brown-skinned Guatemalan
morenas or morenos. The articles, while including fantasy fare and write-in
advice columns, tend to focus on instruction, as if in apology for providing
smut to a desirous marketplace, whose desires are revealed in the personal
ads section.[50] A how-to on "Sexo solitario" appears beside a lesbian photo
essay;[51] a dictionary of sexual perversions, including bestiality, fetishism,
and necrophilia, among others, accompanies a piece on "Prostitución mas-
culina," noting that male hustling "requires a very special personality, a way
of seeing life without prejudice or blame."[52]

Sexo Libre is, beyond the Internet, the most publicly visible element of a
smut universe that otherwise includes strip bars, porn theaters, and the
entire gamut of sex workers. On the surface, Guatemalan culture remains
extremely conservative. Inasmuch as the sexual revolution has arrived, it

has come in secret. Groups like the Colectiva de Lesbianas Liberadas—Lesbiradas are exceptions to the rule. In the middle of the first decade of the new millennium, the Lesbiradas were occasionally holding performances highlighting discrimination at venues like the hip Bodeguita del Centro in zone 1,[53] and there was one gay rights and AIDS activism group, OASIS. In May of 2000 two unknown men grabbed the director of OASIS, Jorge López, and threw him into a white truck with polarized windows. López somehow managed to escape, but has continued to suffer threats and violence. In the same period a mass murderer or group of murderers was systematically slaughtering transvestites and other gay sex workers in zone 1.[54]

Globalized sexual and pop culture discourses abound in Guatemala but remain largely beneath the surface. Of more immediate importance are the high rates of incest and abuse.[55] As early as 1991 a survey of Guatemala City street children between seven and seventeen years of age reported that 100 percent had been sexually abused, over 80 percent by a family member.[56] But rape is hardly confined to the ranks of the homeless. Development has brought a globalization-borne fragmentation of Guatemalan public culture, reflected, to be sure, in the contrasts of piousness and porn, of sexual liberation and sexual abuse, of lowbrow entertainment and foreign rock and centuries-old traditions. But nowhere is the fragmentation seen more clearly than in criminality, a growing danger that now defines the landscape.

"A Savagery that Defies All Imagination":
An Ever More Dangerous World

Everyday violence in Guatemalan society has reached epidemic and patho-logical levels. The effects of the war, state terror, and grinding poverty have combined to create a social landscape in which safety and security, in-asmuch as they ever existed, are things of the past. The problem is at its worst in the cities but is hardly confined there. As we have seen, the campesinos are forming vigilante bands (usually called *rondas* in other countries, though the word is used infrequently in the Guatemalan media), and vicious acts of retribution are common.[57] Sometimes the individual or individuals who have outraged the popular sense of justice are lynched. Sometimes the perpetrator is burned alive—a favorite technique of the army in the early 1980s—or dismembered with machetes. Around the nation, and nowhere more so than in the capital, shootings, robberies, and rape are everyday events. When I completed my research and moved out of zone 1, it took my nervous system nearly a month to recover from the constant threat of assault or death. In twelve months I had witnessed three stabbings, two fights with broken bottles, and a shooting. I had seen four dead bodies on the streets.

Violence touches everyone, but women bear the brunt of it: 25,507 cases of domestic violence were reported in 2003, and 360 women were murdered.[58] "We are worried by the brutal forms of violence seen in Guatemala," Yanette Bautista of Amnesty International was quoted in the press as saying in May of 2004. "They show a savagery that defies all imagination, that is linked to indifference, to the poor social origin of the victims, and to the lack of action on the part of the authorities." Bautista added that of all the savagery, the growing rate of violence against women was most alarming.[59] In November 2004 the discovery of a woman's decapitated corpse in zone 3, dismembered with sharp instruments into half a dozen pieces, gruesomely aided horrified watchdog groups in keeping this trend in the headlines.[60]

In an opinion piece entitled "No salgás m'ijita," or "Don't go out, my daughter," the columnist Carolina Escobar Sarti wrote, "Behind the violence against Guatemalan women there seems to be a clear and well-known message: that the place of decent little women [*mujercitas decentes*] is in their home. . . . Poor men who are out of work, who have fallen into dependency on alcohol, who have no money or who are pressured by the violence that the war has wrought on them, need to let out their frustration and hatred someplace. And what better place than on the bodies of women? What's more, [women] take the blame for wanting their autonomy and for participating actively in the public sphere. Indeed, the [common] phrase 'public woman' [*mujer pública*], relating her to a prostitute, is no accident." Sarti repeated the many reasons for the violence echoed in other sources: poverty, the war, the use of women's bodies as a symbolic territory of conquest—a rape being a punishment of the woman's family or community as a whole. She also related the comment of a Guatemalan official who said there shouldn't be such a fuss because men were dying violently every day as well. "In part he is right," she wrote, "but generally [the men] are not raped or tortured as happens with the women, whose bodies are found with marks and signs that symbolize a greater viciousness toward the female gender."[61]

Rape was a tool of war in Guatemala. The state terror mechanism that peeled the skin off living bodies, that attached electrodes to their extremities and genitals, that asphyxiated them with rubber hoods filled with pesticides, that burned villagers alive, that bayoneted children, also ritualistically violated the female body. It should surprise no one that within the cauldron of postwar, postmodern poverty violence in general and domestic violence and savagery against women in particular are epidemic. This is a society in shock, its very fabric stretched to the breaking point. Among a populace that I, like most, have found to be overwhelmingly kind, giving, and honorable, deep pathologies lurk. The starvation wage, the tumpline, the torture chamber, and the total domination of an exploitative economic system are revisited on the landscape every day. Brutality is having its revenge.

In February 2003 the tabloid *Al Día* reported on the rescue of seven children enslaved in Guatemala City, discovered after two others managed to escape. A man posing as an Evangelical pastor had lured them in and kept them chained up for five months, reportedly forcing them to sell drugs on the street. He and his wife had fed the emaciated kids nothing but bread and water and had beaten them with cables and whips.[62] Perhaps the article was most notable for how quotidian the story was. Just another horror story like all the others in Guatemala City, a metropolis in which every day an average of sixty busses are assaulted and ten people are murdered.[63]

According to popular memory and academic sources alike, crime rates began to grow phenomenally in the 1980s and reached emergency levels by the following decade.[64] As we saw in chapter 4, street gangs, though some had existed in one form or another for several decades, took on the new moniker of *maras* and from the mid-1980s to the present both grew in numbers and became the public scapegoat of cities that, newly freed from martial law, were besieged by everyday crime.[65] Formed at the crossroads of the end of military rule, increased transnational migration, and the spreading of U.S.-influenced consumer culture and of drug culture and the sexual revolution as well, the maras were, in the words of the Asociación para el Avance de las Ciencias Sociales (AVANCSO), a "social invention and cultural expression" alike.[66] Though media commentators quickly linked the gangs with the astronomical numbers of street orphans left homeless by the war, preliminary research indicated that the majority of members had at least one parent and came from either the working class or the *capas medias*, the middle sectors.[67]

The maras have evolved quickly. They spread all over Central America in the last decade and a half of the twentieth century, and for obvious reasons have proved difficult to study systematically. Deborah Levenson, Nora Marina Figueroa, and Marta Yolanda Maldonado, researching for AVANCSO in the late 1980s for a text that was updated in 1998, found that Guatemala City's maras were more than just sites of criminal activity. They were also spaces of solidarity, companionship, cultural and social experimentation, and relative gender freedom. The gangs, they wrote, were groups in which girls and young women could find some relief from the sorts of inhibiting male violence decried so eloquently by Escobar Sarti. They also reported that homosexual relationships, both between men and women, were common and accepted within the ambit of the gangs.[68] A study conducted by social science organizations around Central America and published in 2001 took a more quantitative approach to the topic of the maras in Guatemala, running graphs of family disintegration statistics and possible motivations (drugs, sexual liberty, and so on).[69] Holding that around the isthmus, gangs were "a way of being young" in inner-city neighborhoods,[70] the study's conclusion argued that gangs were "a manifestation of social ills" caused not only "by poverty, but by informality [i.e., the informal economy], uprootedness, multiplying displacements [of populations] and geographic movements."[71] The work also mentioned a critical and yet-to-be studied factor: the transmigration of young people to the United States, particularly Los Angeles, and back to the isthmus.[72]

Gangs are not a social aberration on the landscape. Instead, they reflect the fragmentation–concentration dynamic of the society and economic system at large. For any given individual, the causes and motivations of gang membership are personal and locally rooted; of the two dozen or so *mareros* I have spoken with, most got involved because their relatives or buddies did or simply because it was the thing to do in the neighborhood. Several had tattooed gang insignias on their arms before they ever encountered an actual gang member, a sort of desperate gesture of a need to belong. Others needed money. Gang culture, fluid, local, and as impossible to summarize as it is difficult and dangerous to attempt to study, is as much a fractal expression of globalization in the age of corporate capital dominance as it is a polysemous, multifaceted, bottom-up expression of resistance, survival, and youth culture.

The maras are also part of a greater underground network, in which gang kingpins may have little or no relation with younger, rank-and-file members on the street—the type of kids researchers like me tend to meet. This fact was brutally brought to light just before Christmas 2002, when a gang called Los Cholos led an uprising and took control of El Pavoncito prison in Fraijanes, a municipality in the metropolitan area. Massacring fourteen prisoners, Los Cholos made headlines by decapitating one, stuffing his head between his legs, and later kicking it around the patio and finally parading with it stuck on a pike.[73] "The leaders are big shots," commented one survivor, "because the kids [*la patojada*] would never dare to make these kinds of problems."[74] The Guatemalan tabloids rang in the Yuletide with stories not only of the gruesome prison uprising, but of Christmas Day shootings, car wrecks, and a plane crash in Escuintla. The wrecked aircraft had been ferrying cocaine.[75]

Cocaine is a least common denominator in the Guatemalan underworld.[76] Certainly it is at the heart of cartels like the one that rules El Gallito. From its roots as a working-class beachhead—a site of popular and union organizing, resister of tyranny, voice of a pueblo in demand of justice—Ramón González's neighborhood degraded into one of the city's most dangerous and notorious corners, dominated by gangs of *narcos*. According to *Prensa Libre*, the history began in 1980, when Héctor Leonel Marroquín, "El Coyote," founded the neighborhood's cocaine cartel. Leaders and lieutenants in the decades ahead included men with street names like Marioco, Marín, La Viuda Negra (The Black Widow), and Maco.[77] In 2002, under pressure from the United States, the government disbanded its antinarcotics police, the Departamento de Operaciones Antinarcóticas (DOAN) for rampant corruption, including ties to the El Gallito cartel. At the time, the U.S. embassy was estimating that some 150 tons of narcotics, cocaine and crack chief among them, were trafficked through Guatemala each year.[78] Over time it was revealed that the DOAN had been moving cocaine throughout the nation. The Pavoncito and zone 18 prisons along with upscale discos in zones 9 and 10 were the chief local marketing outlets. The elite police had also been running a protection racket in El Gallito, providing armed security for the neighborhood kingpins.[79] The drug lords managed fine in the wake of DOAN's fall. In February of 2003, for example, six of their soldiers armed with AK-47s attacked police who were attempting to enter the neighborhood.[80] In El Gallito there is no question who is running the show.

Grams, Gates and Garbage: A Story of Two Urban Spaces

Cocaine's many social faces reflect divisions in wealth: crystalline lines for the moneyed; crack (rock, *piedra*, *drapie*) on the streets. Coke morphs form to fit its niche market, and so too does space. The cocaine age itself is part of an era in which the division of space between rich and poor, the *classing* of space into semiprivate enclaves, has become especially acute in the Western world.[81] The rich build guarded districts that serve as public space only to those who have the money and distinction to pass through the phalanx of shotgun-armed men who guard the entryways. Those guards go home, quite often, to neighborhoods that also show the transformation of public into quasi-private space, their own sentries being narcos and mareros and *mafiosos* who keep the territory a place where no *gente decente* would dare to tread.[82]

A pedestrian street named Cuatro Grados Norte, or Four Degrees North, located not far from the Civic Center in zone 4, is built around the Instituto Guatemalteco Americano. Clever college kids, changing one letter and thereby the meaning, call it *Cuatro Gramos Norte*, Four Grams North. This new-millennium so-called cultural center features high-priced bars, discos, and restaurants. In one restaurant diners can accompany their Middle Eastern food with grape-flavored tobacco puffed through a hookah, in preparation for a toot-fueled boogie night next door. Designed by a European transnational, DHV Consultants BV, Cuatro Grados is one of those attractive yet generic arcades that looks like it could be anywhere.[83] There are no shoeshine boys, no beggars. Not even unauthorized mariachis will approach patrons, who can sit outside untroubled, perhaps enjoying the antics of licensed clowns or fire jugglers. For *capitalinos* with money, the place is a safe, pleasant, entertaining refuge, a relaxing urban arcade in which to spend a night out in a dangerous city or to shop by day at a weekend open-air market.

The municipality's participation in planning and zoning Cuatro Grados Norte in 2001 fit into its greater philosophy of designing "a more human city," the architect Fabricio González y González, the muni's chief of planning and design, told me when I interviewed him in 2003.[84] The municipality's other plans included revamping the historic center and polishing up Sexta Avenida as well as improving the already-upscale zone 10. Under Mayor Fritz García-Gallont (2000–4), City Hall also made efforts to rationalize public transport, facilities, and infrastructure in general and the markets in particular.[85] Playgrounds for the wealthy like Cuatro Grados Norte may seem superfluous or even criminal in a city with problems on the scale of Guatemala's, but the logic behind such spaces is undeniable. On the one hand, if the city is to support a white-collar class and be "livable" in any sense of the word, it needs safe recreational facilities. On the other, the acute division of wealth and space, replete with its aesthetic scales, reflects global changes far greater than the power of any mayor to affect. González lent me one of his guiding lights, a copy of *Upgrading Urban Communities*, a CD put out by the World Bank that promotes designed neighborhoods like Cuatro Grados while at the same time underscoring the need for sewers, running water, and other essential infrastructure.[86] A city planner's job is not to address the underlying causes of poverty and its reproduction, but to humanize the spaces in which the divided society moves and lives.

According to González, the municipality's first major step toward integrated planning came in 1995, with the publication of *Metrópolis 2010*. At the time, Oscar Berger Perdomo, one of the founders of the PAN and president of Guatemala from 2004 to 2008, was Guatemala City's mayor (1991–96 and 1996–2000).[87] A prime example of postmodern urban planning, *Metrópolis 2010* was produced with the intellectual and sometimes financial support of a board of consultants that included the nation's major social science and development institutes, numerous foreign governments and NGOs, and national and international public service companies and corporations alike.[88] Grass-roots and neighborhood associations were overlooked. Ambitious and technical, the plan paid specific attention to land use and integrated planning that recognized the embeddedness of the zone within the city (actually a conglomeration of cities in a metropolitan area) and the city within the nation as a whole. It most notably planned a significant role for private investment in urban development, reflecting both the economic thinking of the day and the financial reality of the municipality's limited budget.[89]

Metrópolis 2010 summed up the issue succinctly: "Problem: a lack of sustainable urban–rural development both at a nationwide and city level. Cause: The models of development applied in Guatemala do not address the problem at a nationwide level. Effect: Low level of human development. Objective: To orient the dynamic of urbanization of the city and of its metropolitan area toward a process of development sustainable in human function."[90]

At present there is little evidence that the holistic overhaul of Guatemala City's infrastructure, environment, transportation grid, services, and web of public spaces is going to succeed, despite the sophisticated thinking and good intentions of its planners. Structural factors that produce and reproduce mass poverty, along with cultural elements that stymie rationalization (street vending is not just a necessity but a way of life, for example), consistently undercut strategies that for all their attention to the latest intellectual currents still reproduce the high-modernist ideology of social engineering from above. Planners mean well, but they cannot keep up with conditions on the ground. The economic system both produces the conditions that they address and turns their addressing of it into a white-collar industry that spans continents. NGOs and states and organizations and associations plan, and people pay for the planning. Academics write books and get grants to do so. And day after day, Guatemala City creeps over its fringe of mountains, claims the space around it, and writes misery on that space, writes pain, writes the entirety of social relations of production and exchange that the fragmented planners and critics are unwilling or unable to change.

Land invasions are an ongoing symptom of Guatemala's woes. The earthquake in 1976 occasioned land occupations, such as that in Tierra Nueva, increased rural-to-urban migration, and contributed to a rise in grass-roots popular organizing. It was also a hallmark in the entry of NGOs into Guatemala. These trends and city expansion continued into the 1980s. A housing deficit already acute at the beginning of the decade was exacerbated by spending cutbacks and structural readjustment during the Christian Democratic period from 1986 to 1990.[91] Land invasions increased as well. One of the biggest was in March of 1984, when a group that grew to some fifty thousand people took the land in front of Colonia El Mezquital south of the city in the urban municipality of Villa Nueva.[92] New arrivals would invade the surrounding areas four years later, and the entire area was the subject of a World Bank–UNICEF sustainable development project from 1994 to 1997 that reportedly benefited over thirty-seven thousand people and used community base organizations and revolving funds to ensure its continuity.[93]

In January 1986, two days after President Cerezo took office, invaders from Tierra Nueva (see chapter 5) in Chinautla launched an invasion of neighboring land soon to be known as Tierra Nueva II. Their leader was Dennis Mencos. A law student at USAC and the son of a Tierra Nueva I invader, Mencos was seventeen years old at the time of the invasion. His leadership would not last long. The community—which within a few months had grown to over seven hundred families—was shot through with conflict. Various associations and groups, including the Committees for Urban–Rural Development set up by the Christian Democratic government, vied for control. Even the gangs went to war, with Los Cobras defeating Los Nenes. The Christian Democrats founded an organization called La Quetzalí, which proved to be Mencos's greatest rival. There were assaults, fights, and robberies, and in the end Mencos gave up and went to the United States. The presence of state institutions, including the Banco Nacional de la Vivienda (BANVI), the housing bank, and the CRN, NGOS like La Fundación, La Federación de Jóvenes Cristianos, and La Organización para la Promoción Integral de los Niños, committees and organizations ranging from Alcoholics Anonymous to sports, and religious and women's groups did little to help. They could not prevent the community from disintegrating and exhibiting every woe of urban poverty. This was true even though the neighborhood remained semirural into the 1990s. It had no paved streets and was dotted with plots of corn.[94]

This sort of rural–urban landscape is characteristic of Guatemala City's urban sprawl from the 1980s forward. After the Pan-American and Atlantic highways were completed, the metropolitan area grew to embrace both suburbs and periurban spaces, or peripheral rural areas that form part of the urban fabric and socially reflect urban phenomena like subcultures, styles, gangs, and so on. Sharply fragmented by wealth, the new city spaces include high-class mansions and middle-class housing developments along with the commercial landscape of malls and shops that accompany them and, most notably, shantytowns, colonias, and humble periurban communities where the poor live.[95] The urban area expanded from eighteen thousand hectares in 1988 to twenty-four thousand in 1990 to thirty-five thousand in 1998.[96] According to the census of 1994, the total population was about 1.2 million. A great number lived in poverty, though statistics (notoriously unreliable) vary greatly in their estimates. One reliable source claims that in the early 1990s some 700,000 city dwellers were dwelling in shantytowns and fully half the population lived in deficient housing.[97]

From above, the valley of Guatemala looks beautiful. Descending the escarpment, one sees its uneven rills spangled with development—a combination of the majesty of the landscape and the mechanisms of man that could promise all the adventure and culture that Central America's largest city might have to offer. Soaring birds, *zopilotes*, spread their wings and ride the updrafts, giving the city center an avian halo visible from afar. Zopilotes, though, do not evoke the angelic. They are turkey vultures, and they are circling the dump, the *relleno sanitario* in zone 3, not far from the graveyard and El Gallito.

The zone 3 dump, ringed by nine shantytowns, is a must-see site for social activists. Over two thousand tons of garbage arrive in nearly five hundred trucks every day, and from this detritus scores of people make a living. The muni claims, probably underestimating, that there are about 850 of them, of whom more than 300 are little children.[98] Walking, often barefoot, through the rot and stench, they pick the garbage for salable items. For these people, the poorest of Guatemala City's poor, the dump is both a business and a home.

The muni has made efforts to help the children. In 1989 they opened the Jardín de Niños Santa Clara, a school and recreation center that gave kids education, food, and medical and psychiatric aid. Since then, a playground and a second primary school have been christened. The Boy Scouts set up a troop in 1999, in the same year that the NGO Safe Passage, the area's most successful project, was born.[99] The image of imparting the sorts of civic virtues the Boy Scouts promote in this postapocalyptic landscape borders on the surreal. More easily grasped are the proliferation of gangs, the ubiquity of glue sniffing, and the stunning rates of rape and murder and theft. To me, what is most astonishing about this most brutal of places is that few people seem to believe anymore that the structural problems that keep it in existence will ever go away. This was not the case when I first visited in 1991. There were still guerrillas in that year, and Cuatro Grados Norte and the towering malls had yet to be invented. Countless people told me about their visions of social change in which this horror would be gone. Not so in the new millennium. Now there is just the hope that the NGOs or maybe the Evangelicals will somehow bestow a little comfort on these children.

This chart is reproduced directly from the archival source with only slight changes to the spelling of some company names, not all of which may be accurate. While the exact source and date are unknown and while the information may be incomplete, the list is fascinating for its attempt to chart and document the extent of foreign penetration of the economy during an epoch of intense political violence. Source: "Anexo: Lista de empresas transnacionales en Centroamérica (1978)." CIRMA: Antigua, Guatemala. Clasificación Infostelle 09/02/04. "Relaciones económicas; empresas extranjeras/multinacionales en Guatemala/CA."

North American Capital

Food and Agroindustry

1. Beatrice Foods, Inc.: (i) Fábrica de Productos Alimenticios René, S.A. (ii) Asunto Carimba (iii) Fábrica de Productos Alimenticios Peter Pan, S.A.
2. Bemis: Bemis Internacional, S.A.
3. Borden, Inc: Compañía Internacional de Ventas Centroamericana, S.A.
4. Central Soya: (i) Central Soya de Guatemala, S.A. (ii) Industria Nacional de Concentrados Integrales Centroamericanos.
5. Coca-Cola: (i) Industria de Café, S.A. (INCASA); (ii) Productos Alimenticios Sharp, S.A. (iii) Industrias del Pacífico, S.A. (iv) Tenco.
6. CPC International: Productos de Maíz de Alimentos, S.A.
7. Del Monte: (i) Bandegua: Subsidiaria de la Canadian Canners Ltd.; (ii) Del Monte Internacional, Inc. y Cía. Ltd.
8. Foremost-McKesson: Foremost Dairies de Guatemala, S.A.

9. General Mills: (i) Industria Harinera Guatemalteca, S.A. (ii) Industria del Maíz, S.A. (iii) General Mills de Guatemala.
10. Kellogg's: Kellogg's de Centroamérica.
11. Nabisco: J. B. William y Cía. Ltda.
12. Pet, Inc.: Compañía American D.A. Refrigeration.
13. Philip Morris: Tabacalera Centroamericana, S.A. (TACASA).
14. Pillsbury: (i) Molinos Modernos, S.A. (ii) Productos Alimenticios Imperial, S.A. (iii) Fábricas Kurts, Matéu, Guarin y Cía. Ltda.
15. Ralston Purina Co.: (i) Auto Cafés Purina, Ltda.; (ii) Incubadoras Centroamericanas, S.A. (iii) Purina de Guatemala, Ltda.
16. Riviana Foods, Inc. (Tex.): (i) Alimentos Kerns de Guatemala, S.A. (ii) Envases Industriales, S.A.; (iii) Empresa Agro-Mercantil y de Servicio (iv) Agencia Marítima, S.A.
17. Standard Brands: (i) Dely, S.A. (ii) Pan-American Standard Brands, Inc.
18. Stratford of Texas, Inc.: Plantadores Ornamentales Unidos, S.A. Dependiente de la Green Thumb Corp.
19. United Brands: (i) United Fruit Co. (ii) Cía. Agrícola de Guatemala (iii) Numar, S.A. (iv) Unimar, S.A.
20. Universal Foods: (i) Central Products Universal (ii) Levaduras Universal.
21. Warner Lambert: Productos Adams.

Chemicals and Pharmaceuticals

1. Abbott Laboratories: Abbott Laboratorios, S.A.
2. A. H. Robins Co., Inc. (Va.): (i) Industrial Santa Agape, S.A. (ii) Cyanamid—Inter-American Corp. (iii) Shuton, S.A.
3. American Home Products Corp. (N.Y.): Productos del Hogar, S.A.
4. Avon Products, Inc. (N.Y.): Productos Avon de Guatemala, S.A.
5. Boise Cascade: (i) Bolsas de Papel, S.A. (ii) Industria Papelera Centroamericana, S.A. (iii) Empresa Comercial e Industrial Hispania, S.A. (iv) Litografía de Guatemala, S.A.
6. Bristol Myers: Bristol Myers de Guatemala, S.A.
7. Celanese Corporation: Cía. Comercial e Industrial Celanesa Guatemala, S.A.
8. Chesebrough-Pond's: Chesebrough-Pond's International Ltda.
9. Colgate Palmolive: (i) Colgate Palmolive (Central America) Inc. y Cía. Ltda. (ii) Industria Química, S.A. (iii) Temco, S.A.
10. Dart Industries: Plásticos Centroamericanos Tupperware, S.A.

11. Eli Lilly & Co.: Eli Lilly de Centroamérica, S.A.

12. Exxon: (i) Essochem de Centroamérica, S.A. (ii) Esso Standard Guatemala, Inc. (iii) Esso Central America, S.A.

13. E. I. DuPont de Nemours Co.: Química DuPont Centroamérica, S.A.

14. Firestone Tire and Rubber Co.: (i) Firestone Plantation Co. (ii) Firestone de Guatemala.

15. Gulf Oil Corporation: Petróleos Gulf de Guatemala, S.A.

16. H. B. Fuller Co.: (i) Kativo de Guatemala, S.A. (ii) Fuller y Cía de Centroamérica, S.A.

17. Helena Rubinstein (Colgate Palmolive): Helena Rubinstein de Centroamérica, S.A.

18. Johnson & Johnson: Cía. de Productos para la Salud, Johnson & Johnson, S.A.

19. Norton Simon, Inc., (N.Y.): Max Factor de Centroamérica, S.A.

20. Miles Laboratory: (i) Miles Overseas Inc., Guatemala (ii) Laboratorios Miles de Centroamérica.

21. Monsanto Co. (St. Louis): (i) Monsanto Centroamérica (Guatemala), S.A. (ii) Monoil Guatemala, Inc.

22. Pfizer, Inc.: Pfizer Corporación.

23. Revlon: Revlon Guatemala, S.A.

24. Richardson-Merrell, Inc. (i) Vick Chemical; (ii) Richardson Interamericana, Inc.

25. SCM: (i) Pinturas Centroamericanas, S.A. (PINCASA) (ii) Industria Química Guatemalteca de Adhesivos y Derivados (INDUCOL) (iii) Empresa Nacional de Plásticos (ENAPLA).

26. Squibb: (i) Laboratoria Farmacéutico Squibb, S.A. (ii) Squibb Mathieson International.

27. Standard Oil (Calif.): (i) Refinería Petrolera de Guatemala-California Inc. (GUATCAL) (ii) Refinería de Asfaltos Chevron, Inc. (iii) Cía. Petrolera Chevron, Ltda.

28. Sterling Drugs: Sterling Products International, S.A.

29. Texaco: (i) Texaco Petroleum, Co. (ii) Texaco Guatemala Inc.

30. The Goodyear Tire & Rubber Co.: (i) Gran Industria de Neumáticos de Centroamérica, S.A. (GINSA) (ii) Plantaciones de Hule Goodyear, S.A., Finca las Delicias (iii) Goodyear International Corporation.

31. The Dow Chemical Co. (Mich.): Dow Química de Guatemala, Ltda.

32. The Diversey Corp. (Chicago): Diversey Química Ltda.

33. United Brands: Polymer [sic].

34. Upjohn: (i) Cía. Farmacéutica Upjohn, S.A. (ii) Upjohn Company.
35. Warner Lambert: Laboratorios Productos Farmacéuticos, S.A.

Banks and Financial Institutions

1. American International Group: (i) American International Underwriters (Guatemala) S.A. (ii) La Seguridad de Centroamérica, Cía. de Seguros, S.A. (iii) La Seguridad de Centroamérica, Cía. de Finanzas, S.A.
2. Bank of America: Banco de América N.T. & S.A.
3. Bank of California: Banco de Comercio e Industria, S.A.
4. First National Boston Corp.: Servicios Comerciales e Industriales, S.A.
5. The Continental Corp.: (i) Seguros Universales, S.A. (ii) Comercial Aseguradora Suizo-American, S.A. (CASA).

Appliances, Parts, Equipment

1. Bendix Corporation: Industria Filtros FRAM de Centroamérica, S.A.
2. Cluett Peabody & Co. Inc. (N.Y.): (i) Arrow de Centroamérica Ltd. (ii) Arrow Interamérica y Cía. Ltda.
3. Colt Industries (N.Y.): Industria Fairbanks Morse Centroamérica, S.A.
4. ESB Inc. (Philadelphia): (i) ESB Dúrales, S.A. (ii) Distribuidora M.A. Nícol y Cía. Ltda.
5. Genesco, Inc.: Formfit de Guatemala y Cía.
6. General Telephone & Electronics Corp. (Minn.): G.T.E. Sylvania, S.A.
7. Gillette: (i) Gillette de Centroamérica, S.A.
8. Hobart Manufacturing: (i) Electrodos de Centroamérica Ltda. (Hobart Ayau y Cía. Ltda.)
9. IU International Corp. (Wilmington, Del.): (i) Empresa Agropecuaria Patzulin, S.A. (ii) Monte de Oro, S.A. (iii) International (Guatemala), S.A. (iv) Industria Guatemalteca de Macadamia, S.A. (Inguamasa).
10. Otis Elevator Co.: Otis Elevator Co.
11. PET: Cía. Americana de Refrigeración de Centroamérica, S.A.
12. Pittsburgh–Des Moines Steel: (i) Transformadora de Acero Tissor, Pittsburg–Des Moines & Co., S.A. (TIPIC) (ii) Cilindros de Centroamérica, S.A. (CILCASA).
13. SCM Corporation (N.Y.): (i) Galvanizadora Centroamericana, S.A. (GALCASA) (ii) Servicios Mínimas, S.A. [sic] (iii) Pinturas Centroamericanas, S.A.
14. Singer: Singer Sewing Machine Co.
15. Tappan Co.: Industria Metalúrgica Centroamericana, S.A. (IMCA).

16. The Stanley Works: Herramientas Collins, S.A.
17. U.S. Freight: Tropical Gas Co. Inc. (Tropigas).
18. Weyerhaeuser: Cajas y Empaques de Guatemala, S.A.

Business and Services

1. Foremost-McKesson: Cocinas Foremost.
2. Gulf & Western Industries: Cinema International Corp.
3. IBM Corp. (N.Y.): IBM de Guatemala, S.A.
4. ITT Corp. (N.Y.); (i) Avis de Guatemala, S.A. (ii) ITT de Guatemala, S.A.
5. Minnesota Mining & Manufacturing: Minnesota 3M International, Inc.
6. National Cash Register Company (Ohio): Cajas Registradoras Nacional Azmitia y Cía. Ltda.
7. Pillsbury: Pillsbury Holdings Canada, Ltd.
8. Xerox: Xerox de Guatemala, S.A.

Minerals and Forestry

1. Hannah Mining: Exploraciones y Explotaciones Mineras Izabal, S.A.
2. Minnesota Mining & Manufacturing: Minas de Oriente, S.A. (MINORSA).
3. United States Steel Corp. (Pittsburgh): Industria de Tubos y Perfiles, S.A.
4. Koppers Co.: (i) Impregnadora de Madera de Guatemala, S.A. (ii) Maderas del Norte.

Transportation and Tourism

1. Pan American World Airways: Pan American Airways.
2. Riviana Foods: Agencia Marítima, S.A.
3. U.S. Freight: Coordinated Caribbean Transport, Inc. (CCT).
4. The Interpublic Group of Companies, Inc. (N.Y.): Publicidad McCann-Erickson Centroamericana (Guatemala), S.A.
5. Rolling Inc. (N.Y.): Orkin International, Inc. Cía. Exterminadora Orkin de Guatemala, S.A.
6. J. Walter Thompson (N.Y.): APCU Thompson Asociados, S.A.
7. UAL: (i) Hoteles Baltimore de Guatemala, S.A. (ii) Hotel Camino Real.

Construction

1. Dravo: Cía. Minera de la Sierra (COMISA).

Dutch Transnationals

Chemical-Pharmaceutical

1. A.C.F. Holding N.V. (Amsterdam): (i) ACF Guatemala, S.A. (ii) Ensayos Agrícolas, S.A.
2. Royal Dutch Petroleum Company: (i) Distribuidora Guatemalteca Shell (ii) Guatemalteca Shell (iii) Refinería Petrolera de Guatemala-California, Inc. (iv) Shell Química de Guatemala.

Business and Services

1. Handel en Industrie Maatschappij "CETECO" (Ceteco Trading and Industrial Corporation) N.V. Ámsterdam: Comercial Curaçao de Guatemala, S.A.

English Transnationals

Food and Agroindustry

1. Dalgety, Ltd. (Londres): Agrovita, S.A.

Banks and Finance

1. Lloyds Bank, Ltd. (London): Almacenadora Guatemalteca, S.A.
2. Sun Alliance and London Insurance, Ltd. (London): Alianza Compañía Anglo-Centroamericana de Seguros, S.A.

Other

1. Reed International, Ltd. (London): Firgos (Guatemala), S.A.

Japanese Transnationals

Food and Agroindustry

1. Mitsubishi Corp. (Tokio): Pesca, S.A.

Appliances, Parts, Equipment

1. Chori Company, Ltd. (Osaka): Chori Co.
2. Marubeni Corp. (Osaka): Motores Hino de Guatemala, S.A.
3. Matsushita Electric Industrial Co., Ltd. (Osaka): National de Guatemala, S.A. [sic].

West German Transnationals

Chemical-Pharmaceutical

1. Beiersdorf (Hamburg): Beiersdorf de Centroamérica, S.A.
2. Henkel (Dusseldorf): Henkel Centroamericana, S.A.
3. Hoechst (Frankfurt): Química Hoechst de Guatemala, S.A.
4. Merck (Frankfurt): Merck Centroamericana, S.A.
5. Shering (Berlin): Shering Guatemalteca, S.A.
6. Schlubach (Hamburg): Shlubach de Guatemala, Ltda.

Banks and Finance

1. Dresdner Bank (Frankfurt): Financiera Industrial y Agropecuaria, S.A. (FIASA)

Canadian and U.S.-Canadian Transnationals

Mining and Forestry

1. Inco Ltd. (Toronto): Explotaciones y exploraciones Mineras Izabal, S.A.
2. Mineral Resources International Ltd. (Toronto): Azufres de Guatemala, Ltd.

Transportation and Tourism

1. Westcoast Transmission Co., Ltd. (Vancouver): Cía. Zamora, S.A.

Other

1. Mohawk Industries Ltd. (Vancouver): Cabos Caribe Guatemala, Cía. Ltda.

French Transnationals

Chemical-Pharmaceutical

1. Chimio S.A. (Paris): Roussel Centroamericana.

Swiss Transnationals

Food and Agroindustry

1. Nestlé: Savory, S.A.

Introduction

1. Two works powerfully influenced my approach: Camus, *Ser indígena en la Ciu-dad de Guatemala*, and Cronon, *Nature's Metropolis*. Camus studied Maya in a variety of gritty Guatemala City spaces; most work on this population focuses on remote, rural locations. Cronon's book views urban and rural phenomena as a cohesive whole tied together in a complex matrix of relations of production and exchange. "A city's history," writes Cronon, "must also be the history of its human countryside, and of the natural world within which city and country are both located. . . . Nature's Metropolis and the Great West are in fact different labels for a single region and the relationships that defined it. By erasing the false boundary between them, we can begin to recover their common past" (19). Numerous geographers have also influenced my thinking: Allen, Massey, and Cochrane, *Rethinking the Region*; Diamond, *Collapse*; Harvey, *The Condition of Postmodernity*; Lovell, *Conquest and Survival in Colonial Guatemala*; Sahlins, *Boundaries*; and Soja, *Postmodern Geographies*. On social space, see Lefebvre, *The Production of Space*, a work discussed further in chapter 3.

2. Statistics on Guatemala are unreliable and are rounded off throughout this book. Of the 80 percent of the population that is impoverished, two in three live in extreme poverty, earning under two dollars a day, and with chronic malnutrition. Infrastructure, health care, and education are sorely lacking. Figures can be found on the U.S. Department of State and World Bank websites: http://dev data.worldbank.org (see genderstats and hnpstats) and www.state.gov.

3. Development is an organizing and central theme in Guatemalan culture, poli-tics, and public discourse. The word itself, *desarrollo*, means so many things to different people that it has been emptied of its real-world meaning. I make a key distinction: infrastructure building vs. development. The first is just what the word implies: a sewer, a school, a highway. Development, however, is a cultural phenomenon: a sewer so we won't be a backward nation, a school so children learn middle-class values, a Pan-American Highway so we bring democracy and

prosperity to all. Development, besides referring to what has become a contemporary industry in its own right, is a word that evokes a diverse set of values, goals, and belief systems—a word located where culture and infrastructure meet.

4. I borrow this term from Herf, *Reactionary Modernism*.

5. The birth of the modern state dates to 1871, when, after spending most of the colonial and early national periods casting about for an economic motor, the elite finally landed upon coffee, and liberal growers took the government by arms. A liberal-dictatorial state persisted until 1944, with a short break, a moment of possibility, in the 1920s. In general, the liberals looked to agroexport-led economic growth fueled by infrastructure development like roads, ports, railroads, etc., forced labor, and debt peonage. They were positivist and anticlerical. Under their rule, a nationalist military began to flourish even as foreign penetration of the economy increased. From the late nineteenth century onward, German coffee and U.S. banana concerns entered Guatemala, and into the twentieth century the U.S.-based United Fruit Company (UFCO), came to own much of the nation's lowlands as well as nearly all its railroads, even as other foreign firms owned the telephones, telegraphs, and electric company. Much of this U.S. entry into the economy dates to the twenty-two-year regime of the dictator Manuel Estrada Cabrera (1898–1920), and it is with his fall and the brief fluorescence of democracy that followed that this book begins.

6. Monzón Lemus, *Camino de adolescente*. The title translates as "Way of the Adolescent: The Life of Ramón González in the Barrio El Gallito."

7. Ibid., 1.

8. Estimates of the number of people killed during the war (nearly all by the army) vary from roughly two hundred thousand to over three hundred thousand.

9. No serious historian agrees with the pop culture conception that dates globalization to the late twentieth or early twenty-first century; it has deeper roots. Still, undeniable phenomena underpin the everyday use of the word, which is often trotted out along with its bedfellows, *post-Fordism* and *postmodernism*. Money and data flash across borders. A cyber-world hovers like an aura above the physical. Media mixes cultures. There's marimba in McDonald's. Malls make an archipelago of generic, could-be-anywhere-space on an ever more transnational planet. It's hard to describe the phenomenon of globalization better than Moreton, "It Came from Bentonville," 57–58. On post-Fordism and postmodernism, see Harvey, *The Condition of Postmodernity*, esp. 141–97. Harvey grounds postmodernity in a transition from "Fordist" to "flexible accumulation." Opposing interpretations are Lyotard, *The Postmodern Condition*, and Habermas, *The Philosophical Discourse of Modernity—Twelve Lectures*. For a history of theoretical debates, see Bertens, *The Idea of the Postmodern*. On late capitalism, see Mandel, *Late Capitalism*, and for a defense of modernity, Berman, *All That Is Solid Melts Into Air*. On the mechanics of globalization, see Grewal, *Network Power*. Finally, in a book that deploys such sweeping terms as *globalization*, *neoliberalism*, *development*, and the like, some disclaimers are in order. In no way

do I maintain that Guatemala would not benefit from middle-class growth and all that occasions and accompanies it. Instead, I argue that a particular kind of development—always conditioned and mediated by the social, cultural, economic, and political environment in Guatemala—has historically produced more misery than upward mobility. The forces behind this kind of development are myriad and far from homogenous. I use phrases like *global corporate capital*, *corporate discourse*, and *neoliberal development* as shorthand to refer to a universe of businesses, institutions, networks, and projects as complex, incomplete, and varied as the ground-level Guatemalan structures I spend my time examining. I do not consider capital—either its global, neoliberal, corporate varieties or its grass-roots, small-business, entrepreneurial varieties—to be an autonomous social actor in some functionalist sense; and this book is not a critique of capitalism per se. My shorthand in no way implies that global corporate capital is not run by people, that it and not the Guatemalan ruling class bears responsibility for many of the nation's problems, or that it determines what happens on the ground level with one-to-one causality.

10. A trenchant analysis of contemporary democracy as a product of Cold War terror can be found in Grandin, *The Last Colonial Massacre*.

ONE. Making the Modern Anti-Modern

1. Interview, Arquitecto Fabricio González y González, Jefe de Planificación y Diseño, Municipalidad de Guatemala, 16 May 2003. It was not González who made the comments quoted farther along in the text.

2. Quijano, "Colonialism of Power, Eurocentrism, and Latin America," explores race as "a mental category of modernity" originating in the Americas. For further exploration of these ideas, see Schwartz, ed., *Implicit Understandings*.

3. See Herf, *Reactionary Modernism*.

4. See *El Imparcial*, 15 September 1925, 10, and 19 October 1929, 6, for examples of many such images. For a history of the city's commercial space, see Gellert and Pinto Soria, *Ciudad de Guatemala*.

5. Leach, *Land of Desire*, 103.

6. *Acacia: Órgano de divulgación de la Gran Logia de Guatemala*, Year 1, Vol. 1 (December 1947), 3.

7. "Maximón: El santo más insólito," *El Globo* (Guatemala: Editorial Heraldo, S.A.), 28 March 2003.

8. *Esotérika* (Guatemala: Akelarre/Grupo Extra), Week 4 (2003).

9. *Estudio: Revista mensual de ciencias y filosofía transcendental* (Guatemala), 1:1 (15 March 1922), 45–56, and passim. *Estudio's* editors were Rodolfo Leiva and Carlos Wyld Ospina, both leaders of the movement in Guatemala. For a complete treatment, see Causús Arzú and García Giráldez, *Las redes intelectuales centroamericanas*.

10. For a sample of spiritist publications, see *Brahma-Vidya: Revista teosófica, órgano de las Logias Gnosis y Atma* (1925), and *Luz del Porvenir: Revista de propaganda,*

órgano de la Federación Espiritista de Guatemala (1927). *El Imparcial* frequently covered theosophy: 10 March 1923, 19 (with selections from a speech given by Rodolfo Leíva, president of the Gnosis Lodge, on its founding—an excellent sample of how positivist science and "reason" met "Divine Wisdom"); 5 May 1923, 10 (in which Wyld Ospina opines on theosophy's modernity); 7 February 1924, 5 (algebra and Arabs); 23 February 1924; 30 June 1924, 7 (on masons).

11. *Estudio* 1:1 (15 March 1922), 25, 87–89.

12. *El Imparcial*, 7 August 1929, 1, 2. A complete history of vitalism and eugenics may be found in Causús Arzú and García Giráldez, *Las redes intelectuales*.

13. Vela, *Retóricas de post-guerra*. This book, published by Vela's heirs, reprints his articles in *El Imparcial* on high thought and culture from 1932. The last essay, "La palabra que pronunciara América," covers Pan-Americanism. See 108–14.

14. Guatemalan students founded a cultural club in 1928, naming it—as did their counterparts in many countries—Ariel, in honor of Rodó's work, already over a quarter century old. *El Imparcial*, 8 February 1928. A summary of relevant literature is found in Williamson, *The Penguin History of Latin America*, 284–310, 513–49. See also Causús Arzú and García Giráldez, *Las redes intelectuales*, 152–61.

15. *Bulletin of the Pan-American Union* [hereafter BPAU], (May 1928), 497–504, and (March 1930), 226 (citation); *Chronology of the Pan-American Highway Project* (Washington: Pan-American Union, Technical Unit on Tourism, Department of Economic Affairs, 1963), 1–2; *El Imparcial*, 19 March 1927 and 1 January 1930, 3.

16. *El Imparcial*, 14 October 1922, 9–11, 29 August 1925, 3 and 3 February 1928.

17. This does not imply that there was not rural organizing; there was. See Grandin, *The Last Colonial Massacre*, 27–30.

18. *Más de cien años del movimiento obrero urbano en Guatemala*, vol. 1, *Artesanos y obreros en el período liberal (1877–1944)*, 31–34, 71, 106; *Páginas Sindicales Guatemala* (n.p.: Iepala Editorial, n.d.), 4–5. This document is a well-substantiated history of the Guatemalan labor movement from its inception to the end of the 1970s, donated anonymously to CIRMA, a research institution in Antigua, Guatemala (indexed under "Donativos").

19. Bushnell and Macaulay, *The Emergence of Latin America in the Nineteenth Century*, 284–85; McCreery, *Rural Guatemala, 1760–1940*, 168–69; *Más de cien años*, 1:16, 20–21, 25, 27, 329–38; *Páginas Sindicales Guatemala*, 5–6. On the oligarchy, including histories of families like the Castillos (the beer factory) and the Novellas (cement) back to the colonial period, as well as for insightful comments on racism, social structure, and economy in Guatemala, see Causús Arzú, *Guatemala: Linaje y racismo*.

20. *Boletín Internacional* (México: Frente Popular 31 de Enero, FP-31), May 1982, 9; *Más de cien años*, 1:16, 20–21, 25, 27, 31–39, 64–72, 329–39; *Páginas Sindicales Guatemala*, 6.

21. In 1911 labor leaders from around the isthmus had met in the Primer Congreso Obrero Centroamericano in El Salvador, where they debated strategies to improve their economic conditions. They resolved to use mutual aid and cultural-

educational activities to improve their lot instead of going on strike or forming political parties. *Más de cien años*, 1:49–60.

22. *Boletín Internacional*, May 1982, 9; *Páginas Sindicales Guatemala*, 7–9.

23. *Más de cien años*, 1:125–26; *Páginas Sindicales Guatemala*, 8. The AFL sponsored a Pan-American labor meeting in 1918 that contributed to the formation of a major Guatemalan labor confederation. Workers in this organization soon helped to overthrow Estrada Cabrera.

24. *Más de cien años*, 1:128, 141–44, 203–5.

25. *Páginas Sindicales Guatemala*, 8. CIO-organized sailors for UFCO supported Guatemalan UFCO workers, in one notable example of how international solidarity, when it went beyond paperwork and congresses, could prove its power at the grass roots.

26. *El Imparcial*, 6–17 February 1923, passim; *Más de cien años*, 1:333–35, 339; *Páginas Sindicales Guatemala*, 9.

27. *El Imparcial*, 15 January 1925, 22 August 1925, 29 August 1925, 4 September 1925, 30 November 1925, 15 December 1925, 16 December 1925, and 22 December 1925, 3; *Más de cien años*, 1:190, 339; *Páginas sindicales Guatemala*, 9.

28. This is a greatly simplified gloss of complex labor politics covered at great length in the sources cited here, especially *Más de cien años del movimiento urbano*. *El Imparcial*, 3 February 1926, 29 March 1926; *Más de cien años*, 1:116, 206–16, 235, 335–39.

29. Very dubious statistics indicate that as much as 12 percent of the nonagricultural, urban workforce may have organized by 1927. *Más de cien años*, 1:238–39.

30. *Más de cien años*, 1:144, 211, 217–18, 246, 260.

31. Obando Sánchez, *Memorias*, 11–33.

32. Ibid., 36. Kemmerer missions enforced fiscal orthodoxy and essentially constituted an early form of IMF restructuring programs.

33. Ibid., 34–75; *El Imparcial*, 15 October 1926, 12 November 1926, 19 April 1927; *Más de cien años*, 1:222, 251–52.

34. Obando Sánchez, *Memorias*, 161, and 76–161 passim.

35. The phrase "laboring of culture" comes from Denning, *The Cultural Front*.

36. See Nelson, *A Finger in the Wound*, 46–50, 381.

37. *El Imparcial*, 7 August 1922.

38. The Universidad Popular was inaugurated with state support in March of 1923. *El Imparcial*, 2 March 1923. The dictator Jorge Ubico eliminated it early in his rule, in June of 1932. *Más de cien años*, 1:294.

39. On Le Bon, the generation of the 1890s, philosophy, and fascism, see Hughes, *Consciousness and Society*, 33–42 and 63–104 passim; Lees, *Cities Perceived: Urban Society in European and American Thought, 1820–1940*, 170–71; and, most importantly, Sternhell, *Neither Right nor Left*, 35–37 and passim. From the beginning, one of the goals of the Popular University was to educate campesinos as well as urban workers. In 1923 administrators sent thousands of leaflets for basic literacy and arithmetic to fincas. *El Imparcial*, 8 June 1923. Wyld Ospina quota-

tion is from "Obrerismo y el problema obrero en Guatemala," *El Imparcial*, 19 September 1925, 6.

40. *Más de cien años*, 1:240. The union movement spread throughout all of urbanized Guatemala during the 1920s, though its most important node remained Guatemala City, followed by Quetzaltenango. The UFCO and IRCA workers brought unionism to the ports, docks, and plantations as well. The state and local strongmen actively discouraged rural organizing, but, as we have seen, there were strikes on the fincas by the turn of the decade. It is reasonable to suppose that the rural workers might have forged solidarity with the urban, not vice versa—a process that during the Revolution of 1944–54 remains understudied.

41. AGCA B/22231 (Fomento: Lotificaciones [Lot.]), 1923, Expediente [hereafter abbreviated Exp.] 3373. The government responded that the workers should frame their request according to the Expropriation Law of 1899.

42. AGCA B (Fomento), passim.

43. AGCA B /22237 (Fomento: Lot. El Gallito), 1 October 1930, Rafael Hernández to Aguilar V.

44. For example, see "Normas para la construcción de casas para obreros: Es hora de redimir a las clases trabajadores," *El Imparcial*, 31 May 1924, 7.

45. AGCA B /22231 (Fomento: Lotificaciones), 1928, Exp. 3979.

46. AGCA B /22058 (Fomento: Asociaciones, Sociedades), July 1931, Exp. (F.O.R.); *Más de cien años*, 1:259–62.

47. AGCA B /22058 (Fomento: Asociaciones, Sociedades), July 1931, Exp. (F.O.R.).

48. Causús Arzú and García Geráldez, *Las redes intelectuales*, 289.

49. Herf, *Reactionary Modernism*.

50. De León Aragón, *Caída de un régimen*; Sieder, "Paz, Progreso, Justicia y Honradez," 283–302. For an excellent example of Ubiquista modernist discourse and the cult of leadership, see "Diez años de progreso, 1931–1941," Supplement to *Luz* (Guatemala, 14 February 1941).

51. These state projects had extremely mixed results that varied regionally. For an excellent overview and an examination of the impact among the K'iche' elite of Quetzaltenango, see Grandin, *The Blood of Guatemala*, 194–96. See also Sieder, "Paz, Progreso, Justicia y Honradez."

52. On the banking system and currency (the quetzal replaced the peso in 1924), see *El Imparcial*, 19 September 1925, 7; *Más de cien años*, 1:33–34. A detailed description of the Central Bank and National Mortgage Bank can be found in BPAU (July 1937), 555–63.

53. *Más de cien años*, 1:264, 338.

54. The regime even decapitated the Federación Obrera Guatemalteca, a strong, openly anticommunist union affiliated with both the PAU's labor confederation and the AFL. Dosal, *Power in Transition*, 66; *Más de cien años*, 1:270–74, 277–93; Obando Sánchez, *Memorias*, 75–109.

55. Banana plantation strikes sparked both a near general strike and an army coup attempt in Honduras; Sandino was irritating the Nicaraguan Somoza regime;

and while San Salvadoran workers and citizens—hard hit by the precipitous fall of coffee prices at the onset of the Depression—were flooding the streets with waves of protests, the campesinos unleashed an uprising, and the specter of Farabundo Martí and a Communist-controlled popular revolution loomed large. *Más de cien años*, 1:272.

56. *Revista Lacandones*, the magazine of the explorer's club of the same name, whose stated goal of "producing strong men, scientifically and morally prepared," noted the rapid growth of the clubs and associations around Guatemala. They also promoted the Boy Scouts' national Explorers Day, to be celebrated with team sports competitions in October of 1935. *Revista Lacandones*, 1:1 (1 August 1935), 1 (citation); 1:2 (1 September 1935), 1, 14; *El Imparcial*, 9 December 1924, 8; 18 February 1927, 5; 22 September 1927, 7; 18 February 1928, 2d section, 1. For an examination of similar dynamics in Germany, see Fritzsche, *A Nation of Fliers.*

57. *El Imparcial*, 17 January 1931; *Más de cien años*, 1:256–58; "News Survey of the Month," *The Inter-American* 3, no. 8 (August 1944), 3.

58. Alarmed by events in Europe, the U.S. State Department, under Secretary of State Cordell Hull, and the PAU held an Inter-American Conference for the Maintenance of Peace in Buenos Aires in 1936. The conference was a watershed for the institutionalization of corporate-capitalist ideology and for the transnational creation of space. All nations agreed to work toward the speedy completion of the Pan-American Highway, aided by propaganda such as a Pan-American radio hour in every country. Other conventions covered Promotion of Inter-American Cultural Relations; Interchange of Publications; Artistic Exhibitions; Peaceful Orientation of Public Instruction; and Facilities for Educational and Publicity Films. BPAU (February 1937), 100, 87–109 passim (citation 107–8).

59. *La Aurora, Revista dedicada a nuestra Feria Nacional de Noviembre 1935*, Year 1, no. 2 (November 1935).

60. *Ferias*, or fairs, are extremely important in Guatemalan culture. Each town has a feria on (and around) its saint's day; Ubico's attempt to co-opt and remake this tradition was no small act. The November fairs serve as a reminder of the contradictions of the age: capitalist promotion fueled by forced labor; capitalist development driven by finca agriculture and a foreign banana enclave; and capitalist cultural engineering dressed up with "fascist aesthetics" and civic groups but based, ultimately, on violence. The topic of fascist aesthetics is taken up in Golsan, ed., *Fascism, Aesthetics and Culture*. On commodities, exhibitions, and capitalism, see Richards, *The Commodity Culture of Victorian England*. For a good example of analysis of state pageantry, including beauty contests, see Grandin, *The Blood of Guatemala.*

61. See González Orellana, *Historia de la educación en Guatemala*, 369–73; Grandin, *The Blood of Guatemala*, 195; Kobrak, *Organizing and Repression in the University of San Carlos, Guatemala, 1944 to 1996*, 11–13.

62. This from an address of 1940 by a PAU officer to the Rotary Club of Grand Rapids, Michigan. BPAU (February 1941), 116–24.

63. Students saw films, planted trees, delivered compositions, and put on plays. In Guatemala the Rotary Club sponsored a special issue of the newspaper *Nuestro Diario* to commemorate the festivities. In the United States, the Los Angeles Chamber of Commerce sponsored an event, in league with the Advertising Club of Los Angeles, the Foreign Trade Club of Southern California, and the Pacific Geographic Society. The president of Pomona College delivered a speech entitled "Building International Friendship." Meanwhile, the U.S. Bureau of Foreign and Domestic Commerce distributed materials to boards of education around the United States, and schools also got help from local Rotary Clubs, who sent members into the classroom. BPAU (September 1936), 710–20.

64. *Boletín Vial Panamericana* (June 1937), 96–97.

65. See Cambranes, *Café y campesinos en Guatemala, 1853–1897*, and Williams, *States and Social Evolution*.

66. *Etcétera: Revista Popular* (June 1938), 14.

67. Grandin, *The Blood of Guatemala*, 54.

68. *Modern Mexico/México Moderno* (New York: Mexican Chamber of Commerce of the U.S.), V:50 (March 1934): 15. Compare the work of Esther Born, a promoter of modernism who likened the lines of the pyramid of Cuicuilco to the architecture of Le Corbusier. Born, *The New Architecture in Mexico*, 2.

69. *Modern Mexico/México Moderno*, 1:7 (August 1930), 25.

70. BPAU (July 1939), 387–412.

71. AGCA 3/Caja Clas. 631, 950.1, 128.11, No. Ord. 47404, 47601, 47156 (MCOP 1939–46), 29 August 1939, Exp. (Luis Fernando Flores).

72. Rubenstein, "On Not Performing: Chichicastenango, 1934," manuscript. With thanks to the author.

73. Ibid.

74. Eben F. Comins, "Indians That I Have Drawn," BPAU (July 1939), 368–79 (citation, 369).

75. Ibid., 369–70.

76. See Grandin, *The Blood of Guatemala* and *The Last Colonial Massacre*. For an examination of "procedural culture," or "the associations, understandings, and conventional behavior that emerge from recurring social interactions across local and translocal boundaries" during state formation in late nineteenth-century Guatemala, see Watanabe, "Culturing Identities." The most comprehensive source on ethnic, economic, and social relations in the Guatemalan countryside remains McCreery, *Rural Guatemala, 1760–1940*. Covering Momostenango, but an invaluable source in general, is Carmack, *Rebels of Highland Guatemala*.

77. Indigenismo hardly promoted an advanced rhetoric in Guatemala in the 1930s. According to Viriginia Garrard-Burnett, under Ubico's rule, "the theoretical conflation of alcoholism and indigenismo was fully evolved," such that the drunken Indian majority was held responsible for Guatemala's underdevelopment. Garrard-Burnett, "Indians are Drunks and Drunks are Indians," 341.

78. BPAU (October 1940), 708.

79. Handy, *Revolution in the Countryside*, 50–51 (citation, 50). See also BPAU (October 1940), 702–12. At first, no Indians were going to be invited to the Congress on Indian Life. "The attendance of various Indian groups was one of the most notable and distinguishing aspects of the Congress," the BPAU reported. "In the beginning there had been no little skepticism over the idea of inviting Indians to be present, but the merit and astuteness of the proposal became clearly evident during the Congress. The Indian groups established among themselves a great bond of companionship and sympathy. . . . A letter was read from an Indian named Jasper Hill of the Council Fire of Canada which was a most extraordinary document for its sentiments of human dignity, its poetic expression, and the pride with which it sought for the members of the indigenous races the title of the first Americans." BPAU (October 1940), 706.

80. On the Juntas, the *jefe político* of the department would serve as the minister of agriculture's liaison and would nominate all members to the minister, with the exception of the mayor (*alcalde I°*) of the departmental capital (*cabecera*). The alcalde would fill the same function on the local committees. "Reglamento de las Juntas Departamentales de Agricultura y Caminos," 16 July 1931, in *Boletín de Agricultura y Caminos* (Guate.), X:7 (July 1931), 251–55.

81. This assertion is based on readings of decades of AGCA documents from the Ministerio de Agricutura y Caminos, Fomento, and the Ministerio de Comunicaciones y Obras Públicas. All sources, including the trade press and government propaganda of the era, confirm finqueros' centrality in the road-building process.

82. *Más de cien años*, 1:305.

83. AGCA B / 22574 (Fomento: Corresp. J. P. Dpto. Guate., 1930–38), 24 August 1933, Jefe Política to Fomento. Readings of Fomento and MCOP expedientes in general show a booming correspondence to the government to get exemptions from road duty for infirmity or single parenthood; a small percentage were successful.

84. Pellecer, *Memoria en dos geografías*, 74.

85. Ibid., 75.

86. Ibid.

87. Guzmán Böckler, *Donde enmudecen las conciencias*, 159; *El Imparcial*, 19 October 1923, 3; *Más de cien años*, 1:9, 227, 303.

88. BPAU (May 1933), 394; Handy, *Revolution in the Countryside*, 69; *Más de cien años*, 1:301; "Anexo: Lista de empresas transnacionales en Centroamérica (1978)," in CIRMA (Antigua, Guatemala), Clasificación Infostelle 09 / 02 / 04.

89. Depression-era deflation and the contemporaneous fall of the Salvadoran dictator Hernández Martínez also merit mention. See Orieta Alvarez, "Antecedentes históricos del proceso revolucionario de 1944–1954 en Guatemala," 1:17–23; *Más de cien años*, 1:2:2–4; Saavedra, *El color de la sangre*, 15–17.

90. See Bethell and Roxborough, eds., *Latin America between the Second World War and the Cold War, 1944–1948*; and Grandin, *The Last Colonial Massacre*.

91. BPAU (February 1941), 94–108. A timeline can be found in *Chronology of the Pan*

American Highway Project. The Pan-American Highway became a major issue in the early 1930s as a result of U.S. government support for businesses expanding abroad: U.S. investment in 1933 was just under $5 billion, about $3.3 billion of it in direct investments and the rest in bonds. In 1934 concentrated construction work on the Inter-American began, thanks to a U.S. congressional appropriation of $1 million for the effort and increased cooperation from Central American governments. At the time, less than half of the route consisted of all-weather roads. *Boletín de la Carretera Panamericana* (April 1934), 1; BPAU (April 1934), 294, (May 1935), 383, and (March 1936), 272; *El Imparcial*, 24 June 1934; "Resoluciones y otros documentos del Sexto Congreso Interamericano de Turismo relacionados con el tránsito automotor y el establecimiento de servicios en las rutas del Sistema Panamericano de Carreteras" (Washington: Unión Panamericana, Congresos Panamericanos de Carreteras, Secretaria Permanente, 1956), 5; J. Philip Van Ness, *Report on the Pan American Highway* (Washington: Department of State, 20 June 1944), 4.

92. *Design and Construction of Pan American Highway: Final Project Report* (San Francisco: [U.S. Army] War Department, Corps of Engineers, April 1944).

93. *Design and Construction of Pan American Highway*, passim (citation, 232).

94. García Vettorazzi, "El crecimiento espacial de la Ciudad de Guatemala," 10–11. The War Department's Pioneer Road/Pan-American Highway through Escuintla and Retalhuleu, later known as the Pacific Highway, was one axis of the new agroeconomy; the Atlantic Highway, begun under Arbenz in the early 1950s, was the other.

TWO. Chaos and Rationality

1. Good accounts of the invasion can be found in Gleijeses, *Shattered Hope*, and Schlesinger and Kinzer, *Bitter Fruit*.

2. For a good introduction to interpretive literature on the Revolution, see Forster, *The Time of Freedom*, and Handy, *Revolution in the Countryside*.

3. AGCA 3/Caja Clas. 121.11, No. Ord. 47082 (MCOP: Lot. Gallito y Palmita, 1943–46), 28 September 1946, Exp. (Ing. Juan Prera, Reurbanización de El Gallito), vecinos, petition, 12 September 1946.

4. Ibid., Enrique Prera H., "Proyecto de reurbanización del barrio El Gallito," June 1946.

5. Ibid.

6. Ibid.

7. Ibid., León Yela to Director General of Public Works de Dios Aguilar, 17 September 1946.

8. Ibid.

9. AGCA B/22256 (Fomento: Lot. El Gallito 1942), Memo, "Datos relacionados con la compra-venta de la Finca 'El Gallito' "; Morán Mérida, *Condiciones de vida y tenencia de la tierra en asentamientos precarios de la ciudad de Guatemala*, 18, 137–39; *Más de cien años*, I:227–46.

10. All the relevant legislation can be found in the appendix of Morán Mérida, *Condiciones de vida*. See government *Acuerdos* of 11 February 1928, 4 June 1928 and 14 June 1928, 135–41.

11. AGCA B/22237 (Fomento: Lotificación El Gallito), 30 September 1930, Exp. (Moradores de El Gallito).

12. Ibid., February 1931, Exp. (Vecinos del barrio El Gallito).

13. Ibid., October 1931, Exp. (Manuel Alvarez).

14. AGCA B/22238 (Fomento: Lot. El Gallito), June 1932, Exp. (Susana Flores R.). In 1941 the government began more systematic enforcement of building codes in El Gallito, but the measure does not appear to have resulted in a great number of lots becoming available. *Acuerdo* of 9 April 1941, in Morán Mérida, *Condiciones de vida*, 141.

15. AGCA B/22240 (Fomento: Lot. El Gallito 1934), 3 October 1934, Ministerio Público, Rosa Gómez Archila.

16. AGCA B/22237 (Fomento: Lot. El Gallito), September 1931, Exp. (Soledad Girón de C.).

17. AGCA B/22238 (Fomento: Lot. El Gallito), June 1932, Exp. (Moradores El Gallito).

18. AGCA B/Caja Clas. 121.11, No. Ord. 47082 (MCOP: Lot. Gallito y Palmita, 1943–46), 2 February 1946, DGOP informe. According to Public Works, the excavations were causing landslides and creating mosquito breeding grounds.

19. AGCA B/22238 (Fomento: Lot. El Gallito), June 1932, Exp. (Moradores El Gallito).

20. AGCA B/22249 (Fomento: Lot. El Gallito [and La Palmita] 1937), February 1937, Exp. (Joaquín Chigüil Tecún). The comment on names is based on personal experience. Many of my Mayan friends who are not middle or upper class have a *cédula* (i.d.) name and a street name. Many have told me that everyone in the village changed his or her name during the violence of the 1980s; in Santiago Atitlán, the villagers burned the municipal hall of records. While this was a direct response to the genocide, documents from earlier in the century show that there has been a long-standing tradition of evading state control and surveillance through opaque naming conventions.

21. Scott, *Weapons of the Weak*. See also Scott, *Domination and the Arts of Resistance*; Guha, *Elementary Aspects of Peasant Insurgency in Colonial India*; and Guha and Spivak, eds., *Selected Subaltern Studies*.

22. AGCA 3/Caja Clas. 121.11, No. Ord. 47082 (MCOP: Lot. Gallito y Palmita, 1943–46), February 1943, Exp. (re Julio Díaz).

23. AGCA B/22240 (Fomento: Lot. El Gallito 1934), March 1934, Exp. (Rafael Hernández).

24. AGCA 3/Caja Clas. 121.11, No. Ord. 47082 (MCOP: Lot. Gallito y Palmita, 1943–46), 28 September 1946, Exp. (Ing. Juan Prera, Reurbanización de El Gallito), de Dios Aguilar to Ministro de Comunicaciones y Obras Públicas, 28 September 1946.

25. Ibid., 14 April 1945, Guardia Civil.

26. Ibid.

27. Ibid.

28. Ibid., 23 October 1946, Guardia Civil.

29. Ibid., May-June 1946, DGOP; passim.

30. Ibid., 23 October 1946, Guardia Civil.

31. Ibid., 23 October 1946, Guardia Civil, and passim; AGCA 3/Caja Clas. 121.13, 121.11, No. Ord. 47085, 47083 (MCOP: Colonias, 1947/50), 4 September 1947, MCOP/DGOP re El Gallito Evictions.

32. AGCA 3/Caja Clas. 121.11, No. Ord. 47082 (MCOP: Lot. Gallito y Palmita, 1943–46), 23 October 1946, Guardia Civil.

33. AGCA 3/Caja Clas. 121.13, 121.11, No. Ord. 47085, 47083 (MCOP: Colonias, 1947/50), 14 April 1948 (Gobernación re La Palmita), 30 March 1948, Guardia Civil informe.

34. Ibid., June 1948, Exp. (Cayetano Villalta García y comps.). There are at least three extensive packets of related expedientes and correspondence in the archive, all out of chronological order.

35. Ibid., 16 May 1947, Exp. (Flavio Villalta C. et al.).

36. PAR Secretary General José Manuel Fortuny helped to refound the Communist Party in 1947 and became one of its leaders when it emerged as the PGT in 1949. AGCA 3/Caja Clas. 121.13, 121.11, No. Ord. 47085, 47083 (MCOP: Colonias, 1947/50), 9 September 1947, Fortuny to MCOP; Alcira Goicolea, "Los diez años de primavera," 6:25; *Más de cien años del movimiento obrero urbano*, vol. 2, *El protoganismo sindical en la construcción de la democracia (1944–1954)* (Guatemala: ASIES, 1992), 137, 174.

37. AGCA 3/Caja Clas. 121.13, 121.11, No. Ord. 47085, 47083 (MCOP: Colonias, 1947/50), June 1948, Exp. (Cayetano Villalta García y comps.), 17 March 1948, Villalta G. to President Arévalo.

38. This could be an example of the Guardia playing politics to make the PAR-friendly government take its side, but the overall tenor of the documents, along with the depth of FPL organizing in the barrios during the time period, makes this seem less likely. Villalta and his neighbors were probably dealing with both parties. AGCA 3/Caja Clas. 121.13, 121.11, No. Ord. 47085, 47083 (MCOP: Colonias, 1947/50), 14 April 1948, Gobernación re La Palmita, 18 March 1948, Mayor Guerra Orellana, Jefe de la 5a. Estación de la Guardia Civil to Guardia Civil Director General Coronel Sandoval.

39. Ibid., 14 April 1948 (Gobernación re La Palmita), 27 March 1948, Villalta to Arévalo, and 30 March 1948, Guardia Civil informe.

40. Ibid., July 1947, Exp. (Vecinos, 3a C. del Bosque Final). Interestingly, legally settled neighbors in El Gallito filed suit against the invaders, making reference to their dirty habits and their open-air defecation; they referred to them as an "immoral mob." Ibid., November 1948, Exp. (Celia de la Roca y comps.).

41. AGCA B 3/Caja Clas. 161/64, 16.1, 163 (MCOP: Camp., Col., y Esc. 1951), 8 August 1951, Sec. de Obras Públicas. The colonia was in the immediate La Palmita area.

42. AGCA 3/Caja Clas. 121.13, 121.11, No. Ord. 47085, 47083 (MCOP: Colonias, 1947/50), 10 May 1948, Exp. (Soc. "Pedro Molina Flores" et al., re La Palmita, Col. Labor).

43. The CHN was charged with sales and distribution of houses; it did not own these properties until later in the decade. AGCA 3/Caja Clas. 161/64, 16.1, 163 (MCOP: Camp., Col., y Esc. 1951), 8 August 1951, Sec. de Obras Públicas; AGCA 3/Caja Clas. 161/64, 16.1, 163 (MCOP: Camp., Col., y Esc. 1951), February 1951, Exp. (Andres Samayoa Santos); AGCA 3/Caja Clas. 161/64, 16.1, 163 (MCOP: Camp., Col., y Esc. 1951), 9 May 1951, Sec. Priv. de la Presidencia.

44. AGCA 3/Caja Clas. 121.13, 121.11, No. Ord. 47085, 47083 (MCOP: Colonias, 1947/50), September 1947, Exp. (Lupe Porras Q. y comps.); 9 September 1947, Fortuny (PAR) to MCOP; AGCA 3/Caja Clas. 121.13, 121.11+ (MCOP: Colonias, 1947/50), 20 August 1947, Asturias V., Frente Popular Libertador, to Chacón P., MCOP; AGCA 3/Caja Clas. 121.13, 121.11, No. Ord. 47085, 47083 (MCOP: Colonias, 1947 / 50), 13 November 1948 (Partido Frente Popular Libertador); *Más de cien años*, 2:137–40, 174, 244.

45. The first comprised the Union of Automotive Drivers, the Postal and Telecommunications Employees, and Public Works garage workers, and the second, the teachers' union, the presidential joint chiefs of staff, railroad workers, municipal employees, and (keeping at least one original) the Union of Automotive Drivers.

46. AGCA 3/Caja Clas. 121.13, 121.11, No. Ord. 47085, 47083 (MCOP: Colonias, 1947/50), 13 November 1948 (Partido Frente Popular Libertador), 8 November 1948 letter, Ing. Amílcar Gómez Robelo, Jefe de Urbanismo, to Sub-Director de O.P. Ing. Carlos Cipriani.

47. AGCA 3/Caja Clas. 161/64, 16.1, 163 (MCOP: Camp., Col., y Esc. 1951), 11 April 1951, Memo, CHN to MCOP; AGCA 3/Caja Clas. 161/64, 16.1, 163 (MCOP: Camp., Col., y Esc. 1951), July 1951, Exp. (Pro-Colonia de Pilotos Automovilistas).

48. AGCA 3/Caja Clas. 07, 09, 011, 011.3 (MCOP: Acuerdos y decretos; planificación proyecto Desarrollo Socioeducativo Rural, 1955), 14 January 1955, Memo, Humberto Zelaya, DGOP, "Proyecto para la construcción de casas baratas para obreros, colonias rurales y edificios multifamiliares."

49. AGCA 3/Caja Clas. 121.13, 121.11, No. Ord. 47085, 47083 (MCOP: Colonias, 1947/50), 13 November 1948 (Partido Frente Popular Libertador), 8 November 1948 letter, Ing. Amílcar Gómez Robelo, Jefe de Urbanismo, to Sub-Director de O.P. Ing. Carlos Cipriani; *Actas de la Municipalidad de Guatemala*, 6 September 1961, Acta 76.

50. *Horizontes*, Órgano de publicidad de 50. grado de la Escuela Experimental Indoamericana, Colonia Bethania, no. 1, Year 1 (20 July 1953), 3; Morán Mérida, *Condiciones de vida*, 94.

51. A dutifully anticommunist neighborhood improvement committee arose soon after the invasion in 1954 but to little effect. AGCA 3/Caja Clas. 121.1 (MCOP: Col. y Camp., 1955), June 1955, Exp. (Sub-Comité de Vivienda, Comité Pro-Mejoramiento de la Colonia Bethania).

52. Nelson, *A Finger in the Wound*, 348, and passim.

53. Noble, *America by Design*. Following Herbert Marcuse, Noble (xxiii) argues that "the history of modern technology in America [i.e., the United States] is of a piece with that of the rise of corporate capitalism."

54. There is no way of knowing what the agrarian reform and all the political superstructure it entailed might have accomplished in Guatemala, though scholars view it positively. I am no exception. I believe that lower-class citizens had begun to exert control over development and that they would have continued to do so—and, indeed, that they *did*, under the very different conditions of the Cold War state.

55. The charter of the OAS was signed on 30 April 1948. A copy of the charter, along with an organizational flowchart and propagandistic editorial analysis of the act, can be found in BPAU, July 1948, 360–75. See 364–66 for a discussion of the role of the PAU within the OAS. The PAU remained in charge of the Pan-American Highway project and continued to promote agrarian and scientific education and research projects—a long-standing function of the organization conducted in tandem with U.S. corporations' investing in Latin America. For example, UFCO contributed to the foundation of the PAU's agricultural school in El Zamorano, Honduras, in 1942. *El Imparcial*, 12 May 1942; AGCA MAC/450 (Universidades, Facultades, Institutos y Escuelas del País y Extranjeros, 1944–1955), 18 February 1947, Min. Agric. to Popenoe, Escuela Agrícola Panamericana.

56. A history of international financial institutions written for a popular audience is Ellwood, *The No-Nonsense Guide to Globalization*.

57. During the Revolution of 1944–54 Guatemalans formed 536 unions, 15 labor federations, and 2 confederations. *Páginas Sindicales Guatemala*, 14.

58. Elite resistance to allegedly communist politics included not only the great planters and the Catholic Church hierarchy, but also high-ranking army officers and university students, many of them in self-imposed exile, as well. Numerous anticommunist demonstrations around the nation show that these varied factions had grass-roots support—a phenomenon described in Grandin, *The Last Colonial Massacre*, 82–86. Guatemala City municipal market vendors, for example, demonstrated on behalf of Col. Carlos Castillo Armas, who led the invasion in 1954. For examples of grass-roots anticommunism in the markets and around Guatemala, see *Correo del Occidente* (Quetzaltenango), 24 March 1952, and *El Imparcial*, 5 October 1954. On the anticommunist archbishop Mariano Rossell y Arellano and the Church in general, see *El Imparcial*, 20 April 1951, 7 November 1953, 9 April 1954; *Más de cien años*, 2:355–58; Saavedra, *El color de la sangre*, 71–72. Information on the students' Comité de Estudiantes Universitarios Anti-

comunistas can be found in "Estamos enteramente de acuerdo," Sección a cargo
del Comité de Estudiantes Universitarios Anticomunistas Guatemaltecos en
Exilio (CEUAGE), Sección de Honduras, *La República* (Tegucigalpa), I:23 (22
December 1953), 5; and CEUAGE, "Nuestras aspiraciones: Principios básicos de
nuestro programa político," *El Imparcial*, 14 January 1954, 12. Activities of the
business community are discussed in *Correo del Occidente*, May and June 1952,
passim; *El Imparcial*, 14 May 1952; García Añoveros, *Jacobo Arbenz*, 90–91; *Más
de cien años*, 2:170–80. The literature on army factionalism and anticommunism
is large, and much of it revolves around Col. Francisco Arana, one of the leaders
of the October Revolution. Arana was assassinated in 1949; supposedly, he was
planning a coup against Arévalo, and Arbenz was reported to be behind his
death, an ongoing but unconfirmed scandal in Guatemalan history. See *El Imparcial*, 7 July 1954; Gleijeses, *Shattered Hope*, 53–72; *Más de cien años*, 2:219–29.

59. The politics of modernization and the restructuring of the agrarian economy,
here summed up for brevity's sake, were extremely complex. On the indigenous
elite, who also opposed reforms, and for a trenchant analysis of conflict and
community, see Grandin, *The Blood of Guatemala*, and "Everyday Forms of State
Decomposition: Quetzaltenango, Guatemala, 1954."

60. *Más de cien años*, 2:116–17, 119–21; *Ley de Fomento Industrial*, 23 December 1947,
in *Recopilación 66* (1947–48), 136–39.

61. Plans included building highways and a port at Santo Tomás and forming a
National Electric Energy Commission (implying a threat to Electric Bond and
Share's monopoly) that would construct hydroelectric dams, beginning with the
Jurún–Marinalá facility on the Michatoya River in Escuintla. See *Octubre* (Guate-
mala: Communist Party), 25 October 1951, 5; 5 March 1953, 6; Castillo de León,
"Objetivos de Gobierno del Coronel Jacobo Arbenz Guzmán." Arbenz-era developmentalism overtly linked high-modernist engineering projects with Guatemala's
anti-modern landscape of regional specialization and local production and trade.
Constant examples of this are in government propaganda. For example, in late 1952
Campanillas, a prorevolutionary humor magazine, ran a government-written piece
touting the Atlantic Highway. The highway had touristic importance; it showed the
patriotism of the army, which was helping to build it; most of all, it would serve the
local economy of places like San Agustín Acasaguastlán and Río Hondo (fruit
producers), Estanzuela and Teculután (*panela* [brown sugarloaf]) and cheese
makers), and Gualán and La Unión (tobacco and coffee producers). "Not only will
they be able to intensify a beneficial commercial interchange among themselves,"
the editorial said, "but also, socially, their inhabitants can achieve a better mutual
understanding and a straightforward and beautiful way to fraternize." *Campanillas:
Revista Humorística* (Guatemala: October 1952), 7–9.

62. In 1949 Arévalo had signed Decree 712, the Law of Forced Rental, which empowered campesinos to compel landowners to rent them fallow lands, two years
at a time, in return for 10 percent of the harvest. "Decreto No. 712 del Congreso:

Arrendamiento obligatorio de parcelas de terreno en fincas rústicas, por dos años," *Recopilación* 68 (1949–50), 173–74. For an example of calls for agrarian reform during the Arévalo period, see *Cooperación, Revista del Departamento de Fomento Cooperativo* (Guatemala), I:2 (May 1949), 3.

63. Decreto No. 900 del Congreso, "Ley de Reforma Agraria" of 17 June 1952, *Recopilación* 71 (1952–53), 20–31; Guerra-Borges, "Semblanza de la Revolución Guatemalteca de 1944–1954," 6:14; Handy, *Revolution in the Countryside*, 26, 38–39, 74, 81; *Más de cien años*, 2:244. According to Handy (39), Arbenz's economic program was extensively based on the thinking of George Britnell, a Canadian economist who had prepared a report on Guatemala's economy for the International Bank for Reconstruction and Development, that is, the World Bank, in 1950.

64. "Arbenz reafirmó su programa de tierra, pan e industrialización," *Octubre* (Guatemala: Communist Party), no. 121 (5 March 1953), 5–6. Seventy-eight kilometers of the Atlantic Highway had been paved in the last year.

65. Paradoxically, the very population being engineered—the campesinos, whose organizing had caused the agrarian reform in the first place—was arguably the nation's most dynamic sector. Guatemalans eat, to this day, because nonexporting farmers grow and market food.

66. ABC: *Revista de Alfabetización* (August–November 1947); *Misiones Culturales: Revista de Misiones Ambulantes de Cultura Inicial* (April 1949), 5 (citation); Handy, *Revolution in the Countryside*, 51–52. See also Knight, "The Rise and Fall of Cardenismo, c. 1930–c. 1946," 267–72. The influence of Cardenismo on Guatemalan developments has probably been underestimated. For similar analysis of these types of state projects, see the essays in Joseph and Nugent, eds., *Everyday Forms of State Formation.*

67. Guinea, *Armas para ganar una nueva batalla*, 1–31. According to the same source, the invasion in 1954 occasioned the return of the *núcleos* program, of SCIDE, and of Griffith himself, who advised the Castillo Armas administration on how to educate the peasantry. The *núcleos escolares* were linked with progressive plans coming out of the Ministry of Education, which began to stress getting out of the classroom and learning by doing, citing Maria Montessori and Joseph Dalton as inspirations. *Horizontes Rurales: Vocero del Núcleo Escolar Campesino Número 12* (Guatemala: El Tejar, Chimaltenango), 1:1 (August 1949), 1–3, and AGCA MAC / 450 (Universidades, Facultades, Institutos y Escuelas del País y Extranjeros, 1944–1955), "El Sembrador" (Escuela Industrial 'Cirilo López,' San Pedro Sacatepéquez, San Marcos, May 1950).

68. Fishman, "The Student is a Citizen."

69. On this issue, see Grandin, "Everyday Forms of State Decomposition: Quetzaltenango, Guatemala, 1954," 319; Paredes Moreira, *Reforma agraria: Una experiencia en Guatemala*, 57–60, 73; *Quitar el agua al pez*, 30.

70. The Indigenous Economy Institute had been operating as a wing of INFOP for several years. AGCA 3 / Caja Clas. 12, 0118, 016.1 (MCOP: Proyecto de leyes varios

del Instituto de la Vivienda, 1953), 15 July 1953, Min. de Economía y Trabajo, internal memo, "Creación Oficial del Instituto Nacional de Economía Indígena."

71. AGCA MAC/427 (Planificación Agrícola 1955), 16 January 1954, Robert Dillon, Ing. Agrónomo, Experto Técnico de la O.I.T. de la Naciones Unidas, "Confidencial: Informe sobre la reforma agraria en Guatemala."

72. Grandin convincingly argues that the growth of the Communist PGT, not the agrarian reform, spurred the United States to invade. See *The Last Colonial Massacre*, 52.

THREE. Gender and the Informal Economy

1. AGCA 3/Caja Clas. 121.11/13 (MCOP Camp. y Col., 1957), April 1957, Expediente (Antonia Iba Alonzo [Alonzo Abá]). As in many of the personal accounts in this chapter, the last names (Abá, in this case) hint at Mayan ancestry, although the documents do not specify the Mayanness of the family (is the woman in *traje*, for example?).

2. Black et al., *Garrison Guatemala*, passim; Gleijeses, *Shattered Hope*, 346–47; "Texto de la renuncia del Presidente Jacobo Arbenz Guzmán," in Villagrán Kramer, *Biografía política de Guatemala: Los pactos políticos de 1944 a 1970*, 157. The best history of militarism is Schirmer, *The Guatemalan Military Project*.

3. Berger, *Political and Agrarian Development in Guatemala*, 92–93; "Constitución de la República," 2 February 1956 (in effect 1 March), *Recopilación* 74 (1955–56), 17–48; Dosal, *Power in Transition*, 113; *El Guatemalteco*, 21 July 1954, 945, 26 August 1954, 209–10, and 27 December 1954, 305; and passim, 1954–57 for legislation in general; *El Imparcial*, passim, 1954–57; Le Bot, *La guerre en terre maya*, 154–58; *El pensamiento del Presidente Castillo Armas* (Guatemala: Secretaría de Divulgación, Cultura y Turismo, 1955).

4. *El Guatemalteco*, passim, 1963–66 (see especially "Carta Fundamental del Gobierno," and "Ley de Defensa de las Instituciones Democráticas," 10 April 1963, 457–59); *El Imparcial* 29 July 1957, 21 October 1957, 12 February 1958 (and passim for the period). A thorough list of related texts may be found in the bibliography. One of the first classics on the period was Adams, *Crucifixion by Power*. For a dissenting interpretation of Ydígoras, see Ebel, *Misunderstood Caudillo*. An account from within Guatemala is Rosada-Granados, *Soldados en el poder*; see also Amaro, *Guatemala: historia despierta*.

5. *El Imparcial*, 19 October 1974, 11.

6. Briggs, *Reproducing Empire*.

7. Dependency theory's first center was in the UN's Comisión Económica para América Latina (CEPAL), which promoted import-substituting industrialization (ISI) as a way to overcome structural underdevelopment brought about by the exploitation of the economic periphery by the colonialist economic core. As ISI—statist, protectionist, nationalist, and not unlike the Guatemalan Revolution's programs in its execution—failed to bring prosperity to Latin America, dependency theory's tenets would gradually be transformed by the rising New

Left. Their class-based dependency theories of periphery and core evolved dialogically with the neo-Marxism of the 1960s and 1970s. Bulmer-Thomas, *The
Economic History of Latin America Since Independence*, 264; Hoogvelt, *Globalization and the Postcolonial World*, 37–43, 223–25. For an overview, see Williamson,
The Penguin History of Latin America, 331–41, and for political effects in Guatemala, Grandin, *The Last Colonial Massacre*, 13. Arrayed against dependency was
a similarly evolving body of modernization theory, which informed not only
President Harry Truman's Four Point Program of Development Aid (1949), but
also U.S. policy and foreign aid in Latin America in the decades ahead. Essentially promoting a linear model of development in which the United States and
Europe represented the future toward which traditional, undeveloped Latin
American (and other) countries were developing, modernization theory's most
influential tract would ultimately be W. W. Rostow's *The Stages of Economic
Growth: A Non-Communist Manifesto* (1960). The burgeoning development industry was broadly split between these evolving theoretical poles, with the U.S.
government, corporations, and culture industry working in tandem to promote
the latter. In the words of Ankie Hoogvelt, under modernization theory—and, I
would add, under the entire apparatus of U.S.-led development as part of the
culture industry—"progress became a matter of ordered social reform." Its practitioners "helped to strengthen the illusion of independence and of the sovereignty of the national developmental state, since they were ensconced in a
theoretical framework which accorded integrity to 'society' as a self-regulating
'social whole' within which social and political institutions, cultural values
as well as economic organisations, were comprehended as constituent parts."
Hoogvelt, *Globalization and the Postcolonial World*, 35.

8. Scott, "Gender: A Useful Category of Historical Analysis" (citations from 1067
and 1069, respectively). Joan Scott went on to publish a collection of her essays
on gender and history that greatly influenced further debate—*Gender and the
Politics of History*. Among Latin American historians influenced by Scott was
Stern (*The Secret History of Gender*), who highlighted a "contested patriarchal
pact" that was at once shaped from below even as it mediated social and political
relationships. For further work on gender, power, and politics, see the Special
Issue on Gender of the *Hispanic American Historical Review* 81:3–4 (August–
November 2001), and collections including French and James, eds., *The Gen-
dered Worlds of Latin American Women Workers*, and Dore and Molyneux, eds.,
Hidden Histories of Gender and the State in Latin America.

9. Chen, "Rethinking the Informal Economy." Hart coined the term, Chen writes,
in a journal article in 1971; the ILO used it in 1972.

10. "Encuesta nacional de empleo e ingresos 2002," Instituto Nacional de Estadística.

11. Ibid.; *Prensa Libre*, 5 October 2002, 19. Even registered businesses in Guatemala
have an informal feel. Bus drivers flee the scenes of the accidents they so reg-

ularly cause because the bus company has no record of their names. There is a whole informal sector of *tramitadores* (processors) who make their living by getting government paperwork done, a nightmarish procedure, for individuals and businesses.

12. *Prensa Libre*, 11 October 2002, 23. The informal sector figure comes from the *Encuesta nacional de empleo e ingresos 2002. Prensa Libre* cited the ILO in reporting that 937,500 children under the age of eighteen were working in the informal sector, and that child labor produced 20 percent of Guatemala's GDP. Figures from the ILO for 2003 show that 876,924 children under the age of fifteen were economically active: 155,098 from birth to nine years old, and 721,826 from ten to fourteen. See ILO, Statistical Information and Monitoring Programme on Child Labour, "Estudio cualitativo sobre el trabajo infantil en Guatemala: Informe final, 2003," available at http://www.ilo.org/ipecinfo. The informal economy is not just an urban phenomenon but includes nearly the entirety of the economic activity that keeps the rural majority alive.

13. Before the time period under discussion, the spread of the coffee economy and liberal rule from 1871 forward was the biggest factor in structuring family and economy alike. See Cambranes, *Café y campesinos*, and Williams, *States and Social Evolution*.

14. For more on globalization, the informal economy, and women's labor and their role in development, see Acosta-Belén and Bose, "U.S. Latina and Latin American Feminisms," as well as the edited volume by the same authors: *Women in the Latin American Development Process*.

15. *El Imparcial*, 22 August 1972 (clip).

16. AGCA B/22240 (Fomento: Lot. El Gallito 1934), 25 November 1934, Ministerio Público, Felipe Cárdenas.

17. AGCA B/22244 (Fomento: Lot. El Gallito 1936), December 1936, Exp. (Jesús Aragón Ruano).

18. AGCA B/22244 (Fomento: Lot. El Gallito 1936), August 1936, Exp. (Bernarda Cardona).

19. AGCA 3/Caja Clas. 121.11, No. Ord. 47082 (MCOP Lot. Gallito y Palmita, 1943–46), February 1943, Exp. (Bartola de Ibañez).

20. See Briggs, *Reproducing Empire*; Findlay, "Love in the Tropics"; Grandin, *The Blood of Guatemala* and *The Last Colonial Massacre*; Miller Klubock, *Contested Communities*; Lavrín, *Women, Feminism, and Social Change in Argentina, Chile, and Uruguay, 1890–1940*; Nelson, *A Finger in the Wound*; and Scott, *Gender and the Politics of History*.

21. *A Case History of Communist Penetration: Guatemala* (U.S. Department of State, Publication Number 6465, April 1957); *Penetration of the Political Institutions of Guatemala by the International Communist Movement: Threat to the Peace and Security of America and to the Sovereignty and Political Independence of Guatemala*. (Information submitted by the Delegation of the United States of America to

the Fifth Meeting of Consultation of Ministers of Foreign Affairs of the American Republics, serving as Organ of Consultation; June 1954); James, *Red Design for the Americas*, 56; Schlesinger and Kinzer, *Bitter Fruit*, 51.

22. The CIA had first planned to provide Castillo Armas with tactical and air support, along with strategic assassinations, in mid- to late 1952, under operation code name PBFORTUNE. Director of Central Intelligence Walter Bedell Smith terminated this mission after a security breach, but his successor, Allen Dulles, with the approval of his brother, the secretary of state, brought it back to life in late 1953 and dubbed it PBSUCCESS. Cullather, *PBSUCCESS: The United States and Guatemala, 1952–1954*, 99–101; Haines, "CIA and Guatemala Assassination Proposals, 1952–1954 , 2–3.

23. Cullather, *PBSUCCESS*, 45; Gleijeses, *Shattered Hope*, 221–22; "Guatemalan Communist Personnel to be Disposed of During Military Operations of Calligeris"; McClintock, *The American Connection*, vol. 2, *Guatemala*, 28–29; *El Imparcial*, 13 October 1953, 29 October 1953, 6 November 1953. The description of Peurifoy as pistol-packing comes from a jingle his wife, Betty Jane, wrote after Arbenz's fall: "Sing a song of Quetzals / Pockets full of peace / The junta's in the palace— / They've taken out a lease. / The Commies are in hiding / Just across the street: / To the embassy of Mexico / They beat a quick retreat. / And pistol-packing Peurifoy / Looks mighty optimistic, / For the land of Guatemala / Is no longer Communistic." Reprinted in "In Wife's Jingle He is Pistol-Packing Peurifoy," *Daily People's World* (San Francisco), 2 August 1954, 8.

24. Bernays was aided in spreading anticommunist hysteria by such figures as Sen. Henry Cabot Lodge of Massachusetts, who owned UFCO stock, and Thomas G. Corcoran, a well-connected Washington lawyer contracted by UFCO as a lobbyist, who is reported to have been one of the driving forces behind PBFORTUNE. García Añoveros, *Jacobo Arbenz*, 98–100; Gleijeses, *Shattered Hope*, 90; Schlesinger and Kinzer, *Bitter Fruit*, 80. None of this denies the critical role of the Communist PGT in Guatemala during the Revolution, a topic Grandin treats thoroughly in *The Last Colonial Massacre*.

25. Theodore Geiger, *Communism versus Progress in Guatemala*, 1.

26. The fact that there were probably no more than two thousand or twenty-five hundred self-declared Communists in Guatemala and that they held "only four of the government's 51 seats" was immaterial, the NPA declared, because "the leadership of all the other Government parties is permeated with concealed Communist sympathizers." From their hidden positions of influence, communists "wield[ed] a vastly disproportionate influence." Astonishingly, the NPA claimed that agrarian reform was especially necessary in Guatemala. However, the experts opined, it should not be accomplished by breaking up banana and coffee plantations, since those two products provided over 85 percent of the nation's foreign exchange. Instead, the NPA recommended resettling highland Indians, who were responsible for "uneconomic use of the land," in underpopulated coastal regions and in the jungles of Petén—the underdeveloped north-

eastern province bordering Belize. This is exactly the type of so-called agrarian reform that governments after the invasion would undertake. Ibid., inside front cover, 8, 19, 33.

27. See UN Security Council Document S/3232 (1954), Cablegram dated 19 June 1954 from the Minister for External Relations of Guatemala [Guillermo Toriello] to the President of the Security Council, 1, 2; UNSC Document S/3238 (1954), Cablegram dated 20 June 1954 from the Minister for External Affairs of Guatemala addressed to the President of the Security Council; UNSC Draft Resolutions S/3236/Rev.1 and S/3237 (adopted by the Security Council 20 June 1954).

28. *Communist Aggression in Latin America: Guatemala*, 83rd Cong., 2nd sess., 27–29 September, 8 October, and 14–15 October 1954, 9–68.

29. James, *Red Design for the Americas*, 56. James's tract is based in large part on a U.S. State Department report from 1957 entitled *A Case History of Communist Penetration: Guatemala* (op. cit.). This, in turn, borrows long passages verbatim from the literature's seminal text—a government document circulated even as the U.S.-sponsored invasion of Guatemala was beginning, called *Penetration of the Political Institutions of Guatemala by the International Communist Movement: Threat to the Peace and Security of America and to the Sovereignty and Political Independence of Guatemala*. Many of the claims originating in this dodgy body of propaganda were regurgitated in the above-cited House Subcommittee testimonials, and since have made their way into standard political histories.

30. Over the years, ever more wild yarns about Arbenz would enter the literature. Carlos Manuel Pellecer, for example—a labor leader in the Arbenz era who later renounced communism—would write in his memoir of 1997 that the first lady had been cuckolding her husband by carrying on an affair with one Ennio de la Roca, a Cuban refugee and CIA-employed double agent who was specially trained "to seduce the wives of powerful men." Pellecer, *Arbenz y yo*, 261–63, 277 (citation).

31. Scott, "Gender," 1070.

32. Women had made significant political gains during the Revolution, winning the first steps toward full electoral franchise and demanding recognition for the special needs of mothers and children. They also took leadership positions in the formation, maintenance, and supply of city neighborhoods. Families and family needs, meanwhile, were a revolutionary focus as well. During the 1944–54 era, for example, the Instituto Guatemalteco de Seguridad Social (IGSS) was created, the first social workers appeared, state-run day-care centers were instituted, and the first genuine effort to educate nonelite children was made. The government, the left, and the anticommunist bloc all made public appeals to women and used gendered images, many of them machista, to make their cases to the public. Anticommunist students, for example, wrote pamphlets specifically for women claiming that Communism would destroy the family. See, e.g., "Manifesto de la agrupación anti comunista altaverapacense." For a good example of Communist Party rhetoric on gender, see "La mujer guatemalteca y el 2do.

Congreso del Partido," *Octubre,* 4 December 1952, 9. The Alianza Femenina Guatemalteca (AFG) was a vocal defender of women's rights on the ground. Organizing among Guatemala City market vendors, probably with little success, given the sector's conservatism and right-wing links at midcentury, the AFG decried the lack of children's cafeterias, schools, and day-care centers in the markets. The organization helped to construct a makeshift hall for children in Mercado No. 2 (today Sur 2), to be used until the municipality built the promised nursery. It also advocated for installing roofing on outdoor stalls so children wouldn't be exposed to the elements. *Mujeres* (Alianza Femenina Guatemalteca) 1:8 (20 June 1952), 1.

33. Charge of murder in *El Imparcial,* 7 July 1954.

34. All of the following are front-page stories from *El Imparcial* featuring doña Odilia: "Hospital para los incurables," 27 July 1954; "La Señora de Castillo Armas observa trascendental labor para la infancia," 21 August 1954; "Odilia de Castillo Armas visitó el hospital infantil de Barrios," 24 August 1954. See also de la Guardia, *Castillo Armas, libertador y mártir,* and Paiz Herrera, *1931–1978: Años de la vida política de Guatemala.* María Vilanova de Arbenz, by way of contrast, had almost never been mentioned in *El Imparcial.* Several accounts tell of her activities as first lady, but none are substantiated. See Weymann Fuentes, "Jacobo Arbenz: Un perfil del ex-presidente de Guatemala," 2:179.

35. AGCA SASP-SBS P4:1961–62/T6 (DBI, Solicitudes de Ayudas), passim; AGCA SASP-SBS P 4:1961/T4 (ASCP, Solicitudes de Ayudas), passim.

36. According to Graciela Quan, delegate to the United Nations and advisor to the Castillo administration on social projects, the Consejo Nacional was an outgrowth of Previsión Social de la Casa Presidencial (presidential social welfare program), an affair managed by the nation's first ladies since the time of Arévalo. *El Imparcial,* 15 November 1955, 28 August 1956, 5, 1 October 1956, 4 October 1956, 6 October 1958, 7 October 1958.

37. AGCA SASP-SBS P 9:1967/T3 (DBI, Recortes de Prensa), *El Gráfico,* undated clip.

38. The First International Congress of Social Economy was held in Buenos Aires in 1924. According to PAU propaganda, this conference gave rise to the idea of opening schools of applied sociology to train social workers, the first of which in Latin America debuted in Santiago de Chile in 1925. BPAU, November 1924, 1096–1106 and December 1948, 580–81.

39. The First Pan-American Congress of Social Service was held in Santiago in 1945 and the second in Rio de Janeiro four years later. BPAU, April 1945, 206–10. Social welfare and applied social science were, at the institutional level, major Inter-American concerns in the 1940s. In 1942, for example, fifteen Latin American "leaders of social thought and action" gathered with their North American counterparts in several U.S. cities for an Inter-American Seminar on Social Studies sponsored by the National Catholic Welfare Conference. The featured

discussions covered "The Americas and the Crisis of Civilization." *The Inter-American Monthly*, September 1942, 45.

40. The birth and growth of the UN and the OAS accompanied not only the rise of the CIA, but of vast U.S. development investment projects ranging from the Marshall Plan to the work of USAID. President John F. Kennedy created USAID in 1961, after Congress passed the Foreign Assistance Act of the same year. Although USAID was a new institution, its functions had been long standing in other agencies: the Department of Agriculture's Food for Peace program (distribution of agricultural surplus); the International Cooperation Agency (economic and technical assistance); the Export-Import Bank (local currency functions); and the Development Loan Fund. See http://www.usaid.gov/about _usaid. The postwar period brought the demise of the popular front and the dismantling of leftist politics alike, even as new technologies, including the hydrogen bomb, air and automotive travel, and television, transformed societies. In the industrialized world, advertising, marketing, public relations, industrial design, mass retail, and mass media and entertainment took their still-recognizable forms. The development industry became a vast employer as it used these technologies dialogically to promote liberal, consumerist individualism.

41. There are no reliable statistics available, so this observation is based purely on readings of the primary documents and applies specifically to the poor, that is, the vast majority of the population. All of the cited AGCA collections show a marked predominance of split families and single parents, even correcting for expedientes from El Gallito and La Palmita, where the government gave special preference to single mothers.

42. This comment is based upon the reading of multiple police reports of the 1930s, from which many of the family histories presented in this work are taken. Interestingly, as police reports gave way to social workers' reports from the late 1940s forward, *women's* loose sexual behavior began to emerge as a trope.

43. Monzón Lemus, *Camino de adolescente*, vi, 5–6, 10, 18–19.

44. My research here bears out phenomena documented by Greg Grandin (in *The Blood of Guatemala*) as far back as the late colonial period. "Quetzalteco women were highly visible and active in the public sphere and participated in nearly every facet of production and trade," he writes. "Through trade and credit, women created a world of countervailing power that mitigated the vicissitudes of patriarchy" (38). Grandin goes on to develop these themes quite broadly, and his entire work is essential reading in this regard.

45. AGCA 3 / Caja Clas. 121.1 (MCOP Col. y Camp., 1955), May 1955 (María Tranquilina Díaz).

46. AGCA 3 / Caja Clas. 121.11 / 13 (MCOP Camp. y Col., 1957), July 1957, Exp. (Emeteria Varela v. de González).

47. "Informe social" on Emeteria Varela, and "Informe social" on Rosa Roca de Morán, Dirección del Servicio Social, MCOP, 12 June 1956, in AGCA 3 / Caja Clas.

121.11/13 (MCOP Camp. y Col., 1957), July 1957, Exp. (Emeteria Varela v. de González).

48. AGCA 3/Caja Clas. 121.11, No. Ord. 47082 (MCOP Lot. Gallito y Palmita, 1943–46), March-April 1946, Juzgado 30. de Paz (re Lucía Morataya).

49. AGCA SASP-SBS P8:1963/T8 (DBI, Cierre de Casos, Serv. Social), 9/13/63 (Gloria Ortíz G.).

50. AGCA SASP-SBS P 8:1963/T8 (DBI, Cierre de Casos, Serv. Social), 3/19–6/24/63 (Caso, 3 ninos Orellana Vásquez).

51. AGCA SASP-SBS P4:1961–62/T5 (ABI, Informes Misceláneos), Sección de Estudio Mental. Reportes Generales de Casos, Guardería No. 3, 1962 (A.C.H., name omitted for privacy); AGCA SASP-SBS P4:1961–62/T5 (ABI, Informes Misceláneos), Sección de Estudio Mental. Reportes Generales de Casos, Guardería No. 3, 1962 (S.G.: name omitted); AGCA SASP-SBS P4:1961–62/T5 (ABI, Informes Misceláneos), Sección de Estudio Mental. Reportes Generales de Casos, Guardería No. 3, 1962 (L.A.F.G.: name omitted for privacy); AGCA SASP-SBS P4:1961–62/T5 (ABI, Informes Misceláneos), Sección de Estudio Mental. Reportes Generales de Casos, Guardería No. 3, 1962 (A.M.M.S.: name omitted).

52. Guinea, *Armas para ganar una nueva batalla*; *El Imparcial*, 13 November 1954, 1 June 1955.

53. *El Imparcial*, 21 May 1964. Projects such as ICD were squarely rooted in nineteenth-century, even eighteenth-century, colonialism, imperialism, and economic doctrine. For background and global context, see Cowan and Shenton, *Doctrines of Development*. A review of theories is found in Hoogvelt, *Globalization and the Postcolonial World*.

54. *El Imparcial*, 24 May 1956.

55. Guzmán Böckler, *Donde enmudecen las conciencias*, 176–77.

56. *Desarrollo integral de las comunidades rurales en Guatemala*, 41, 77, passim.

57. Lefebvre, *The Production of Space*, 325.

58. On politics, power, and gender, see Scott, "Gender"; Stern, *The Secret History of Gender*; and, for a succinct overview, Deutsch, "Gender and Sociopolitical Change in 20th-Century Latin America."

59. Lefebvre, *The Production of Space*, 376. Lefebvre was arguing against structuralism's determinism, propensity to classify, and tendency to see the public, not the private, sphere as leading development.

FOUR. Making the Immoral Metropolis

1. *Extra* (Guatemala: Grupo Extra, S.A.), 17–23 August 2003, 1, 3. More salient information on the gangs can be found in *Maras y pandillas en Centroamérica*, vol. 1.

2. *Prensa Libre*, 19 August 2003, 4–5.

3. AGCA SASP-SBS P 8:1963/T8 (DBI, Cierre de Casos, Serv. Social), 9/18/63–8/25/64 (Caso, Leonarda Cristina Bor Aroche).

4. See Grandin, *The Last Colonial Massacre*, 6–17, 92–104.

5. AGCA 3 / Caja Clas. 650.2 (MCOP: Carreteras 1961), 6 July 1961, Highways of the World to MCOP. Dossiers like that of HOTW's John McCormack show the geography of this vital step in globalization; he had built modern thoroughfares first as a soldier in Guam and then in Saudi Arabia, Thailand, Cambodia, Laos, and Ecuador. A leader in global road engineering and standardization was the International Road Federation. Based in London, Washington, and Paris, it was a consultative organ of the UN and a cooperative agency with the OAS and the Organization of European Economic Cooperation. *Carreteras del Mundo,* 13 March 1961.

6. The contracted leg of the highway ran from Colotenango to the border. Guatemala paid $712,500, and the United States, $1,425,000. AGCA 3 / Caja Clas. 07, 09, 011, 011.3 (MCOP: Acuerdos y decretos; planificación proyecto Desarrollo Socioeducativo Rural, 1955), 18 January 1955, U.S. Bureau of Public Roads, Inter-American Regional Office, to MCOP.

7. *Programa regional de carreteras centroamericanas,*1: 29–30; AGCA 3 / Caja Clas. 650.2 (MCOP: Carreteras 1958), 12 June 1958, DGC Financial Report. By 1958, the United States had invested $138,703,000 in the Interamerican Highway since the project's inception. *Chronology of the Pan American Highway Project,* 10. For the ICA and agriculture, see Paredes Moreira, *Reforma agraria,* 136–37. Its programs most clearly demonstrate the links between planning in highways, agriculture, and rural education and social engineering.

8. The contractors included Thompson Cornwall, Fisher de Guatemala, La Panamericana, Oceanic Constructors, Contica International, Asturias Vizcaíno, El Aguila, and Johnson Drake. These companies worked not only on the Pan-American, but also the Atlantic and Pacific highways. Thompson Cornwall built the bulk of what today is the Mexican–Central American section of the Pan-American Highway network.

9. AGCA 3 / Caja Clas. 650.2 (MCOP: Carreteras 1958), 13 June 1958, "Gobierno . . . Frente al Problema de 'El Tapon.'" Blasting on the Tapón began in early 1961. AGCA 3 / Cajas Clas. 650.2 (MCOP: Carreteras, 1961), 2 February 1961, Thompson Cornwall to MCOP.

10. Interviews, "don Ossiel," Antigua, Guatemala, 2/10/03 and 2/24/03. Don Ossiel's story illustrates greater historical trends. Migrating from the countryside to Guatemala City at around the time of the Castillo Armas invasion, he began an "automobile age" career, learning to drive and do basic repairs as an apprentice mechanic. After moving to his wife's hometown of Antigua and spending many years as a Thompson Cornwall employee, he launched a complex web of money-making activities in the informal economy, most of which keep him wheeling up and down the highway he helped to build.

11. "Construction of the Unfinished Sections of the Pan American Highway," Council of the Organization of American States Special Committee to Study to Formulation of New Measures for Economic Cooperation Working Group, CECE / Subgroup 4; Working Paper No. 11 (Washington: OAS, 11 February 1959), 7.

12. Ibid., 5; AGCA 3 / Caja Clas. 650.2 (MCOP: Carreteras 1958), 23 May 1958, Ing. Carlos Von Ahn, Sub-Director Ejectivo, DGC, to Ing. Otto E. Becker M., Sub-Secretario del MCOP.

13. AGCA 3 / Caja Clas. 650.2 (MCOP: Carreteras 1958), September 1958, Exp. (D. Villatoro, Aldea Michicoy, Huehue).

14. Ibid. Occasionally villagers opposed the construction of feeder roads, usually because of right-of-way issues. AGCA 3 / Caja Clas. 650.2 (MCOP: Carreteras 1958), November 1958, Exp. (El Progreso, Jutiapa); ibid., July 1958, Exp. (Cantón 'Tunayac', Momostenango).

15. AGCA 3 / Caja Clas. 650.2 (MCOP: Carreteras 1958), ICA Project Documents.

16. For example, ibid., May 1958, Exp. (Dpt. de Sta. Rosa).

17. AGCA 3 (MCOP: Carreteras), 1954–63, passim.

18. *Programa regional de carreteras centroamericanas*, 1:22, 29. In 1953 CEPAL and the UN's Administración de Asistencia Técnica did a study on Central American transport with an eye to the common market, recommending a network of ten highways to integrate the region (ibid., 28). Meanwhile, the still-to-be-completed Interamerican Highway was an ongoing concern for Central American public works ministers, who requested a comprehensive study from the International Road Federation in 1959. *Chronology of the Pan American Highway Project*, 11.

19. *El Imparcial*, 4 February 1964 ("economic blood"), 18 June 1966, 16 November 1968, 23 December 1971, 10 June 1974.

20. U.S. imperialism: *Boletín Internacional* (México: Frente Popular 31 de Enero, FP-31), May 1982, 10–11.

21. *El Guatemalteco*, 5 June 1961, 33. Central America had been united during the colonial era and was a single nation for roughly the first two decades of independence. To this day, reunification, however unlikely, is a powerful political theme. See *El Imparcial*, 29 April 1958, 25 September 1958, 17 October 1958, 6 February 1960, 9 June 1960; and *El Guatemalteco*, 5 March 1959, 923.

22. Guzmán Böckler, *Donde enmudecen las conciencias*, 173. The CACM fell apart after the football war of 1969 between Honduras and El Salvador.

23. 23 December 1947, "Ley de Fomento Industrial," *Recopilación* 66 (1947–48), 136–39; 28 July 1948, "Ley Orgánica del Instituto de Fomento de la Producción," *Recopilación* 66 (1948–49), 88–100; *Más de cien años*, 2:119–21; Dosal, *Power in Transition*, 95. INFOP outlived the Revolution and by 1963 was enmeshed in a web of state agencies and banks—including the Revolution-created Agrarian Bank and the National Institute of Agrarian Transformation—working on an integrated program to bring credits to indigenous farmers, finish the Pan-American Highway, improve feeder roads, and foment industrial production. See *El Imparcial*, 10 May 1963.

24. Dosal, *Power in Transition*, 118. Resistance to taxation that could have funded national industrial growth was another factor in producing the illusory growth that failed to enrich the Guatemalan formal economy as a whole. Paradoxically, the resistance was spearheaded by Guatemala's most important trade organiza-

tion, Coordinador de Asociaciones Agrícolas, Comerciales, Industriales, y Financieras, formed in January 1957, near the twilight of the Castillo Armas regime. Dosal, *Power in Transition*, 114. Other trade associations of the era included the lasting and politically influential Cámara de Industria de Guatemala—(Guatemalan Chamber of Industry, 1958), the Asociación de Azucareros (sugar, 1957), ANACAFE (coffee, 1960), and the post-Ydígoras Consejo Nacional de Algodón (cotton council, 1965). Dosal, *Power in Transition*, 114–15; *El Guatemalteco*, 11 November 1960, 361, and 10 May 1961, 769; Guzmán Böckler, *Donde enmudecen las conciencias*, 173.

25. Petras, "Cambios en la estructura agraria de la América Latina," 111. According to Petras, companies expanding into Mexico and Central America during this period also included General Foods, Anderson Clayton, Ralston Purina, King Ranch, Caterpillar Tractor, Borden, John Deere, Monsanto, Dow Chemicals, and others.

26. "Anexo: Lista de empresas transnacionales en Centroamérica (1978)," in CIRMA (Antigua, Guatemala), Clasificación Infostelle 09/02/04 ("Relaciones económicas; empresas extranjeras/multinacionales en Guatemala/CA, Conatipro," n.p.: 1978 [?]). See also ibid., untitled list of subsidiary businesses in Guatemala with parent industries—a typewritten list from an anonymous donor that appeared in 1981 in a guerrilla publication: *Guatemala en Lucha* (Guatemala: Fuerzas Armadas Rebeldes [FAR]), No. 1, Yr. 1 (July 1981), 8–9.

27. Morán Mérida, *Condiciones de vida*, 20. Colonias El Esfuerzo, El Limoncito, 15 de Agosto, Lourdes I, and Lourdes II date to this invasion. By 1968 about sixty thousand families were living in *asentamientos precarios* in Guatemala City, mostly in zones 3, 5, 6, and 7 (ibid., 21).

28. Ibid., 153–55.

29. Specifically redone were Calle Martí, the in-city leg of the Atlantic Highway, and Avenida Petapa, which runs to the modern university campus. The engineering and positioning problems with the drainage and sewers are ironically symbolic. Ultimately, the Trébol's *aguas negras* (black waters) were released into the ravine behind the cemetery, which backs onto the slums around El Gallito. This is the same area where the municipal dump provides housing and employment for thousands of garbage pickers, many of them children and all of them among the hemisphere's most miserable. AGCA 3/Caja Clas. 650.2 (MCOP: Carreteras 1958), 19 December 1958, Internal Memo, Otto E. Becker Meyer, Jefe del Proyecto 13-B; AGCA 3/Caja Clas. 128 (MCOP: Préstamos, Carreteras, 1960), 5 February 1959, Roberto Woolfolk, Jefe de Expropiaciones to Ydígoras; AGCA 3/Caja Clas. 650.2 (MCOP: Carreteras 1958), 14 May 1958, Mejicanos, DGC, to MCOP, re Ave. Petapa; *El Imparcial*, 9 March 1959.

30. An excellent journalistic account can be found in Schlosser, *Fast Food Nation*.

31. *EDOM 1972–2000*, 168; *El Imparcial*, 14 September 1962, clip. The grain market is known as El Granero; an area dedicated to the sale of tomatoes and chile also developed, known as El Tomatero.

32. *El Imparcial,* 14 January 1959 (clip), 14 August 1959 (clip); *La Hora,* 12 May 1959 (clip).

33. Morán Mérida, *Condiciones de vida,* 21.

34. *El Imparcial,* 22 May 1963 (clip).

35. *Prensa Libre,* 19 February 1969, 38–39.

36. *El Imparcial,* 29 November 1973 (clip).

37. See Camus, *Ser indígena en la Cuidad de Guatemala,* 111–12, and more broadly, 93–151, for an excellent ethnography of the market at the turn of the millennium.

38. In the proletarian novel *Camino de adolescente,* Ramón's idea of becoming a truck-driving corn merchant fits this dynamic. Camus, *Ser indígena,* 100–101; Mérida Morán, *Condiciones de vida,* 21.

39. AGCA 3 / Caja Clas. 654.1.650 (MCOP: Carreteras, Reparaciones, 1959), Folder 650.3.149.220.357: October 1959, Exp. (J. Ignacio Bran).

40. AGCA 3 / Caja Clas. 121.1 / 121.11 (MCOP: Solic. de Camp. y Col., 1963), 1962, Exp. No. 5892.

41. García Vettorazzi, "El crecimiento espacial," 4–5; Rodas Maltéz, *Producción de suelo habitacional y de los servicios básicos en la periferia metropolitana de la Ciudad de Guatemala,* 82.

42. Camus, *Ser indígena,* 61–62; Mérida Morán, *Condiciones de vida,* 36–38. It is a rule of thumb in Guatemalan scholarly literature that rural-to-urban migration before the earthquake of 1976 was largely by Ladinos. However, statistics for the period are unreliable, and close readings of archived documents indicate that there well may have been a much higher percentage, though still likely a minority, of Mayan migrants in the 1950s and 1960s than is commonly supposed.

43. Camus, *Ser indígena,* 99; Rodas Maltéz, *Producción del suelo,* vii.

44. AGCA SASP-SBS P28:1969/T1 (Dirección de Bienestar Infantil y Familiar, Contratos Máquinas), passim. The examples are from 1969. For commercial leisure space throughout the 1960s, see, for example, AGCA SASP-SBS P4:1961–62/T7 (DBI, Traganíqueles); and AGCA Secretaría Asuntos Sociales de la Presidencia / Secretaría de Bienestar Social, Paquete 9:1965–66/Tomo 4 (Dirección de Bienestar Infantil, Providencias Secretaría General).

45. Since I lived next door to this *centro comercial,* the Capitol on Sexta Avenida in zone 1, I spent a great deal of time in it, checking e-mail, buying dinner, and trying to figure out what was going on. The individual quoted, an eighteen-year-old man, had been hanging out in the area for about two years. He grew up in a stable nuclear family, poor but housed and fed, in zone 3, on Avenida Centroamérica near El Gallito. He dropped out of school at sixteen. He never divulged how he made his money but given his in-depth descriptions of life in the mall, teased out over plates of Chinito Veloz Chinese fast food (paid for by me), I suspect he ran crack from El Gallito for clients afraid to go there or possibly turned tricks with Guatemalan businessmen and foreign city dwellers, many linked with the U.S. military, a major source of business for young hustlers. No one I spoke to confirmed the existence of a coherent *mara* (gang) that

considered the mall its turf. However, my informant's comments about the *maquintas* being the entryway for youth into a seedy underworld was one I heard numerous times, both from kids involved with the process and from critics of delinquency in society at large.

46. See Segrue, *The Origins of the Urban Crisis*.

47. Guatemala; Mixco, Villa Nueva; Petapa; Villa Canales; Amatitlán; Santa Catarina Pinula; San José Pinula; Fraijanes; Palencia; San Pedro Ayampuc; Chinautla; San Raimundo; San Juan Sacatepéquez; San Pedro Sacatepéquez; Chuarrancho; and San José del Golfo. Not all are fully urbanized, so people define the AMG differently (see Camus, *Ser indígena*, 86n15; García Vettorazzi, "El crecimiento espacial," 2).

48. García Vettorazzi, "El crecimiento espacial," 1.

49. *El Imparcial*, 6 October 1967, 21 July 1971; Municipalidad de Guatemala, Depto. de Ingenería, Oficina de Urbanismo, "Nomenclatura de barrios vías y numeración de casas para la Cd. de Guatemala," Aprobado por el Consejo Municipal el 25 de enero de 1952.

50. EDOM 1972–2000: *Plan de desarrollo metropolitano* (Guatemala: Municipalidad de Guatemala, 1972). See also Rodas Maltéz, *Producción de suelo*, introduction, 1–2; *Actas de la Municipalidad de Guatemala*, 7/6/61, Acta 57.

51. EDOM 1972–2000, 377–79.

52. Sereseres, "The Guatemalan Legacy," 26–27; Rodas Maltéz, *Producción de suelo*, introduction, 1–2; *El Imparcial*, 22 March 1979. The mayor behind EDOM's creation, Manuel Colom Argueta (1970–74), founder of a social democrat opposition party known as the United Revolutionary Front, would be machine-gunned by the right in 1979. As mayor, Colom Argueta never hesitated to voice public disagreement with the military regime of Arana Osorio. See, e.g., *El Imparcial*, 16 January 1974, 10.

53. EDOM 1972–2000, 167–68, 179.

54. EDOM 1972–2000, 383.

55. The census listed a total population of 586,698 in these municipalities. By the time of the census of 1973, Amatitlán, Villa Canales, Santa Catarina Pinula, and Chinautla had been added to the list, with a population of 899,172. García Vettorazzi, "El crecimiento espacial," 4. On Mixco, see Camus, *Ser indígena*, 154, 158. Mixco is located on the Pan-American Highway between the old capital city, Antigua, and the current capital, settled in 1773. Camus points out the importance of Mixco's agricultural heritage; though heavily indigenous, its proximity to the capital area meant that *hacienda* (finca/big plantation) agriculture predominated. Farther west toward Mexico along the Pan-American, in Chimaltenango, for example, Mayan communities were better able to preserve their landholdings.

56. AGCA 3/Caja Clas. 143 (MCOP: Caminos y O.P., 1960), 16 July 1959 (Aldea Loma Alta, San Juan Sacatpéquez); Camus, *Ser indígena*, 159; Morales, *La articulación de las diferencias o el síndrome de Maximón*, 369.

57. AGCA 3/AGCA 3/Cajas Clas. 650.2 (MCOP: Carreteras, 1958), May 1958, Exp. (Empresas Alianza y Eureka); Camus, *Ser indígena*, 157, 157nn5, 6.

58. AGCA 3/Cajas Clas. 650.2 (MCOP: Carreteras, 1958), July 1958, Exp. (Colonia Belén, Mixco, Guate.). In July 1958 the community, forty-eight families large, was eight months old. Last names on the petitions include a mix of Spanish and Mayan, though Spanish last names are not necessarily an indicator that the family does not speak a Mayan language.

59. Camus, *Ser indígena*, 160–61. The Listex and Bon Max factories are two of La Brigada's largest. In her ethnography of this neighborhood, Camus details the tensions between arriving and passive migrants, who became city dwellers by default as the area was transformed from rural to urban.

60. Ibid., 167.

61. Ibid., 161.

62. Morán Mérida, *Condiciones de vida*, 21.

63. Camus, *Ser indígena*, 62.

64. *El Imparcial*, 5 November 1974; Levenson-Estrada, *Trade Unionists against Terror*, 56. According to Levenson-Estrada, the greatest numbers of rural migrants came from Escuintla, where "capitalist export agriculture" was growing at the fastest pace (59–60).

65. *El Imparcial*, 5 November 1974, 8.

66. Ibid.

67. Ramírez, *La guerra de los 36 años*, 256. See chapter 6 for further discussion of the gangs; research indicates that many of their members in the 1990s and 2000s came from stable homes, not from the streets.

68. Ibid., 72.

69. Ibid., 46–47.

70. FUEGO was formed to replace the older Federación de Estudiantes Secundarios. See ibid., 69.

71. Ibid., 69–75. FUEGO encompassed both state and private schools.

72. The Zacapa contingent rallied to near success, but the newly trained Cuban pilots bombed them as troops mobilized around the country's northeast, throughout Zacapa, and from Puerto Barrios in Izabal to the Honduran border. Black et al., *Garrison Guatemala*, 65; Dosal, *Power in Transition*, 119; Dunkerley, *Power in the Isthmus*, 441–42; Grandin, *The Last Colonial Massacre*, 91–91; *El Guatemalteco* 160:42 (14 November 1960), 337; *El Imparcial*, 4 May 1960 (on MLN) and 14–16 November 1960, passim. For Ydígoras's version, consult Ydígoras Fuentes, *My War with Communism*, 183–207. According to Chiqui Ramírez, the original leader of the November uprising was Alejandro de León Aragón, who was killed late in 1961 (76–77).

73. *El Imparcial*, 22 July 1959, 3 September 1959, 19 July 1960, 21 July 1960, 22 November 1960, 23 November 1960. Threats of military coups were the norm. In August 1959 rumors of a forthcoming *golpe* were so prevalent that the army publicly declared its good intentions toward the government. This drama unfolded again

in February of 1960, supposedly involving at least twenty high-ranking officers, and then once more in June of the next year, resulting in the arrest of Col. Oscar Domingo Valle, an ex-member of the defense ministry and one-time governor of Quetzaltenango. *El Imparcial*, 1 August 1959, 2 February 1960, 12 June 1961, 14 June 1961.

74. Levenson-Estrada, *Trade Unionists against Terror*, 43.

75. Interestingly, it was not until 1964 that "from a stance originally nationalistic and anti-imperialistic, the [MR-13] leaders came to accept Marxism as the best method for analysis and action and socialism as the struggle's goal." *Revolución socialista en Guatemala*, 9. Berger, *Political and Agrarian Development in Guatemala*, 106; *El Imparcial*, 12 July 1961. For in-depth details, see the autobiography of the guerrilla César Montes, the nom de guerre of Julio César Macias: Macías, *Mi camino: la guerrilla*, 1–45.

76. Barry, *Inside Guatemala*; *El Imparcial*, 14–15 March 1962, 28 March 1962; *El Guatemalteco*, 18 April 1962, 521; Sereseres, "The Guatemalan Legacy," 32.

77. ORIT started in 1951, is the AFL's Inter-American Regional Organization of Workers, originally founded in 1948 as the Confederación Interamericana de Trabajadores, or Interamerican Workers' Confederation. ORIT had been attempting to organize within Guatemala before the invasion in 1954 but had its greatest successes just after. See Berger, *Political and Agrarian Development in Guatemala*, 92–93; *Boletín Internacional* (Mexico City: Frente Popular 31 de Enero, FP-31), May 1982, 10; Le Bot, *La guerre en terre maya*, 158–59; Levenson-Estrada, *Trade Unionists against Terror*, 29–31; *Más de cien años*, 2:290–99, 358–75; *Páginas Sindicales Guatemala*, 17–18.

78. *El Guatemalteco*, 25 January 1962, 817.

79. *El Guatemalteco* 14 March 1962, 273, and 21 March 1962, 321–22; *El Imparcial*, March 1962, passim; *Páginas Sindicales Guatemala*, 18–19; Ramírez, *La guerra de los 36 años*, 92.

80. *El Guatemalteco*, 18 April 1962, 521; *El Imparcial*, 16 April 1962; *Páginas Sindicales Guatemala*, 19; Ramírez, *La guerra de los 36 años*, 91–109.

81. Interview, 12 February 2005, Carlos Ramos, Guatemala City. Name changed at subject's request. Don Carlos is typical of the older men I've met who migrated to the United States and later returned. "There," he says, "I was 'Charley.' Here I'm *don* Carlos." When I met him he was counseling two teenage boys to carry skateboards in the United States to fool the *migra* into thinking they were U.S.-born Latino kids.

82. The information on the RRS-MR-13 comes from Ramírez, *La guerra de los 36 años*, 94. Other information has been culled from Adams, *Crucifixion by Power*, 275; Amaro, *Guatemala: Historia Despierta*, 217–18; Levenson-Estrada, *Trade Unionists against Terror*, 43; Dosal, *Power in Transition*, 119. Three opposition parties were crying for Ydígoras's resignation, charging anarchy and corruption. Meanwhile, the military high command engineered a virtual takeover of his administration; Ydígoras's cabinet emerged in late March with nine of ten posts

filled by military officers. The new cabinet's official declaration stated that it was above politics, corruption, and self-interest and had intervened on behalf of the nation in the fight against Communism. The text is reproduced in *El Imparcial*, 2 May 1962.

83. Ydígoras allowed Juan José Arévalo—the exiled first president of the Revolution —to run in the presidential elections of 1963. On 29 March 1963 Arévalo landed on Guatemalan soil. Two days later the military overthrew Ydígoras and canceled the elections. Dunkerley, *Power in the Isthmus*, 443; *El Imparcial*, 1 May 1959, March 1963, passim; Gleijeses, *Shattered Hope*, 393; Gleijeses, "Guatemala: Crisis and Response," 52.

84. Peralta, a Guatemala City native, graduated from the Escuela Politécnica, an elite army academy, in 1929 as an infantry lieutenant. He pursued an additional degree in military studies in Santiago de Chile and served as military attaché to embassies in Mexico, Chile, Costa Rica, El Salvador, and Cuba. Peralta first served Ydígoras as head of the INTA's predecessor, the Dirección General de Asuntos Agrarios (Department of Agrarian Affairs), which was the anticommunists' replacement for the Departamento Agrario Nacional, the agrarian reform's agricultural department. At the end of 1960 Peralta became minister of defense, a promotion that indicates not only his personal political ambitions and connections, but also the increasing link between agrarian transformation and national military projects in the wake of the Cuban Revolution. Berger, *Political and Agrarian Development*, 93–95, 121–22; *El Guatemalteco*, 5 March 1959, 925; Héctor Alejandro Gramajo Morales, *De la guerra ... a la guerra*, 100; Haeussler Yela, *Diccionario General de Guatemala*, 3:1218; *El Imparcial*, 5 March 1958, 25 March 1958, 5 May 1958, 6 May 1958, 1 July 1958, 12 May 1958, 4 October 1958, 3 January 1959, 9 February 1959, 17 March 1959, 16 July 1959, 20 July 1959, 27 July 1959, 9 September 1959, 2 November 1959, 7 November 1959, 8 December 1959, 15 December 1959, 5 May 1960, 15 June 1960, 6 July 1960; McClintock, *The American Connection*, 2:50; Painter, *Guatemala: False Hope, False Freedom*, 37–47; *Recopilación 79* (1960–61), 84.

85. "Anteproyecto de un plan para el desarrollo socio-económico de Guatemala en 21 años," 37, 55; Berger, *Political and Agrarian Development in Guatemala*, 111; *El Imparcial*, 3 January and 2 July 1958, 9 February, 6 July and 21 October 1959, 26 September 1962; *Informe* of Ydígoras Fuentes on agrarian transformation, *El Guatemalteco*, 5 March 1959, 932; "Ley de Transformación Agraria," in *El Guatemalteco*, 19 October 1962, 1281–90; Villacorta Escobar, *Apuntes de economía agrícola*, 49–51.

86. Civic action's creators date it to Operation Pan America, an OAS production of 1958 billed as an inter-American effort to solve the dilemmas of structural poverty. In 1960, as part of the operation, the OAS christened civic action with the Act of Bogotá, setting off a storm of government and military initiatives in Guatemala and around Latin America. The Act of Bogotá, wrote the OAS secretary general, expressed "the governments' determination to launch a massive,

across-the-front attack on underdevelopment." *Organization of American States 1960 Annual Report*, 4. The "across-the-front attack," *El Imparcial* reported, was applauded by nations around the Americas, "with the notable exception of Cuba," as "a new 'Marshall Plan' of millions of dollars to eliminate poverty, ignorance, and social injustice in the nations of Hispanic America" (7 September 1960). The paper did not, however, note the irony of the fact that the plan called for "replacing the large-estate / small-farm system with a fair ownership system" (38), the very sort of agrarian reform for which the United States had overthrown Arbenz just six years before. A summary of civic action can be found in the military's own propaganda: *Ejército de Guatemala: 365 días al servicio de la patria* (Guatemala: Departamento de Información y Divulgación del Ejército, 1991), insert in *Siglo Veintiuno* (Guatemala), 30 June 1991. See also *El Imparcial*, 5 September 1960, 2, and 7 September 1960; Díaz Cardona, *Fuerzas armadas, militarismo y constitución nacional en América Latina*; Nunn, *The Time of the Generals: Latin American Professional Militarism in World Perspective*; and, most important, Schirmer, *The Guatemalan Military Project*. For background on the Alliance for Progress and its role in agrarian transformation throughout Latin America, see Restrepo Fernández, "¿Reforma agraria o modernización agrícola?," 527–48. On links with U.S. strategy in Vietnam and on the Alliance for Progress, see Barry and Preusch, *The Soft War*. Finally, for an account from a Guatemalan perspective, see Rosada-Granados, *Soldados en el poder*.

87. *Ejército de Guatemala: 365 días al servicio de la patria*, 4.

88. Peralta's civic action projects included Operación Escuela, in which troops built schoolhouses, and Programa de Unidades Móviles en Areas Rurales, which sent doctors into the countryside. On rural army commissioners, see Carmack, *Rebels of Highland Guatemala*, 285 and passim; and Grandin, *The Last Colonial Massacre*, 87–88, 115–16, 128, 132.

89. As head of state, Peralta accelerated civic action. He deployed troops to work on road projects, school-building programs, literacy workshops, and public works. While funded by the Alliance for Progress and administered by cabinet ministries, each headed by colonels, these programs were actualized with military manpower and materiel under the banner of civic action. Haeussler Yela, *Diccionario general*, 3:521; *El Imparcial*, 23 April 1963, 2 May 1963, 23 May 1963, 25 June 1963, 16 July 1963, 29 July 1963, 2 August 1963, 4 February 1964, 7 March 1964, 23 May 1964, 20 March 1965, 20 April 1965.

90. *El Guatemalteco*, 6 April 1963, 425–26, 19 April 1963, 502; *El Imparcial*, 1 April 1963, 2 April 1963, 17 May 1963; "Carta Fundamental del Gobierno," in *El Guatemalteco*, 10 April 1963, 457–58; "Ley de Defensa de las Instituciones Democráticas," in *El Guatemalteco*, 10 April 1963, 458–59.

91. *El Imparcial*, 19 April 1963, 14 May 1963, 17 May 1963.

92. Ramírez, *La guerra de los 36 años*, 125–26.

93. *Revolución socialista en Guatemala: Primera declaración de la Sierra de las Minas*, 9.

94. Congressman Menéndez de la Riva managed to escape from his captors, who he

said were the FAR, but suffered a nervous breakdown shortly thereafter. *El Imparcial*, 3 July 1964, 8 May 1965, 22 May 1965, 7 December 1965, 1 March 1966, 1 June 1966, 10 June 1966.

95. President Julio César Méndez Montenegro represented the Partido Revolucionario (PR), a party stung by the assassination in November 1965 of its former leader, his brother, Mario Méndez Montenegro. Julio César Méndez, the dean of the Law School at USAC, picked up the party's banner. Previously, he had participated in the politics surrounding the Revolution of 20 October 1944. Vice President Marroquín, meanwhile, the editor of the Guatemalan newspaper *La Hora*, had served as minister of agriculture for both Arévalo and Ydígoras. *Guatemala: Elecciones '95*, 75; *El Guatemalteco*, 11 May 1966, 571–72; *El Imparcial*, 10 May 1966.

96. The secret pact, signed by the military's highest-ranking officers, by the politicians-elect, and by the PR secretary general, delineated the terms under which the Méndez government could function if it wished to prevent a military takeover. All anticommunist laws were to be enforced, and all understandings and treaties with insurgents were forbidden. Meanwhile, the PR was neither to enjoy unilateral rule at the expense of parties more favored by the army nor to interfere politically with the army. The pact lessened the president's authority and jurisdiction over the armed forces as well. *El Imparcial*, 28 May 1964; "Pacto Secreto de 1966," in Villagrán Kramer, *Biografía política de Guatemala*, 459–61 (see also 408–10).

97. *Ejército de Guatemala: 365 días al servicio de la patria*, 4. In Méndez's first six months as president, two pan–Latin American conventions were held in Guatemala City, one of agricultural credit managers and one of agronomists, showing the nation's centrality in instituting the remade campesino and reengineered countryside as bulwarks against communism.

98. The United States also provided "Army Special Forces personnel" and "helicopter gunships and fixed-wing aircraft" to the Zacapa–Izabal campaign. *El Imparcial*, 6 December 1966, 14 February 1966, 6 August 1968; McClintock, *The American Connection*, 2:79–87 (citations).

99. By the time of the Méndez presidency, bombings, abductions, and assassinations were everyday events. In January 1968 insurgents killed two members of the U.S. military mission in Guatemala, including its chief, John Webber, and wounded a third. In August of the same year a group called Resistencia de la Ciudad (Resistance of the City), supporters of the FAR, killed Ambassador John Gordon Mein of the United States in a botched attempt to kidnap him. The plan had been to trade him for the release of the recently captured FAR chief, Camilo Sánchez, the nom de guerre of Carlos Ordóñez. The ambassador's death sparked even greater waves of violence as the right sought revenge, and, as the government imposed a state of martial law, firefights broke out all over the city in the weeks ahead. Not long afterward, security forces began house-to-house and car-to-car searches in the capital, hunting for subversive materials. See "Asesinato de

un embajador," in "Magazine Veintiuno," a supplement to *Siglo Veintiuno* (Guatemala), 23 August 1998, 19, 26–27; *El Guatemalteco*, 29 August 1968, 513; *El Imparcial*, 16 January 1968, 2 February 1968, 28–29 August 1968, 9 September 1968. For another version of Mein's assassination, see McClintock, *American Connection*, 96.

100. Grandin, *The Last Colonial Massacre*, 74. On Operation Cleanup, see ibid., 74–75, 96–104.

101. Handy, *Gift of the Devil*, 162–64; McClintock, *The American Connection*, 2:85. *Mano*, meaning "hand," also served as an acronym for Movimiento de Acción Nacionalista Organizada.

102. Ball, Kobrak, and Spirer, *State Violence in Guatemala, 1960–1996*, 98; *Quitar el agua al pez*, 37n6. MLN belligerency was well known; in early November 1966, for example, the police raided an MLN arsenal in Guatemala City's zone 2, seizing dynamite, rifles, and machine guns; several party leaders were arrested. *El Imparcial*, 3 November 1966.

103. *El Imparcial*, 25–26 May 1967, 2 June 1967, 30 August 1967. By August over one hundred university professors, students, union organizers, and political activists in Quetzaltenango, Retalhuleu, San Marcos, and other departments found that their names were on the death lists.

104. Dunkerley, *Power in the Isthmus*, 460; Saavedra, *El color de la sangre*, 159–61; Simon, *Guatemala: Eternal Spring, Eternal Tyranny*, passim.

FIVE. Executing Capital

1. Berger, *Political and Agrarian Development*, 157, 169n4; Dosal, *Power in Transition*, 132; *El Imparcial*, 2 March 1970, 21 March 1970, 22 June 1970, 29 June 1970, 8 March 1972; Dunkerley, *Power in the Isthmus*, 459, *El Guatemalteco*, 3 April 1970, 193–94; *Violencia y contraviolencia*, 78.

2. The government created a host of new state agencies and authorities, many of which were managed by military officials and all of which would occasion a nearly 300 percent rise in the state budget by 1978. New agencies and authorities launched by 1975 included Corporación Financiera Nacional (CORFINA), GUATEXPRO, an export-promoting agency, Instituto Guatemalteco de Turismo (INGUAT), Banco Nacional de la Vivienda (BANVI, the National Housing Bank), Banco Nacional de Desarrollo Agrícola (BANDESA, the National Agricultural Development Bank), Dirección General de Servicios Agrícolas (DIGESA), Instituto Nacional de Comercialización Agrícola (INDECA), Comité Permanente de Exposiciones (COPEREX), Empresa Guatemalteca de Aviación (AVIATECA), an airline, Instituto de Fomento de Hipotecas Aseguradas (FEGUA), a mortgage insurance board, and Instituto de Energía Nuclear (INEN). *El Imparcial*, 18 February 1969, 26 April 1969, 8 May 1969, 2 June 1969, 9 June 1969, 12 June 1969, 10 July 1969, 20 December 1969, 7 January 1970, 3 July 1970, 13 July 1970, 16 July 1970, 17 July 1970, 12 August 1970, 10 December 1971, 16 June 1975, 32.

3. *El Guatemalteco*, 16 September 1970, 664; *El Imparcial*, 31 July 1970, 21 August 1970; *Recopilación* 90 (1970–71), 193. Arana launched the agrarian development plan in Santa Cruz del Quiché at the commencement ceremony of an agricultural school run by Centro Nacional de Desarrollo, Adiestramiento y Productividad (CENDAP, the National Center of Development, Training and Productivity). The choice of venues for the event is instructive. The school, called the Tecún Umán Federation, had offered courses to 497 campesinos by radio broadcast—a sort of learning-at-a-distance technique by which social planners hoped to exponentially extend their reach.

4. *El Imparcial*, 25 November 1970; *Recopilación* 90 (1970–71), 253. A concise history of agrarian credit in Guatemala from 1944 to the early 1970s—a history in which the Banco Nacional Agrario, INFOP (the production institute), and the Servicio Cooperativo Interamericano de Crédito Agrícola Supervisado (SCICAS) all played major roles but in which the disenfranchised rarely found access easy— can be found in Villacorta Escobar, *Apuntes de economía agrícola*, 73–77.

5. *El Imparcial*, 4 August 1970, 21 November 1970, 25 November 1970, 21 March 1971, 3 May 1971, 1 February 1972.

6. *El Imparcial*, 10 May 1973, 10 October 1974, 8; *Recopilación* 92 (1972–73), 93–97. In 1975, under Laugerud García, both INDECA and BANDESA touted their regionalization, indicating that they had developed a sophisticated national network (BANDESA, for example, had twenty-nine regional seats by 1975). In that same year, Col. Enrique Ruata Asturias took control of INDECA, a passage to military control that both of the centrist parties, the Christian Democrats and the PR, praised, after a year of vocal denunciations of corruption and irregularities in all three agricultural agencies. *El Imparcial*, 14 March 1973, 20 September 1974, 2 January 1975, 12, 30 July 1975.

7. Dosal, *Power in Transition*, 134; *El Imparcial*, 15 July 1971, 20 December 1971, 21 December 1971.

8. The Centro Interamericano de Exportaciones (CIPE) was an OAS division headquartered in Bogotá, and in August 1972 it was directed by Vicente de Areaga. *El Imparcial*, 1 August 1972.

9. Dosal, *Power in Transition*, 134–35.

10. *El Imparcial*, 18 December 1972, 3 February 1973, 6 February 1973.

11. In 1975, when Gen. Fausto David Rubio Coronado, minister of defense, was relieved of his position and appointed as minister of agriculture, his first public statements concerned the scarcity of basic grains. The new minister said that INDECA was the only branch of the government's agricultural bureaucracy that would not be subject to overhaul and reform. *El Imparcial*, 18 May 1971, 21 May 1971, 1 February 1975, 30 July 1975, 18 October 1975, 2, 16 July 1976.

12. *Guatemala en Lucha* Year 2, no. 3 (September 1982), 14.

13. Ibid., 12–14. The popular movement's campesino magazine, *De Sol a Sol*, further claimed that BANDESA was giving huge credits to cattle ranchers since 1975, leaving small farmers with nothing. *De Sol a Sol*, no. 26 (March 1979), 3. On DDT

and other pesticides, see *Revista Envio*, online, November 2004, "Centroamér-ica: Una región en crisis ecológica," http://www.envio.org.ni/ar ticulo. Nu-merous websites have watchdog information about the continued exportation of deadly chemicals banned in the North to the global South as well as about the deaths and birth defects that result from the use of even approved agrochemicals without the proper protective equipment. For one example, see Ulises Sadoul, "Los trabajadores rurales: entre la espada y la pared," http://www.nodo50 .org/pretextos/Laespada.htm.

14. About three-quarters of the ranches were located on the Costa Sur, but a steady displacement toward the Petén was noted, both for reasons noted in the text and because of the new economic successes in sugar, which was taking up coastal land, and rubber, which was drawing population to the Petén. Berger, *Political and Agrarian Development*, 110, 126–27, 147–50; Dunkerley, *Power in the Ist-humus*, 473; Grupo Subsectorial de Trabajo de la Carne (GSTC), "Propuesta de creación de la Asociación Nacional Ganadera (ANAG)," Collection Melgar Zamboni (hereafter Coll. Melgar Z.), 8.

15. Interview, Carlos Melgar, 8/13/03.

16. See EDOM 1972–2000, 386.

17. Interview, Carlos Melgar, 8/13/03. *Vos* is the superinformal "you." *Mirá, vos* means, in speech between friends, "Hey, look."

18. In 1998 the four companies complying with USDA standards were EXGUAPA-GRA, INDUPESCA, INPRACSA, and PROCASA. Coll. Melgar Z., 43–46; inter-view, Carlos Melgar, 8/13/03.

19. Interviews, Carlos Melgar, 7/16/03 and 8/13/03. On La Fragua, see Royal Ahold website, 2003, http://www.ahold.com and related subpages. In 2005 Royal Ahold sold its shares of Paiz Ahold to Wal-Mart Stores, Inc.

20. Interview, Carlos Melgar, 8/13/03.

21. *El Imparcial*, 22 August 1972, 9 April 1974; interview, Carlos Melgar, 8/13/03.

22. Interview, Carlos Melgar, 8/13/03. Bit by bit, more information comes out. They had met with César Montes, one of the nation's most important guerrilla leaders. Several meat vendors did join the movement. According to Chiqui Ramírez's book, a meat vendor named Percy Jacobs who turned guerrilla (and may have been code-name Canción) later left the movement to open a meat business in a Mexico City market. While there, he was *ajusticiado* (read: killed) by the guerrillas for having purloined their funds. See Ramírez, *La guerra de los 36 años*, 225. Another meat vendor from Mercado La Presidenta (I omit the name, since I have not found it in the left's own publications) left the group to join the guerrillas; his code name was Iguana.

23. On the MCI, see *El Imparcial*, 24 August 1970. For a (perhaps edited) collection of Laugerud's speeches, see *Pensamiento de General Laugerud*, vol. 1: *Candidato Presidencial*.

24. The government launched the bank on a five-million-dollar initial investment capitalized by the Instituto de Previsión Militar, the army's financial wing, and by

tax revenues. The bank later cofinanced with the Bank of America the Santa Rosita military housing project in the capital, which offered eight hundred luxury units to higher-ups in the military. *El Imparcial*, 11 February 1972; Black, *Garrison Guatemala*, 52; "Ley Orgánica del Banco del Ejército," in *Recopilación* 90 (1970–71), 326–32. The military's account can be found in Escobar Argüello, "El Banco del Ejército," in *Revista Militar* 11, no. 3 (January/March 1974), 79–85. According to the article, the bank would develop and strengthen the army's welfare system, relieving the state of that financial burden. Its goal was to improve conditions for the population as a whole by advancing loans to small and midsized businesses, especially those involved in ISI. The bank was also to invest in scientific research, helping the country to utilize its natural resources more effectively.

25. Schwartz, *Forest Society: A Social History of Petén, Guatemala*, 287; *Ejército de Guatemala: 365 días al servicio de la patria*, 4; *El Guatemalteco* 165:64 (6 September 1962), 801; *El Imparcial*, 5 February 1964, 10 February 1964, 27 May 1964, 2 June 1964, 18 June 1964, 30 June 1964, 7 March 1967, 15 July 1967, 27 September 1967, 8 October 1968, 7 February 1970, 30 March 1970, 16 April 1970, 17 April 1970; "La franja transversal del norte," in *Guatemala: Revista Cultural del Ejército* 8:20–21 (30 June 1980), 83–86.

26. *El Imparcial*, 24 June 1975.

27. The first issue of *Guatemala: Revista Cultural del Ejército* (Army Cultural Magazine) included articles on social projects and civic action, such as an army wives' club that made donations to schools and to antituberculosis efforts and military medical teams treating highland toddlers. Future issues had astonishing headlines such as "Human Rights: Peace as the Fundamental Principle of Coexistence in the Universe." *Guatemala: Revista Cultural del Ejército* 1:1 (30 June 1975), 11, and 2:6–7 (31 December 1976), 37. Increasingly two-headed, civic action included not only literacy and aid programs, but also direct construction and engineering work. The military had recently institutionalized the Cuerpo de Ingenieros del Ejército de Guatemala (CIEG, Army Corps of Engineers), uniting various units under one command. The CIEG would manage ground-level construction in what was fast becoming a spree of development and corruption in the FTN, the country's northern region. *Recopilación* 94 (1973–74), 281.

28. *Guatemala: Revista Cultural del Ejército*, 6:16–17 (30 June 1979), 5. Jennifer Schirmer writes about the military's promotion of the "sanctioned Mayan"—see *The Guatemalan Military Project*—and, besides styling itself as protector and tutor of the Maya, the army drew on faux-Mayan mystic customs as far back as the Revolution; see, for example, issues from 1949 of the Escuela Politécnica newsletter, *Xol Bei* (AGCA Hemeroteca paq. 1247).

29. "Acción Cívica Militar: anotaciones del Mayor César Octavio Noguera Argueta y del Subtte. As. y Doctor Luís Sieckavizza," *Revista Militar* 11, no. 9 (July/September 1975), 53–58. A case in point of how youth could go astray, the army article said, was what had happened with Crater. Crater, the Centro de Capacitá-

ción Social (Center for Social Training), had been founded in the 1960s at USAC. Inspired by Vatican II, it was an outreach program of the Roman Catholic Church oriented toward liberation theology. With the help of the Maryknoll priest Blase Bonpane, students formed base communities and organized in the city and the highlands alike throughout the decade, using techniques based on Paulo Friere's Pedagogy of the Oppressed. Though originally in league with the Christian Democratic party, Crater members became increasingly conscious of social inequity through their work with the poor. By 1967 scores of students and *cursillo* (course) members, terrorized by death squads, were joining organizations like the FAR. See Bonpane, *Guerrillas of Peace*, 23–32, 56–57.

30. *Central America Report* (Guatemala: Inforpress Centroamericana) [hereafter CAR] (13 December 1974), 129, (14 March 1975), 89–90. The bulk of cooperativists were organized in two umbrella groups: Federación Nacional de Cooperativas de Ahorro y Crédito (FENACOAC, National Federation of Savings and Credit Cooperatives), with about sixty thousand members, and the Federación de Cooperativas Agrícolas Regionales (FECOAR), with eleven thousand. CAR (17 November 1975), 329.

31. State agencies, meanwhile, rallied to the cooperative cause: BANDESA and CORFINA advanced loans and ran development programs, while INTECAP (the Professional Training Institute) helped, among other things, to promote wheat production in the highlands. As early as January 1975 Congress was debating plans to create a national cooperative institute to control events, but these plans would not be actualized until after Lucas took office. *El Imparcial*, 30 November 1974, 28 January 1975, 31 January 1975, 14 March 1975, 2 May 1975, 1 July 1975, 28 October 1975, 26 March 1976, 29 October 1976.

32. McClintock, *The American Connection*, 2:133 (citation), 132–34.

33. CAR (11 February 1976), 41–46; *El Imparcial*, 5 February 1976, 9 February 1976; Jonas, *The Battle for Guatemala*, 95.

34. CAR (11 February 1976), 41–43.

35. Ibid., 41–42.

36. *Prensa Libre*, 1 November 2002, Nacional, online.

37. Tierra Nueva I (a second one was born in 1985) was planned as an idealist, communitarian, socialist community, but it erupted in conflicts, and the system fell apart. A study of both Tierra Nueva I and II is AVANCSO, *"Aquí corre la bola:" Organización y relaciones sociales en una comunidad popular urbana*. The information used here is from pages 11–19. See also Camus, *Ser indígena*, 157.

38. McClintock, *The American Connection*, 2:136.

39. *De Sol a Sol: Periódico campesino*, no. 11 (March 1976), 1, 4.

40. The CRN, originally created in 1969, by most accounts provided relatively honest and efficient fiscal administration. It was headed by Gen. Ricardo Peralta Méndez, commander of the Guatemalan navy, who had links to the Christian Democrats. Amaro, *Guatemala: Historia Despierta*, 222; CAR (29 March 1976), passim, and (11 February 1976), 43, 46; *Ejército de Guatemala: 365 días al servicio*

de la patria, 5; *El Imparcial*, 8 September 1969, 30 September 1969 (includes a copy of the decree creating the CRN), 16 February 1976, 27 May 1976; *Recopilación* 91 (1971–72), 106, 300, 95 (1975–76), 489, 525–26, 96 (1976–77), 422.

41. *El Imparcial*, 19 March 1976, 30 April 1976; Barry and Preusch, *The Soft War*, 113–15; Peckenham, "Land Settlement in the Petén"; *Recopilación* 96 (1976–77), 115.

42. Schirmer, *The Guatemalan Military Project*, 36–37. In some ways, the CRN was structured like the National Agrarian Department (DAN) that had managed Arbenz's agrarian reform in the early 1950s.

43. Harvey, *The Condition of Postmodernity*.

44. For a brief summary, see Ellwood, *The No-Nonsense Guide to Globalization*, and Hoogvelt, *Globalization and the Postcolonial World*. An overview written during the time period can be found in *Nueva Sociedad* (San José, Costa Rica), no. 29 (March–April 1977), 5–11. On Laugerud's cabinet nominations, see *El Imparcial*, 24 June 1974.

45. *El Imparcial*, 8 May 1976, 15 May 1976, 18 March 1977, 21 October 1977, 2 December 1977; Schirmer, *The Guatemalan Military Project*, 37.

46. CAR 3:34 (30 August 1976), 265.

47. The EGP broadsheet expressed solidarity with the Salvadoran rebels and attacked the neocolonialism of the IDB and its "soft loans" to Guatemala. *El Imparcial*, EGP Manifesto, 31 May 1977, 13.

48. Ramírez, *La guerra de los 36 años*, 246; *Páginas Sindicales Guatemala*, 29. For an in-depth study, see Kobrak, *Organizing and Repression in the University of San Carlos, Guatemala, 1944 to 1996*.

49. *Boletín Internacional* (México: Frente Popular 31 de Enero, FP-31), May 1982, 11; *Páginas Sindicales Guatemala*, 27–29; *Quitar el agua al pez*, 33. State terror had failed to quash grass-roots organizing after the coup in 1954. Paradoxically, anticommunism often either provided cover for organizers or launched initiatives with serious radical potential. The Autonomous Federation of Guatemalan Unions (FASGUA), the Central of Federated Workers (CTF), and the Central Nacional de Trabajadores (CNT) are good examples. Anticommunist trade unionists founded FASGUA right after the coup, but its member unions, hiding behind the shield of conservative umbrella leadership, remained Communist in orientation. By the 1960s, albeit with low membership (only fifteen unions were affiliated by 1968), FASGUA was a leader of leftist workers' organization in Guatemala. During Laugerud's presidency, meanwhile, members of the CTF (the new name of CONTRAGUA/CONSIGUA, which had been formed with ORIT and AIFLD support) bucked their conservative leadership and followed the radical trade unions in the 1970s in both philosophy and tactics. The very foundation of the AIFLD in 1962 had been promoted to combat the new and growing Confederación Latino-Americana de Trabajadores (CLAT), an initiative of the Christian Democrats. Yet in Guatemala, even the CLAT and the Christian Democrats proved too centrist to hold their membership in the 1970s. In 1968 the CLAT had founded the CNT, which organized both urban workers

and peasant leagues. By 1973 the CNT was distancing itself from the Christian Democratic party, and in 1978 it broke with the CLAT altogether. Some of its leadership went on to work with the FAR. *Boletín Internacional* (Mexico City: Frente Popular 31 de Enero, FP-31), May 1982, 11; Levenson-Estrada, *Trade Unionists against Terror*, 33–39.

50. Ball, Kobrak, and Spirer, *State Violence in Guatemala, 1960–1996*, 20.

51. *Boletín Internacional* (September 1982), 17–18; *Quitar el agua al pez*, 33; *Páginas Sindicales Guatemala*, 29.

52. CAR (23 January 1978), 29; Gleijeses, "Guatemala: Crisis and Response," 54; *El Imparcial*, EGP Campo Pagado, 4 January 1978, 5.

53. The state workers were organized in an emergency committee composed of employees in health, mail, telegraphs, education, courts, and even the Labor Ministry itself. They were soon joined in sympathy strikes by metalworkers and bakers. *El Imparcial*, 23 February 1978, 27 February 1978; *Páginas Sindicales Guatemala*, 30; Levenson-Estrada, *Trade Unionists*, 144–45.

54. CAR (20 March 1978), 91, 5:13 (3 April 1978): 97–98; *Recopilación 97* (1977–78), 65–66.

55. CAR (5 June 1978), 169; *El Imparcial*, 9 June 1978, 19 (army ad), and 12 June 1978; *Páginas Sindicales Guatemala*, 31; *El Rano Chapín: Los pobladores en pie de lucha* (Guatemala: FP-31, n.d. [1982 or 1983—during the Ríos Montt dictatorship]), 6. The best source on Panzós is Grandin, *The Last Colonial Massacre*, for this period, see 147–59.

56. CAR (3 July 1978), 203; Dunkerley, *Power in the Isthmus*, 473; López Rivera, *Guatemala: Intimidades de la pobreza*, 9–10. For an excellent discussion of Guatemala's agrarian landscape, with some reference to the history discussed here, see AVANCSO, *Regiones y zonas agrarias de Guatemala*.

57. Grandin, *The Last Colonial Massacre*, 19.

58. *Boletín Internacional*, FP-31, May 1982, 11, September 1982, 17–18.

59. Dunkerley, *Power in the Isthmus*, 471–72; *El Imparcial*, 10 August 1978, 17 August 1978, 2–5 October 1978, passim; *Páginas Sindicales Guatemala*, 31.

60. CAR (4 June 1979), 174, and (18 June 1979), 187–90.

61. CAR (9 July 1979), 212.

62. CAR (17 September 1979), 294.

63. CAR (1 October 1979), 307, (22 October 1979), 332–33, and (10 January 1980), 6–7 (citation). By this time Arana was leader of the Central Auténtica Nacional (CAN) political party.

64. CAR (11 February 1980), 41, 43, CAR (18 February 1980), 49, and CAR (31 March 1980), 99; "Gobierno condena enérgicamente masacre terrorista ocurrida en Embajada de España" and "Bomba Molotov por parte de ocupantes provocó incendio en Embajada Española," *El Imparcial*, 1 February 1980; *De Sol a Sol*, no. 32 (February 1980), 6; *Obrero en lucha* (Guatemala: FTG), no. 1 (April 1980), 2–5.

65. *Boletín Informativo* (Guatemala: Frente Democrático Contra La Represión),

(April 1980), 3–6; *Boletín Socialista Democrático* (Guatemala), 1, no. 14 (March 1980), 1; CAR (3 March 1980), 65, (10 March 1980), 74, (14 April, 1980), 106, (12 May 1980), 139 (citation), (19 May 1980), 146–47.

66. CAR (8 September 1980), 273–74; CAR (3 December 1979), 377–78; CAR (1 November 1980), 341–42; *Recopilación* 100 (1980–81), 22.

67. CAR (29 August 1981), 269–70; Jonas, *The Battle for Guatemala*, 138; Sereseres, "The Guatemalan Legacy," 35–36.

68. There is an enormous literature on the violence in Guatemala, ranging from human rights reports and investigations to testimonials. Most important, see Comisión para el Esclarecimiento Histórico, *Guatemala: Memoria del silencio* (Guatemala, 1999)—the Truth Commission report. Particularly moving is Falla, *Masacres de la selva*.

69. Grandin, *The Last Colonial Massacre*, xv.

70. CAR (11 June 1982), 171 (citation); Dosal, *Power in Transition*, 149; Figueroa Ibarra, "El contenido burgués y reaccionario del golpe de estado en Guatemala," 122, 128; Handy, *Gift of the Devil*, 183; "Proclama del Ejército de Guatemala al Pueblo," 9 June 1982, in *Recopilación* 101 (1981–82), 112–13.

71. Barry, *Inside Guatemala*, 56 (citation); *Guatemala: Security, Development, and Democracy* (Guatemalan Church in Exile, 1989), 3, 9, 57. For events in the Ixcán, see Falla, *Masacres de la selva*.

72. The CRN served as the military's liaison with the wave of Private Volunteer Organizations (PVOS) that began appearing in the heady Evangelical days of Ríos Montt. Their first numbers included Love Lift International, Youth with a Mission, and Pat Robertson's Christian Broadcast Network. Sen. Jack Kemp, a Republican, was also on hand. Ríos revived the CRN with AID, IDB, and UN World Food Program money. CAR (19 November 1982), 359–60; Barry and Preusch, *The Soft War*, 113–15, 120, 134, 236; *Recopilación* 102 (1982–83), 18–19, 33–34.

73. CAR (4 February 1983), 34.

74. CAR (5 August 1983), 223–24.

75. CAR (12 August 1983), 241–42.

76. "Proclama del Alto Mando y del Consejo de Comandantes Militares," in *Recopilación* 103 (1983–84), 58–59. On the restrictive nature of democracy in Guatemala after 1985, see Grandin, *The Last Colonial Massacre*.

77. Barry, *Inside Guatemala*, 58.

78. CAR (28 November 1981), 371–72, and 10:6 (11 February 1983), 44; José Maria Mayrink, "O apoio civil na luta antiguerrilha na Guatemala"; *Recopilación* 103 (1983–84), 229–30. Commentary on model villages based on author interviews and visits.

79. The agencies included INDE, INACOP, INDECA, BANVI, CONE, and the CRN.

80. *Recopilación* 103 (1983–84), 633–37.

81. CAR (6 April 1984), 108–9; *Recopilación* 103 (1983–84), 311–13.

82. CAR (14 December 1984), 389, and (22 February 1985), 52–53; *Recopilación* 104 (1984–85), 106–13.

83. *Verdad: Órgano del Comité Central* PGT (Guatemala: Partido Guatemalteco del Trabajo), no. 280 (January 1985), 6–7.

84. Nelson, "Chisec, Alta Verapaz," and "Coban, Alta Verapaz," from field research report, 80, 90–91, and passim. Chisec, for example, had developed largely through the colonization of the FTN, and most of its population consisted of newcomers to the area. The Mayan mayor, Nelson reported, was viewed as politically impotent, and the Inter-Institution Coordinators simply as individuals whose job it was to keep the army informed of local goings-on.

85. Barry and Preusch, *The Soft War*, 118, quotation from "Transforming the Indian Highlands" (London: Latin American Regional Report, May 6, 1983). The reasons for the government's interest in nontraditional exports were clear: the sector had grown an incredible 46.8 percent in 1979 (though coffee and cotton continued to provide over half the country's foreign exchange), while petroleum, the nation's great hope, was performing sluggishly. The real explosion, however, came in 1980, when the government began selling small lots to unspecified recipients in the FTN for the symbolic price of one quetzal, expressly for the cultivation of crops such as cardamom, coffee, cacao, pepper, and citrus fruits. The government provided free cardamom seedlings to numerous highland cooperatives. Guatemala actually beat most other Latin American countries to the nontraditional export trend, which blossomed in the hemisphere only after the Baker Plan of 1985 and the Brady Plan of 1989 had rescued major nations from the critical debt crisis kicked off by Mexico's threatened loan default of 1982—the same year in which Guatemala had created a guaranty fund to extend credit to the agroexport sector. Ironically, Guatemala escaped the brunt of the debt crisis thanks to its revolution, the United States, and the major IFIS (international financial institutions) made sure that the state remained sufficiently liquid fiscally to avoid going the way of Cuba and Nicaragua. Bulmer-Thomas, *The Economic History of Latin America Since Independence*, 364–65, 373–75, 383; CAR (18 February 1980), 50, (12 May 1980), 140; *El Guatemalteco*, 16 August 1968, 369; *Recopilación* 100 (1980–81), 111, 221. For a more positive view of nontraditional agroexport development, see Paus, ed., *Struggle Against Dependence*.

86. Despite relative army unity and unprecedented army counterinsurgency efforts, both popular resistance sectors and the guerrillas saw gains in 1984 and 1985. Guatemala's famed yearlong strike and occupation of the Coca-Cola bottling plant was a major landmark in labor history. During the months that the members of the Bottling Union steadfastly held their ground, insurgency and popular unrest increased. The summer of 1984 saw not only a rash of assassinations and kidnappings, but pitched battles between the army and guerrillas, including a confrontation in August in San Marcos in which two ORPA contingents, four hundred men strong, challenged the military. Guerrilla activity

escalated in 1985 as insurgents scored successes throughout the highlands. Just
months before the presidential elections in 1985, Guatemala City erupted in
violence as massive protests and riots forced bus companies to rescind fare
increases. Union workers, stung by inflation, joined the fray, as did university
students, which led to an army occupation of the university campus. CAR (8 June
1984), 175, (10 August 1984), 245, (15 February 1985), 41–42, and (6 September
1985), 265–68; Levenson-Estrada, *Trade Unionists Against Terror*, 3 and passim.

87. *Elaboración de productos cárnicos.*

88. The Asociación de Expendedores de Carne de Res, or Beef Vendors' Association, formed in 1985, represented some thirty-six butchers in about a dozen
markets. It combated high beef prices, served as a watchdog on meat-packing
plants, and began internal *capacitación*, or job training. ASEC, formed in 1992,
included all types of meat vendors. Interviews, Carlos Melgar, 6/16/03 and
8/13/03; Expendedores de Carne de Res, minutes and meeting notes, April
1985–April 1986 (Coll. Melgar Z.): Acta 3, 17 April 1985, and passim; *Prensa Libre*,
12 March 1986, 12; "Informe sobre la situación de la Asociación de Expendedores
de Carne, ASEC, desde el inicio de la consultoría en julio de 1998 hasta el mes de
agosto de 1999," unpublished report (Guatemala: Unidentified government
agency [division of MAGA?], 1999) (Coll. Melgar Z.), 1–8, Seminario de Planificación ZOPP, "El sector minorista: los beneficios y compromisos incorporándose al PROMECA," Guatemala, 27–31 May 1991, Salón de Conferencias
INTECAP (Guatemala: Dirección de Servicios Pecuarios, DIGESEPE / Cooperación Técnica Alemana GTZ, 1991), conference handout (Coll. Melgar Z.).
PROMECA was coadministrated by GTZ—the Deutsche Gesellschaft für Tech-
nishe Zusammarbeit GmbH—and MAGA, or the Ministerio de Agricultura,
Ganadería y Alimentación (through DIGESEPE, or Dirección General de Servicios Agropecuarios). Public sector organizations involved included INTECAP
(Instituto Técnico de Capacitación y Productividad) and the Facultad de Me-
dicina Veterinaria y Zootécnica de la Universidad de San Carlos de Guatemala.
For the private sector were the Asociación para el Mejoramiento de la Industria
Pecuaria (ASINPEGUA) and the Centro de Carnes Sociedad Anónima
(CECARSA), along with a number of trade organizations representing both
wholesalers (such as the Asociación de Porcinocultores de Guatemala [AP-
OGUA]) and retailers.

89. PROMECA consumer education proposals (minutes, notes, proposals), 26–29
October 1992 (Coll. Melgar Z.).

90. ASEC, "Reglamento para el uso de los recursos del Fondo Rotatorio," 9 April
1992, modified June 1993, April 1994 (Coll. Melgar Z.); "Plan de acción 1993,
Asociación de Expendedores de Carne, ASEC," (Coll. Melgar Z.), internal document, Junta Directiva Provisional, ASEC, 1993.

91. Carlos Melgar, Personal ASEC minutes and meeting notes, 1994 (Coll. Melgar
Z.): "Editorial: Nostalgia," c. 20 November; Melgar, handwritten letter draft.

92. Carlos Melgar, Personal ASEC minutes and meeting notes, 1994 (Coll. Melgar Z.): 13 October; minutes, Reunión de Trabajo de la ASEC.

93. Inside the new Centro de Tecnología de la Carne (CETEC), erected as part of PROMECA and run by the meat wholesalers' trade organization, ASEC and INTECAP cosponsored events on quality control, human relations, hygiene, and small business administration and on the various aspects of processing livestock. In 1996, when the Guatemalans and Germans founded the Federación Guate-malteca de Grupos Organizados del Sector Cárnico (FEGOSCA) to provide various meat interests with services in administration, finance, promotion, train-ing, and modernization, ASEC was both a founding member and a client. ASEC, mixed internal paperwork (Coll. Melgar Z.): Invitation to INTECAP-ASEC total quality control seminar, 10 May 1993; Poster, "ASEC- CETEC eventos de capaci-tación, 1995," FEGOSCA brochure, c. 1997–98; ASEC, Legal documents and paperwork (Coll. Melgar Z.); notarized legal agreement, FEGOSCA-ASEC, 30 October 1996; Interviews, Carlos Melgar, 7/16/03, 8/13/03.

94. "Informe sobre la situación de la Asociación de Expendedores de Carne, ASEC, desde el inicio de la consultoría en julio de 1998 hasta el mes de agosto de 1999," unpublished report by government assessor of ASEC Auto-Abastecimiento Proj-ect (Guatemala: Unidentified government agency, 1999) (Coll. Melgar Z.), 16 March 1999; Lic. Juan Luis Orantes, Asesor Coordinador del Proyecto, to ASEC Junta Directiva (Coll. Melgar Z.).

95. Interview, Carlos Melgar, 8/13/03.

96. In the planning for at least five years with the help of advisors from Spain, INTECAP began operations in 1972, despite stiff private-sector opposition both because of its cost and because of a history of lackluster results derived from the already-existing CENDAP. Finally, the private sector was invited to help write the status. In 1976 INTECAP claimed that it expected to serve sixteen thousand students, a 65 percent increase over its enrollment during the previous two years. By 1977 the agency, thanks to Spanish and West German aid, had opened twenty-seven branches around the country. INTECAP initially offered classes like "Psychology for Secretaries" and "Modern Methods of Planning, Organiza-tion and Control of Productive Processes," showing a clear emphasis on provid-ing subsidized job training for business and industry. Quickly, however, popular demand won out, and courses such as "Diesel Mechanics," "Home Appliance Repair," "Hand Weaving," and "[Making] Artificial Flowers" appeared. *El Impar-cial*, 30 October 1970, 2 February 1971, 16 November 1971, 29 April 1972, 17 May 1972, 1–2 August 1972, 6 January 1973, 4, 14 February 1973, 29 January 1974, 8 February 1974, 10, 4 December 1974, 6 December 1974, 9 December 1975, 29 January 1976, 26 January 1977.

97. *Prensa Libre*, 5 October 2002, 22.

98. CONMIGUAT's parent organization, COCEMI, the Comité Coordinador de Em-presarios de la Microempresa de la Región Central de América (Coordinating

Committee of Small Business Owners of the Central American Region), formed in Heredia, Costa Rica, in 1993. Within five years the organization had over 50,000 members in 126 organizations grouped into 6 national committees. COCEMI got financial support from the government of Holland and the International Labor Organization, CONMIGUAT from the European Union. *Micro-empresa* (Guatemala: CONMIGUAT), September 1997, passim; "La micro-empresa por el desarrollo de la región: Plataforma de acción, versión popular" (Costa Rica: COCEMI [Comité Coordinador de Empresarios de la Micro-empresa de la Región Central de América], 1998), 28.

99. "La microempresa por el desarrollo de la región," 28.
100. Ibid., 19.

SIX. A Society of Vendors

1. Goldin, "Organizing the World through the Market," 1–2, 94; Swetnam, "The Open Gateway: Social and Economic Interaction in a Guatemalan Market-place," 5–6, passim.

2. Interview, Carlos Melgar, 7/16/03. This overview is also based on a close reading of boxes full of ASIMEM papers, comparing actual results to the yearly "action plans" drawn up by the leadership and presented to the membership as a whole for discussion and approval.

3. Interview, Siriaca Subuyuj, Mercado Cervantes, 7/15/03. The phrase means "she calls herself Julia."

4. Ibid.

5. Interview, Blanca Alicia González Farfán, Mercado Cervantes, 7/15/03.

6. Note her use of *el pueblo* and how her family story exemplifies a whole range of migratory and economic activity seen throughout the twentieth century in Guatemala.

7. I am omitting the name of the offender—one of the group's highest officers— since it is not relevant to this history and because including it would violate one of my prime directives, namely, not to get involved in Guatemalan political squabbles. There is, however, ironclad proof of the embezzlement. Melgar managed to negotiate a peaceful settlement through which the organization was reimbursed. Comecer, Minutes, ASIMEM Meetings, 13 April–30 November 1999 (Coll. Melgar Z.): 13 April 1999; 8 October 1999, Organismo Judicial, Acuerdo Final, ASIMEM and [name omitted] (Coll. Melgar Z.).

8. ASIMEM, "Reglamento interno provisional de la Asociación de Inquilinos de los Mercados Municipales," c. 28 February 1993 (Coll. Melgar Z.); 11 November 1993, Acta Notarial de Asociación de Inquilinos de Mercados Municipales— ASIMEM/Nuevo Amanecer, Min. Gobernación, Instrumento Público Núm. 46, Expediente T-930320 (Coll. Melgar Z.): sheet 8.

9. 11 November 1993, Acta Notarial de Asociación, ASIMEM (Coll. Melgar Z.): sheet 8.

10. "The markets run at a defecit," a municipal official told me. "They pay thirty quetzales per square meter per month. Nowhere else in the *world* is it so cheap!" At the time of the interview, that figure worked out to slightly under US$4.00. Interview, Ing. Civil Said Tapia, Subdirector de Abastos, Dirección General de Abastos, CENMA [Central de Mayoreo], Guatemala City, 6/03/03.

11. Interview, Carlos Melgar, Guatemala City, 6/16/03. See also Camus, *Ser indígena*, 103. Privatization rumors were behind numerous upsets in Guatemala City. In 1999, for example, Mayor García-Gallont had flyers posted in all the markets insisting that "the municipal markets under no circumstances will be privatized, as members of the political opposition have maliciously reported." In 2001 privatization rumors caused two strikes that shut down all municipal markets in the metropolitan area for days, and over five thousand vendors demonstrated in the streets. October 1999, PAN, Flyer, Fritz García-Gallont Promises No Privatization (Coll. Melgar Z.); *Nuestro Diario*, 4 April 2001, 5; *Prensa Libre*, 5 April 2001, 2 and 28 September 2001, Nacional, online.

12. Interview, Carlos Melgar, 6/16/03; Interviews, Beatriz Cux López and Blanca Alicia González Farfán, Mercado Cervantes, 7/15/03.

13. Mercado Cervantes, Reuniones Generales y Notas Administrativas, 10 February 1999–6 June 2001 (Coll. Melgar Z.): 14 October 1999.

14. Interviews: Carlos Melgar, 6/16/03, 7/16/03, and Beatriz Cux López and Blanca Alicia González Farfán, Mercado Cervantes, 7/15/03; Registro Civil de la Capital, Inscripción de Nombramiento, Libro 4 anex. PI, Folio 327, Acta 382, 9 June 1999 ["Melgar Samboni" (*sic*) named Presidente de la Junta Directiva y Representante Legal de ASIMEM] (Coll. Melgar Z.).

15. Comecer, ASIMEM Minutes, 11 January 2000–27 March '01 (Coll. Melgar Z.): 13 March 2001 (new junta directiva elected, ASIMEM); 27 May 2001, Letter of Resignation, Junta Directiva Mercado Cervantes to Junta Directiva ASIMEM (Coll. Melgar Z.).

16. Interview, Ing. Civil Said Tapia, Subdirector de Abastos, Dirección General de Abastos, CENMA [Central de Mayoreo], Guatemala City, 6/03/03.

17. *Prensa Libre*, 6 August 1979 (clip). The article covers the acute lack of markets and its impact on daily life at the neighborhood level.

18. Interview, Beatriz Cux López, 7/15/03. For fine-grained ethnographies of the markets and city neighborhoods alike, see Camus, *Ser indígena*.

19. *El Imparcial*, 17 January 1976 (clip); 18 March 1976 (clip); 22 March 1976 (clip); 24 June 1983 (clip; citation).

20. An article in *La Hora* on the history of Guatemala City markets read as follows: "The entrances [of the mule trains] were: the Guarda del Golfo, the Guarda of Chinautla, the Guarda of Incienso and mainly, the Guarda Viejo, where they arrived with black beans from Parramos, and from Antigua, Guatemala, with magnificent oranges, corn, broad-beans and such fare. . . . [T]hrough the other Guardas [they came] with charcoal, firewood, pine torches, and in general

everything necessary for commerce." *La Hora,* 10 September 1975 (clip). For a scholarly version, see Gellert and Pinto Soria, *Ciudad de Guatemala,* 56.

21. *El Imparcial,* 14 May 1963 (clip).

22. *Prensa Libre,* 9 August 1968 (clip), 14 August 1968 (clip; police citation); *El Imparcial,* 14 August 1968.

23. EDOM 1972–2000, 141.

24. EDOM 1972–2000, 177, 179; *El Imparcial,* 29 July 1971 (clip) and 2 December 1974. In 1972 the muni did a poll of vendors and reported that there were 1,132 in satellite markets and 7,329 with licenses renting puestos. According to the statistics, 80 percent of the informal vendors were single women with small children (*El Imparcial,* 22 August 1972).

25. *El Imparcial,* 22 December 1971 (clip).

26. *Microempresa* (Guatemala: CONMIGUAT): September 1997, 8.

27. Comecer, ASIMEM Minutes, 11 January 2000–27 March 2001 (Coll. Melgar Z.): 15 February 2000, 14 March 2000, 27 March 2000, 5 September 2000.

28. ASIMEM, "Capitulo III: Economía complementaria," Working paper, n.d. [c. 1999–2000] (Coll. Melgar Z.).

29. Mercado Cervantes, Reuniones Generales y Notas Administrativas, 10 February 1999–6 June 2001 (Coll. Melgar Z.): 9 October 2000.

30. Interview, Carlos Melgar, 6/16/03.

31. Interview, Carlos Melgar, 7/16/03.

32. Interview, Carlos Melgar, 7/16/03.

33. Mercado Cervantes, Reuniones Generales y Notas Administrativas, 10 February 1999–6 June 2001 (Coll. Melgar Z.): 2 April 2001.

34. Comecer, Reuniones, 11 October 2000–5 September 2001 (Coll. Melgar Z.): 18 April 2001.

35. 24 April 2001, Ex-miembros de la Junta Directiva to Junta, ASIMEM (Coll. Melgar Z.).

36. Comecer, Reuniones, 11 October 2000–5 September 2001 (Coll. Melgar Z.): 22 May 2001; 27 May 2001, Letter of Resignation, Junta Directiva Mercado Cervantes to Junta Directiva ASIMEM (Coll. Melgar Z.).

37. Interviews, Carlos Melgar, 6/16/03 and 7/16/03; Interview, Ing. Civil Said Tapia, Subdirector de Abastos, Dirección General de Abastos, CENMA [Central de Mayoreo], Guatemala City, 6/03/03. Confirming membership is *Prensa Libre,* 7 September 2002, Económicas, online.

38. The municipal administrator within each market often has to deal with routine keeping of the peace. "Your kids are always playing in the aisles and they broke a vendor's goods," the Cervantes administrator wrote to one of the seasonal renters who had a spot on the sidewalk outside. "Please control your children's behavior, and remember that you might not have the opportunity to sell here next Christmas if you don't." Melgar, Mixed Misc. Paperwork (Coll. Melgar Z.): 16 December 1999, Roberto Menéndez, Admin., Cervantes, to Blanca Morataya and César Augusto Morataya.

39. *El Imparcial*, 5 October 1954 (clip). As we saw in chapter 4, most of the city's markets were constructed in the 1960s, so the political geography varies greatly depending on which market is under consideration.

40. Camus, *Ser indígena*, 294.

41. See ibid., 93–150.

42. Comecer, ASIMEM Minutes, 25 September 1997–9 March 1999 (Coll. Melgar Z.): 31 March 1998, 25 July 1998.

43. Comecer, ASIMEM Minutes, 25 September 1997–9 March 1999 (Coll. Melgar Z.): passim and 3 March 1998 (citation).

44. Camus, *Ser indígena*, 94n3.

45. Ibid., 102–3.

46. Melgar, Mixed Misc. Paperwork (Coll. Melgar Z.): Flyer, posted Mercado Sur 2, c. October 1999, PENNAT and Proc. de los Derchos Humanos. Sur 2, nested between the municipal and national government civic center of zone 4, the Fifth Avenue and Sixth Avenue street markets, and the enormous street bazaar at 18 Calle (all zone 1), was at the time the home of ASIMEM headquarters.

47. Comecer, ASIMEM Minutes, 13 April–30 November '99 (Coll. Melgar Z.): 16 November 1999.

48. Interview, anonymous (OASIS), June 2004.

49. The Fundación Ayúdame, for example, held such an event in Mercado Cervantes in May 2000. Additionally, social workers came by periodically to hold meetings on disease prevention and hygiene. Comecer, ASIMEM Minutes, 11 January 2000–27 March 2001 (Coll. Melgar Z.): 16 May 2000; Melgar, Mixed paperwork (Coll. Melgar Z.): 29 October 1999, Isabel Castañeda de Irume, Trabajadora Social, Distrito Municipal de Salud, Centro de Salud Zona 3, to Comité, Mercado Cervantes.

50. Comecer, ASIMEM Minutes, 13 April–30 November 1999 (Coll. Melgar Z.): 23 November 1999.

51. Comecer, ASIMEM Minutes, 11 January 2000–27 March 2001 (Coll. Melgar Z.): 3 February 2001.

52. Melgar, Mixed Misc. Paperwork (Coll. Melgar Z.): 1 June 1999, Ministerio de Liturgia, Parroquia de la Santísima Trinidad, to Director, Cervantes.

53. They call the group Acción Católica, which, in the documents, caused me no end of confusion and excitement until I found out that it's just a name, nothing more, no connections.

54. Comecer, ASIMEM Minutes, 25 September 1997–9 March 1999 (Coll. Melgar Z.): 27 January, 17 February, and 19 June 1998, respectively.

55. Comecer, ASIMEM Minutes, 11 January 2000–27 March 2001 (Coll. Melgar Z.): 22 February 2000.

56. Comecer, ASIMEM Minutes, 13 April–30 November 1999 (Coll. Melgar Z.): 29 June 1999.

57. Comecer, ASIMEM Minutes, 11 January 2000–27 March 2001 (Coll. Melgar Z.): 27 January and 1 February 2000.

58. Comecer, ASIMEM Minutes, 13 April–30 November 1999 (Coll. Melgar Z.): 23 November 1999.

59. Comecer, ASIMEM Minutes, 11 January 2000–27 March 2001 (Coll. Melgar Z.): 13 June 2000; Interview, Carlos Melgar, 7/16/03.

60. Interview, Beatriz Cux López, 7/15/03. Her import supplier is the Frutería Vidaurri, Sociedad Anónima de Capital Variable, Sucursal Guatemala. She gives me the receipt for the previous week's buy, which, at 5,540 quetzales (about US$710)—around three months' salary for a low-level white-collar worker—drives home how important it is for her to plan carefully. Imported goods are not uncommon; they can be found at major markets even in rural areas of Guatemala that are well connected to the highway network.

61. This is a thumbnail sketch, based on innumerable interviews and thousands of hours spent in markets all over the city and the nation. In this summary, I followed Carlos Melgar, Interview, 6/16/03.

62. On carteros, see Camus, Ser indígena, 114–15.

63. Interview, "Abelardo," cartero, CENMA, 06/03/03.

64. Interview, Ing. Civil Said Tapia, Subdirector de Abastos, Dirección General de Abastos, CENMA, Guatemala City, 6/03/03. At the time of our interview, Josué Enríquez Dardón—ASIMEM's first president back in the 1990s—was president of the committee inside the market. La Florida, according to Tapia, has the city's worst desborde, or spillage onto the street. There are two hundred vendors inside and one thousand outside. Not long before, the outside vendors had organized a union, the Sindicato de Vendedores del Mercado La Florida.

65. Interview, Marcia Yunixa Laz Cienfuegos, Delegada Municipal, Mercado Cervantes, 7/15/03.

66. Prensa Libre, 29 May 2001, Nacional, online.

67. Prensa Libre, 29 April 2000, 3.

68. Prensa Libre, 5 May 2000, 8.

69. Al Día, 22 October 2001, 1, 4–5; Nuestro Diario, 22 October 2000, 1–4; Prensa Libre, 22 October 2000, 1–3.

70. Abel Pérez, Presidente, Comité de Inquilinos y Vendedores del Mercado La Terminal, public statement reproduced as flyers (Coll. Melgar Z.): October 2000.

71. Comecer, ASIMEM Minutes, 11 January 2000–27 March 2001 (Coll. Melgar Z.): 21 November 2000; Interview, Marcia Yunixa Laz Cienfuegos, Delegada Municipal, Mercado Cervantes, 7/15/03; Mercado Cervantes, Reuniones Generales y Notas Administrativas, 10 February 1999–6 June 2001 (Coll. Melgar Z.): 7 February 2001; Prensa Libre, 27 October 2000, 3. See also the muni's propaganda paper, especially the issues from 2002–3. El Chapín (Guatemala: Municipalidad de Guatemala.), Year 1 (2002), passim.

72. Comecer, ASIMEM Minutes, 11 January 2000–27 March 2001 (Coll. Melgar Z.): 21 November 2000. For a basic description of how the muni works, including the functions of the alcaldes auxiliares, see "¿Qué hace nuestra Muni?"

73. Comecer, ASIMEM Minutes, 25 September 1997–9 March 1999 (Coll. Melgar Z.): 11 November 1997.

74. Comecer, ASIMEM Minutes, 25 September 1997–9 March 1999 (Coll. Melgar Z.): 16 June 1998.

75. Interview, Carlos Melgar, 7/16/03; Comecer, ASIMEM Minutes, 13 April–30 November 1999 and passim (Coll. Melgar Z.): 30 September 1999 (extensive information on Servicios Públicos); Comecer, ASIMEM Minutes, 11 January 2000–27 March 2001 and passim (Coll. Melgar Z.): 5 September 2000 (introduction of Desarrollo Social).

76. *Al Día*, 27 March 2000, 5; Comecer, ASIMEM Minutes, 11 January 2000–27 March 2001 (Coll. Melgar Z.): 27 March 2000.

77. Comecer, ASIMEM Minutes, 11 January 2000–27 March 2001 (Coll. Melgar Z.): 4–25 April 2000.

78. 15 May 2000, Junta Directiva de ASIMEM to Dr. Julio Eduardo Arango Escobar, Procurador de los Derechos Humanos (Coll. Melgar Z).

79. 3 July 2001, Muni/ASIMEM. "Convenio de censo en los 23 mercados del Municipio de Guatemala y mercados satélites reconocidos por la Municipalidad de Guatemala" (Coll. Melgar Z.); Comecer, Reuniones, 12 September 2001–25 September 2002 (Coll. Melgar Z.): 12 September 2001; Interview, Carlos Melgar, 7/16/03.

80. Comecer, ASIMEM Minutes, 13 April–30 November 1999 (Coll. Melgar Z.): 23 February–13 April 1999.

81. Comecer, ASIMEM Minutes, 13 April–30 November 1999 (Coll. Melgar Z.): 27 May 1999.

82. Interview, Carlos Melgar, 7/16/03.

83. Comecer, ASIMEM Minutes, 13 April–30 November 1999 (Coll. Melgar Z.): 27 May 1999.

84. Interview, Carlos Melgar, 7/16/03. Four years had passed since the Pollo Rey battle when I spoke with Melgar, and there still wasn't a *depósito* in Mercado Roosevelt or in Cervantes, either, for that matter. No markets were model, either.

85. *La Hora*, 2 May 2002, online. Alvizúrez was opposing a plan of the Asociación Nacional de Municipalidades (ANAM).

86. Comecer, ASIMEM Minutes, 11 January 2000–27 March 2001 (Coll. Melgar Z.): 23 May 2000.

87. *Al Día*, 27 May 2006, 6. *Al Día* is a lowbrow news magazine that features car wrecks, crime, football, pop culture, and cheesecake. Highly graphic, it is, together with *Nuestro Diario*, the best medium through which the government can speak to the pueblo, featuring as it does a design that makes it readable even by people who don't know how to read.

88. *Prensa Libre*, 30 May 2000, 6. While it is a commentary on Guatemalan political life that a demonstration of four thousand people in front of Congress is page-six news, the fact nonetheless remains that the FRG formed an opposition block against the bill after the demonstration.

89. Comecer, ASIMEM Minutes, 11 January 2000–27 March 2001 (Coll. Melgar Z.): 6 June 2000.

90. *Prensa Libre*, 21 July 2000, 4.

91. For the blow-by-blow, see *Prensa Libre*, 1 August 2000, 6; 3 August 2000, 5; 4 August 2000, 5.

92. Comecer, Reuniones, 11 October 2000–5 September 2001 (Coll. Melgar Z.): 20 June 2001.

93. Comecer, Reuniones, 11 October 2000–5 September 2001 (Coll. Melgar Z.): 11 July 2001. The original reads as follows: "Los proyectos [del comité] estarán que tengamos nuevas ideas como Higiene. Que las personas sean mas higiénicas que haya control de calidad. Limpieza de pasillos."

94. Comecer, Mixed paperwork, 2001 (Coll. Melgar Z.): page proofs, advertisements, "Mercados del Nuevo Milenio," July 2001; Comecer, Reuniones, 11 October 2000–5 September 2001 (Coll. Melgar Z.): 2 August 2001, 8 August 2001; Interview, Beatriz Cux López, 7/15/03. The lack of follow-up was not for lack of trying. Under Alvizúrez, ASISM took up the project, trying even to institute a unified pricing system in the markets. See *Prensa Libre*, 7 September 2002, Económicas (online).

95. *Prensa Libre*, 4 April 2003, Nacional, online. The market research firm, Gauss, used a sample of 7,376 homes in the capital, out of a universe of over two million.

96. Interviews, Carlos Melgar, 7/16/03 and 8/13/03; *Prensa Libre*, 16 March 2003, 6–7; Royal Ahold website, 2003, http://www.ahold.com and related subpages. In 2005 Royal Ahold sold its shares of Paiz Ahold to Wal-Mart Stores, Inc.

97. Interview, Carlos Melgar, 6/16/03.

SEVEN. Fragmentation and Concentration

1. See Berger, *Political and Agrarian Development*; Camus, *Ser indígena*; Dosal, *Power in Transition*.

2. AVANCSO, *El Proceso de crecimiento metropolitano*, 101, 114. According to XI *Censo nacional de población y VI de habitación (Censo 2002)*, the AMG population —that is, the population of the entire department of Guatemala—in 2002 had grown to over 2.5 million. All numbers are rounded to the nearest thousand and should be taken as a relative guide.

3. See Castañeda, *Utopia Unarmed*, 175–235, 358–90, and passim.

4. Ibid., 237–66.

5. See, for example: *Acuerdos de paz*, "Acuerdo sobre fortalecimiento del poder civil y función del ejército en una sociedad democrática"; ONGs, *sociedad civil y Estado en Guatemala: Elementos para el debate*; Smith, "The Militarization of Civil Society in Guatemala." Both the Constitution of 1985 and the Peace Accords of 1996 made, at least on paper, real steps toward demilitarizing society, freeing public discourse and association, and recognizing the rights of women and the Maya.

6. A brief political summary follows. The winner of the elections in 1985 was Vinicio

Cerezo Arévalo, a Christian Democrat who had participated in the student movements of the 1960s and who weathered numerous coup attempts during his term (1986–91). Jorge Serrano Elías (1991–93) of the Movimiento de Acción Solidaria won the elections in 1990 and took office in 1991. The nation was in turmoil, the economy was in crisis, and the civil war was still being waged. Faced with an opposition Congress, on 25 May 1993 Serrano pulled off the "self-coup" that led to his exile in Panama, where he became a successful mall developer. In early July 1993 Congress elected the human rights official Ramiro de León Carpio, the Procurador de los Derechos Humanos, to the presidency, which he held until January of 1996. His successor—a signatory to the Peace Accords with the guerrillas—was Alvaro Arzú Irigoyen (1996–2000), the mayor of Guatemala City from 1986 to 1990 and the figure around whom the Partido de Avanzada Nacional (PAN) had organized in 1989. The party of the new right, the PAN represented urban professionals and technocrats along with big capital, most notably the nation's relatively new sugar elite. Besides winning the presidency for Arzú, the party also installed Oscar Berger Perdomo as the capital's mayor. Groomed as Arzú's successor, Berger held City Hall for two terms (1991–96 and 1996–2000), and, after the term of the corrupt FRG man Alfonso Portillo Cabrera (2000–4), was elected president in 2003 on the Gran Alianza Nacional (GANA) ticket. In 2007 Álvaro Colom Caballeros (2008–12) of the center-left Unidad Nacional de la Esperaza (UNE) party defeated the retired general Otto Perez Molina of the Partido Patriota (PP) with just under 53 percent of the vote. General information can be found in Escobar Medrano and González Camargo, *Historia de la cultura de Guatemala*, 2:284–309; Gaitan A., *Los Presidentes de Guatemala*, 149–64; *Historia sinóptica de Guatemala*, 454–64; *Quién es quién: Catálogo electoral 1999*, passim. Particularly useful is *La economía de Guatemala ante el ajuste estructural a comienzos de los '90*, 28–37, 69–70, and passim. Finally, a brief summary of Guatemalan contemporary politics can be found on the U.S. Department of State website, http://www.state.gov, in the Background Reports section. On Cerezo and the Christian Democrats, see CAR, 15 August 1975, 222–23, 4 December 1978, 380–81, 27 August 1979, 269–71, 1 November 1980, 341–42, 6 July 1984, 201; ONGS, *sociedad civil y Estado*, 23–25; *Quién es quién, Catálogo electoral 1999*, 48–52, 121–23; Ramírez, *La guerra de los 36 años*, 72. On Christian Democrats and unions, see Levenson-Estrada, *Trade Unionists against Terror*, 33 and passim, as well as Berger, *Political and Agrarian Development*, 125; and Le Bot, *La guerre en terra maya*, 158–59. See also *Historia sinóptica de Guatemala*, 454–56.

7. WOLA Policy Brief, "Military Intelligence and Human Rights in Guatemala: The Archive and the Case for Intelligence Reform" (Washington: Washington Office on Latin America, 30 March 1995), ms. 2–9, 13. The manuscript is housed in CIRMA. Early in the 2000s, President Berger was attempting to reduce the EMP's power.

8. *Siglo Veintiuno*, 12 May 2003, 2–3.

9. *Prensa Libre*, 3 November 2002, 6.

10. "ONG deben regularse," *Prensa Libre*, 30 March 2004 (online).

11. Maite Rico and Bertrand de la Grange, journalists, article published in *Real Instituto Elcano*, 15 April 2004, reproduced on http://www.nuevamayoria.com.

12. Many NGOs bypass the national government and work directly with municipalities, which, under the current Constitution, receive 8 percent of public expenditure and thus have some economic autonomy. *ONGs, sociedad civil y Estado en Guatemala*, 33–35. See also Nelson, *A Finger in the Wound*, 105–6, 291–92, 299–301. A summary can be found in Gálvez Borrell and Gellert, *Guatemala: Exclusión social y estrategias para enfrentarla*, 93–108.

13. Moreton, *To Serve God and Wal-Mart*.

14. Most notably, see Warren, *Indigenous Movements and their Critics*. Also extremely useful is Nelson, *A Finger in the Wound*.

15. *El Periódico*, 12 October 2002, 3; *Prensa Libre*, 12 October 2002, 2, 13 October 2002, 6. Guatemala ratified CAFTA in 2005; it went into effect in mid-2006.

16. *Prensa Libre*, 14 October 2002, 10. A wide ranging and lively debate on the PPP was constantly being updated on the Internet.

17. *¡Alerta!—Petén Despierta*, Year 1, no. 1 (March–April 2002), 1. This publication provided a simple but sophisticated partisan overview not only of the PPP, but of neoliberalism in general, including a discussion of the feminization of poverty (2). Also covered were the economic weight of transnationals and various proposed trade agreements, including Free Trade Area of the Americas/Área de Libre Comercio de las Américas (FTAA /ALCA).

18. *Nuestro Diario*, 21 January 2003, 2–3; *Prensa Libre*, 21 January 2003, 2–3, 26 February 2003, 2–5.

19. *Prensa Libre*, 2 October 2002, 2–3, 3 October 2002, 2–4, 18 December 2003 (online), 5 August 2004 (online).

20. *Siglo Veintiuno*, 12 October 2002, 8.

21. Mattson and Ayer, "La maquila en Guatemala: Hechos y tendencias," STITCH report, 2004 (www.stitchonline.org/archives/maquila.html); "Trade Unions and the Maquila Sector," Peace Brigades International—Guatemala, Special Report, September 1996 (http://www.hartford-hwp.com). Peace Brigades International, founded in 1981, is headquartered in London. STITCH is the name of a group of women organizers and activists in solidarity with Central America; it is based in Washington.

22. Human Rights Watch, 2002 Report on Guatemalan Maquila Sector, "Las trabajadoras se enfrentan a la discriminación" (http://www.hrw.org/spanish/informes).

23. Mattson and Ayer, "La maquila en Guatemala."

24. Figures vary widely from source to source. According to the Centro Interamericano de Investigación y Documentación sobre Formación Profesional CINTERFOR of the International Labor Organization), which used figures from the Ministry of Economy, accumulated employment in the maquila sector from

1995 to 2000 was 147,211, with 22,180 new jobs being added in the year 2000. This figure, however, does not necessarily indicate the total level of employment at any given moment. I have rounded numbers and double-checked them wherever possible. CINTERFOR, "Proyecto Mejoramiento de las condiciones laborales y de vida de las trabajadoras de la maquila en Centroamérica: Informe de avance," January 2001 (http://www.ilo.org/public/spanish).

25. Human Rights Watch, 2002 Report on Guatemalan Maquila Sector; Mattson and Ayer, "La maquila en Guatemala."

26. "To the United States Trade Representative: Petition and Request for Review of the GSP Status of Guatemala Under the Worker Rights Provisions of the Generalized System of Preferences" (1 June 1991), 16. Petitioners: International Labor Rights Education and Research Fund (ILRERF); U.S./Guatemala Labor Education Project (U.S./GLEP); United Electrical, Radio & Machine Workers of America (UE); Amalgamated Clothing and Textile Workers Union (ACTWU); United Food and Commercial Workers International Union (UFCW); International Union of Food and Allied Workers' Associations (IUF), North America. Antigua, Guatemala: CIRMA. Cuadro de Clasificación Infostelle, 09/02/05, Relaciones económicas; maquiladoras.

27. Ibid., 16–18.

28. "Trade Unions and the Maquila Sector."

29. Amorín, "Maquila se escribe con 'm' de muerte," *Rel-Uita* (Uruguay, November 2004), reproduced on http://www.solidaridad.net; Human Rights Watch, 2002 Report on Guatemalan Maquila Sector; Cumes Salazar and Chocoyo Chile, *Nos hace llorar: Jóvenes trabajadoras en las maquilas coreanas de San Lucas, Sacatepéquez a El Tejar, Chimaltenango* (Guatemala: Programa de Apoyo para la Salud Materno Infantil y para la Salud de Otros Grupos de Riesgo, publicada gracias al apoyo USAID, November 1997); Gema Palencia, "Maltrato en Maquilas," April 2004, on http://www.latinoamerica-online.it; "Trade Unions and the Maquila Sector." A common refrain of the maquiladoras' defenders is that the salaries that sound so low in dollars are actually adequate, given the cost of living in the host country. This is simply untrue. At the time of this writing, a can of dog food costs over one dollar, the cheapest meat is over two dollars a pound, antibiotics in a pharmacy can cost over five dollars a pill, and a five-gallon jug of potable water costs nearly two dollars. Anyone doubting that basic survival costs have far outpaced salaries can consult reports on the consumer price index, periodically updated by the Instituto Nacional de Estadística.

30. "El temor a que el 'monstruo' nos deje sin ropa," *El Periódico*, Edición Dominical, 8 August 2004 (online).

31. *Prensa Libre*, 25 November 2002, 20.

32. *Prensa Libre*, 30 October 2000, 22, 13 November 2002, 23. For U.S. State Department support of overseas franchising, see Schlosser, *Fast Food Nation*, 229–30.

33. From http://www.dominos.com.gt.

34. *Prensa Libre*, 29 July 2002, Económicas (online).

35. "Grupo Roble con las cadenas más grande de centros comerciales en Centroamérica," *Moneda* (25–29 August 2003), 6.

36. In translation, García Canclini, *Hybrid Cultures*. See especially chapter 7, "Hybrid Cultures, Oblique Powers."

37. *Alux* means *duende*, which translates as "sprite" or "spirit," and *Nahual* is the personal animal-spirit guide that all Maya are said to have. Alvarado, "Presto non troppo: Para la historia del rock," *Prensa Libre*, 11 June 2004 (online). Guatemalan rock has notably featured a number of death metal, heavy metal, and trash metal bands, such as Sangre Humana (Human Blood), founded in the mid-1970s, whose hits include "Visión satánica" (1981), and Necropsia, started in 1995, a group whose first demo was "Das Ende der Welt" (The End of the World). Details from the 1960s forward can be found in Castañeda Maldonado, "Historia del Rock en Guatemala."

38. *Expresión Juvenil, El periódico de la juventud*, February 2003; *Extra* (Guatemala: Grupo Extra, S.A.), 3–9 August 2003; *El Globo*, 28 March 2003; *Lucha 3000* (Guatemala: Grupo Nova), 6 August 2003 and 18 August 2003.

39. Garrard-Burnett, *Protestantism in Guatemala*.

40. As always, statistics vary. "100 años de protestantismo: De Justo Rufino Barrios a Ríos Montt," *Siglo Veintiuno* (insert, *Magazine 21*), 10 September 1995, 4–5; *La Hora*, 18 July 1900, 9; "Los protestantes en Guatemala" (CIRMA, Colección Documentos 2565, n.p., June 1991); Sarasa, *Los protestantes en Guatemala*, 28–55. Thorough collections of related clippings can be found in CIRMA, particularly in Colección Inforpress.

41. U.S. Department of State (http://www.state.gov).

42. I relayed this remark to two Kaqchikel friends. One, informally involved with pan-Mayanism, commented, "No, it's people who have lost their customs." Another, a devout Catholic, said virtually the same thing but was referring to Catholic, not Mayan, customs.

43. Indeed, the first significant period of growth of the religion dates to the turbulence around the Arbenz presidency. In 1952 the magazine of the Evangelical Assemblies of God had the Statue of Liberty on its cover—an indication of the ideology the U.S.-based missionary magazine's backers were attempting to spread in Latin America. The Evangelical grade school Colegio Evangélico "Francisco G. Penzotti" was founded in Guatemala City in 1951 and published its first school newspaper only weeks after the invasion of 1954. With an enrollment of two hundred students from the first to the sixth grades, the colegio was one of only three Evangelical primary schools in the city, which had a population of "four thousand or more" Evangelicals at the time, according to the paper. "And us?" asked an article on the back cover. "Are we making sure that our children are learning the sublime truths of the *Evangelio* in the home and in the classroom? It is said . . . that in light of the communist danger that looms over Latin America, the Vatican will increase the number of priests in these countries. . . . The

increase of Catholic education is also suggested, which would mean the opening of more schools directed by the Roman Church. And us? What are we doing?" *Escuela Evangélica*, 1:1 (August 1954), 1–4 (citation from 4); *La Luz Apostólica* 36:2 (October 1952), cover. Catholic officialdom in this era was also highly anti-Communist and conservative and was also actively engaged in organizing youth around rightist political principles, particularly through Catholic Action. One popular rightist midcentury Catholic youth organization was the girls' organization Cadettes de Cristo, a self-described movement of "growing conquest to recruit the entire 'mass' of youth [young women] with social influence on behalf of the Father, of the Church, and of Christ." *Cadette*, 11:10 (c. October 1946), 4.

44. See, for example, Iglesia Guatemalteca en el Exilio, untitled report on Evangelical Protestantism in Guatemala (Guatemala, CIRMA: Archivo Histórico, Colección Plumstock, no. 16, January 1983).

45. *Prensa Libre*, 10 November 2002, 21.

46. *La Palabra, Voz del nuevo milenio* (Guatemala), 22–28 June 2003, 3, passim.

47. *La Palabra*, 22–28 June 2003, 19; *La Verdad*, 17–23 August 2003, 14.

48. *La Palabra*, 17–22 August 2003, 4–6.

49. *La Palabra*, 22–28 June 2003, 12.

50. For example, two issues I surveyed offered advice to parents on sex education for their children and covered the importance of tenderness in lovemaking, male virginity, the multiple male orgasm, the dangers of drug use during pregnancy, sex after menopause, and the benefits of Nonoxynol-9. *Sexo Libre*, nos. 174 and 179 (2003), passim.

51. *Sexo Libre*, no. 156 (2003), 6–7, 10–11.

52. *Sexo Libre*, no. 159 (2003), 11 (citation), 2–6.

53. Colectivo de Lesbianas Liberadas—*Lesbiradas*, flyer, Guatemala City, March 2003.

54. *El Periódico*, 17 June 2003, 17. *Campo pagado* (paid advertisement) signed by dozens of national and international human rights groups as well as by individuals.

55. *Prensa Libre, Revista Domingo*, 6 April 2003, 8–10.

56. *Expresión Juvenil*, February 2003, 3. The survey population was 143 children.

57. One example among many: "Todos Santos Cuchumatán Under People's Law. The inefficiency of the National Civil Police in the population of Todos Santos Cuchumatán, Huehuetenango, propelled the community to create the Committee of Local Security, which has imposed its own law. Among the principal points of its protection plan [are enforcing] a '*toque de queda*' [curfew] beginning at 9:00 every day. . . . Curiously, [this municipality] had the same controls during the armed internal conflict. . . . [Members] indicate that during that period there were patrollers who undertook the work of security . . . just as is happening today, when groups of approximately 20 people make *rondas* in various districts." *Prensa Libre*, 20 February 2003, cover, 8.

58. *Prensa Libre*, 8 March 2004 (online).

59. *Prensa Libre*, 28 May 2004 (online).

60. Telecast, *Noticiero Guatevisión*, 7 December 2004.

61. *Prensa Libre*, 26 June 2004 (online).

62. *Al Día*, 10 February 2003, 1, 3.

63. *Prensa Libre*, 22 January 2003, 2, 11 May 2003, 6.

64. Morán Mérida, *Condiciones de vida*, 73–75.

65. Until the 1980s street gangs were known as *pandillas*, not *maras*, and were common in the 1970s. See AVANCSO, *Por sí mismos: Un estudio preliminar de las "maras" en la Ciudad de Guatemala*, 7–10.

66. Ibid., 17 (citation), 1–17 passim.

67. Ibid., 17.

68. Ibid., passim.

69. *Maras y pandillas en Centroamérica*, 1:109–95.

70. Ibid., 436.

71. Ibid., 438.

72. Ibid., 440. "18" and "13," two of the largest gangs at the time of this writing, are both named after streets in Los Angeles.

73. *Nuestro Diario*, 24 December 2002, 26 December 2002, 27 December 2002, 5; *Prensa Libre*, 27 December 2002, 14 February 2003, 3, 15 April 2003, 2–4.

74. *Prensa Libre*, 28 December 2002 (online).

75. *Nuestro Diario*, 26 December 2002.

76. An overview of the nation's cartels and their activities circa 2002 can be found in *Prensa Libre*, 27 October 2002 (online).

77. *Prensa Libre*, 13 November 2002, 12.

78. *Prensa Libre*, 18 October 2002, 3.

79. *Prensa Libre*, 11 November 2002, 6.

80. *Prensa Libre*, 27 February 2003 (online).

81. Davis, *City of Quartz*, covers this subject.

82. An overview of the sharpened division of space along economic lines (the authors call it "una dualización metropolitana profunda") can be found in AVANCSO, *El proceso de crecimiento metropolitano de la Ciudad de Guatemala*, 125 and passim.

83. DHV Consultants, Guatemala (Grupo DHV, Germany), "Presentaciones, Ante-proyecto, y Proyecto Cuatro Grados Norte," (DHV to Municipalidad de Guate-mala: June–July 2001), courtesy of Municipalidad de Guatemala. Note that Cuatro Grados gained a reputation for seediness and was nearly shut down toward the end of the first decade of the 2000s.

84. Interview, Arq. Fabricio González y González, Jefe de Planificación y Diseño, Municipalidad de Guatemala, 5/16/03. At the time of the interview, the muni was attempting to overhaul transportation, based on a study conducted in the late 1990s by the Japan International Cooperation Agency (JICA). Agencia de Cooperación Internacional de Japon, *El estudio de factibilidad sobre el proyecto de transportación urbana*.

85. Interview, González y González, 5/16/03; *El Chapín*, Year 1, no. 2 (August 2002).

86. "Upgrading Urban Communities: A Resource for Practitioners," compact disc, 2001 edn. (World Bank, 1999–2001), passim.

87. *Metrópolis 2010: Plan de desarrollo metropolitano.* PAN, a neoliberal party with right-wing roots, organized around ex-mayor (1986–91) and President Alvaro Arzú Irigoyen (1996–2000) in 1989. See *Quién es quién: Catálogo electoral 1999,* 48–52, 103–8.

88. *Metrópolis 2010.* The contributors included Gobierno de México, Gobierno de Holanda, Koinberg/Suecia, IELAB/Holanda; GUATEL and EMPAGUA (telephones and water); and, from the private sector: Aviateca, Banco Industrial, Electricidad ENRON de Guatemala, Europa Motors Company, Shell de Guatemala, Texaco Guatemala, et al.

89. Ibid.; *El proceso de crecimiento metropolitano de la Ciudad de Guatemala,* 163–65.

90. *Metrópolis 2010,* 3.

91. Morán Mérida, *Condiciones de vida,* 23, 37–39.

92. These invasions became Colonias La Esperanza, Monte de Olivos, Tres Banderas, El Esfuerzo, and El Exodo and were regularized by the state (through BANVI) in 1985. AVANCSO, *Aquí corre la bola,* 20–21; Quesada S., "Invasiones de terrenos en la Ciudad de Guatemala," 6–8; Morán Mérida, *Condiciones de vida,* 22–23, 95. Estimates of the number of original invaders vary widely, but most exceed twenty thousand.

93. Basurto, "Fighting Urban Poverty: Promoting Community Organization"; "Invasiones de tierras (1986–1990): Un desborde popular en tiempos de Democracia," in *Boletín del Centro de Estudios Urbanos y Regionales,* no. 9 (November 1990), 3.

94. AVANCSO, *"Aquí corre la bola,"* 22–85.

95. AVANCSO, *El proceso de crecimiento metropolitano de la Ciudad de Guatemala,* 32, 120–39.

96. García Vettorazzi, "El crecimiento espacial de la Ciudad de Guatemala," 2.

97. AVANCSO, *El proceso de crecimiento metropolitano de la Ciudad de Guatemala,* 126. The total population figure can be found in various sources. It appears in this source on page 114. Statistics are extremely unreliable (see pages 111–13 for an extensive list of problems in the data). In short, census taking is slipshod at best and corrupt at worst; variables have not been kept consistent: for example, are people counted where they live or where they happen to be during the census? The definition of what areas constitute the city is not agreed upon and often is not indicated in tandem with any given statistic; and the population itself is extremely mobile and particularly difficult to count. *El proceso* points out that in 2002 the municipality was claiming that 3.5 million people lived in the metropolitan area, while the Instituto Nacional de Estadística (INE) was reporting that only 2.6 million lived in the entire department of Guatemala. The U.S. State Department (2005) puts the nation's total population at 14.3 million, and the metropolitan area's at 2.5 million (Background Notes, http://www.state .gov/r/pa/ei/bgn).

98. *El Chapín* (August 2002), 4. The government later banned children from the dump.

99. Ibid.

altiplano—highlands

asentamientos precarios—precarious settlements; shantytowns

barraca—hut, humble dwelling; in the countryside, called a *rancho*

barranco—ravine

barrio—neighborhood; sometimes has the sense of a poor or working-class neighborhood

cabecera—the capital of a department (*departamento*) or municipality (*municipio*)

camino—road, way, or path

campesino—country person, farmer; often translated as "peasant," a term avoided in this text because of its European connotations, which do not apply to the situation in Guatemala

cantina—a lower-class bar, typically serving only men

capitalino/a—a person from Guatemala City

carretera—highway

centro comercial—depending on the historical period, translates as "shopping center" or "mall"

chapín—slang word meaning "Guatemalan"

chavo/a—dude, fellow, young guy or girl

comedor—a lower-class restaurant or eatery

costumbre—literally, "custom," but popularly used to refer to the various rituals and practices of Maya in general and Mayan shamans specifically

covacha—hovel, hut; in the countryside, called a *rancho*

departamento—department, the political division in Guatemala equivalent to a state in the United States; there are twenty-two departments in the country

desarrollo—development

don, doña—an honorific, similar to "Sir" or "Madam" but used before a first name

finca—large farm or farming estate

finquero—the owner of a finca

huipil—the sleeveless woven blouse worn by Mayan women, accompanied by a skirt known as a *corte*; men referring to a woman in traditional dress will often say she is "de corte"

Indio—Indian, a racist slur; the politically correct equivalent is *indígena*

inquilino/a—literally, "tenant," but in this book used to refer to a vendor who rents a stall in a municipal market

junta directiva—council of leaders; leadership group, similar to the board of directors of an organization, such as a neighborhood improvement committee

Ladino—in Guatemala, any person who is not ethnically or culturally Mayan

lámina—corrugated metal used for roofing

maquila/maquiladora—export reassembly plant; in Guatemala, almost all produce textiles

mara—gang, street gang

mercado—market

mestizo—of mixed Native American and Spanish (or other) heritage

milpa—a corn field or corn-and-bean field; refers to a smallholding, or *minifundia*

muni—short for *municipio*; *la muni* refers to City Hall

municipalidad—municipality; similar to a county in the United States (or parish, in Louisiana); there are 331 municipalities in Guatemala's twenty-two departments

onda—vibe; *buena onda*, good vibe; *mala onda*, bad vibe; *¿Qué onda?* means "What's up?"

pandilla—an older term for street gang, now virtually replaced by "mara"

patojo/a—kid, youngster (a Guatemalan word); a group of kids is a *patojada*

pila—an apparatus in which laundry is washed by hand; usually a concrete structure with a central, water-holding well flanked by two shallow washboard-like basins

pisados—the downtrodden (vulgar)

pobladores—squatters; land invaders

el pueblo—the people or folk, but a word with a strong sense of solidarity that invokes the lower-class mass majority; also can mean "village" or "town"

pues—literally, "then"; a very commonly used word in Guatemala, as in *sí pues*, which means "yes, then" but translates as "sure," "of course," or, emphatically, "uh-huh!"

puesto—means "place" (and is the past participle of the verb "to put") but refers to a vendor's place or booth within a market

tenis—tennis shoes; sneakers

típica—handcrafts or artisan goods, usually Mayan-made

tortilla—flat, round, thin pancake of corn mush fried on a *comal* (griddle) or other type of grill; the staple food in Guatemala

trabajador/a—worker

traje—traditional Mayan dress

vendedor—seller, salesperson

vos—the most informal form of second-person singular address ("you")

Bibliographic Note

Research for this book was primarily conducted in the Archivo General de Centro América (AGCA) in Guatemala City. Other document collections, record sets, and libraries consulted in Guatemala City include those of the Biblioteca Nacional, the Museo Nacional de Historia of the Instituto Nacional de Antropología e Historia, the Instituto Nacional de Estadística, the Municipalidad de Guatemala, and the private collection of Carlos Melgar Zamboni. Also cited are sources from the historical archive of the Centro de Investigaciones Regionales de Mesoamérica (CIRMA) in Antigua, Guatemala, which also houses a Fototeca, or historic photographic archive. In the United States, researchers may find many cited documents in the Latin American Library of Tulane University in New Orleans and in the Columbus Library of the Pan-American Union in Washington.

Periodicals cited in the notes are listed below. Most may be found in the AGCA *hemeroteca* (press repository), including sources such as school newspapers and smaller-run magazines. Publications consulted for multi-year periods include the *Bulletin of the Pan-American Union* (BPAU); the *Central America Report* of Inforpress Centroamericana (CAR); *El Guatemalteco*, the official newspaper of the Guatemalan government; *El Imparcial*, the nation's main newspaper through most of the twentieth century; *El Periódico*; *Prensa Libre*; *Revista Militar*, the magazine of the Guatemalan Army; and *Siglo Veintiuno*. Citations from *El Imparcial* only include a page number if the article is not on the front page. The references marked "(clip)" come from the indexed collection at CIRMA, which houses nearly all the resistance movement publications cited and is in general the best source for information on the popular movements.

In citing AGCA documents, I have tried to facilitate the difficult work of any researcher wishing to consult the original material. All the collections examined, with the exception of the Ministerio de Fomento (see the list of abbreviations below), are unindexed, and include many boxes, or *legajos*, with the same numbers and names. The notes give the folio (if one exists), the legajo name, and the *expediente*, or document packet, within the legajo (expedientes are bound packets, usually featuring numerous documents related to a single issue). Expedientes were rarely numbered. I have identified them with the most prominent date on their cover, along with the name of the party listed. Only in cases where necessary for clarity's sake have I included the citations of individual documents within expedientes. For example, the note that reads "AGCA 3/Caja Clas. 121.11, no. Ord. 47082 (MCOP: Lot. Gallito y Palmita, 1943–46), 28 September 1946, Expediente [Exp.] (Ing. Juan Prera, Reurbanización de El Gallito), vecinos, petition, 12 September 1946" refers to the Archivo General de Centro América (AGCA), folio 3, legajo (classified by the numbers given) pertaining to the Ministry of Communications and Public Works (MCOP), with the words "Lotificación El Gallito y Palmita" written on it. What follows describes the expediente within the legajo—its cover date and name (in parentheses)—and the document within the expediente, in this case, a petition submitted by neighbors on 12 September 1946.

Abbreviations

A.—Acta
ABI—Asociación de Bienestar Infantil
AGCA—Archivo General de Centro América (General Archive of Central America)
ASCP—Oficina de Asuntos Sociales, Casa Presidencial
Caja Clas.—Caja Clasificada or Cajas Clasificadas
Camp. y Col.—Campamentos y Colonias
CAPE—Central America Printed Ephemera Collection, Tulane University Latin
    American Library, New Orleans, LA
CIRMA—Centro de Investigaciones Regionales de Mesoamérica, Antigua,
    Guatemala
Coll. Melgar Z.—Private collection of Carlos Melgar Zamboni, Guatemala City
DBI—Dirección de Bienestar Infantil
DGC—Dirección General de Caminos
DGOP—Dirección General de Obras Públicas
Esc.—Escuelas
Exp.—Expediente
INE—Instituto Nacional de Estadística
Lot.—Lotificación or Lotificaciones
MAC—Ministerio de Agricultura y Caminos (Ministry of Agriculture and Roads)
MCOP—Ministerio de Comunicaciones y Obras Públicas (Ministry of
    Communications and Public Works)
no. Orden—Número de Orden
O.P.—Obras Públicas
P.—Paquete. The unorganized SASP-SBS files are identified by these codes,
    although not systematically.
SASP—Secretaría de Asuntos Sociales de la Presidencia (Presidential Secretariat of
    Social Affairs)

SBS—Secretaría de Bienestar Social (Secretariat of Social Welfare)
Serv.—Servicio
T.—Tomo

Periodicals

ABC: *Revista de Alfabetización*. Guatemala. 1947.

Acacia. Órgano de divulgación de la Gran Logia de Guatemala. Guatemala. 1947.

¡Alerta!—Petén Despierta. Year 1, no. 1. March–April 2002.

La Aurora, Revista dedicada a nuestra Feria Nacional de Noviembre 1935. Guatemala.
    1935.

Boletín de la Carretera Panamericana. Washington: Pan-American Union,
    Confederación Panamericana de Educación Vial. 1934–35. Continued as *Boletín
    Vial Panamericana*.

Boletín Informativo. Guatemala: Frente Democrático Contra La Represión. April
    1980.

Boletín Internacional. Mexico City: Frente Popular 31 de Enero, FP-31. 1981–82.

Boletín Socialista Democrático. Guatemala. 1980.

Boletín Vial Panamericana. Washington: Pan-American Union, Confederación
    Panamericana de Educación Vial. 1936–37. Continuation of *Boletín de la Carretera
    Panamericana*.

Brahma-Vidya: Revista Teosófica, Órgano de las Logias Gnosis y Atma. Guatemala.
    May 1925.

Bulletin of the Pan-American Union. Washington: Union of American Republics.

Cadette. Guatemala: Cadettes de Cristo [Catholic Action]. October 1946.

Campanillas: Revista Humorística. Guatemala.

Carreteras del Mundo. London, Washington, Paris: International Road Federation.

Central America Report. Guatemala: Inforpress Centroamericana.

El Chapín. Guatemala: Municipalidad de Guatemala. 2002.

Cooperación, Revista del Departamento de Fomento Cooperativo. Guatemala. 1949–51.

Correo de Occidente. Quetzaltenango, Guatemala. 1952.

Daily People's World. San Francisco: Communist Party. 1953–54.

Al Día. Guatemala.

"Diez años de progreso, 1931–1941." Suplemento *Luz*. Guatemala, 14 February 1941.

Escuela Evangélica. Guatemala: Colegio Evangélico "Francisco G. Penzotti." August
    1954.

Estudio: Revista mensual de ciencias y filosofía transcendental. Guatemala. 1922.

Esotérika. Guatemala: Akelarre / Grupo Extra, S.A.

Etcétera—Revista Popular. Revista Centroamericana. Guatemala: Centro Editorial.
    1938.

Expresión Juvenil, El periódico de la juventud. Guatemala.

Extra. Guatemala: Grupo Extra, S.A.

El Gráfico. Guatemala.

Guatemala en Lucha. Guatemala: Fuerzas Armadas Rebeldes [FAR]. 1981–82.

Guatemala: Revista Cultural del Ejército. Guatemala: Relaciones Públicas del Ejército de Guatemala.

El Guatemalteco. Guatemala: Gobierno de la República de Guatemala.

La Hora. Guatemala.

Horizontes. Órgano de publicidad de 50. grado de la Escuela Experimental Indoamericana Colonia Bethania. Year 1, no 1. 20 July 1953.

Horizontes Rurales: Vocero del Núcleo Escolar Campesino Número 12. Guatemala: El Tejar, Chimaltenango. Year 1, no. 1. August 1949.

El Imparcial. Guatemala.

The Inter-American Monthly. Washington: Foreign Policy Association. 1942–46.

Lucha 3000. Guatemala: Grupo Nova, 2003.

La Luz Apostólica. San Antonio: Latin American District Council of the Assemblies of God; Casa Evangélica de Publicaciones. October 1952.

Luz del Porvenir: Revista de propaganda, Órgano de la Federación Espiritista de Guatemala. Guarda Viejo, Guatemala. April 1927.

Misiones Culturales: Revista de Misiones Ambulantes de Cultura Inicial. Guatemala. April 1949.

Mujeres, Boletín de la Alianza Femenina Guatemalteca. Guatemala. 1952–53.

Nuestro Diario. Guatemala.

Obrero en lucha: Periódico obrero de la Federación de Trabajadores de Guatemala. Guatemala. 1980.

Octubre. Guatemala: Communist Party. 1951–53.

La Palabra, Voz del nuevo milenio. Guatemala.

El Periódico. Guatemala.

Prensa Libre. Guatemala.

El Rano Chapín: Los pobladores en pie de lucha. Guatemala: Frente Popular 31 de Enero. c. 1982–83.

Revista de la Asociación Lacandones. Guatemala. 1935.

Revista Militar. Guatemala: Editorial del Ejército.

El Sembrador. San Pedro Sacatepéquez: Escuela Industrial "Cirilo López." May 1950.

Sexo Libre. Guatemala.

Siglo Veintiuno. Guatemala.

De Sol a Sol: Periódico campesino. Guatemala: Comité Pro Justicia y Paz. 1975–80.

La Verdad. Guatemala: Publicaciones La Verdad.

Verdad, Órgano del Comité Central PGT. Guatemala: Partido Guatemalteco del Trabajo. 1984–85.

Works Cited

Abell, Peter. "Sociological Theory and Rational Choice Theory." *The Blackwell Companion to Social Theory*, 2d edn., ed. Bryan S. Turner. Oxford: Blackwell, 2000.

"Acción Cívica Militar: Anotaciones del Mayor César Octavio Noguera Argueta y del Subtte. As. y Doctor Luís Sieckavizza." *Revista Militar* 11, no. 9 (July/September 1975): 53–58.

Acosta-Belén, Edna, and Christine E. Bose. "U.S. Latina and Latin American Feminisms: Hemispheric Encounters." *Signs* 25, no. 4 (summer 2000): 1113–19.

Acosta-Belén, Edna, and Christine E. Bose, eds. *Women in the Latin American Development Process.* Philadelphia: Temple University Press, 1995.

Actas de la Municipalidad de Guatemala. 1918–2003.

"Acuerdo sobre fortalecimiento del poder civil y función del ejército en una sociedad democrática." *Acuerdos de paz,* 3d edn. Guatemala: Universidad Rafael Landívar, Ministerio de Educación, Secretaria de la Paz, Gobierno de Suecia, June 1998.

Acuerdos de paz. 3d edn. Guatemala: Universidad Rafael Landívar, Ministerio de Educación, Secretaria de la Paz, Gobierno de Suecia, June 1998.

Adams, Richard. *Crucifixion by Power: Essays on Guatemalan National Social Structure, 1944–1966.* Austin: University of Texas Press, 1970.

Adams, Richard, and Santiago Bastos. *Las relaciones étnicas en Guatemala, 1944–2000.* Antigua, Guatemala: CIRMA, 2003.

Agencia de Cooperación Internacional de Japón (JICA). El estudio de factibilidad sobre el proyecto de transportación urbana en el área metropolitana de Guatemala, Informe final a la Municipalidad de Guatemala. Tokyo: Yachiyo Engineering Co., Ltd., and Chodai Co., Ltd., March 1997. Unpublished report. Courtesy of the Municipalidad de Guatemala.

Aguilera Peralta, Gabriel. *El fusil y el olivo: La cuestión militar en Centroamérica.* San José: FLACSO, 1989.

Allen, John, Doreen Massey, and Alan Cochrane. *Rethinking the Region.* London: Routledge, 1998.

Alvarado, Paulo. "Presto non troppo: Para la historia del rock." *Prensa Libre,* 11 June 2004.

Alvarez, Orieta. "Antecedentes históricos del proceso revolucionario de 1944–1954 en Guatemala." *La Revolución de Octubre: Diez años de lucha por la democracia en Guatemala, 1944–1954.* Vol. 1, ed. Eduardo Antonio Velásquez Carrera. Guatemala: Universidad de San Carlos de Guatemala, Centro de Estudios Urbanos y Regionales, 1994.

Alvarez, Sonia E., Evelina Dagnino, and Arturo Escobar, eds. *Cultures of Politics, Politics of Cultures: Re-visioning Latin American Social Movements.* Boulder: Westview Press, 1998.

Amaro, Nelson. *Guatemala: Historia Despierta.* Guatemala: IDESAC, 1992.

Amorín, Carlos. "Maquila se escribe con 'm' de muerte." *Rel-Uita* (Uruguay, November 2004). Reproduced on http://www.solidaridad.net.

Anderson, Benedict. *Imagined Communities: Reflections on the Origin and Spread of Nationalism.* Rev. ed. London: Verso, 1991.

Anteproyecto de un plan para el desarrollo socio-económico de Guatemala en 21 años. Guatemala: Dirección General de Cartografía, February 1964.

Appadurai, Arjun. *Modernity at Large: Cultural Dimensions of Globalization.* Minneapolis: University of Minnesota Press, 1996.

ASIES. *Más de cien años del movimiento obrero urbano en Guatemala*. Vol. 1: *Artesanos y obreros en el período liberal (1877–1944)*. Guatemala, 1991.

——. *Más de cien años del movimiento obrero urbano*. Vol. 2: *El protagonismo sindical en la construcción de la democracia (1944–1954)*. Guatemala, 1992.

——. *Más de cien años del movimiento obrero urbano en Guatemala*. Vol. 3: *Reorganización, auge y desarticulación del movimiento sindical (1954–1982)*. Guatemala, 1992.

AVANCSO. *El proceso de crecimiento metropolitano de la Ciudad de Guatemala: Perfiles del fenómeno y ópticas de gestión*. Guatemala, 2003.

——. *Regiones y zonas agrarias de Guatemala: Una visión desde la reproducción social y económica de los campesinos*. Guatemala, 2001.

——. *Por los caminos de la sobrevivencia campesina*. Vol. 1: *Las estrategias de producción y reproducción campesina en la Zona Agropecuaria, Comercial y Fronteriza del Departamento de San Marcos*. Guatemala, 1999.

——. *Por sí mismos: Un estudio preliminar de las "maras" en la Ciudad de Guatemala*. 2d edn. Guatemala, 1998.

——. *La economía de Guatemala ante el ajuste estructural a comienzos de los '90*. Guatemala, January 1998.

——. *"Aquí corre la bola:" Organización y relaciones sociales en una comunidad popular urbana*. Cuadernos de Investigación no. 9. Guatemala, 1993.

Ball, Patrick, Paul Kobrak, and Herbert F Spirer. *State Violence in Guatemala, 1960–1996: A Quantitative Reflection*. Washington: American Association for the Advancement of Science, 1999.

Barry, Tom. *Inside Guatemala*. Albuquerque: The Inter-Hemispheric Education Resource Center, 1992.

Barry, Tom, and Deb Preusch. *The Soft War: The Uses and Abuses of U.S. Aid in Central America*. New York: Grove Press, 1988.

Bastos, Santiago, and Manuela Camus. *Quebrando el silencio: Organizaciones del pueblo maya y sus demandas*. Guatemala: FLACSO, 1992.

Basurto, Paolo. "Fighting Urban Poverty, Promoting Community Organization: The Case of 'El Mezquital' in Guatemala City." In *Upgrading Urban Communities: A Resource for Practitioners*. Compact disc ed. 2001. World Bank: 1999–2001.

Bell, Daniel. *The Cultural Contradictions of Capitalism*. 1976; reprint, New York: Basic Books, 1996.

Berger, Susan A. *Political and Agrarian Development in Guatemala*. Boulder: Westview Press, 1992.

Berman, Marshall. *All That Is Solid Melts into Air: The Experience of Modernity*. London: Penguin, 1988.

Bertens, Hans. *The Idea of the Postmodern*. London: Routledge, 1995.

Bethell, Leslie, and Ian Roxborough, eds. *Latin America between the Second World War and the Cold War, 1944–1948*. Cambridge: Cambridge University Press, 1992.

Bhabha, Homi K. *The Location of Culture*. London: Routledge, 1994.

Black, George, et al. *Garrison Guatemala*. New York: Monthly Review Press, 1984.

Bonpane, Blase. *Guerrillas of Peace: Liberation Theology and the Central American Revolution.* 2d edn. Boston: South End Press, 1987.

Born, Esther. *The New Architecture in Mexico.* New York: William Morrow, 1937.

Bourdieu, Pierre. *Distinction: A Social Critique of the Judgment of Taste.* 1979; reprint, Cambridge: Harvard University Press, 1984.

Briggs, Laura. *Reproducing Empire: Race, Sex, Science, and U.S. Imperialism in Puerto Rico.* Berkeley: University of California Press, 2002.

Bulmer-Thomas, Victor. *The Economic History of Latin America since Independence.* New York: Cambridge University Press, 1994.

———. *The Political Economy of Central America since 1920.* New York: Cambridge University Press, 1987.

Bushnell, David, and Neill Macaulay. *The Emergence of Latin America in the Nineteenth Century.* 2d edn. New York: Oxford University Press, 1994.

Camacho, Luis, et al. *Cultura y desarrollo desde América Latina.* San José: Universidad de Costa Rica, 1993.

Cambranes, Julio C. *Café y campesinos en Guatemala, 1853–1897.* Guatemala: Editorial Universitaria, 1985.

Camus, Manuela. *Ser indígena en la Cuidad de Guatemala.* Guatemala: FLACSO, 2002.

Carmack, Robert M. *Rebels of Highland Guatemala: The Quiché-Mayas of Momostenango.* Norman: University of Oklahoma Press, 1995.

A Case History of Communist Penetration: Guatemala. U.S. Department of State, Publication Number 6465, April 1957.

Castañeda, Jorge G. *Utopia Unarmed: The Latin American Left after the Cold War.* New York: Vintage, 1994.

Castañeda Maldonado, Mario Efraín. "Historia del rock en Guatemala: La música rock como expresión social en la ciudad de Guatemala entre 1960 a 1976." Undergraduate thesis, Universidad de San Carlos de Guatemala, Escuela de Historia, 2008.

Castillo de León, Otto Sergio. "Objetivos de Gobierno del Coronel Jacobo Arbenz Guzmán: Guatemala, 1951–1954." Thesis, Universidad de San Carlos de Guatemala, 1992.

Caulfield, Sueann. "The History of Gender in the Historiography of Latin America." *Hispanic American Historical Review* 81, nos. 3–4 (August–November 2001): 449–90.

Causús Arzú, Marta. *Guatemala: Linaje y racismo.* 2d edn. San José, Costa Rica: FLACSO, 1995.

Causús Arzú, Marta, and Teresa García Giráldez. *Las redes intelectuales centroamericanas: Un siglo de imaginarios nacionales (1820–1920).* Guatemala: F&G Editores, 2005.

Chen, Martha Alter. "Rethinking the Informal Economy." 2003. http://www.india-seminar.com/2003.

Chomsky, Aviva, and Aldo Lauria-Santiago, eds. *Identity and Struggle at the Margins of the Nation-State: The Laboring Peoples of Central America and the Hispanic Caribbean*. Durham: Duke University Press, 1998.

Chronology of the Pan-American Highway Project. Washington: Pan-American Union, Technical Unit on Tourism, Department of Economic Affairs, 1963.

"100 años de protestantismo: De Justo Rufino Barrios a Ríos Montt." *Siglo Veintiuno* (insert, *Magazine 21*), 10 September 1995.

Clark, Shannan. "The Creative Class: White-Collar Workers and the Culture of Consumer Capitalism in Modern America." Forthcoming.

Coatsworth, John H. *Growth Against Development: The Economic Impact of Railroads in Porfirian Mexico*. Dekalb: Northern Illinois University Press, 1981.

Cohen, Lizabeth. *A Consumer's Republic: The Politics of Mass Consumption in Postwar America*. New York: Knopf, 2003.

"Colectivo de Lesbianas Liberadas—Lesbiradas." Flyer. Guatemala City, March 2003.

Comisión para el Esclarecimiento Histórico. *Guatemala: Memoria del silencio*. Guatemala, 1999.

Comité de Estudiantes Universitarios Anticomunistas. "Estamos enteramente de acuerdo." Sección a cargo del Comité de Estudiantes Universitarios Anticomunistas Guatemaltecos en Exilio (CEUAGE), Sección de Honduras. *La República* (Tegucigalpa), 1, no. 23 (22 December 1953): 5.

———. "Nuestros aspiraciones: Principios básicos de nuestro programa político." *El Imparcial*, 14 January 1954, 12.

Communist Aggression in Latin America: Guatemala. Congress, House, Subcommittee on Latin America of the Select Committee on Communist Aggression, Ninth Interim Report. 83rd Cong., 2nd sess. (27–29 September, 8 October, and 14–15 October 1954).

"Construction of the Unfinished Sections of the Pan-American Highway." Council of the Organization of American States Special Committee to Study the Formulation of New Measures for Economic Cooperation Working Group. CECE/Subgroup 4; Working Paper no. 11. Washington: Organization of American States, 11 February 1959.

Cooper, Frederick, et al. *Confronting Historical Paradigms: Peasants, Labor, and the Capitalist World System in Africa and Latin America*. Madison: University of Wisconsin Press, 1993.

Coronil, Fernando. *The Magical State: Nature, Money, and Modernity in Venezuela*. Chicago: University of Chicago Press, 1997.

Cortés Conde, Roberto, and Shane J. Hunt, eds. *The Latin American Economies: Growth and the Export Sector, 1880–1930*. New York: Holmes and Meier, 1985.

Cottam, Martha L. *Images and Intervention: U.S. Policies in Latin America*. Pittsburgh: University of Pittsburgh Press, 1994.

Cowan, M. P., and R. W. Shenton. *Doctrines of Development*. London: Routledge, 1996.

Cronon, William. *Nature's Metropolis: Chicago and the Great West*. New York: W. W. Norton, 1991.

Cullather, Nicholas. PBSUCCESS: *The United States and Guatemala, 1952–1954.* Washington: History Staff, Center for the Study of Intelligence, Central Intelligence Agency, 1994. Released as sanitized 1997.

Cumes Salazar, Helidoro, and Teresa Chocoyo Chile. *Nos hace llorar: Jóvenes trabajadoras en las maquilas coreanas de San Lucas, Sacatepéquez a El Tejar, Chimaltenango.* Guatemala: Programa de Apoyo para la Salud Materno Infantil y para la Salud de Otros Grupos de Riesgo, publicada gracias al apoyo USAID, November 1997.

Davis, Mike. *City of Quartz.* New York: Verso, 1990.

Decreto no. 900 del Congreso: "Ley de Reforma Agraria." 17 June 1952. *Recopilación de las leyes de la República de Guatemala* 71 (1952–53), 20–31.

De la Guardia, César Manuel. *Castillo Armas, libertador y mártir.* Guatemala: Biblioteca Indoamericana, 1957.

De León Aragón, Oscar. *Caída de un régimen: Jorge Ubico–Federico Ponce; 20 de octubre de 1944.* Guatemala: FLACSO, 1995.

Denning, Michael. *The Cultural Front.* London: Verso, 1997.

Desarrollo integral de las comunidades rurales en Guatemala: Labor de la Dirección General de Desarrollo Socioeducativo Rural. Guatemala: Editorial del Ministerio de Educación Pública, 1957 [Crónicas de Diario de Centroamérica, September 1956].

Design and Construction of the Pan-American Highway: Final Project Report. San Francisco: [U.S. Army] War Department, Corps of Engineers, April 1944. Housed in the Columbus Library of the Pan-American Union.

Deutsch, Sandra McGee. "Gender and Sociopolitical Change in Twentieth-Century Latin America." *Hispanic American Historical Review* 71, no. 2 (May 1991): 259–306.

DHV Consultants, Guatemala (Grupo DHV, Germany). "Presentaciones, Anteproyecto, y Proyecto Cuatro Grados Norte" (DHV to Municipalidad de Guatemala: June–July 2001). Unpublished proposal. Courtesy of Municipalidad de Guatemala.

Diamond, Jared. *Collapse: How Societies Choose to Fail or Succeed.* New York: Viking, 2005.

Díaz Cardona, Francia Elena. *Fuerzas armadas, militarismo y constitución nacional en América Latina.* Mexico City: Universidad Nacional Autónoma de México, 1988.

Dillon, Robert. "Confidencial: Informe sobre la reforma agraria en Guatemala." AGCA MAC/427 (Planificación Agrícola 1955), 16 January 1954.

Dore, Elizabeth, and Maxine Molyneux, eds. *Hidden Histories of Gender and the State in Latin America.* Durham: Duke University Press, 2000.

Dosal, Paul J. *Power in Transition: The Rise of Guatemala's Industrial Oligarchy, 1871–1994.* Westport, Conn.: Praeger, 1995.

Dunkerley, James. *Power in the Isthmus: A Political History of Modern Central America.* London: Verso, 1988.

Ebel, Roland H. *Misunderstood Caudillo: Miguel Ydígoras Fuentes and the Failure of Democracy in Guatemala.* Lanham, Md.: University Press of America, 1998.

Elaboración de productos cárnicos. Mexico City: Editorial Trillas, 1984.

Ellwood, Wayne. *The No-Nonsense Guide to Globalization*. Oxford: New Internationalist Publications/Verso, 2001.

Escobar, Arturo. *Encountering Development: The Making and Unmaking of the Third World*. Princeton: Princeton University Press, 1995.

Escobar Medrano, Edgar, and Edna González Camargo. *Historia de la cultura de Guatemala*. 2 vols. Guatemala: Editorial Orión, 2003.

Esquema director de ordenamiento metropolitano (EDOM) 1972–2000: Plan de desarrollo metropolitano. Guatemala: Municipalidad de Guatemala, 1972.

Falla, Ricardo. *Masacres de la selva: Ixcán, Guatemala, 1975–1982*. Guatemala: Editorial Universitaria, 1992.

Featherstone, Mike. *Consumer Culture and Postmodernism*. London: Sage Publications, 1990.

Ferguson, James. *Expectations of Modernity: Myths and Meanings of Urban Life on the Zambian Copperbelt*. Berkeley: University of California Press, 1999.

———. *The Anti-Politics Machine: "Development," Depoliticization, and Bureaucratic Power in Lesotho*. Minneapolis: University of Minnesota Press, 1994.

Figueroa Ibarra, Carlos. "El contenido burgués y reaccionario del golpe de estado en Guatemala." In *La Crisis Política en Guatemala*. Mexico City: Universidad Autónoma del Estado de México, 1983.

Findlay, Eileen J. "Love in the Tropics: Marriage, Divorce, and the Construction of Benevolent Colonialism in Puerto Rico, 1898–1910." *Close Encounters of Empire: Writing the Cultural History of U.S.–Latin American Relations*, ed. Gilbert M. Joseph, Catherine C. LeGrand, and Ricardo D. Salvatore. Durham: Duke University Press, 1998.

Fishman, Peter. "The Student Is a Citizen: Constructing Schooling in Guatemala's Western Highlands, 1944–1954." Undergraduate thesis, Yale University, 2006.

FLACSO. *Sombras de una batalla: Familias desplazadas por la violencia en Ciudad de Guatemala*. Guatemala, 1994.

Flores, Marco Antonio. *Fortuny: Un comunista guatemalteco*. Guatemala: Oscar de León Palacios, Palo de Hormigo y Universitaria, 1994.

Foreign Policy Association. *The Inter-American Monthly*. Washington, 1942–46.

Forster, Cindy. *The Time of Freedom: Campesino Workers in Guatemala's October Revolution*. Pittsburgh: University of Pittsburgh Press, 2001.

French, John D., and Daniel James, eds. *The Gendered Worlds of Latin American Women Workers: From Household and Factory to the Union Hall and Ballot Box*. Durham: Duke University Press, 1997.

Fritzsche, Peter. *A Nation of Fliers: German Aviation and the Popular Imagination*. Cambridge: Harvard University Press, 1992.

Gaitan A., Héctor. *Los Presidentes de Guatemala*. Guatemala: Editorial Artemis Edinter, 1992.

Gálvez Borrell, Víctor, and Gisela Gellert. *Guatemala: Exclusión social y estrategias para enfrentarla*. Guatemala: FLACSO, 2000.

García Añoveros, Jesús M. *Jacobo Arbenz*. Madrid: Historia 16, 1987.

García Canclini, Néstor. *Culturas híbridas: Estrategias para entrar y salir de la modernidad*. Mexico City: Editorial Grijalbo, 1990.

——. *Hybrid Cultures: Strategies for Entering and Leaving Modernity*. Translated by Christopher L. Chiappari and Silvia L. López. Minneapolis: University of Minnesota Press, 1995.

García Vettorazzi, Silvia. "El crecimiento espacial de la Ciudad de Guatemala: ¿Un desorden permitido?" *La Ciudad de Guatemala y su área de influencia urbana: Perfiles de problemas y líneas de solución*. Serie Temas Urbanos 2000, no. 1. Guatemala: AVANCSO, 2000.

Garrard-Burnett, Virginia. "Indians are Drunks and Drunks are Indians: Alcohol and Indigenismo in Guatemala, 1890–1940." *Bulletin of Latin American Research* 19, no. 3 (July 2000): 341–56.

——. *Protestantism in Guatemala: Living in the New Jerusalem*. Austin: University of Texas Press, 1998.

Geiger, Theodore. *Communism versus Progress in Guatemala*. Planning Pamphlet no. 85. Washington: National Planning Association, 1953.

Gellert, Gisela, and J. C. Pinto Soria. *Ciudad de Guatemala: Dos estudios sobre su evolución urbana, 1524–1950*. Guatemala: USAC/CEUR, 1990.

Gleijeses, Piero. "Guatemala: Crisis and Response." *Report on Guatemala: Findings of the Study Group on United States–Guatemalan Relations*. SAIS Papers in International Affairs, no. 7. Boulder: Westview/Foreign Policy Institute, Johns Hopkins University, 1985.

——. *Shattered Hope: The Guatemalan Revolution and the United States, 1944–1954*. Princeton: Princeton University Press, 1991.

Goldin, Liliana R. "Organizing the World through the Market: A Symbolic Analysis of Markets and Exchange in the Western Highlands of Guatemala." Ph.D. diss., State University of New York at Albany, 1985.

Golsan, Richard J., ed. *Fascism, Aesthetics, and Culture*. Hanover, N.H.: University Press of New England, 1992.

González Orellana, Carlos. *Historia de la educación en Guatemala*. Guatemala: Editorial José de Pineda Ibarra, 1970.

Gootenberg, Paul. *Imagining Development: Economic Ideas in Peru's "Fictitious Prosperity" of Guano, 1840–1880*. Berkeley: University of California Press, 1993.

Gordon, Linda. "Review of Joan W. Scott, *Gender and the Politics of History*." *Signs* 15, no. 4 (summer 1990): 853–58.

Gould, Jeffrey L. *To Lead as Equals: Rural Protest and Political Consciousness in Chinandega, Nicaragua, 1912–1979*. Chapel Hill: University of North Carolina Press, 1990.

Gramajo Morales, Héctor Alejandro. *De la guerra . . . a la guerra: La difícil transición política en Guatemala*. Guatemala: Fondo de Cultura Editorial, 1995.

Grandin, Greg. *The Last Colonial Massacre: Latin America in the Cold War*. Chicago: University of Chicago Press, 2004.

———. *The Blood of Guatemala: A History of Race and Nation*. Durham: Duke University Press, 2000.

———. "Everyday Forms of State Decomposition: Quetzaltenango, Guatemala, 1954." *Bulletin of Latin American Research* 19, no. 3 (July 2000): 303–20.

Greenblatt, Stephen. *Marvelous Possessions: The Wonder of the New World*. Chicago: University of Chicago Press, 1991.

Grewal, David Singh. *Network Power: The Social Dynamics of Globalization*. New Haven: Yale University Press, 2008.

Grupo de Apoyo Mutuo y Centro Internacional para Investigaciones en Derechos Humanos. *Quitar el agua al pez: Análisis del terror en tres comunidades rurales de Guatemala, 1980–1984*. Guatemala, 1996.

"Grupo Roble con las cadenas más grandes de centros comerciales en Centroamérica." *Moneda* (25–29 August 2003): 6.

Grupo Subsectorial de Trabajo de la Carne (GSTC). "Propuesta de creación de la Asociación Nacional Ganadera (ANAG): Modernización y competitividad de la cadena agroalimentaria de la carne." Trabajo de consultoría realizado por Lic. Jorge Mario Búcaro M., Zootecnista. Guatemala: unpublished report, November 1998. Coll. Melgar Z.

Guatemala: Security, Development, and Democracy. Guatemalan Church in Exile, 1989.

"Guatemalan Communist Personnel to be Disposed of during Military Operations of Calligeris." Washington: Central Intelligence Agency, n.d. [c. 1954]. Declassified 1997.

Guerra-Borges, Alfredo. "Semblanza de la Revolución Guatemalteca de 1944–1954." *Historia general de Guatemala*, 4:14. Guatemala: Asociación de Amigos del País, 1997.

Guha, Ranajit. *Elementary Aspects of Peasant Insurgency in Colonial India*. Durham: Duke University Press, 1999.

Guha, Ranajit, and Gayatri Chakravorty Spivak, eds. *Selected Subaltern Studies*. New York: Oxford University Press, 1988.

Guinea, Gerardo. *Armas para ganar una nueva batalla*. Guatemala: Tipografía Nacional, 1957.

Guzmán Böckler, Carlos. *Donde enmudecen las conciencias: Crepúsculo y aurora en Guatemala*. Mexico City: Secretaria de Educación Pública, Consejo Nacional de Fomento Educativo, 1986.

Haeussler Yela, Carlos C. *Diccionario General de Guatemala*. 3 vols. Guatemala: n.p., 1983.

Haines, Gerald K. "CIA and Guatemala Assassination Proposals, 1952–1954: CIA History Staff Analysis." Washington: Central Intelligence Agency, 1995. Released as sanitized 1997.

Halperin-Donghi, Tulio. "Dependency Theory and Latin American Historiography." *Latin American Research Review* 17, no. 1 (1982): 115–30.

Handy, Jim. *Revolution in the Countryside: Rural Conflict and Agrarian Reform in Guatemala, 1944–1954*. Chapel Hill: University of North Carolina Press, 1994.

———. *Gift of the Devil: A History of Guatemala*. Boston: South End Press, 1984.

Harvey, David. *The Condition of Postmodernity: An Enquiry into the Origins of Cultural Change*. Oxford: Basil Blackwell, 1990.

Herf, Jeffrey. *Reactionary Modernism: Technology, Culture, and Politics in Weimar and the Third Reich*. Cambridge: Cambridge University Press, 1984.

Historia sinóptica de Guatemala. Guatemala: Elaborado por Asociación Amigos del País, para uso exclusivo del Ministerio de Educación, 1999.

Holston, James. *The Modernist City: An Anthropological Critique of Brasilia*. Chicago: University of Chicago Press, 1989.

Hoogvelt, Ankie. *Globalization and the Postcolonial World: The New Political Economy of Development*. Baltimore: Johns Hopkins University Press, 1997.

Hughes, H. Stuart. *Consciousness and Society: The Reorientation of European Social Thought, 1890–1930*. New York: Alfred A. Knopf, 1961.

Human Rights Watch. "Las trabajadoras se enfrentan a la discriminación." 2002 Report on Guatemalan Maquila Sector. On http://www.hrw.org.

Hutchison, Peter, ed. *Central America and Mexico Handbook 2002*. Bath: Footprint Handbooks, 2001.

Iglesia Guatemalteca en el Exilio. Untitled report on Evangelical Protestantism in Guatemala. Guatemala, CIRMA: Archivo Histórico, Colección Plumstock, no. 16, January 1983.

"Informe sobre la situación de la Asociación de Expendedores de Carne, ASEC, desde el inicio de la consultoría en julio de 1998 hasta el mes de agosto de 1999." Unpublished report by government assessor of ASEC Auto-Abastecimiento Project. Guatemala: Unidentified government agency, 1999. Coll. Melgar Z.

Instituto Nacional de Estadística. República de Guatemala. "Indice de precios al consumidor—IPC, 1995–2000."

International Labor Organization. SIMPOC: Statistical Monitoring Programme on Child Labour. "Estudio cualitativo sobre el trabajo infantil en Guatemala: Informe final, 2003." http://www.ilo.org/ipecinfo.

"Invasiones de tierras (1986–1990): Un desborde popular en tiempos de Democracia." *Boletín del Centro de Estudios Urbanos y Regionales*, Universidad de San Carlos de Guatemala, no. 9 (November 1990).

James, Daniel. *Red Design for the Americas: Guatemalan Prelude*. New York: Day, 1971.

Jameson, Fredric, and Masao Miyoshi, eds. *The Cultures of Globalization*. Durham: Duke University Press, 1998.

Jay, Martin. *The Dialectical Imagination: A History of the Frankfurt School and the Institute of Social Research, 1923–1950*. 1973; reprint, Berkeley: University of California Press, 1996.

Jonas, Susanne. *The Battle for Guatemala: Rebels, Death Squads, and U.S. Power*. Boulder: Westview, 1991.

Jonas, Susanne, and David Tobis, eds. *Guatemala*. New York: North American Congress on Latin America, 1981.

Joseph, Gilbert M., Catherine C. LeGrand, and Ricardo D. Salvatore, eds. *Close Encounters of Empire: Writing the Cultural History of U.S.–Latin American Relations*. Durham: Duke University Press, 1998.

Joseph, Gilbert M., and Daniel Nugent. "Popular Culture and State Formation in Revolutionary Mexico." *Everyday Forms of State Formation: Revolution and the Negotiation of Rule in Modern México*, ed. Gilbert M. Joseph and Daniel Nugent. Durham: Duke University Press, 1994.

Joseph, Gilbert M., and Daniel Nugent, eds. *Everyday Forms of State Formation: Revolution and the Negotiation of Rule in Modern Mexico*. Durham: Duke University Press, 1994.

Kaplan, Amy, and Donald Pease, eds. *Cultures of U.S. Imperialism*. Durham: Duke University Press, 1993.

Kay, Cristóbal. *Latin American Theories of Development and Underdevelopment*. London: Routledge, 1989.

Knight, Alan. "The Rise and Fall of Cardenismo, c. 1930–c. 1946." *Mexico since Independence*, ed. Leslie Bethell. Cambridge: Cambridge University Press, 1991.

Kobrak, Paul. *Organizing and Repression in the University of San Carlos, Guatemala, 1944 to 1996*. New York: American Association for the Advancement of Science, 1999.

Lavrín, Asunción. *Women, Feminism, and Social Change in Argentina, Chile, and Uruguay, 1890–1940*. Lincoln: University of Nebraska Press, 1998.

Leach, William. *Land of Desire: Merchants, Power, and the Rise of a New American Culture*. New York: Vintage, 1993.

Le Bot, Yvon. *La guerre en terre maya: Communauté, violence et modernité au Guatemala*. Paris: Éditions Karthala, 1992.

Lees, Andrew. *Cities Perceived: Urban Society in European and American Thought, 1820–1940*. Manchester: Manchester University Press, 1985.

Lefebvre, Henri. *The Production of Space*. Translated by Donald Nicholson-Smith. Oxford: Blackwell, 1991.

Levenson-Estrada, Deborah. *Trade Unionists against Terror: Guatemala City, 1954–1985*. Chapel Hill: University of North Carolina Press, 1994.

Lewis, Tom. *Divided Highways: Building the Interstate Highways, Transforming American Life*. New York: Viking, 1997.

Lock, Margaret, and Deborah R. Gordon, eds. *Biomedicine Examined*. Dordrecht: Kluwer Academic, 1987.

López Rivera, and Oscar Augusto. *Guatemala: Intimidades de la pobreza*. Guatemala: Universidad Rafael Landívar, Instituto de Investigaciones Económicos y Sociales, 1999.

Lovell, W. George. *Conquest and Survival in Colonial Guatemala: A Historical Geography of the Cuchumatán Highlands, 1500–1821*. Montreal: McGill–Queens University Press, 1992.

Macleod, Murdo J. *Spanish Central America: A Socioeconomic History, 1520–1720*. Berkeley: University of California Press, 1973.

Mallon, Florencia E. *Peasant and Nation: The Making of Postcolonial Mexico and Peru*. Berkeley: University of California Press, 1995.

——. "The Promise and Dilemma of Subaltern Studies: Perspectives from Latin American History." *American Historical Review* 99 (December 1994): 1491–1515.

Mandel, Ernest. *Late Capitalism*. London: New Left Books, 1975.

"Manifesto de la agrupación anti comunista altaverapacense." March 1952. Tulane University Archives: Central America Printed Ephemera Collection 20(435), box 10.

Maras y pandillas en Centroamérica. Vol. 1. Managua: UCA Publicaciones, 2001.

Marx, Karl. *Capital: A Critique of Political Economy*. 3 vols. Translated by Ben Fowkes. London: Penguin, 1990.

——. *Grundrisse*. Translated by Martin Nicolaus. London: Penguin, 1993.

Mattson, Corey, and Marie Ayer. "La maquila en Guatemala: Hechos y tendencias." STITCH report, 2004. On http://www.stitchonline.org/archives/maquila.html.

Mayrink, José Maria. "O apoio civil na luta antiguerrilha na Guatemala." In *O Estado de São Paulo*. São Paulo, 3 March 1982.

McClintock, Anne. *Imperial Leather: Race, Gender and Sexuality in the Colonial Conquest*. London: Routledge, 1995.

McClintock, Michael. *The American Connection*. Vol. 2: *Guatemala*. London: Zed Books, 1985.

McCreery, David. *Rural Guatemala, 1760–1940*. Stanford: Stanford University Press, 1994.

Menchú Tum, Rigoberta. *Me llamo Rigoberta Menchú y así me nació la consciencia*. Edited by Elizabeth Burgos. Mexico City: Siglo Veintiuno Editores, 1985.

Metrópolis 2010: Plan de desarrollo metropolitano. Guatemala: Municipalidad de Guatemala, 1995.

Miller Klubock, Thomas. *Contested Communities: Class, Gender, and Politics in Chile's El Teniente Copper Mine, 1904–1951*. Durham: Duke University Press, 1998.

Montes, César (nom de guerre of Julio César Macias). *Mi camino: La guerrilla*. Mexico City: Planeta, 1998.

Monzón Lemus, Cristóbal. *Camino de adolescente: La vida de Ramón en el barrio "El Gallito."* Guatemala: Delgado Impresos, 1990.

Moore, Brian L. *Cultural Power, Resistance and Pluralism: Colonial Guyana, 1838–1900*. Kingston: University Press of the West Indies, 1995.

Morales, Mario Roberto. *La articulación de las diferencias, o el síndrome de Maximón: Los discursos literarios y políticos del debate interétnico en Guatemala*. 2d edn. Guatemala: Editorial Palo de Hormigo, 2002.

Morán Mérida, Amanda. *Condiciones de vida y tenencia de la tierra en asentamientos precarios de la Ciudad de Guatemala*. 2d edn. Guatemala: Ediciones CEUR-USAC, 2000.

Moreton, Bethany E. "It Came from Bentonville: The Agrarian Origins of Wal-Mart Culture." *Wal-Mart: The Face of Twenty-First-Century Capitalism*, ed. Nelson Lichtenstein. New York: New Press, 2006.

——. *To Serve God and Wal-Mart: The Making of Christian Free Enterprise.* Cambridge: Harvard University Press, 2009.

Municipalidad de Guatemala. 2005. http://www.nuestramuni.com.

Nelson, Diane. *A Finger in the Wound: Body Politics in Quincentennial Guatemala.* Berkeley: University of California Press, 1999.

——. "Chisec, Alta Verapaz," and "Coban, Alta Verapaz." Field research reports. Antigua, Guatemala: CIRMA, n.d. [after 1986].

Noble, David F. *America by Design: Science, Technology, and the Rise of Corporate Capitalism.* Oxford: Oxford University Press, 1977.

Nunn, Frederick M. *The Time of the Generals: Latin American Professional Militarism in World Perspective.* Lincoln: University of Nebraska Press, 1992.

Obando Sánchez, Antonio. *Memorias: La historia del movimiento obrero en Guatemala en este siglo.* Guatemala: Editorial Universitaria, 1978.

ONGs, sociedad civil y Estado en Guatemala: Elementos para el debate. Guatemala: AVANCSO-IDESAC, March 1990.

Organización Internacional del Trabajo. Centro Interamericano de Investigación y Documentación sobre Formación Profesional (CINTERFOR). "Proyecto Mejoramiento de las condiciones laborales y de vida de las trabajadoras de la maquila en Centroamérica: Informe de avance." January 2001. On http://www.ilo.org/public/spanish/region.

Organization of American States 1960 Annual Report of the Secretary General to the Council of the Organization. Washington: Pan-American Union, 1961.

Páginas Sindicales Guatemala. Guatemala: Iepala Editorial, n.d. CIRMA, Donativos.

Painter, James. *Guatemala: False Hope, False Freedom.* London: Catholic Institute for International Relations, Latin American Bureau, 1989.

Paiz Herrera, Federico. *1931–1978: Años de la vida política de Guatemala.* Guatemala: n.p., 1978.

Palencia, Gema. "Maltrato en maquilas." April 2004. On http://www.latinoamerica-online.it.

Paredes Moreira, José Luis. *Reforma agraria: Una experiencia en Guatemala.* Guatemala: Imprenta Universitaria, 1963.

Paus, Eva, ed. *Struggle against Dependence: Nontraditional Export Growth in Central America and the Caribbean.* Boulder: Westview, 1988.

Peckenham, Nancy. "Land Settlement in the Petén." *Latin American Perspectives* (spring–summer 1980).

Pellecer, Carlos Manuel. *Arbenz y yo.* Guatemala: Editorial Artemis y Edinter, 1997.

——. *Memoria en dos geografías.* 2d edn. Mexico City: Costa-Amic, 1964.

——. *Renuncia al comunismo.* Mexico City: Costa-Amic, 1963.

Penetration of the Political Institutions of Guatemala by the International Communist Movement. Information submitted by the Delegation of the United States of America to the Fifth Meeting of Consultation of Ministers of Foreign Affairs of the American Republics, serving as Organ of Consultation. June 1954.

Pensamiento de General Laugerud. Vol. 1: *Candidato Presidencial.* Guatemala: Relaciones Públicas de la Presidencia, n.d. [mid-1970s].

El pensamiento del Presidente Castillo Armas. Guatemala: Secretaría de Divulgación, Cultura y Turismo, 1955.

Petras, F. "Cambios en la estructura agraria de la América Latina." *Desarrollo agrario y la América Latina*, ed. Antonio García. Mexico City: Fondo de Cultura Económica, 1981.

Pike, Frederick B. *The United States and Latin America: Myths and Stereotypes of Civilization and Nature*. Austin: University of Texas Press, 1992.

Pratt, Mary Louise. *Imperial Eyes: Travel Writing and Transculturation*. London: Routledge, 1992.

Programa regional de carreteras centroamericanas: informe preliminar. 2 vols. Tegucigalpa and Guatemala City: BCIE, SIECA, January 1963.

"Los protestantes en Guatemala." CIRMA, Colección Documentos 2565, n.p., June 1991.

"¿Qué hace nuestra muni?" Guatemala: Municipalidad de Guatemala, c. 2003.

Quesada S., and Flavio J. "Invasiones de terrenos en la Ciudad de Guatemala." Guatemala: Centro de Estudios Urbanos y Regionales, Universidad de San Carlos de Guatemala, February 1985.

Quién es quién: Catálogo electoral 1999. Guatemala: Acción Ciudadana et al., October 1999.

Quijano, Aníbal. "Colonialism of Power, Eurocentrism, and Latin America." *Nepantla: Views from the South* 1, no. 3 (2000): 533–80.

Ramírez, Chiqui. *La guerra de los 36 años: Vista con ojos de mujer de izquierda*. Guatemala: Editorial Oscar de León Palacios, 2001.

Recopilación de las leyes de la República de Guatemala. Guatemala, 1872–1993. Includes all constitutions and laws.

Report on Guatemala: Findings of the Study Group on United States–Guatemalan Relations. SAIS Papers in International Affairs, no. 7. Boulder: Westview/Foreign Policy Institute, Johns Hopkins University, 1985.

Resoluciones y otros documentos del Sexto Congreso Interamericano de Turismo Relacionados con el tránsito automotor y el establecimiento de servicios en las rutas del Sistema Panamericano de Carreteras. Washington: Unión Panamericana, Congresos Panamericanos de Carreteras, Secretaria Permanente, 1956.

Restrepo-Fernández, Iván. "¿Reforma agraria o modernización agrícola? Reflexiones sobre la Reunión Mundial de Reforma Agraria." *Desarrollo agrario y la América Latina*, Antonio García (comp.). Mexico City: Fondo de Cultura Económica, 1981.

Revolución socialista en Guatemala: Primera declaración de la Sierra de las Minas. Montevideo: Dirección del Movimiento Revolucionario 13 de Noviembre; Edición del Comité Bancario de Lucha Antimperialista, 1965.

Richards, Thomas. *The Commodity Culture of Victorian England: Advertising and Spectacle, 1851–1914*. Stanford: Stanford University Press, 1990.

Rodas Maltéz, Francisco. *Producción de suelo habitacional y de los servicios básicos en la periferia metropolitana de la Ciudad de Guatemala: Estudio de los municipios de Mixco, Santa Catarina Pinula y San José Pinula*. Guatemala: CEUR et al., 1996.

Rosada-Granados, Héctor. *Soldados en el poder: Proyecto militar en Guatemala, 1944–1990.* Amsterdam: Thela, 1998.

Roseberry, William. "Hegemony and the Language of Contention." *Everyday Forms of State Formation: Revolution and the Negotiation of Rule in Modern Mexico,* ed. Gilbert Joseph and Daniel Nugent. Durham: Duke University Press, 1984.

Roseberry, William, ed. *Anthropologies and Histories: Essays in Culture, History, and Political Economy.* New Brunswick: Rutgers University Press, 1989.

Roseberry, William, and Jay O'Brien, eds. *Golden Ages, Dark Ages: Imagining the Past in Anthropology and History.* Berkeley: University of California Press, 1991.

Ross, Kristin. *Fast Cars, Clean Bodies: Decolonization and the Reordering of French Culture.* Cambridge: MIT Press, 1996.

Rostow, W. W. *The Stages of Economic Growth: A Non-Communist Manifesto.* Cambridge: Cambridge University Press, 1960.

Rouquié, Alain. *The Military and the State in Latin America.* Translated by Paul E. Sigmund. Berkeley: University of California Press, 1987.

Saavedra, Alfredo. *El color de la sangre: 40 años de represión y de resistencia en Guatemala.* Guatemala: Grupo de Apoyo Mutuo y el apoyo de NOVIB de Holanda, 2001.

Sahlins, Peter. *Boundaries: The Making of France and Spain in the Pyrenees.* Berkeley: University of California Press, 1989.

Said, Edward W. *Orientalism.* New York: Vintage, 1978.

Sarasa, Jesús María. *Los protestantes en Guatemala.* 2d edn. Guatemala: n.p., December 1992.

Schirmer, Jennifer. *The Guatemalan Military Project: A Violence Called Democracy.* Philadelphia: University of Pennsylvania Press, 1998.

Schlesinger, Stephen, and Stephen Kinzer. *Bitter Fruit: The Untold Story of the American Coup in Guatemala.* New York: Anchor Press / Doubleday, 1984.

Schlosser, Eric. *Fast Food Nation.* New York: HarperCollins, 2002.

Schnapp, Jeffrey T. *Staging Fascism: 18 BL and the Theater of Masses for Masses.* Stanford: Stanford University Press, 1996.

Schneider, Ronald M. *Communism in Guatemala, 1944–1954.* 1958; reprint, New York: Octagon Books, 1979.

Schooley, Helen. *Conflict in Central America.* Harlow, Essex: Longman Group UK, 1987.

Schwartz, Norman B. *Forest Society: A Social History of Petén, Guatemala.* Philadelphia: University of Pennsylvania Press, 1990.

Schwartz, Stuart B., ed. *Implicit Understandings: Observing, Reporting, and Reflecting on the Encounters between Europeans and Other Peoples in the Early Modern Era.* Cambridge: Cambridge University Press, 1994.

Scott, James C. *Domination and the Arts of Resistance: Hidden Transcripts.* New Haven: Yale University Press, 1990.

——. *Seeing Like a State: How Certain Schemes to Improve the Human Condition Have Failed.* New Haven: Yale University Press, 1998.

———. *Weapons of the Weak: Everyday Forms of Peasant Resistance.* New Haven: Yale University Press, 1985.

Scott, Joan Wallach. *Gender and the Politics of History.* New York: Columbia University Press, 1988.

———. "Gender: A Useful Category of Historical Analysis." *American Historical Review* 91, no. 5 (December 1986): 1053–75.

Segrue, Thomas J. *The Origins of the Urban Crisis: Race and Inequality in Postwar Detroit.* Princeton: Princeton University Press, 1996.

Seminario de Planificación ZOPP. "El sector minorista: los beneficios y compromisos incorporándose al PROMECA." Guatemala, 27–31 May 1991. Salón de Conferencias INTECAP. Guatemala: Dirección de Servicios Pecuarios, DIGESEPE/Cooperación Técnica Alemana GTZ, 1991. Conference handout.

Sereseres, César D. "The Guatemalan Legacy: Radical Challengers and Military Politics." *Report on Guatemala: Findings of the Study Group on United States– Guatemalan Relations SAIS Papers in International Affairs.* no. 7. Boulder: Westview/Foreign Policy Institute, Johns Hopkins University, 1985.

Sieder, Rachel. "'Paz, Progreso, Justicia y Honradez': Law and Citizenship in Alta Verapaz during the Regime of Jorge Ubico." *Bulletin of Latin American Research* 19, no. 3 (July 2000): 283–302.

Silva Girón, César Augusto. *Guatemala en la historia contemporánea.* Guatemala: Editorial Litografia Seguricheques de Guatemala, 1992.

Simon, Jean-Marie. *Guatemala: Eternal Spring, Eternal Tyranny.* New York: W. W. Norton, 1987.

Smith, Carol A. "The Militarization of Civil Society in Guatemala: Economic Reorganization as a Continuation of War." *Latin American Perspectives,* Issue 67, Vol. 17, no. 4 (fall 1990): 8–41.

Smith, Carol A., ed. *Guatemalan Indians and the State, 1540–1988.* Austin: University of Texas Press, 1990.

Soja, Edward. *Postmodern Geographies: The Reassertion of Space in Critical Social Theory.* London: Verso, 1989.

Spivak, Gayatri. "Can the Subaltern Speak?" *Marxism and the Interpretation of Culture,* ed. Cary Nelson and Lawrence Grossberg. Urbana: University of Illinois Press, 1988.

———. *A Critique of Postcolonial Reason: Toward a History of the Vanishing Present.* Cambridge: Harvard University Press, 1999.

Stern, Steve J. "Feudalism, Capitalism, and the World-System in the Perspective of Latin America and the Caribbean" and "Reply: 'Ever More Solidarity.'" With Immanuel Wallerstein, "Comments on Stern's Critical Tests." *American Historical Review* 93:4 (October 1988), 829–97

———. *The Secret History of Gender: Women, Men and Power in Late Colonial México.* Chapel Hill: University of North Carolina Press, 1995.

Sternhell, Zeev. *Neither Right nor Left: Fascist Ideology in France.* Translated by David Maisel. Princeton: Princeton University Press, 1986.

Stoll, David. *Between Two Armies in the Ixil Towns of Guatemala*. New York: Columbia University Press, 1993.

——. *Rigoberta Menchú and the Story of All Poor Guatemalans*. Boulder: Westview, 1999.

Swetnam, John S. "The Open Gateway: Social and Economic Interaction in a Guatemalan Marketplace." Ph.D. diss., University of Pennsylvania, 1975.

Taracena Arriola, Arturo, Gisela Gellert, and Robert W. Clegman, Richard N. Adams, and Santiago Bastos Amigo. *Etnicidad, Estado y nación en Guatemala, 1808–1945*. 2 vols. Antigua, Guatemala: CIRMA, 2002.

Taracena Arriola, Arturo, and Jean Piel, eds. *Identidades nacionales y estado moderno en Centroamérica*. San José: FLACSO, 1995.

Thorner, Daniel, Basile Kerblay, and R. E. F. Smith, eds. *A. V. Chayanov on the Theory of Peasant Economy*. Madison: University of Wisconsin Press, 1986.

"To the United States Trade Representative: Petition and Request for Review of the GSP Status of Guatemala Under the Worker Rights Provisions of the Generalized System of Preferences." June 1, 1991. Petitioners: International Labor Rights Education and Research Fund (ILRERF); U.S./Guatemala Labor Education Project (U.S./GLEP); United Electrical, Radio & Machine Workers of America (UE); Amalgamated Clothing and Textile Workers Union (ACTWU); United Food and Commercial Workers International Union (UFCW); International Union of Food and Allied Workers' Associations (IUF), North America. Antigua, Guatemala: CIRMA. Cuadro de Clasificación Infostelle, 09/02/05, Relaciones económicas; maquiladoras.

Torres Rivas, Edelberto. *Crisis del Poder en Centroamérica*. Costa Rica: Editorial Universitaria Centroamericana (EDUCA), 1981.

"Trade Unions and the Maquila Sector." Peace Brigades International–Guatemala. Special Report, September 1996. On http://www.hartford-hwp.com/archives. Peace Brigades International: London.

Turner, Bryan S. "Cultural Sociology and Cultural Sciences." *The Blackwell Companion to Social Theory*, 2d edn., ed. Bryan S. Turner. Oxford: Blackwell, 2000.

Turner, Bryan S., ed. *The Blackwell Companion to Social Theory*. 2d edn. Oxford: Blackwell, 2000.

Unión Guatemalteca de Agencias de Publicidad. http://www.ugap.com.

United Nations Security Council. Document S/3232 (1954). Cablegram dated 19 June 1954 from the Minister for External Relations of Guatemala to the President of the Security Council.

——. Document S/3238 (1954). Cablegram dated 20 June 1954 from the Minister for External Affairs of Guatemala to the President of the Security Council.

——. UNSC Draft Resolutions S/3236/Rev.1 and S/3237. Adopted by the Security Council 20 June 1954.

Van Ness, Philip J. *Report on the Pan-American Highway*. Washington: Department of State, 20 June 1944.

Vela, David. *Retóricas de post-guerra*. Guatemala: Editorial Cultura, 2001.

Venturi, Robert, Denise Scott-Brown, and Steven Isenour. *Learning from Las Vegas: The Forgotten Symbolism of Architectural Form.* Cambridge: MIT Press, 1977.

Villacorta Escobar, Manuel. *Apuntes de economía agrícola.* Guatemala: Editorial Universitaria, 1973.

Villagrán Kramer, Francisco. *Biografía política de Guatemala: Los pactos políticos de 1944 a 1970.* Guatemala: FLACSO, 1993.

Violencia y contraviolencia: Desarrollo histórico de la violencia institucional en Guatemala. Guatemala: Editorial Universitaria, 1980.

Wallerstein, Immanuel. *The Modern World System: Capitalist Agriculture and the Origins of the European World-Economy in the Sixteenth Century.* New York: Academic Press, 1976.

Warren, Kay. *Indigenous Movements and Their Critics: Pan-American Activism in Guatemala.* Princeton: Princeton University Press, 1998.

Watanabe, John M. "Culturing Identities: The State and National Consciousness in Late Nineteenth-Century Western Guatemala." *Bulletin of Latin American Research* 19, no. 3 (July 2000): 322–40.

——. *Maya Saints and Souls in a Changing World.* Austin: University of Texas Press, 1992.

Weaver, Frederick Stirton. *Inside the Volcano: The History and Political Economy of Central America.* Boulder: Westview, 1994.

Weymann Fuentes, Eduardo Humberto. "Jacobo Arbenz: Un perfil del ex-presidente de Guatemala." *La Revolución de Octubre: Diez años de lucha por la democracia en Guatemala,* ed. Eduardo Antonio Velásquez Carrera. 2 vols. Guatemala: Universidad de San Carlos de Guatemala, 1994.

Williams, Raymond. *The Long Revolution.* London: Penguin, 1965.

——. *Marxism and Literature.* Oxford: Oxford University Press, 1989.

——. *The Politics of Modernism: Against the New Conformists.* London: Verso, 1989.

Williams, Robert G. *States and Social Evolution: Coffee and the Rise of National Governments in Central America.* Chapel Hill: University of North Carolina Press, 1994.

Williamson, Edwin. *The Penguin History of Latin America.* London: Penguin Books, 1992.

WOLA Policy Brief. "Military Intelligence and Human Rights in Guatemala: The Archive and the Case for Intelligence Reform." Washington: Washington Office on Latin America, 30 March 1995. Manuscript housed in CIRMA.

"Women of the World Fight for Democracy against Warmongers." *For a Lasting Peace, For a People's Democracy.* Bucharest: Organ of Information of the Bureau of the Communist and Workers' Parties, 1 March 1953.

Woodward, Ralph Lee Jr. *Central America: A Nation Divided.* 2d edn. New York: Oxford University Press, 1985.

World Bank. Development data. http://devdata.worldbank.org/hnpstats and http://devdata.worldbank.org/genderstats.

Ydígoras Fuentes, Miguel. *My War with Communism: As Told to Mario Rosenthal.* Englewood Cliffs, N.J.: Prentice-Hall, 1963.

J. T. WAY, a faculty affiliate of the University of Arizona, lives and works in Guatemala. He is a member of the team of directors at the Centro de Investigaciones Regionales de Mesoamérica (CIRMA), where he also works as a professor of history and dean of a program for foreign undergraduate and graduate students.

Library of Congress Cataloging-in-Publication Data

Way, John T. (John Thomas)
The Mayan in the mall : development, globalization, and the making of modern Guatemala / John T. Way.
p. cm.
Includes bibliographical references and index.
ISBN 978-0-8223-5120-7 (cloth : alk. paper)
ISBN 978-0-8223-5131-3 (pbk. : alk. paper)
1. Economic development—Social aspects—Guatemala.
2. Globalization—Social aspects—Guatemala.
3. Globalization—Economic aspects—Guatemala.
4. Guatemala—Economic conditions—1985–
I. Title.
HC144.W39 2012
972.8105'2—dc23   2011038525